Praise from the Experts

"Katherine has taken an industry-wide requirement for SAS® and contributed a much desired reference from which users, beginner to guru, will profit. She has expertly taken a complex subject and simplified it in step-by-step format while satisfying us with understandable examples. I found her approach appropriate, straight forward, and undemanding to comprehend…. I strongly advocate this superior manuscript for use in training as well as employing SAS."

Greg H. Smith, OCP DBA
Lead Instructor - DBA & DA Programs
SAIT (Southern Alberta Institute of Technology)

"The section in Chapter 6 on the SQL optimizer and use of indexes in queries is a perfect example of an often difficult concept for analysts to understand (and thus, often overlooked), yet critical to writing efficient code. The book presents the optimizer and indexing topics clearly, with good query examples and how to interpret SAS® logs… What Katherine illustrates in her book is how powerful and important PROC SQL is to SAS and that it can often be more efficient to use than other SAS code when performing database tasks."

The Essential PROC SQL Handbook for SAS® Users is the ideal reference for a SQL programmer (novice to expert) new to working in the SAS environment. This book will be the single source reference for PROC SQL within our Data Quality group."

Sean O'Neill
Vice President - Data Quality Management
Citi Cards, Information Business

"I think this book is very interesting and educational. It has a logical progression that would fit well as an educational textbook. I may add this book to the curriculum, but would definitely recommend it as another reference textbook for my DBA program."

Mark Perry, Oracle Database Administrator
(DBA) Program Coordinator
Southern Alberta Institute of Technology (SAIT)

SAS Publishing

The Essential PROC SQL Handbook

For SAS® Users

Katherine Prairie

The Power to Know.

The correct bibliographic citation for this manual is as follows: Prairie, Katherine. 2005. *The Essential PROC SQL Handbook for SAS® Users.* Cary, NC: SAS Institute Inc.

The Essential PROC SQL Handbook for SAS® Users

ISBN 978-1-59047-571-3

SAS Institute Inc., SAS Campus Drive, Cary, North Carolina 27513-2414

1st printing, March 2005
2nd printing, August 2011

Contents

Foreword

This book is designed to introduce PROC SQL to programmers who are working with database-specific SQL and who would like to try working with SAS. For those with SAS experience, it is an introduction to the powerful PROC SQL toolkit. There are some examples comparing PROC SQL statements to SAS procedures and DATA step statements. However, the focus is on the accomplishment of common tasks using PROC SQL.

For those experienced in database-specific SQL, it provides a gentle introduction to the flexibility offered by SAS. Within a single SAS session a user can connect to multiple databases simultaneously, issuing queries with added flexibility and functionality unique to SAS. Although this book does not cover other SAS procedures and Base SAS, it does introduce some SAS concepts outside of PROC SQL.

For all users, there are examples of every feature of PROC SQL and plenty of tips and hints. There is sufficient coverage of database concepts that you should have no difficulty accessing tables stored in relational databases using PROC SQL. Information on both the SQL Pass-Through Facility and the SAS/ACCESS LIBNAME engine are provided.

A Quick Reference has been provided at the back of the book. In this section you will find key details for every major concept and term presented in the book together with page references.

Technical notes

A single set of tables with data applicable to a small ficticious book publishing company, Bluesky Publishing, is used throughout the book. Table names have been italicized to distinguish them in written paragraphs. Details on the table structure and data are included in Appendix A, "Bluesky Publishing Tables."

Throughout the program examples, capitalization, indentation, and space have been added for readability. PROC SQL statements are not case-sensitive; only quoted strings included in SQL statements are case-sensitive. In SQL statements a single space is required between and after keywords, aliases, and other character elements that are not separated by a delimiter such as a quote, parenthesis, or comma. Additional space added for readability does not affect the execution of an SQL statement.

PROC SQL, QUIT, LIBNAME, and TITLE statements have been included in examples where appropriate for completeness. A PROC SQL statement invokes the SQL procedure, and each subsequent statement ending in a semicolon is executed. PROC SQL remains active until a QUIT statement is encountered.

A LIBNAME statement can be issued before or after the PROC SQL statement. It remains in effect for the duration of the SAS session unless it is cleared or another LIBNAME statement is issued changing the libref. TITLE statements can also be issued before or after the PROC SQL statement and remain in effect until changed.

When syntax is provided, an ellipsis (…) is used to indicate more of the same option repeated any number of times. A single vertical bar (|) is used to separate items, each of which is a valid option. Optional clauses are enclosed in angle brackets (<>) within statement syntax.

In the code used in this book the following OPTIONS statement was issued at the start of the SAS session to control the PROC SQL output shown throughout the book unless otherwise indicated.

```
OPTIONS linesize=256 nocenter nonumber stimer nodate;
```

All PROC SQL statements included in this book were run in both SAS Version 8 and SAS Version 9. Testing in SAS Version 9 was conducted in all versions up to and including SAS Version 9.1.2 (TS1M2). Enhancements made to PROC SQL in SAS Version 9 are outlined in Chapter 8, "PROC SQL Enhancements in SAS Version 9." Most of the SQL statements in this book can also be run in earlier SAS versions such as SAS Version 6 or 7.

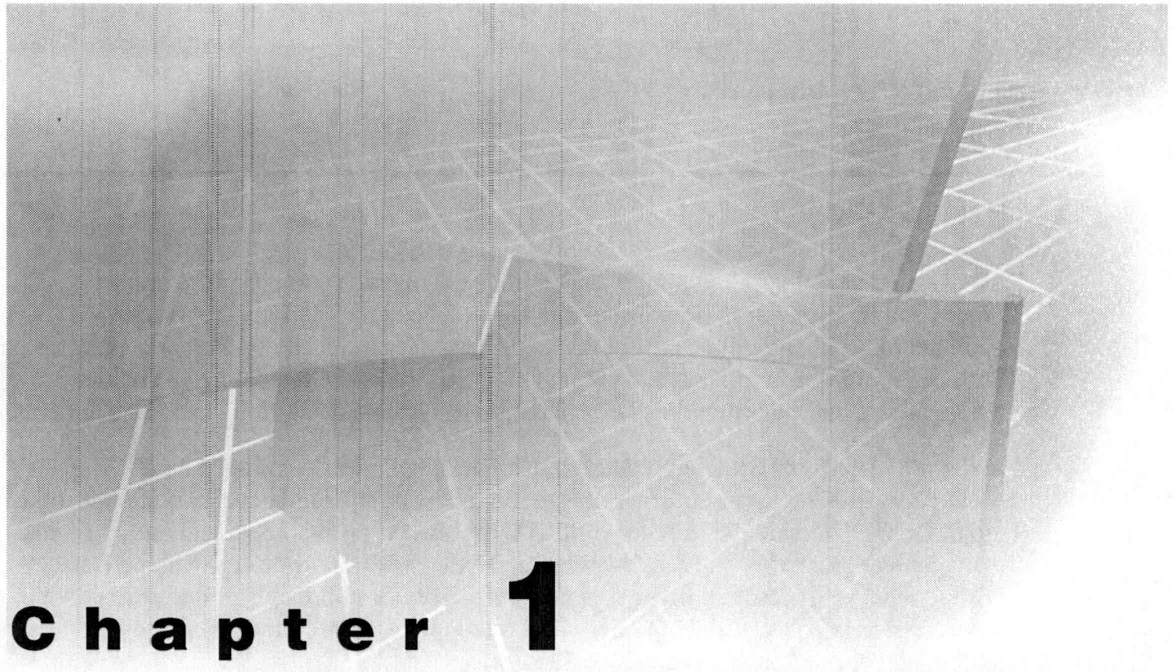

Chapter 1

Introduction to PROC SQL

A little history

SQL is a powerful, flexible, fourth-generation sublanguage that enables complex processing through a few simple statements. You need only to indicate the desired outcome rather than outline each of the steps necessary to reach that outcome because SQL is a nonprocedural language. SQL statements allow for the complete creation, maintenance, and reporting of relational database systems using English-like statements.

In the mid-1970s the Structured Query Language (SQL) was developed by IBM researchers in San Jose, California, to support a new relational database model. In June 1970, Dr. E. F. Codd, a researcher with IBM, published his mathematical theory of data management in a paper entitled "A Relational Model of Data for Large Shared Data Banks." His ideas resulted in the definition of a new form of data storage structure, a table consisting of rows and columns. The relational database model was thus born from tables and the relationships between tables.

SQL was designed to enable access to data stored in a relational database. It allows you to create, alter, and delete tables as well as modify or delete existing records or add new records to tables.

By the late 1980s and early 1990s, each database vendor had its own version of SQL. In an effort to minimize the inconsistencies and provide portability of SQL statements, the American National Standards Institute (ANSI) developed a set of international standards to be applied to the language. Several standards have been published by ANSI since 1986, including SQL-89, SQL-92, SQL-99 and SQL-2003.

Each successive SQL language release extends functionality. However, the foundations of the SQL language have remained mostly unchanged. Vendors that are compliant with the ANSI SQL-92 standard, for example, are also compliant with the SQL-99 core function standards.

The power and ease-of-use of SQL has resulted in its use in hundreds of database products today. Companies such as Oracle, Microsoft, Sybase, and IBM depend heavily on SQL in their database products regardless of operating system. As a result, anyone working with databases today must be proficient in SQL. The ANSI standards have resulted in a set of more or less common statements with agreed upon functionality from each vendor. However, many different ideas and syntactical differences are found in each flavor of SQL.

PROC SQL underwent major change in SAS Version 8, resulting in a more versatile procedure that is also more closely in line with the ANSI SQL-92 standard. The new version extends the functionality of the SQL language with elements from Base SAS.

PROC SQL statements

There are approximately 40 statements in SQL which can be grouped into several categories. Data Definition Language (DDL) statements such as CREATE, ALTER, and DROP are used to create and maintain tables and other objects such as indexes and views in a relational database. Data Manipulation Language (DML) statements such as SELECT, INSERT, UPDATE, and DELETE are used to retrieve and maintain rows of table data. The final group of statements, COMMIT, ROLLBACK, GRANT, and REVOKE are all Data Control Language (DCL) statements, which are focused on database security.

This book concentrates on the DDL and DML statements that support reporting or selection of data and the creation and maintence of tables and views. With knowledge of just seven statements, you have the powerful functionality of SQL at your fingertips.

Why learn PROC SQL?

Why learn PROC SQL instead of continuing to use the SAS programming language and the standard procedures? A single SELECT statement may encompass selection, manipulation, merging, sorting, summary, filtration, and reporting processes, eliminating several SAS procedures and DATA steps in your programs.

You will find that you can apply many of the concepts you already know to PROC SQL. Whether it is retrieving data from a data set or database, the SQL procedure treats everything as though it were a two-dimensional table composed of rows and columns. This is similar to the SAS data set where the observations are rows and variables are columns.

The SQL procedure completes many tasks with a single SQL statement while the more traditional SAS solution may involve several SAS procedures and DATA steps.

> **Tip:** A table generated in PROC SQL can be referenced in a DATA step in exactly the same way as a data set. The reverse is also true; data sets created in a DATA step can be used in PROC SQL.

PROC SQL allows you to modify and maintain tables within a database from the SAS session. Statements to modify existing records, add new records, and delete records can all be incorporated into a PROC SQL statement and applied via the SQL Pass-Through Facility or LIBNAME engine.

The compact nature of a SQL statement allows for quick updates of programming code if the data changes. SQL statements can also include macro variables allowing for a generic program that can be dynamically updated.

Reporting that suits your needs

A PROC SQL query generates a summarized, sorted report without a call to any other procedures. The SELECT statement automatically produces printed output, eliminating the need for a PRINT procedure. The SELECT statement also sorts the result set without a call to PROC SORT.

SAS standard formats and user-defined formats created in PROC FORMAT may be applied within a SELECT statement.

Output Delivery System (ODS) destinations may be specified for the reports generated by a SELECT statement. A single SELECT statement may generate several formatted reports such as HTML and PDF reports using ODS statements. A document destination may also be specified, providing for flexible output options without the need to re-execute the query.

The TEMPLATE procedure may be used to create custom styles for reports. Other SAS procedures such as PROC TABULATE and PROC REPORT may operate on tables created by the SQL procedure.

Tip: A simple SELECT statement produces a printed report unless you specify the NOPRINT option. SELECT statements that are part of a subquery in a CREATE, ALTER, or UPDATE statement do not generate output. In each of these cases, the output returned by the SELECT statement is used as input to the CREATE, ALTER, or UPDATE statement.

The power to create

The PROC SQL CREATE statement provides for the creation of tables, views, and SAS data sets in either a database or a native SAS library from within a SAS session. Users working within a database require appropriate privileges in order to execute a CREATE statement in a database. The new tables can be created within a database or stored in a native SAS data library.

There are several options available for the creation of tables in PROC SQL. Each column and column modifier can be specified much in the same way as empty fields in a data set can be established in a DATA step. However, tables can also be created using the structure of an existing table or data set as a template, but leaving an empty table. Alternatively, the CREATE statement can mimic the DATA step data set creation process, taking both structure and data from an existing table or data set.

Views provide the ability to selectively allow users to see columns and rows of information in one or more tables and data sets. Views can be generated from a complex SELECT statement that retrieves information from one or more tables or data sets. However, you issue a simple SELECT statement against the view, retrieving up-to-date information because the view is re-created each time it is queried. The dynamic nature of views makes them invaluable for reporting applications.

> **Tip:** Most table creation in a database can be accomplished using PROC SQL statements. If additional database-specific statements are required, they can be passed directly to the Relational Database Management Systems (RDBMS) for processing using the SQL Pass-Through facility. Only those users with appropriate database privileges can successfully submit CREATE statements.

Ease of maintenance

PROC SQL statements such as ALTER, INSERT, UPDATE, DROP, and DELETE provide for the addition of new data and the modification or update of existing data in a table. From within a SAS session, tables in a database as well as tables and data sets stored in native SAS libraries can be maintained by users with appropriate database privileges.

New rows can be added to tables directly using the INSERT statement, or they may be taken from one or more tables or data sets in any active library, including a database. One or more criteria can be set, limiting the rows taken from the other sources.

In PROC SQL, a single UPDATE statement applies the changes to existing rows in a table without creating a new table or data set. The rows modified by the UPDATE statement can be limited through WHERE clause criteria based on values within the same table or other tables. Moreover, updates can be easily applied from records in one or more other data sets or tables.

Existing tables and data sets can also be altered using the ALTER statement to include additional columns and add column modifiers such as labels or formats. In each case, the work is done on the existing table without the need to create a new table or data set.

Security

USER, a special keyword, when added to a PROC SQL INSERT or UPDATE statement can be used to store the user ID associated with the action in a table. Such statements can be triggered by specific events to execute in the background of applications, allowing for the creation of an effective audit table. Dates and other information collected from the SAS session can also be added to the entry.

Database security is also maintained. A user must have the appropriate security to create tables, views, and indexes within a database. Only those users with appropriate database privileges can successfully submit INSERT, UPDATE, ALTER, and DELETE statements. In addition, only those users with read-access to tables may report from them or views built from those tables using the SELECT statement.

Data integrity checks

Integrity constraints such as primary key, foreign key, check, unique, and not null can all be added either at the time a table is created or later with an ALTER statement. Once set, they automatically check all incoming data values.

Primary key integrity constraints check for duplicate values as data is entered into one or more columns of a table. Foreign key integrity constraints prevent data from being entered into the column of one table unless the value is already in another. This form of constraint is useful for ensuring that each row of your incoming data has a valid code such as a state abbreviation.

The check integrity constraint can be used to check all incoming data against one or more criteria. For example, it can be used to limit your incoming data to a specific date range. The NOT NULL integrity constraint can be applied to prevent the entry of null values.

Foreign key constraints make the task of synchronizing column values common to two tables or data sets effortless through the specification of referential actions. When a value in the parent or reference table is modified, the value in the linked or child table is automatically modified in the same way. In addition, the constraint can be set up so that the value in the child table is changed to a missing value if the value in the linked parent table is deleted.

Optimized performance

The PROC SQL optimizer automatically works out a plan for executing SQL statements in the most efficient manner possible. Indexes can be built to provide better performance for your queries. In addition, directions for the optimizer may be added as statement options.

Performance optimization is important when tables are stored in one or more databases as well as native SAS libraries. The SQL optimizer determines whether processing should be transferred to the database or be handled by SAS. Options such as DBMASTER, new in SAS 9, assist in the optimizer in efficient handling of queries involving tables residing in different database locations.

Adaptability

Flexibility in a changing environment

We all know how unstable the computing environment in companies is today. Your company may decide to implement a new data warehouse using Sybase instead of DB2. A new package may be introduced to generate reports from your Oracle database.

If you are using a SAS/ACCESS LIBNAME statement to connect to a database, the only change needed regardless of the database is to the LIBNAME connection string required to establish a connection to the database.

Using the familiar SAS interface, you can easily create new tables and update and retrieve your data. There is no need to learn another product or interface such as Oracle SQL*Plus or ISQL. Moreover, the information extracted using SQL is directly available for further processing in a SAS DATA step or other SAS procedures.

SAS PROC SQL allows you to apply your standard SAS output formats and labeling options and almost all of the SAS functions. In fact, if you are a SAS programmer, you already know more about SQL statements than most other programmers!

Table merges and Cartesian products

One of the strengths of SQL is its ability to join or merge two or more tables, generating result sets or new tables that include data from one or more of the tables. Criteria can be built from any column in the joined tables as well. Unlike the SAS data set merge, the tables do not have to be presorted or indexed on a key variable in order to accomplish the join. With PROC SQL, the procedure sorts and merges the tables in the same step.

There are several ways to accomplish a join or merge in SQL. It is possible to match common values in a column in two or more tables. However, it is also possible to produce a Cartesian product of all combinations of all rows from all of the tables.

Two or more tables can also be joined using outer joins which retrieve nonmatching rows from one or both tables along with the unique matching rows. Set operations provide additional merge or join functionality based on intersect, union, and exception operations.

Fuzzy logic

A wide range of criteria can be applied to SQL queries thereby limiting the rows retrieved or manipulated by the query. However, often the criteria we wish to apply cannot be written in a simple fashion using mathematical operators such as =, <, or >.

PROC SQL WHERE clauses may include conditions that require fuzzy logic or inexact matching.

Fuzzy logic can be applied to pattern-matching criteria in an SQL query. SAS functions such as SCAN and CONTAINS allow us to parse a string for the inclusion of various characters. The LIKE operator can be used in conjunction with wildcard symbols to restrict character string matches to a particular position within a column value. For criteria based on a range, the BETWEEN operator can be used to set the bounds.

PROC SQL may also include the SAS SOUNDEX function in the WHERE clause of a query. This function will match column values that sound similar to the given value.

Criteria built from stored data

Subqueries provide the ability to calculate or retrieve one or more values which are then substituted into a WHERE clause. Essentially they allow report criteria to be built at the time the query is run. Subqueries are executed first, returning one or more values to the main query.

Work within a database from a SAS session

An advantage of the SQL procedure is its ability to establish a connection to a database through SAS/ACCESS and the SQL Pass-Through facility. PROC SQL statements may be submitted interactively within a SAS session directly to a database regardless of its location. For example, database servers can be accessed from client machines, or the database may be distributed between several machines.

In addition, a single SAS session can support multiple connections to one or more databases enabling multisource data delivery for data warehouse extraction, transformation and loading processes and other applications. SAS procedures and DATA steps can seamlessly combine database tables and tables and data sets stored in native SAS libraries.

SQL Pass-Through Facility

SAS took the new tool one step further by incorporating the ability to execute SQL statements generated from within a SAS session directly against a variety of database systems. The SQL Pass-Through Facility enables a user to retrieve information from a database and incorporate it into SAS data sets, all from within the familiar SAS environment.

A database specific CONNECT statement first opens communication with the database. SAS then passes the SQL statements to the database for execution and returns the results to the SAS session. Finally, a DISCONNECT statement closes the database connection.

SAS/ACCESS LIBNAME statement

Since SAS 8, connecting to a database has become even easier with the enhancement of the LIBNAME statement. With PROC SQL and SAS/ACCESS, the export and import steps are eliminated. A LIBNAME statement provides the means to connect to the database, and these tables can be accessed directly by either a DATA step or PROC SQL. Moreover, a data set stored in a native SAS library may be matched to records in tables stored in two different database systems using fields in common between the tables.

The LIBNAME statement specifies the parameters needed to establish a database connection and associate that connection with a libref. Once assigned, the libref can be used as part of two-level names in any SAS procedure or DATA step. In addition, views can store embedded LIBNAME statements making the connection to a database invisible to the user.

Interactive and Web-based applications

Internet and intranet-driven applications can incorporate SQL statements using htmSQL input files that provide access to tables and data sets, both in native SAS libraries and databases. In addition, entire SQL statements can easily be built from parameters passed through interactive Web pages.

In SAS/AF FRAME entry and webAF, objects can be populated through data retrieved from either native SAS libraries or databases using the SQL procedure. Parameters passed through FRAME objects can also be used to set criteria used in SQL statements.

Values retrieved from tables or data sets using SQL queries can also be easily bound to macro variables using the INTO clause. These variables can be passed to macro programs in FRAME source code or other SAS programs.

When not to use PROC SQL

The SQL procedure does not read or write text files directly. Nor is it well suited to the creation of a data set using instream record images.

The SAS DATA step offers a wide range of delimiters and other formatting options commonly encountered in data files. It provides more flexibility when reading files such as spreadsheets that may include missing values when they are imported into SAS. The SAS INPUT statement also allows for named input.

Although the PROC SQL INSERT statement may be used to add rows to a table or data set, a VALUES keyword is required for each row and the complete record must be enclosed in parentheses. In addition, all character and missing variables must be enclosed in quotation marks. Because many files that are imported contain, at best, a delimiter between fields, the added syntax required by the INSERT statement can significantly add to the workload of data imports.

The SAS DATA step is your only solution if you are attempting to import fixed-width columnar data into SAS. PROC SQL does not allow for positional column references in the INSERT statement.

The PROC SQL advantage

SQL is an important component of every database today regardless of its function. It is used for transactional databases as well as data warehouses and data marts supporting data mining activities. The effort you put into learning PROC SQL in SAS provides you with a skill that can be used in environments other than SAS. Once you've completed this book, you will be ready to tackle reporting, table creation, and maintenance in any database system your company decides to implement.

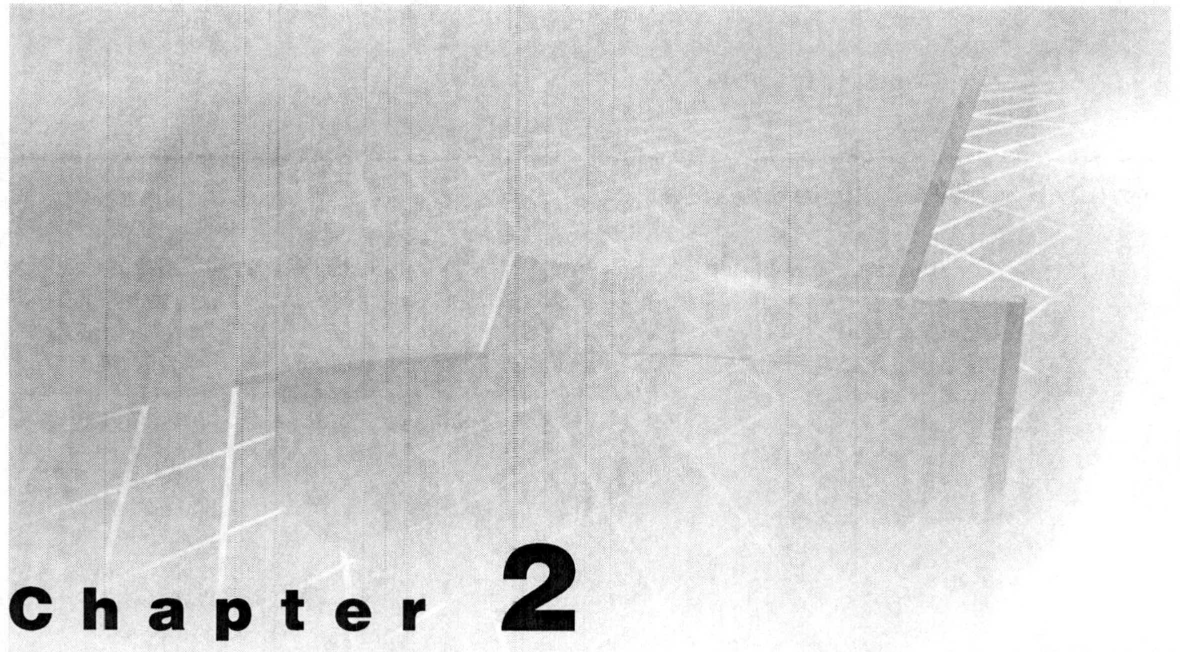

Chapter 2

Working with PROC SQL

PROC SQL concepts

The SQL language was developed to allow operations such as selecting data and inserting new rows of information to be performed on tables stored within a relational data model. The relational data model was first described by Dr. Edgar F. Codd (Codd, 1970). It describes the organization and relationships that define a database.

A relational database uses tables to store information and those tables can be related to one another through keys. A strict rule of relational databases is that each row of information in a table must be unique. This is enforced through a primary key or unique identifier requirement for each row.

In SAS, SQL statements are part of the SQL procedure. PROC SQL may be used to work with tables in a database using SAS/ACCESS or the SQL Pass-Through facility. However, PROC SQL can also be used to create and maintain tables and to report from tables and data sets stored in a native SAS library.

Table structure

Tables and SAS data sets have the same structure; both contain data values and descriptive information about those values. The PROC SORT statement can be applied to either a table or data set; the sorted results may be saved, if desired.

> **Tip:** Whether you use table or data set, you are referring to the same thing. Both have structure, data values, and descriptive information about those values.

Tables contain rows that are identical to data set observations. Each row has one or more columns of data or data set variables. The value of a column for a given row is known as a field. This is equivalent to a SAS observation variable value. A data type such as character, numeric or date is assigned to a column. The data type determines the field values allowed in each column of a table.

> **Tip:** When a new column in a table is assigned a DATE data type, the data inserted into that column are stored in a numeric form corresponding to an internal date. Internal dates differ between systems. In SAS, dates are stored as the number of days between January 1, 1960 and the specified date.
>
> Columns must be declared with a data type of DATE if you want to apply date functions to the column or use dates as part of your selection criteria in SQL statements.
>
> When using dates in PROC SQL statements, SAS informats and formats can be applied. However, care must be taken when using dates in SQL queries submitted against RDBMS tables. For example, when querying a Sybase table

you might use a date format of “21JAN2004” whereas queries written in Oracle would use a format of ’01-JAN-04’.

Caution: If the century is not included in a date, the default century for SAS or the RDBMS is applied.

Three records or rows in the *stock* table of the Bluesky Publishing Company are displayed in the table below. There are three variables or columns defined for each row in the table. The value or field of the category column for the third row is *arts*.

Table name: STOCK		
ISBN	**title**	**category**
1-7890-1072-1	**Decorative Arts**	arts
1-7890-2878-7	The Ultimate Philosophy	arts
1-7890-1256-2	Democracy in America	arts

Row

Column

Field

PRIMARY KEY, FOREIGN KEY, and other constraints

Constraints are an important aspect of PROC SQL, especially when working with database tables. Constraints such as the PRIMARY KEY and FOREIGN KEY are used to facilitate table joins and the FOREIGN KEY, CHECK, and UNIQUE constraints provide automatic data validation mechanisms. These constraints are common in production databases and data warehouses. They are also commonly seen in interactive applications where they either check incoming values entered by the user or provide a list from which the user selects a value.

Tip: Constraints should be applied carefully because they have both a negative and positive effect on performance. Processing of table joins and WHERE clause filters, for example, may be enhanced through the indexes automatically generated when constraints such as the PRIMARY KEY are added. However, each time a data value is modified or new data value is entered into a column upon which a constraint has been applied, the constraint conditions must be checked. For very large tables or those with many constraints, there can be a substantial increase in processing time.

Many constraints are associated with tables to enforce certain rules for the modification of existing data and for incoming data values in table columns. Others prevent you from dropping a table before first dropping the constraint. As a result, the presence of constraints affect statements issued in PROC SQL.

Constraints can be applied to columns in tables created in PROC SQL or in other languages, regardless of where they are stored.

> **Tip:** Constraints can be specified at the time a table is created or applied to existing tables using the ALTER statement in PROC SQL. Alternatively, PROC DATASETS can be used.
>
> SAS/ACCESS and SQL Pass-Through facility users: In order to add constraints to existing tables in a database, you must have the appropriate privileges.

PRIMARY KEY constraint

A primary key is a group of one or more columns in a table which together uniquely identify a particular row within that table. It is this characteristic of unique identification via a primary key that distinguishes a relational database from other forms of storage.

> **Tip:** Indexes are automatically created for primary key columns.

A single PRIMARY KEY constraint is permitted for a table. Once a primary key has been assigned to a column, all values within that column must be unique. It is possible to designate several columns together as a composite primary key. In this situation, the combination of values in the columns must be unique for each row in the table. In the table shown below, the client number uniquely identifies a customer; therefore it has been assigned the role of primary key.

> **Tip:** PRIMARY KEY constraints also prevent the insertion of a null value into the column.

Table name: CLIENT		
clientno	**company**	**phone**
1001	University of Texas	512-495-4370
2010	Chicago State University	312-756-7890
3007	Heffers Booksellers	01223-568568

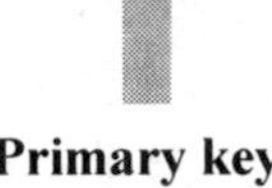

Primary key

But what if a single column is not adequate to uniquely identify a row in a table? In the *orders* table shown below, invoice information for the Bluesky Publishing Company is stored. You might assume from the first row in the table that an invoice number would be a good choice of primary key for this table. However, the next three rows have the same invoice number and order date. Because each invoice represents several book orders, both the invoice number and product code must be used together to uniquely identify a row in this table. This is known as a composite primary key.

Table name: ORDERS			
invoice	**prodcode**	**ord_date**	**clientno**
030207-01	300456	7-Feb-03	1001
030506-01	300680	6-May-03	1001
030506-01	400178	6-May-03	1001
030506-01	500120	6-May-03	1001

Primary keys

Tip: In SAS Version 8 and 9, each of the constraints discussed in this section can be built within PROC SQL. If you are using an earlier version of SAS, the CREATE INDEX statement offers several options for creating constraints. Refer to your SAS documentation for more information on the CREATE INDEX statement.

The PRIMARY KEY constraint can be useful when you want to ensure that you do not have duplicates in a column. All incoming data that matches existing data in a column upon which a PRIMARY KEY constraint is in force will be rejected. If the PRIMARY KEY constraint is built on more than one column, all incoming data that matches the combination of the columns will be rejected.

Tip: Take advantage of PRIMARY KEY or UNIQUE constraints when loading large data files that must have unique values. The PRIMARY KEY constraint can be dropped after the data is loaded if you do not wish to have the added processing overhead.

FOREIGN KEY constraint

A FOREIGN KEY constraint links a table column to a column in a second reference table. The data type of the columns must match and the column in the second table must have a PRIMARY KEY constraint defined for it.

Tip: A single table may have several FOREIGN KEY constraints defined; however, none of the columns may also be associated with a PRIMARY KEY constraint.

Consider how you would associate a customer of the Bluesky Publishing Company with the details of all of his or her orders. The order and client information is stored in separate tables so the tables have to be considered together. If we identify a column containing common values in both the *orders* table and the customer table we can forge a relationship between the tables. This relationship is known as a join, and it will be discussed later.

Table name: ORDERS		
invoice	**prodcode**	**clientno**
030207-01	300456	1001
030506-01	300680	1001
030506-01	400178	1001
030506-01	500120	1001

Table name: CLIENT	
clientno	**Company**
1001	University of Texas
2010	Chicago State University
3007	Heffers Booksellers
4008	National University of Sydney

Primary keys **Foreign key** **Primary key**

Notice the *orders* table has a primary key or unique identifier different from the customer table. Compare the clientno column in each table. The clientno column in the *orders* table contains values in common with the clientno column in the *client* table. The clientno column in the *orders* table is known as a foreign key because it is related to a key value in another table. It is somewhat similar to having a key to someone else's hotel room. If you know the hotel the person is staying in (table) and the room number (foreign key column), you can access the room.

Caution: The data type of each column linked through a foreign key relationship must be the same in order to join the tables in SAS.

A table may have more than one foreign key that allows it to be related to more than one table. In addition, a column may function as both a primary and foreign key as shown in the *client* and *address* tables. These kinds of table relationships are common in data warehouses where look-up tables are used to describe various codes contained in the main data tables.

Table name: ORDERS		
invoice	**prodcode**	**clientno**
030207-01	300456	1001
030506-01	300680	1001
030506-01	400178	1001
030506-01	500120	1001

Primary keys **Foreign key**

Table name: CLIENT	
clientno	**Company**
1001	University of Texas
2010	Chicago State University
3007	Heffers Booksellers
4008	National University of Sydney

Primary key

Table name: STOCK	
isbn	**prodcode**
1-7890-1072-1	300678
1-7890-2878-7	300456
1-7890-1256-2	300289
1-7890-5477-x	300680

Primary key **Foreign key**

Table name: ADDRESS	
clientno	**address**
1001	6015 Pine Street
2010	951 South King Drive
3007	200 Trinity St.
4008	6D Lor Ampas

Primary key

Often primary to foreign key links are referred to as a parent/child relationship; a value cannot exist in the column of the child table unless a similar value is stored in the parent table.

The following gives an example of SQL statements creating two tables, *orders* and *stock*. The product code (prodcode) column (the PRIMARY KEY constraint in the stock table) is used to enforce the values of the product code column in the orders table through a foreign key. Notice that the columns in both tables that are part of the referential integrity constraint have the same data type.

```
CREATE table stock (
       ISBN             char(13),
       title            char(50),
       auth_fst         char(10),
       auth_lst         char(15),
       category         char(20),
       reprint          char(1),
```

```
        stock           num,
        yrPubl          num,
        prodCode        char(6),
        price           num,
    constraint stock_pk primary key(prodcode)
);
CREATE table orders (
        prodCode        char(6),
        ord_date        date,
        quantity        num,
        totsale         num,
        currency        char(3),
        delCode         char(3),
        clientNo        num,
        invoice         char(10),
constraint prod_fk foreign key(prodcode)references stock
on delete set null on update cascade
);
```

Once a FOREIGN KEY constraint has been established, each value entered into the column must be present in the linked column in the reference table.

> **Tip:** For an example of how to create and populate a set of tables with common values in a column linked by a primary key-foreign key relationship, refer to the "Putting it all together" example in Chapter 6, "Creating and Managing Tables and Views."

Data integrity

Foreign keys help ensure data integrity when loading data. All allowed values for a column are stored in a separate validation table linked to the main table by a foreign key relationship. The *stock* table acts as a validation table for the *orders* table. With the foreign key relationship built on the product code (prodcode) column, only orders with a product code in the stock table can be entered.

> **Tip:** Inserting data into tables that have primary and foreign key links requires careful thought. An entry is usually made into the table with the controlling foreign key first. For example, a product code must be entered in the ***stock*** table before an entry in the ***orders*** table for that product can be made. More information on creating tables and inserting data is included in Chapter 6, "Creating and Managing Tables and Views."

Foreign keys are often used in interactive applications where a user is allowed to select a choice from a list or menu. The items in the list are often taken from validation tables that contain unique entries and descriptive details relating to each entry. Details relating to each book are stored in the *stock* table. To access this information, you create a join between the *stock* and the *orders* table. This ensures consistency when descriptions and other information associated with the stock are included in reports. It also keeps storage requirements in check because the main table stores only a code matching an entry in the validation table rather than all the details associated with the item.

> **Tip:** Validation code tables are ideal for interactive applications because the drop-down menus can be populated with labels or codes from the table.

Foreign keys are implemented in data warehouses to establish relationships between fact and dimension tables. Fact tables store measured data while dimension tables provide descriptive details relating to codes stored in dimension tables. The validation code tables referred to here would be dimension tables in a data warehouse.

> **Tip:** If you work with a data warehouse, you may have heard of star and snowflake schemas. These are commonly used models that rely heavily on foreign and primary key relationships between dimension and fact tables.

UNIQUE constraint

A UNIQUE constraint forces each entry in the column to be distinct within the column. PRIMARY KEY constraints are also UNIQUE constraints by default. UNIQUE constraints may be applied to either one column or a combination of two or more columns in a table. A single table may have several UNIQUE constraints defined.

> **Tip:** What is the difference between a PRIMARY KEY and a UNIQUE constraint? Both constraints automatically generate indexes and prevent duplicate values in a column or combination of columns. However, a table may have only a single PRIMARY KEY while any number of UNIQUE constraints is allowed. UNIQUE constraints also allow a single null value within the column or columns while PRIMARY KEY constraints do not.

The creation of a UNIQUE constraint on a column that contains a null or missing value causes an interesting situation. In the SAS System, numeric null values are less than or smaller than all of the non-null values; character null values are designated by a string of blanks. Each of these representations of a null value is still a form of value. Therefore, a column with a UNIQUE constraint will allow one null value within that column.

CHECK constraint

A CHECK constraint is a criterion against which an incoming value is verified. It is similar to a WHERE clause on a SELECT statement or an IF statement in Base SAS.

Any number of CHECK constraints can be included in a single table. The CHECK constraint may reference more than one column in a table.

A range of values, a list of values, or a set of values can be incorporated into the CHECK constraint. A check of the incoming value against the criterion must resolve to true. Otherwise a constraint violation warning is issued in the SAS log.

CHECK constraints may also be applied to an existing table in which rows of data have been loaded. In this case, every stored value in the affected column is checked and the application of the constraint fails if a value fails to meet the criteria of the CHECK constraint.

> **Tip:** CHECK constraints are very useful when loading data. They provide an easy way of confirming that incoming data lies within the expected range.

NOT NULL constraint

This constraint prevents the insertion of a null value into a column. It does not ensure that a unique value for the column is entered. Any number of NOT NULL constraints may be defined in a single table. However, each NOT NULL constraint may be applied to a single column. It is applied automatically to columns designated as primary or foreign keys.

> **Tip:** NOT NULL constraints can be combined with other constraints such as UNIQUE.

PROC SQL versus SAS DATA step

PROC SQL accomplishes many of the same tasks of traditional SAS DATA steps and procedures and often with a significantly reduced number of statements and procedure calls. Performance may also be improved in some cases, when PROC SQL is used.

Let's start by working through a fairly simple task using PROC SQL and the SAS DATA step. In this example PROC SQL is used to produce a report on sales information from the Bluesky Publishing Company. The sample program below shows the same task being completed using a more traditional set of DATA and PROC steps. Both sets of programming code merge two data sets, create a new variable, calculate summary statistics, and print an ordered set of results.

```
TITLE1   "Sales Information by Product Code and Author";
TITLE2  "January 1, 2004 to May 31, 2004";

OPTIONS linesize=256 nocenter nonumber stimer nodate;

PROC SQL stimer;
```

```
LIBNAME bluesky "C:\mydata\bluesky bookstore\";

SELECT    stock.prodcode "Product Code" format=$15. ,
                stock.auth_lst "Author" format=$15.,
          avg(orders.quantity) as mnqty "Average Quantity"
                format=6.0,
          avg(stock.price) as mnprice "Average Price"
                format=comma10.2,
          sum(orders.quantity*stock.price) as smprice
          "Quantity * Price" format=comma10.2
FROM      bluesky.orders, bluesky.stock
WHERE     orders.ord_date between '01JAN2004'd and
          '31MAY2004'd
          and stock.prodcode = orders.prodcode
GROUP BY stock.prodcode, stock.auth_lst
ORDER BY stock.auth_lst;
```

```
Sales Information by Product Code and Author
January 1, 2004 to May 31, 2004
```

Product Code	Author	Average Quantity	Average Price	Quantity * Price
400345	Barry	25	86.00	2,150.00
200145	Bishop	700	56.25	39,375.00
200507	Bole	20	74.50	1,490.00
100890	Clark	260	69.00	17,940.00
100406	Davis	45	15.00	675.00
600125	Dixon	237	6.95	4,948.40
300456	Johnson	55	9.50	522.50
600489	Lillard	25	5.50	137.50
500500	Marossy	70	23.50	1,645.00
400100	Miler	350	43.75	15,312.50
600780	Paul	103	8.60	885.80
400128	Perry	1230	34.00	41,820.00
100345	Sharr	180	65.00	11,700.00
500238	Wilson	200	22.25	4,450.00

```
LIBNAME bluesky "C:\mydata\bluesky bookstore\";

PROC sort data=bluesky.stock;
          by prodcode;

PROC sort data=bluesky.orders;
          by prodcode;

DATA mrgdata;
          merge bluesky.stock bluesky.orders;
          by prodcode;
          keep prodcode auth_lst quantity price totprice;
     if ord_date >= '01JAN2004'd and ord_date <= '31MAY2004'd;
     Totprice = price*quantity;

PROC SUMMARY data=mrgdata nway;
          class prodcode auth_lst;
          var quantity price totprice;
          output out=newstuff mean= mnqty mnprice mntprice
          sum=sqty sqprice sqtprice;

PROC sort data=newstuff;
          by auth_lst;

PROC print data=newstuff noobs label;
          var prodcode auth_lst mnqty mnprice sqtprice ;
          label prodcode = 'Product Code'
               auth_lst = 'Author'
               mnqty = 'Average Quantity'
               mnprice = 'Average Price'
               sqtprice = 'Quantity * Price';
          format prodcode auth_lst $15. mnqty 6. mnprice
                comma10.2 sqtprice comma10.2;
     TITLE1  "Sales Information by Product Code and Author";
     TITLE2  "January 1, 2004 to May 31, 2004";

RUN;
```

```
             Sales Information by Product Code and Author
             January 1, 2004 to May 31, 2004

                                            Average       Average      Quantity
Product Code        Author                 Quantity         Price       * Price

400345              Barry                        25         86.00      2,150.00
200145              Bishop                      700         56.25     39,375.00
200507              Bole                         20         74.50      1,490.00
100890              Clark                       260         69.00     17,940.00
100406              Davis                        45         15.00        675.00
600125              Dixon                       237          6.95      4,948.40
300456              Johnson                      55          9.50        522.50
600489              Lillard                      25          5.50        137.50
500500              Marossy                      70         23.50      1,645.00
400100              Miler                       350         43.75     15,312.50
600780              Paul                        103          8.60        885.80
400128              Perry                      1230         34.00     41,820.00
100345              Sharr                       180         65.00     11,700.00
500238              Wilson                      200         22.25      4,450.00
```

Tip: PROC SQL is an interactive procedure or RUN group. Once it is invoked, it remains active until it is terminated with a QUIT statement or a step boundary is encountered. A RUN statement is not required in a SQL procedure.

There are several significant differences between the programs shown above despite the fact that the reports are identical. Notice that the SQL query generates a summarized, sorted report without a call to any other procedures. The SELECT statement automatically produces printed output, eliminating the need for a PRINT procedure. Both of the programs apply formatting to the report, although the method differs.

Tip: A simple SELECT statement produces a printed report unless you specify the NOPRINT option. More information on options is included later in this chapter.

Another important difference between the two programs is their use of system resources. Both of the data sets or tables are small; the *orders* and *stock* tables have 40 and 30 observations respectively. Yet, if you compare the portion of the SAS log shown in the next example with that shown in the second example following, you will find that the SQL procedure utilized 0.03 seconds of CPU time while the DATA step and SORT procedures utilized a combined total of 0.27 seconds. Although performance differences will not always be apparent, well-written SQL queries should require fewer resources.

SAS log:

```
NOTE: SQL Statement used (Total process time):
      real time           0.03 seconds
      cpu time            0.03 seconds

NOTE: There were 30 observations read from the data set
      BLUESKY.STOCK.
NOTE: The data set BLUESKY.STOCK has 30 observations and 10
      variables.
NOTE: PROCEDURE SORT used (Total process time):
      real time           0.04 seconds
      cpu time            0.04 seconds
```

SAS log:

```
NOTE: There were 40 observations read from the data set
      BLUESKY.ORDERS.
NOTE: The data set BLUESKY.ORDERS has 40 observations and 8
      variables.
NOTE: PROCEDURE SORT used (Total process time):
      real time           0.04 seconds
      cpu time            0.04 seconds

NOTE: There were 30 observations read from the data set
      BLUESKY.STOCK.
NOTE: There were 40 observations read from the data set
      BLUESKY.ORDERS.
NOTE: The data set WORK.MRGDATA has 16 observations and 5
      variables.
NOTE: DATA statement used (Total process time):
      real time           0.07 seconds
      cpu time            0.06 seconds

NOTE: There were 16 observations read from the data set
      WORK.MRGDATA.
NOTE: The data set WORK.NEWSTUFF has 14 observations and 10
      variables.
NOTE: PROCEDURE SUMMARY used (Total process time):
      real time           0.05 seconds
      cpu time            0.06 seconds
```

(continued on the next page)

(continued)

```
NOTE: There were 14 observations read from the data set
      WORK.NEWSTUFF.
NOTE: The data set WORK.NEWSTUFF has 14 observations and 10
      variables.
NOTE: PROCEDURE SORT used (Total process time):
      real time           0.04 seconds
      cpu time            0.05 seconds

NOTE: There were 14 observations read from the data set
      WORK.NEWSTUFF.
NOTE: PROCEDURE PRINT used (Total process time):
      real time           0.02 seconds
      cpu time            0.02 seconds
```

PROC SQL naming convention

Table names, column names, and aliases of up to 32 characters in length are allowed. Column names in tables stored in relational database systems are subject to the restrictions of the database and are not overridden by SAS.

A summary of the valid SAS name rules is as follows:

- Up to 32 alphanumeric characters and the underscore (_) are allowed in names.
- Mixed case is allowed.
- Names must begin with either a character or an underscore.

Reserved words

There are several keywords that carry special meaning within PROC SQL statements. In ANSI Standard SQL, these keywords are reserved which means they cannot be used as column or table names.

SAS/ACCESS and SQL Pass-Through Facility users: The ANSI Standard reserves all SQL keywords regardless of the context. However, each RDBMS adheres to the standard differently. Refer to Appendix C, "Dictionary Table Descriptions," for more information related to database access using PROC SQL.

PROC SQL has a more liberal approach to keywords, reserving few and allowing their usage in some situations but not others. The following summarizes the reserved words:

- The CASE keyword is used to initiate a CASE expression. You cannot use it to indicate a column name on a SELECT statement; however, it can be used as a column alias on a SELECT clause or as a table alias in a FROM clause. It is possible to create a column named CASE using a CREATE statement, but this is problematic. Although a table may contain a column called *case*, it can be referenced in a SELECT statement only when you use an asterisk. For details on the CASE expression, refer to Chapter 3, "Understanding the SELECT Statement."
- The keywords listed below cannot normally be used for table aliases in a FROM clause; however, they can be used as table names as well as column names and column or expression aliases:

AS	INNER	OUTER
EXCEPT	INTERSECT	RIGHT
FROM	JOIN	UNION
FULL	LEFT	WHEN
GROUP	ON	WHERE
HAVING	ORDER	

Tip: The DQUOTE=ANSI option mentioned later in this chapter can be used to work with names that do not meet SAS guidelines. This option also allows you to include reserved words such as CASE in a SELECT statement.

Caution Using keywords for column and table names can make your query difficult to understand and debug. Consider using the SAS RENAME= option to replace column keyword names for use in PROC SQL. Remember, you can create a column heading or alias to identify the column by another name in your reports.

- The USER keyword is reserved for the current user ID. If it is referenced on a SELECT statement, the user ID is displayed once for each row retrieved by the SELECT statement. By default, the column does not have a label, although a label or heading can be applied to it.

Tip: The USER keyword can be very helpful in the creation of audit trail records. A program can be created to automatically add the user ID of the individual issuing certain statements to a table or data set.

PROC SQL comments

Comments of the form /**comment* */ may be added within an SQL statement. The code below gives two examples of this form of comment.

```
LIBNAME bluesky "C:\mydata\bluesky bookstore\";

SELECT *
FROM  bluesky.orders /*This is also a comment*/
/*Here is a comment within a SELECT statement on its own line*/
WHERE prodcode = '500500';
```

Comments of this form are also helpful for temporarily removing sections of your SQL statement. For example, in the code below several conditions are eliminated from processing because they are contained within the commented section.

> **Tip:** Comments within PROC SQL are added in the same way as comments in the rest of your SAS program.

```
LIBNAME bluesky "C:\mydata\bluesky bookstore\";

SELECT *
FROM  bluesky.orders
WHERE     prodcode = '500500' /*or prodcode = '400128' or prodcode
       = '400345'*/;

SELECT prodcode
FROM  bluesky.stock;
```

An alternative form of comment starts with an asterisk and ends with a semicolon. These comments are always indicated on a separate line from the SQL statements. The code below gives an example of this form of comment.

```
LIBNAME bluesky "C:\mydata\bluesky bookstore\";

SELECT prodcode
FROM  bluesky.stock;
*This is an alternate form of comment;
```

LIBNAME statement

General form:
LIBNAME *libref directory-path filename* **| RDBMS** *connection parameters***;**

One or more LIBNAME statements can precede or follow a PROC SQL statement establishing a set of libraries for the session. Once you define the libraries, all objects stored within those libraries are available to the SAS session. The LIBNAME statement syntax and usage with the SQL procedure is the same as that in Base SAS.

When you establish a SAS session, a default WORK storage location is created for all data sets, tables, and other files created during the session. The contents of the WORK library are cleared when the current SAS session ends.

Tip: If a USER library is specified on a LIBNAME statement, it becomes the default library for the SAS session, overriding the WORK library. It can be very helpful to set up a USER library so that you do not have to remember to use two-level names each time you want to permanently save a data set or table. To access the WORK library in this case, you would add WORK as the first-level name.

A LIBNAME statement associates a disk storage location with an alias or libref that remains active during your SAS session. Unlike the WORK library, all files stored in this location remain intact when the SAS session ends.

Tip: LIBNAME statements associating a libref name with a disk storage location can be cleared during an active SAS session using the CLEAR option:

```
LIBNAME bluesky CLEAR;
```

If you wish to clear all library references, add the _ALL_ keyword.

```
LIBNAME bluesky _ALL_CLEAR;
```

To reference a table stored in a permanent library location or to create a new data set or table in a library, you need both a first-level and second-level name. The first-level name refers to the libref name referenced on the LIBNAME statement; the second-level name identifies the specific table in the library.

Tip: Both permanent and temporary SAS data sets created in DATA steps and SAS procedures are available to the SQL procedure. When you're working in versions prior to SAS 9, you access permanent data sets using two-level names. Beginning with SAS 9 you can access a permanent data set by a physical filename.

An example of the storage of a newly created table called *orders* in the BLUESKY library is shown below. This table will be permanently stored in the directory location specified on the LIBNAME statement unless it is deleted using either SAS or system commands.

```
LIBNAME bluesky "C:\mydata\bluesky bookstore\";

CREATE table bluesky.neworder
       (prodcode char(6),
       ord_date date,
       quantity num);
```

Subsequent references to a table stored in a permanent library are made through a two-level name as shown below. Notice that the LIBNAME statement is not repeated. Once a LIBNAME statement has been issued, it remains in effect throughout the current SAS session, even if the SQL procedure is terminated.

```
SELECT    prodcode, ord_date, quantity
FROM      bluesky.orders
WHERE            quantity > 500;
```

prod Code	ord_date	quantity
500120	06MAY03	600
200345	10NOV03	1400
300680	20OCT03	2900
100340	09JAN03	800
500120	06SEP03	1000
200145	12APR04	700
400128	12APR04	1230
600125	05MAY04	600
200678	12JUN04	5000
100601	23JUL04	590
400102	23JUL04	1500

Tip: To reference a networked directory in Windows, use the following form:

```
LIBNAME name '\\host\directory\subdirectory';
```

For example, if Columbus is the name of the machine on which the folder *shared sas* is stored, the LIBNAME statement assigning MYSQL to this location would be as follows:

```
LIBNAME MYSQL '\\columbus\shared sas\tables';
```

DESCRIBE statement

The DESCRIBE statement provides an overview of a table or view. It provides a summary of all of the columns and their corresponding formats, data types, and labels. In addition, any indexes and constraints associated with the table are also indicated.

General form:
DESCRIBE TABLE *<libref>.table* | *view*;

Below is an example of the DESCRIBE statement run against the *orders* table of Bluesky Publishing Company. The CREATE statement for both the table and the index associated with the order date (ord_date) column are reported. Details on the PRIMARY KEY constraint associated with the product code (prodcode) and invoice columns are also reported.

```
LIBNAME bluesky "C:\mydata\bluesky bookstore\";

DESCRIBE TABLE bluesky.orderPend;
```

SAS log:

```
1221  describe table bluesky.orderPend;
NOTE: SQL table BLUESKY.ORDERPEND was created like:

create table BLUESKY.ORDERPEND( bufsize=8192 )
  (
   prodCode char(6),
   ord_date num format=DATE. informat=DATE.,
   quantity num,
   totsale num format=COMMA10.2,
   currency char(3),
   delCode char(3) label='Delivery Code',
```

(continued on the next page)

(continued)

```
   clientNo num,
   invoice char(10)
  );
create index ord_date on BLUESKY.ORDERPEND(ord_date);
create unique index prodinv_pk on
       BLUESKY.ORDERPEND(prodCode,invoice);
```

```
-----Alphabetic List of Integrity Constraints-----

     Integrity
#    Constraint     Type           Variables
__________________________________________________

1    prodinv_pk     Primary Key    prodCode invoice
```

Tip: For details on working with indexes, refer to Chapter 6, "Creating and Managing Tables and Views."

Working with databases

PROC SQL can be used to access tables and other objects stored in a database through a connection established either through SAS/ACCESS or the SQL Pass-Through Facility.

SAS/ACCESS LIBNAME statement

Beginning with SAS 8, the LIBNAME statement can reference a specific relational database as well as disk locations. The link is made possible through the installation of the appropriate SAS/ACCESS product for the RDBMS. Each RDBMS has a different set of connection options that are provided with the SAS/ACCESS documentation for that product.

General form:
LIBNAME *libref RDBMS*
SAS/ACCESS engine RDBMS specific connection options;

SAS/ACCESS and SQL Pass-Through Facility users

Information on the connection options used in SAS/ACCESS LIBNAME statements is provided in Appendix C, "Information for Database Users."

The SAS/ACCESS LIBNAME statement is supported for DB2, Oracle, Informix, Teradata, OLE DB, Sybase, ODBC, and PC files.

The SAS/ACCESS interface to CA-OpenIngres was discontinued in Version 9. In addition, SAS/ACCESS interfaces to DB2 and Oracle under VM and the Rdb interface under Alpha/OpenVMS, OS/2, and OpenVMS VAX platforms have also been discontinued.

Microsoft SQL Server databases are accessed through ODBC in a Windows Environment. SAS Version 9 introduced access to Microsoft SQL Server databases in UNIX environments using the SQL Pass-Through Facility.

A SAS/ACCESS LIBNAME engine, PC files was added in SAS Release 9.1 for Microsoft Access and Excel.

An example of a LIBNAME statement referencing a schema called *bluesky* in an Oracle database called *master* is shown below. The user name and password are included in the LIBNAME statement. By default the schema consists of objects owned by the user which in this case would be *scott*'s schema. The schema option is used here to open access to a collection of objects owned by *bluesky*. Only those objects that the user *scott* has been granted access to in the *bluesky* schema are available.

```
LIBNAME  bluesky ORACLE
         user = scott password = tiger path = master schema =
               bluesky;
```

Subsequent references to a permanent table includes both a first-level and second-level name. The first-level name refers to the library name referenced on the LIBNAME statement. The second-level name identifies the specific table in the database.

> **Tip:** Multiple LIBNAME statements can be issued for a SAS session, allowing for a link to one or more database locations and SAS data libraries.

If the LIBNAME statement references a database, the table will be stored in that database. An example of the creation of a table called *orders* in the *bluesky* schema stored in the *master* database is shown below. The CREATE statement is executed by the user *scott*; it will be successful only if the user has the necessary privileges in the database. The newly created table will belong to the *bluesky* schema.

All database objects created using PROC SQL are associated with the schema of the user indicated in the LIBNAME statement unless the SCHEMA option is set. A schema is a collection of objects owned by a user. Essentially, each database object has a two-level name, with a user ID used as a qualifier. By default, each time you connect to a database you are working within your own schema.

```
LIBNAME  bluesky ORACLE
         user = scott password = tiger path = master schema =
                bluesky;

CREATE table bluesky.neworder
                (prodcode char(6),
                 ord_date date,
                 quantity num);
```

In many cases the objects the user wishes to work with are associated with a different schema. The SCHEMA option in the LIBNAME statement is used to set an existing schema in the database as the default.

Information on working with databases using the SAS/ACCESS LIBNAME statement is included in Appendix C, "Information or Database Users."

When a DBMS connection is made through a LIBNAME statement, all PROC SQL statements are executed by the user indicated in the LIBNAME statement. The user must have the privileges necessary to create a table in order to successfully execute the PROC SQL statement shown above. Although the table is created in the database, SAS-specific SQL rather than database-specific SQL is used in the CREATE TABLE statement. In this example, SAS data types are used instead of Oracle data types.

SAS/ACCESS users

As of SAS 9, SAS/ACCESS views are no longer recommended. The CV2VIEW procedure can be used to convert your SAS/ACCESS views into PROC SQL views. More information on PROC SQL views is presented in Chapter 6, "Creating and Managing Tables and Views."

SQL Pass-Through Facility

The SQL Pass-Through Facility enables a user to retrieve information from a database and incorporate it into SAS data sets and tables, all from within the familiar SAS environment. A database-specific CONNECT statement first opens communication with the database. SAS then passes the SQL statements to the database for execution and returns the results to the SAS session. Finally, a DISCONNECT statement closes the database connection.

Consider again the task illustrated in the next example. What if the inventory and sales data were stored in a database? One option would be to extract the necessary data from the database and store it in a formatted file that can be imported into SAS.

The SQL Pass-Through facility provides the ability to submit database-specific SQL statements from within a SAS session. An example of the use of the SQL Pass-Through Facility to retrieve data from an Oracle database is shown below. The additional statements and syntax required to communicate with the database are highlighted.

```
 PROC SQL;

CONNECT to oracle (user=scott password=tiger path=master);

TITLE1   "Sales Information by Product Code and Author";
TITLE2   "January 1, 2003 to May 31, 2003";

SELECT     prodcode "Product Code" format=$15.,
                    auth_lst "Author" format=$15.,
           mnqty "Average Quantity" format=comma8.,
           mnprice "Average Price" format= comma10.2,
           smprice "Quantity * Price" format= comma10.2
FROM connection to oracle /* determines records returned to the
SAS session*/
    *inner SELECT statement executed by database;

(SELECT    stock.prodcode   ,
                 stock.auth_lst ,
           avg(orders.quantity) as mnqty ,
           avg(stock.price) as mnprice,
           sum(orders.quantity*stock.price) as smprice
FROM       bluesky.orders, bluesky.stock
WHERE      orders.ord_date between '01-JAN-2003' and
           '31-MAY-2003'
           and stock.prodcode = orders.prodcode
GROUP BY stock.prodcode, stock.auth_lst
ORDER BY stock.auth_lst);

DISCONNECT from oracle;
QUIT;
```

You will notice that the syntax in the inner SELECT statement differs from the PROC SQL SELECT statement syntax shown in the earlier section, “PROC SQL versus SAS DATA step.” The query passed to the relational database system must be consistent with the SQL that is native to that DBMS.

> **Tip:** The SELECT statement is covered in detail in Chapter 3, “Understanding the Select Statement.”

PROC SQL options

There are a wide range of SAS system and data set options that can be applied to customize a PROC SQL session. A complete discussion of SAS options is contained in the *SAS Language Reference*: *Dictionary*. Commonly used PROC SQL options and those that behave differently in SQL are summarized in the table below.

Option	Default	Description
DQUOTE=ANSI		Value within double quotation marks is treated as a variable. This option allows you to use reserved words, DBMS names, and other names that do not meet SAS specifications.
DQUOTE=SAS	√	Treats all values within double quotation marks as strings.
NOERRORSTOP[1]	√	Signals PROC SQL to continue execution and check all statement syntax is an error is encountered.
ERRORSTOP		Signals PROC SQL to stop execution but check all statement syntax if an error is encountered.
NOEXEC		Verifies the syntax of an SQL statement but does not execute the statement. Alternative is EXEC (default).
FEEDBACK		Causes the SQL statement to be displayed after all view references are expanded; also expands an asterisk on a SELECT statement to a list of columns.
FLOW=<*n* <*m*>>[2]		Character column values longer than *n* are flowed to multiple lines. If both *n* and *m* are specified, the width is floated between the two values to balance the layout. Alternative is NOFLOW (default).
INOBS=*n*		Limits the number of rows read from all tables listed on FROM clauses to *n*.
LOOPS=*n*		Limits the number of iterations through an inner loop to *n*; More information on this option and its companion macro option SQLOOPS is included in Chapter 7, "Building Interactive Applications."
OUTOBS=*n*		Limits the number of rows in the output to *n*;. This option can also be used to set the number of retrieved rows inserted into a table retrieved from another table.
NOPRINT		Does not print the output generated from the SQL procedure; often used in the assignment of macro variables. Alternative is PRINT (default).

(*continued*)

Option	Default	Description
PROMPT		PROC SQL prompts you to stop or continue each time the number specified on the INOBS, OUTOBS, or LOOPS option is reached.
NOPROMPT	√	PROC SQL stops processing when the limit imposed by INOBS, OUTOBS, or LOOPS is reached.
SORTSEQ=*sort-table*		Specifies a collating sequence for ORDER BY clauses that differs from the system's default collating sequence.
SORTMSG		Messages relating to PROC SQL sort operations will be reported in the log. Alternative is NOSORTMSG (default).
STIMER[3]		Reports real and CPU time information after each statement issued in PROC SQL executes.
NOSTIMER	√	Reports combine real and CPU time information for all statements issued during an invocation of PROC SQL.
THREADS[4]	√	Directs PROC SQL to use threaded processing if available.
NOTHREADS[4]		Directs PROC SQL to not use threaded processing, even if available.
UNDO_POLICY=REQUIRED	√	All inserts or updates that have been done to the point of the error are reversed.
UNDO_POLICY=NONE		All inserts and updates are kept.
UNDO_POLICY=OPTIONAL[5]		Only those updates or inserts that can be reversed reliably are reversed when an error occurs.
NUMBER[6]		Show row numbers in the output. Alternative is NONUMBER (default).

[1] When running in batch mode, the default is ERRORSTOP.

[2] FLOW will not wrap character column values that are longer than the length specified in a format on the SELECT statement.

[3] The STIMER system option must also be set. Refer to the section on system options below for more information.

[4] Once THREADS|NOTHREADS has been set on a PROC SQL statement or a RESET statement, it cannot revert to the default value unless PROC SQL is first terminated.

[5] Reversal cannot be completed if other changes would also be affected. An error message is issued by PROC SQL if an UNDO operation is not executed.

[6] The SAS system option NUMBER is used to control whether page numbers are displayed at the top of each page.

Tip: PROC OPTIONS provides details on SAS system options including the current value. Either all system options, a group of options, or a single option can be reported. Refer to *SAS Language Reference: Dictionary* for details.

If the THREADS option is used and another program has the SAS data set open for reading, writing, or updating, the SQL statement using that data set may fail. A message indicating statement failure is written to the log.

Options can be listed on the statement invoking the PROC SQL procedure or they may be set out separately on a SAS OPTIONS statement either before or after the procedure is run. However, an OPTIONS statement sets SAS system level options only.

Caution: An OPTIONS statement sets SAS system options. If you specify OPTIONS=NUMBER, you will be setting page numbers on. On the other hand the statement PROC SQL NUMBER turns row numbering on.

To change a specific PROC SQL option without quitting and rerunning the procedure, use the RESET statement. For example, the statement RESET NUMBER can be issued from within the SQL procedure.

In the code below the PROMPT and OUTOBS options are set out on the PROC SQL statement. A RESET statement is used to change the OUTOBS value after the execution of the first SELECT statement. Without the specification of a value, the OUTOBS option reverts to its default value. Notice, however, that an equal sign is required for this option whether a value is specified or not.

```
PROC SQL PROMPT OUTOBS=10;
LIBNAME bluesky "C:\mydata\bluesky bookstore\";

SELECT *
       FROM bluesky.orders;

RESET  outobs=;

SELECT *
       FROM bluesky.orders;
```

Tip: In the above example the RESET statement with the OUTOBS option is used to reset the number of observations to the default value of MAX. The RESET statement with OUTOBS=MAX could be used as an alternative. The advantage of using the RESET statement with option= form is that you do not have to know the default value for the option.

Using SAS data set options with PROC SQL

In addition to SAS system options and SQL procedure options, most of the SAS data set options can also be applied to tables and views referenced in an SQL statement. Data set options such as RENAME=, OBS=, KEEP=, and DROP= provide additional functionality within SQL statements.

Data set options are specified immediately following a table on the FROM clause of a SELECT statement. They can also be applied to both stand-alone SELECT statements and those that are used in conjunction with CREATE TABLE or CREATE VIEW statements.

The code below gives an example of a SELECT statement using data set options OBS= and DROP=. The OBS= option is used to limit the number of rows retrieved to three while the DROP= option is used to limit the reported columns.

```
LIBNAME bluesky "C:\mydata\bluesky bookstore\";

SELECT *
FROM   bluesky.orders(obs=3 drop=delcode);
```

prod Code	ord_date	quantity	totsale	currency	clientNo	invoice
100340	09JAN03	800	14400	CAD	8003	030109-01
100340	12JUN04	20	360	CAD	8003	041212-01
100345	10MAR04	180	11700	EUR	7008	040310-01

Tip: The DROP= data set option is great when you want to report all but a few columns from a table with many columns. Without the DROP= option, each column to be included in the report would have to be listed on the SELECT clause.

In the code below, a new *orders* table is created in the WORK library using the *orders* table from the BLUESKY library as a source of both structure and data. The OBS data set option limits the number of rows taken from the original table for the new table to ten. The DROP option causes the currency and delivery code (delcode) columns in the original table to be excluded from the new table. Neither of these options has an impact on the original table; only the newly created table is affected.

```
LIBNAME bluesky "C:\mydata\bluesky bookstore\";

CREATE table orders
  AS  SELECT *
      FROM   bluesky.orders(drop=currency delcode obs=10);

SELECT *
FROM  orders;
```

```
PROC SQL;
CREATE table orders
AS  SELECT *
FROM bluesky.orders(drop=currency delcode obs=10);

NOTE: Table WORK.ORDERS created, with 10 rows and 6 columns.

SELECT *
FROM orders;
```

prod Code	ord_date	quantity	totsale	clientNo	invoice
300456	07FEB03	300	2850	1001	030207-01
300680	06MAY03	150	2175	1001	030506-01
400178	06MAY03	500	32875	1001	030506-01
500120	06MAY03	600	20700	1001	030506-01
200345	10NOV03	1400	76972	4008	031110-01
300680	20OCT03	2900	3390	2010	031020-01
400100	15MAR03	125	5468.75	4008	030315-01
400128	11APR03	200	6800	7008	030411-01
400100	11APR03	200	8750	5005	030411-01
600125	24JUN03	350	2432.5	3007	030624-01

Tip: If you use a KEEP= data set option to control the columns in the new table, the order of the columns in the original table is maintained. If you wish to change the default order of the columns in the table, you must list the columns on the SELECT clause in the desired order.

More information on creating new tables from existing tables in included in Chapter 6, "Creating and Managing Tables and Views."

Data set options relating only to permission such as PW=, ALTER=, READ= and WRITE=, can be used in SELECT statements referencing views. In the code below, a new view called *ordview* is created in the WORK library and a password of *dog* is assigned to read access. When the view is accessed in the SELECT statement, the data set option PW= is used to provide the required password.

```
LIBNAME bluesky "C:\mydata\bluesky bookstore\";

CREATE VIEW ordview
AS SELECT   *
FROM        bluesky.orders(read=dog);

SELECT *
FROM   ordview(pw=dog);
```

Tip: You cannot use data set options other than those relating to permission in a SELECT statement retrieving data from a view or the data dictionary tables. However, you can use data set options in a SELECT statement referenced in a CREATE VIEW statement. More information on views is presented in Chapter 6, "Creating and Managing Tables and Views." Data dictionary tables are covered in Chapter 7, "Building Interactive Applications," and Appendix B, "Dictionary Table Descriptions."

SAS/ACCESS and SQL Pass-Through facility users: You cannot apply SAS data set options to an SQL statement passed to a database for processing using the SQL Pass-Through facility. To limit the number of observations processed, the PROC SQL option **NOOBS=** *<number>* is used instead of **OBS=** *<number>*.

Most SAS data set options apply if the SAS/ACCESS LIBNAME engine is used. More information on options available when using SAS/ACCESS and the SQL Pass-Through facility is provided in Appendix C, "Information for Database Users."

Important SAS system options for PROC SQL users

BUFSIZE option

General form:
BUFSIZE=*n* | *nK* | *nM* | *nG* | *MIN* | *MAX* | *hexX*

The BUFSIZE option specifies the permanent page size to be associated with tables created during that session. The page size sets the amount of data to be transferred to one buffer at a time. A default value appropriate to your operating environment is set automatically for BUFSIZE. The number of buffers available during a session is established by the BUFNO option. This option is set to 1 by default.

The BUFSIZE value can be set to size (*n*) in bytes, kilobytes (K), megabytes (M), or gigabytes (G) in the OPTIONS statement. If you want, you can specify the minimum (MIN) or maximum (MAX) value for your operating system or a hexadecimal (HEX) value.

> **Tip:** Rather than setting a minimum size, set BUFSIZE=0 to have SAS automatically set a default page size appropriate to your operating system.

When a table is created, specify a BUFSIZE value for the table if the default is not suitable. The BUFSIZE value specified for a table cannot be changed after the table has been created. However, the BUFSIZE value for the session can be altered at any time with the OPTIONS statement.

> **Tip:** The default BUFSIZE value optimizes sequential access to your tables. Performance for direct (random) access to your tables can be improved by changing the BUFSIZE values. The SAS documentation for your operating environment contains information about the default setting as well as settings for direct access.

STIMER option

There is a STIMER option at both the PROC SQL and the SAS system level, which controls whether CPU and real timing information are reported in the log. The real and CPU time for each statement issued in PROC SQL is reported to the SAS log only if the SAS system option STIMER is also set. If you use only the SAS system option, timing information for the procedure as a whole is reported when the procedure terminates.

PROC SQL output options

PROC SQL SELECT statements automatically generate output for reporting purposes and headings, formatting, and titles can be applied using standard SAS options. The output can also be used as input to other SAS procedures and DATA steps. A NOPRINT option can be specified in the PROC SQL statement to suppress the printing of the results set.

> **Tip:** Information on headings and formatting options within PROC SQL are included in Chapter 3, "Understanding the SELECT Statement."

PROC SQL output can be formatted using the Output Delivery System (ODS), an alternative available since SAS 7. The advantage? A greater range of output and formatting options, especially valuable when faced with the need to create one or more versions of a report derived from numerous SAS procedures. In the past, several versions of the program would have to be created and run for each report.

> **Tip:** How often have you found yourself re-running a lengthy SAS program in order to make small changes to formatting or output order? ODS allows you to format all of your output in a single step and manipulate the order and contents of your output. I find it especially useful when generating both an HTML and more formal hardcopy version of my analysis reports.

ODS destinations

There are three possible destinations for your output using ODS: SAS output listing, a SAS document, or a SAS data set.

The ODS SAS output listing destination is by default always assigned at the start of your SAS session. With few exceptions, the output listings included in the examples in this book were generated by the default ODS listing option.

ODS provides the ability to create a SAS document, including only the desired output in a specified order. Output from various SAS procedures can be combined in any order within the SAS document, regardless of the order in which they were run. In addition, output can be duplicated or deleted, eliminating the need to re-run programs to generate different versions of your final report. Formatting for the entire document can be set, eliminating the need to re-run your program to reformat one or more parts of your output and ensuring a consistent look and feel.

Finally, an output data set can be generated using the ODS output destination. This alternative is helpful when working with procedures such as PROC PRINT that generate only output and not a data set.

> **Tip:** Additional ODS information and examples are included in Chapter 8, "PROC SQL Enhancements in SAS 9." For more details on usind ODS, refer to the SAS customer support Web site and the SAS 9 product documentation.

Third-party formatted destinations

With ODS, procedure output can be generated using mark-up languages such as HTML or XML, allowing for the distribution of your reports via the Web. The mark-up option is extremely flexible; you can use existing mark-up language tagsets or create your own to suit unique needs. This functionality, as well as the ability to define your own styles, is provided by PROC TEMPLATE.

In the code below an HTML file called *order.html* is generated from the PROC SQL output. This query generates a table showing the total quantity of each book ordered by the Chicago State University by book title. The font, color, and other formatting of the report are drawn from the predefined style *BarrettsBlue*.

```
ODS html file='order.html' style=BarrettsBlue nogtitle;
TITLE "Orders placed by Chicago State University";
LIBNAME  bluesky "C:\mydata\bluesky bookstore\";

SELECT   s.title label="Book Title", sum(o.quantity) "Quantity"
FROM     bluesky.orders o, bluesky.stock s, bluesky.client c
WHERE    o.clientno=c.clientno and c.company='Chicago State
         University'
         and o.prodcode = s.prodcode
GROUP BY s.title;

ODS html close;
```

Tip: Why control the HTML file name? In a dynamic Web page or application, you might want the user to choose the report to be displayed. If each report is stored in a separate HTML file with a unique name, the appropriate report can be linked to each choice presented to the user.

Alternatively, each style attribute such as font, color, and height can be set on the ODS statement. These style attributes are applied to all output until the ODS HTML CLOSE statement is encountered. Style attributes can be overridden on statements such as the TITLE statement. In the code below the BarretsBlue style is set as the overall style for the output, but the attributes of font and color of this predefined style are overridden for the title.

```
ODS html file='order.html' style=BarrettsBlue nogtitle;
TITLE font=italic bold color=black "Orders placed by Chicago State
University";
```

Tip: There are numerous predefined styles available. Use the following query to obtain a list of ODS styles:

```
PROC SQL;
SELECT  style
FROM    dictionary.styles;
```

> More information on dictionary tables is included in Chapter 7, "Building Interactive Applications," and Appendix B, "Dictionary Table Descriptions." The PROC TEMPLATE procedure can also be used to obtain a list of styles or create new styles. Information on PROC TEMPLATE is provided in Chapter 8, "PROC SQL Enhancements in SAS 9."

Often the need is simpler; you might want to include SAS output in a Microsoft Word document for reporting. The rich text format (RTF) destination provides superior results for tables in Word by adjusting the column widths in SAS for the best fit on a Word document page.

Portable Adobe PDF and PostScript files can be created through the PRINTER destination. PDF files can be easily incorporated into Web pages as a download choice, making it possible to distribute SAS generated reports to a world-wide audience.

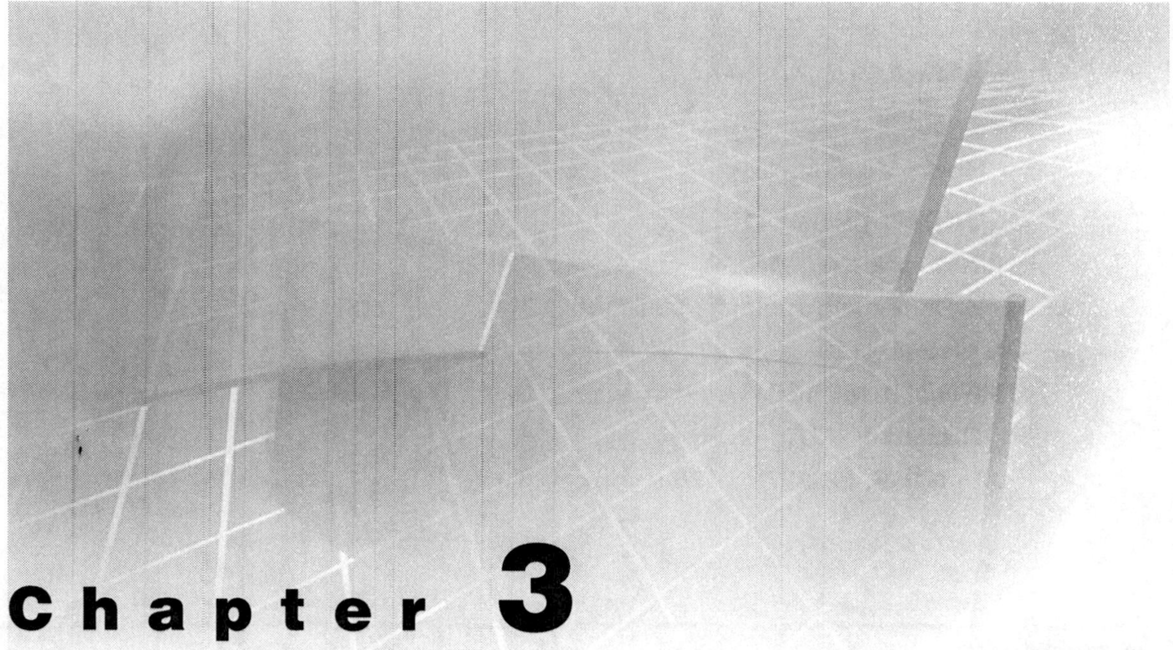

Chapter 3

Understanding the SELECT Statement

SELECT statement

Of all of the statements available in PROC SQL, the SELECT statement is probably the most commonly used. The SELECT statement, also known as a query, allows you to subset, summarize, manipulate, and report information stored in a table or data set.

In its simplest form, it reports the entire contents of a table, listing the contents of every column. However, when additional clauses and options are added it allows for complex forms of queries that list only certain columns or rows. In addition, the SELECT statement allows us to join tables and data sets together. When two or more tables are joined together, we can extract information from all of them simultaneously. Joins may include tables stored in database systems and within a SAS native library.

If you review the general form of the SELECT statement above, you will notice that only the SELECT and FROM clauses are required; all of the other clauses are optional. The SELECT clause indicates the column or columns to be retrieved while the FROM clause indicates the table or view in which the columns are stored.

Tip: The existence of both a SELECT statement and a SELECT clause causes confusion for many users. A SELECT statement is made up of one or more clauses and ends with a semicolon. It includes at minimum a SELECT and FROM clause.

General form:

```
<PROC SQL;>
SELECT   <DISTINCT> * |<table | alias.>column|expression
         <,<table|alias.>column|expression ...>
<INTO    clause>
FROM     <libref.>table <alias>  <JOIN operator> <libref.>table <alias>
<ON           clause>
<WHERE        clause>
<GROUP BY     clause>
<HAVING       clause>
<ORDER BY     clause>
<USING        clause>
     ;

<QUIT;>
```

Tip: The PROC SQL statement is only required if the procedure has not already been invoked. The procedure remains in effect until a QUIT statement is processed.

Syntax description:

- Each line represents a separate clause in a SELECT statement.
- The order in which each clause appears in the SELECT statement is fixed.
- An optional clause, keyword, or item in a clause is enclosed in angle brackets (< >).
- Keywords are shown in uppercase.
- A vertical bar (|), indicates a set of choices.
- If several repetitions of the same item can be included in a clause, an ellipsis is used.
- A column is a single variable in a table whereas an expression includes a function or two or more columns linked by an operator. For example, a column multiplied by another column would form an expression.
- A single semicolon (;) is used to end the SELECT statement.

The order in which each of the clauses shown above can appear in a SELECT statement cannot be altered. The error message you receive if your clauses are in the wrong order can be ambiguous. The next example shows a SELECT statement in which the ORDER BY and FROM clauses have been reversed and the resulting SAS error message. A syntax error is indicated. However, the statement order is not mentioned as one of the possible causes. In this example, the ORDER BY prodcode statement has been interpreted as a set of three columns in the SELECT clause with the required commas between each of the columns missing. Details on the correct syntax for a SELECT clause that includes a list of columns is included in the next section.

```
LIBNAME bluesky "C:\mydata\bluesky bookstore\";

SELECT    *
ORDER BY prodcode
FROM  bluesky.orders;
```

SAS log:

```
    .
    256   SELECT  *
    257   ORDER BY prodcode
    258   FROM bluesky.orders;
               -----
               22
               76
ERROR 22-322: Syntax error, expecting one of the following: ',',
FROM, INTO.

ERROR 76-322: Syntax error, statement will be ignored.
```

Tip: SAS and RDBMS syntax errors relating to SQL can be ambiguous. Check your statement order first; then check the syntax of each clause in your statement starting with the clause before the underlined error message indicator.

A simple SELECT statement might look as follows:

```
SELECT      *
FROM        reprint;
```

This statement would return all columns of information from a table called *reprint* stored in the SAS work library. The output is shown below.

reprint	cutOff
A	0
B	10
C	50
D	100
E	500
F	1000

Compare the previous SELECT statement to one with a few more options shown below.

```
LIBNAME bluesky "C:\mydata\bluesky bookstore\";

SELECT    currency "Currency", mean(exchrate) "Average",
          max(exchrate) "Maximum", min(exchrate) "Minimum"
FROM      bluesky.currency
WHERE     currency IN ('CAD','EUR','SGD')
GROUP BY  currency;
```

Tip: Labels have been added to the columns giving a more readable report. More information on labels is included later in this chapter.

This SELECT statement returns values from the *currency* table; but in this instance the table is in the permanent library location referenced by *bluesky*. The SELECT clause now indicates a specific set of columns that are to be included in the report. A new value is also calculated from two of the columns in the table. In addition, the rows that are retrieved from the table are limited with a WHERE clause. Finally, the results are grouped by the currency variable. The output is shown below.

Currency	Average	Maximum	Minimum
CAD	1.37798	1.54145	1.2966
EUR	0.858131	0.9416	0.79293
SGD	1.728042	1.77712	1.68325

SQL Pass-Through Facility SELECT statement

If you are using the SQL Pass-Through Facility, the syntax changes slightly. The Pass-Through Facility has an outer SELECT statement that controls which columns and rows are available or reported in the SAS session from those returned from the database. The clauses and options included in the outer SELECT statement are specific to PROC SQL.

The inner SELECT statement is passed directly to the relational database for processing. The clauses and options included in the inner SELECT statement are specific to the RDBMS to which the connection is made.

General form:

```
PROC SQL;

          CONNECT TO dbms-name <AS alias>
                     (dbms-argument = value
                     <dbms-argument=value ...>);

Outer Query  SELECT     clause
          FROM       CONNECTION TO
                     dbms-name | alias

Inner Query  (SELECT    clause
          FROM       <owner.>table <alias>
                     <JOIN operator>
                     <owner.>table <alias>
          <optional inner SELECT statement clauses>)

          <optional outer SELECT statement clauses>;

          DISCONNECT FROM dbms-name | alias;

<QUIT>;
```

Tip: Inner SELECT statements are passed directly to the database for processing. As a result, they may include clauses that are not available in SAS and the syntax may differ. Refer to your RDBMS SQL documentation for details.

Both the inner and outer SELECT statements may include optional clauses such as WHERE, GROUP BY, and ORDER BY. Optional clauses in the outer SELECT statement are placed after the closing parenthesis of the inner SELECT statement.

The next example is based on the SQL query in the previous example. The inner SELECT statement shown here is almost identical to the third example in the "SELECT statement" section preceding. However, the SQL language that is specific to Oracle uses the keyword *avg* instead of *mean* to calculate an average from a column of values. The asterisk on the outer SELECT clause causes SAS to report all columns returned from the database table resulting from the execution of the inner SELECT statement. All of the rows returned by the inner SELECT statement are included in the report because the outer SELECT statement lacks a WHERE clause. The ORDER BY clause in the outer SELECT statement is processed by SAS after the rows are retrieved from the database.

```
PROC SQL;

CONNECT TO ORACLE
(user=scott password=tiger path=master);

SELECT    *
FROM      CONNECTION TO ORACLE

(SELECT   currency "Currency", avg(exchrate) "Average",
          max(exchrate) "Maximum", min(exchrate) "Minimum"
FROM      bluesky.currency
WHERE     currency IN ('CAD','GBP','DEM')
GROUP BY  currency
)
ORDER BY  currency;

DISCONNECT FROM ORACLE;

QUIT;
```

SELECT and FROM clauses

- ▶ SELECT
- INTO
- ▶ FROM
- ON
- WHERE
- GROUP BY
- HAVING
- ORDER BY
- USING;

General form:

SELECT <DISTINCT> * | <table qualifer.>column | expression <AS alias> <column-modifier > | constant <, ...>

FROM <libref.>table <alias> <JOIN operator> <libref.>table <alias> <,...>

Note: Column modifiers can only be used when columns are explicitly named in a SELECT clause. They are not available if an asterisk, representing all columns, is used in a SELECT clause.

The SELECT clause contains a list of one or more columns of data values to be retrieved from a table. Arithmetic, statistical and character functions can be applied to any of the columns. A discussion on the use of functions is contained in Chapter 4, "Functions."

The FROM clause identifies the table or tables that contain the columns listed in the SELECT clause. Every SELECT statement must contain these two clauses in order to generate a result set or report from a table or data set. The next example contains a query that specifies the product code (prodcode), order date (ord_date), quantity and total sale price (totsale) columns in the SELECT clause. The resulting report contains only those columns from the *orders* table although there are additional columns in the table. Notice that the sequence of the columns in the report matches the column sequence in the SELECT clause.

Tip: A join operator is added to a FROM clause only if an ON clause is included in the SELECT statement. Information relating to the ON clause is found later in this chapter.

A WHERE clause has been added to this query to limit the number of rows reported. The WHERE clause is covered in detail later in this chapter.

```
LIBNAME    bluesky "C:\mydata\bluesky bookstore\";

SELECT     prodcode, ord_date, quantity, totsale
FROM       bluesky.orders
WHERE      ord_date > '01JUL2004'd;
```

```
prod
Code     ord_date  quantity   totsale
--------------------------------------
500168   20JUL04        335     11390
100601   23JUL04        590   15487.5
400102   23JUL04       1500     82500
400178   23JUL04         10     657.5
500116   23JUL04        400     13600
```

Tip: Character and numeric values can also be specified in a SELECT clause. For example, a comma can be added after each column in an output file if a delimited file is needed. Constant values, both numeric and character, can also be added:

```
PROC SQL;
 SELECT        "Bluesky Publishing Company" ,
               "," , 2004 , "," ,
               ord_date ,  ","  , totsale
 FROM          bluesky.orders;
```

Alternatively, all columns in the table can be retrieved by specifying an asterisk (*) after the SELECT keyword as shown in the following example.

```
LIBNAME    bluesky "C:\mydata\bluesky bookstore\";

SELECT     *
FROM       bluesky.orders
WHERE      ord_date > '01JUL2004'd;
```

prod Code	ord_date	quantity	totsale	currency	del Code	clientNo	invoice
500168	20JUL04	335	11390	AUD	EXP	5005	040720-01
100601	23JUL04	590	15487.5	EUR	EXP	3007	041223-01
400102	23JUL04	1500	82500	AUD	EXP	5005	041223-02
400178	23JUL04	10	657.5	EUR	EXP	6090	041223-03
500116	23JUL04	400	13600	EUR	EXP	7008	041223-04

Tip: When you use the asterisk option in the SELECT clause, you cannot specify alias, label, and formatting for table columns. However, labels and formats associated with each column at the time the table was created will be applied. See Chapter 5, "Working with Two or More Tables," for more information on creating tables.

SELECT clause

► SELECT
INTO
FROM
ON
WHERE
GROUP BY
HAVING
ORDER BY
USING;

General form:

SELECT <DISTINCT> * | <table qualifer.>column | expression
<AS alias> <column-modifier > | constant
<, …>

The SELECT clause controls the columns or expressions passed to the result set. There are several options available for the SELECT clause. If the DISTINCT keyword is added to the SELECT clause, it reports only unique values in the columns included on the clause. It is processed in the same way as a PROC SORT statement with a NODUP option. The SELECT statement in the following code generates a report of unique order dates (ord_date) within the *orders* table for the Bluesky Publishing Company.

Tip: The PROC SORT NODUP and NODUPKEY options operate in the same way as the DISTINCT keyword. A discussion of recommended usage for each is included in this section.

```
LIBNAME   bluesky "C:\mydata\bluesky bookstore\";

SELECT    DISTINCT ord_date
FROM      bluesky.orders
WHERE     ord_date > '01JUL2004'd;
```

```
ord_date
________

20JUL04
23JUL04
```

If several different columns or expressions are included with the DISTINCT keyword, then the report will show all unique combinations of the columns or expressions. Notice that the output shown in the example below includes multiple entries for July 23, 2004. However, each entry for this date is associated with a different client number, making the combination of order date and client number distinct.

```
LIBNAME   bluesky "C:\mydata\bluesky bookstore\";

SELECT    DISTINCT ord_date, clientno
FROM      bluesky.orders
WHERE     ord_date > '01JUL2004'd;
```

```
ord_date  clientNo
__________________

20JUL04       5005
23JUL04       3007
23JUL04       5005
23JUL04       6090
23JUL04       7008
```

Tip: When the DISTINCT keyword is used, it is applied to every column on the SELECT clause. Only the unique combinations of the listed columns or expressions will be included in the report. If an asterisk is included on the SELECT clause, only rows that have a complete set of unique values are included.

PROC SORT versus SELECT DISTINCT

There are several options available in the SORT procedure that eliminate duplicate values from the result set. The SORT procedure's NODUP, NODUPKEY, and NODUPRECS options provide similar functionality to the DISTINCT keyword shown here. However, there are important distinctions among these processes.

PROC SORT overwrites the existing table eliminating the duplicates unless an output table is indicated. Duplicates in the columns specified in the BY statement are identified, and all rows except for the first BY group are eliminated. All of the columns in the original table are kept unless a KEEP or DROP option is added. Alternatively, rows in which all column values are duplicated can be removed.

The PROC SQL SELECT statement with a DISTINCT keyword eliminates the duplicates only from the result set; the table itself remains unchanged. Moreover, the DISTINCT option checks for duplicate values in the specified columns and creates a result set that includes only those columns.

This allows for several queries checking for different duplicate values. In the following example the table is checked for duplicates in the order date (ord_date) and product code (prodcode) columns. Each of the columns is treated separately although they are part of the same SELECT statement. A count of the unique order dates and book product code values is generated. These counts can then be compared to the total number of entries in each column to quickly determine the number of unique values of each.

```
LIBNAME    bluesky "C:\mydata\bluesky bookstore\";

SELECT     count(distinct ord_date)  'Distinct order dates',
           count(ord_date) 'Total number of order dates',
           count(distinct prodcode)'Distinct products',
           count(prodcode)'Total number of products'
FROM       bluesky.orders;
```

```
  Distinct      Total
     order      order  Distinct      Total
     dates      dates  products   products
  ----------------------------------------
        23         40        27         40
```

SELECT DISTINCT also provides an easy method of incorporating complex manipulation involving more than one table and a check for uniqueness in the same step. Consider the next example. In this query, four tables are joined to determine the categories of books sold by client country. This single SELECT statement merges the four tables using different common columns and retrieves the distinct combinations of country and category. The ability to merge two or more tables filter or subset the results, and report unique values in a single statement is unique to PROC SQL.

```
LIBNAME   bluesky "C:\mydata\bluesky bookstore\";

SELECT    DISTINCT address.country, stock.category
FROM      bluesky.client, bluesky.orders,
          bluesky.address, bluesky.stock
WHERE     client.clientno = address.clientno
          and client.clientno = orders.clientno
          and orders.prodcode=stock.prodcode
          and country ne 'USA';
```

country	category
Australia	computer
Australia	medicine
Canada	arts
Canada	computer
Canada	general
Canada	medicine
Canada	science
France	general
France	medicine
France	science
Germany	arts
Germany	engineering
Germany	medicine
Singapore	engineering
Singapore	general
Singapore	medicine
UK	arts
UK	engineering
UK	general
UK	science

As an alternative to overwriting the current table, the OUTPUT option of PROC SORT provides an easy method of creating a new table with the results of the sort. To create a new table populated only with unique values from the currency column of the *currency* table using PROC SQL, a DISTINCT keyword is added to the SELECT clause of the subquery in a CREATE TABLE statement. Compare the equivalent PROC SORT and PROC SQL statements in the following.

```
LIBNAME  bluesky "C:\mydata\bluesky bookstore\";

PROC SORT data=bluesky.currency out=new_table(keep=currency) NODUPKEY;
         by currency;
RUN;

* The following PROC SQL statement performs the same task;

LIBNAME  bluesky "C:\mydata\bluesky bookstore\";

PROC SQL;

CREATE TABLE new_table
          AS   SELECT DISTINCT currency
               FROM bluesky.currency;
QUIT;
```

Tip: A subquery is an SQL statement within another SQL statement. In the above example, the SELECT statement is a subquery because it is part of the CREATE TABLE statement. Subqueries are commonly used in WHERE clauses of SELECT statements. More information on subqueries is found in Chapter 5, "Working with Two or More Tables."

Tip: More details on the CREATE TABLE statement are provided in Chapter 6, "Creating and Managing Tables and Views." Table joins are covered in Chapter 5, "Working with Two or More Tables."

Column modifiers—labels and formatting

The use of column labels and formats can greatly improve reports generated through the SQL procedure. One or both of these column modifiers can be applied to each column or expression in a SELECT clause. They can also be specified for columns or expressions for which an alias has been defined.

Formats

Standard and custom user-defined SAS formatting can be applied to any column in a SELECT clause. The keyword FORMAT must precede the format specification.

In the next example, formats for three of the columns and expressions in the SELECT clause have been specified. A WHERE clause has been added to the query limiting the report to the arts category books currently stocked by the Bluesky Publishing Company.

```
LIBNAME   bluesky "C:\mydata\bluesky bookstore\";

TITLE1    'Report of value of Art Books in Stock';
TITLE2    'Bluesky Publishing Company';

SELECT    title FORMAT = $40.,
          stock,
          price FORMAT= dollar10.2,
          stock*price as totprice FORMAT= dollar12.2
FROM      bluesky.stock
WHERE     category = 'arts'
ORDER     by totprice;
```

```
                 Report of value of Art Books in Stock
                      Bluesky Publishing Company

title                                         stock        price      totprice
------------------------------------------------------------------------------
The Ultimate Philosophy                         100        $9.50       $950.00
Democracy in America                             55       $36.00     $1,980.00
The Underground Economy                        1000       $14.50    $14,500.00
Decorative Arts                                1500       $16.95    $25,425.00
```

Tip: A report title can be specified in a TITLE statement. These titles remain in effect until a new TITLE statement is issued. There are many more reporting options available through ODS. Information on ODS is provided in Chapter 2, "Working with PROC SQL," and Chapter 8, "PROC SQL Enhancements in Version 9."

The rules that apply to the application of a format to a column or expression are as follows:

- The FORMAT keyword must precede the format specification.
- An optional equal sign (=) may be specified after the FORMAT keyword for clarity.

- All SAS standard formats and user-defined formats created in PROC FORMAT are available. Information on SAS formats is included in the *SAS Language: Reference: Dictionary*; PROC FORMAT is covered in the *Base SAS Procedures Guide*.

PROC FORMAT can be used to associate formats with columns listed in a SELECT clause in the same way they are used in Base SAS. However, PROC SQL does not acknowledge formats in either the GROUP BY or ORDER BY clauses.

In the next example PROC FORMAT is used to associate a book category for specified product code ranges.

```
LIBNAME bluesky "C:\mydata\bluesky bookstore\";

PROC FORMAT;
value $category
      'science'='General Science'
      'engineering'='Engineering'
      'arts' ='General Arts'
      'medicine' = 'Medicine'
           'computer' = 'Information Technology'
           'general' = 'General Interest'
;

PROC SQL;

SELECT    distinct category "Category" format= $category.
FROM      bluesky.stock;
```

```
Category
______________________

General Arts
Information Technology
Engineering
General Interest
Medicine
General Science
```

Tip: Formats defined using PROC FORMAT can be included in a SELECT statement to modify the appearance of column values. However, the original data value is used for sorting and grouping in ORDER BY and GROUP BY statements. To use a format value in the ORDER BY or GROUP BY statements, consider using the CASE expression to generate a new variable with the formatted value. Details on the CASE expression and the ORDER BY and GROUP BY statements are included later in this chapter.

Labels

A heading or label can be indicated for each column or expression. Labels are flexible in terms of the allowable length and characters. However, they can only be used to generate a column heading in your report.

In the next example labels and formats have been applied to columns and expressions in the SELECT clause. The LABEL keyword and the equal sign associated with it are both optional. If you check the SELECT clause carefully, you will notice that the stock column associates a label simply by including a quoted string after the column name. On the other hand, the title column uses only the LABEL keyword. The report titles are specified in a TITLE statement in the same way as titles for other Base SAS procedures.

```
TITLE1    'Report on value of Art Books in Stock';
TITLE2    'Bluesky Publishing Company';

LIBNAME bluesky "C:\mydata\bluesky bookstore\";

SELECT    title LABEL 'Book Titles' FORMAT= $40.,
          stock 'Qty of Books',
          price LABEL='Book Price' FORMAT= comma10.2,
          stock*price LABEL= 'Stock Value' FORMAT= comma10.2
FROM      bluesky.stock
WHERE     category = 'arts';
```

```
              Report on value of Art Books in Stock
                    Bluesky Publishing Company

                                          Qty of               Stock
Book Titles                                Books  Book Price      Value
----------------------------------------------------------------------
Decorative Arts                             1500       16.95  25,425.00
The Ultimate Philosophy                      100        9.50     950.00
Democracy in America                          55       36.00   1,980.00
The Underground Economy                     1000       14.50  14,500.00
```

Tip: Labels are often confused with aliases, discussed in the next section. Aliases are also set in the SELECT clause; however, they operate very differently. As a result, when you first start programming in PROC SQL you may find it helpful to use LABEL= *'string'* for all of your labels in order to more clearly distinguish them from aliases.

I do not recommend using the LABEL keyword without the equal sign because it can be confused for a column name by those new to SQL programming. If you want to avoid the extra typing, exclude the LABEL keyword and add your quoted string directly after the column or expression name as was done for the stock column in the above example.

Warning: If you include a quoted label in an ORDER BY clause, SAS will report a warning rather than an error. The ORDER BY clause treats the quoted string as a constant value that occurs in every row and executes the query.

It is always a good idea to check your SAS log for warning messages!

The rules that apply to the use of a heading or label are as follows:

- The keyword LABEL is optional.
- An optional equal sign (=) can be specified after the LABEL keyword for clarity.
- Either must be enclosed in matching single or double quotes
- To include a single quote within the text string, you must enclose the entire heading in double quotes.
- Spaces and special characters including ' , - , / , $, # and @ are allowed.
- Both are case-sensitive.
- Text strings that do not include blanks are never divided between multiple lines.
- Column width in the report will be adjusted to accommodate the longest text string in the heading unless a FORMAT option is also indicated.
- The heading will be spread over several lines with blanks being used to aid separation. The length of the longest string controls the maximum number of characters and spaces that will appear in any single line.

Tip: Formats and labels can be associated with each column in a table at the time of creation. This eliminates the need to specify column modifiers in SELECT statements. Chapter 6, "Creating and Managing Tables and Views," contains details on the options available with the CREATE TABLE statement.

Caution: Formats and labels added in the CREATE TABLE statement are permanently associated with the table. Every SAS procedure accessing the table will use those formats and labels as the default for that table. They can, however, be overridden in SELECT statements or procedures such as PROC PRINT.

SAS/ACCESS and SQL Pass-Through facility users: SAS formats, labels, and lengths applied in a CREATE TABLE statement issued against a database are not passed to the database. More details on creating tables within a database from PROC SQL are included in Appendix C, "Information for Database Users."

Use of column or expression aliases

An alias can be applied to a column or expression in the SELECT clause. When an alias is specified, a new temporary variable with the alias name is created based on the column or expression. An alias is active only for the current SQL statement, unless it is assigned in a SELECT clause that is part of a CREATE TABLE statement.

Tip: If you assign an alias to an expression in a SELECT clause that forms a subquery in a CREATE TABLE statement, the alias becomes the name of the column in the new table.

Once an alias has been assigned, it (rather than the original column or expression) can be referenced in other SELECT clauses such as WHERE and ORDER BY or in subqueries. As a result, aliases can simplify complex queries, especially when expressions based on nested functions are included in a SELECT clause.

Tip: There is a difference between a column heading or label and a column alias. If you do not include the AS keyword, you are associating a column label with the variable. Column labels are used to enhance output only and cannot be referenced within a SELECT statement.

There are several rules that apply to the creation of an alias on a SELECT clause:

- The alias must be preceded by an AS keyword. If the AS keyword is omitted, an error message such as the one shown in the SAS log on page 65 is reported in the SAS log.
- The alias is limited to 32 characters or fewer.
- Standard SAS variable naming conventions apply:

  Only letters, digits, and the underscore are allowed in the name.

  The variable name must begin with a letter or an underscore.
- The alias can be referenced in ORDER BY, GROUP BY, HAVING and WHERE clauses in a SELECT statement. To include an alias in a WHERE or GROUP BY clause you must precede it with the CALCULATED keyword.

In the SELECT statement shown in the next example the stock quantity (stock) is multiplied by the unit price to give a total inventory value. The alias totprice is assigned to the calculation and a column heading is associated with the newly calculated variable.

Tip: Both an alias and a column label can be associated with an expression in a SELECT clause. If you assign an alias to an expression and omit the column label, the alias will appear above the column in the output.

```
LIBNAME bluesky "C:\mydata\bluesky bookstore\";

SELECT    title, stock, price,
          stock*price as totprice 'Total Stock Value'
FROM      bluesky.stock
WHERE     stock > 500
ORDER     by totprice;
```

title	stock	price	Total Stock Value
Women Writers	1000	8.6	8600
Risks in Life - % Gain or Loss?	1000	14.3	14300
The Underground Economy	1000	14.5	14500
Visual Basic for Beginners	600	34	20400
Start a Business Using a Computer	1000	22.25	22250
Free Thinking in Mathematics	900	26.25	23625
Decorative Arts	1500	16.95	25425
Introduction to Computer_Science	1000	32.5	32500
Unconventional treatments	1000	55	55000
The Art of Computer Programming	1600	34.5	55200
Tibetan Medicine	2000	34	68000
Book of Science and Nature	1000	69	69000
Space Sciences	1500	56.25	84375
Engineering Infrastructure Modeling	2400	54.98	131952
Managing Water Resources	6000	45	270000

Tip: If an alias is not assigned to an expression in the SELECT clause, the resulting column will have a blank heading unless a label is specified for the expression. It is good practice to assign aliases to all calculated values generated in a SELECT statement. Although a label will improve the look of the report, it cannot be used in other clauses in the SELECT statement.

If the AS keyword is omitted, the SELECT statement fails and an error message is written to the SAS log, as shown in the next example. In PROC SQL a quoted string is required for every column label specified. Only aliases are included without quotes and they must be preceded by an AS keyword.

SAS log:

```
432   PROC SQL;
433   SELECT  title, stock, price,
434       stock*price totprice
                      --------
                      22
ERROR 22-322: Syntax error, expecting one of the following: !, !!,
  &, *, **, +, ',', -, '.', /, <, <=, <>, =, >, >=, ?, AND, AS,
  CONTAINS, EQ, EQT, GE, GET, GT, GTT, LE, LET, LIKE, LT, LTT,
  NE, NET, OR, ^=, |, ||, ~=.

435   FROM    bluesky.stock
436   WHERE   stock > 500
437   ORDER   by totprice;
```

> **Tip:** In a SELECT clause, quotes are required for column labels; column aliases must be preceded by the AS keyword.

The previous example reports all of the rows or observations in the *stock* table. An alias may also be used in a WHERE clause to limit the reported rows. The alias must be preceded by a CALCULATED keyword as shown in the next example. A more detailed discussion of WHERE clauses can be found in a later section of this chapter.

```
LIBNAME bluesky "C:\mydata\bluesky bookstore\";

SELECT    title, stock,
          price,
          stock*price as totprice
FROM      bluesky.stock
WHERE     CALCULATED totprice < 3000;
```

title	stock	price	totprice
Democracy in America	55	36	1980
The Ultimate Philosophy	100	9.5	950
National Library of Medicine	35	65.75	2301.25
Medications and Maintenance	30	86	2580
Computer: Beginners Guide	100	23.5	2350
The Maestro	100	6.95	695
Mountaineering Skills	200	5.5	1100

Tip: The CALCULATED keyword tells SAS that the variable is not a column in the table, but rather a variable generated by the SELECT clause. It is necessary because the WHERE clause is processed before the SELECT clause. As a result, expressions created in the SELECT clause are unknown to the WHERE clause unless the CALCULATED keyword is included.

CASE expressions

General form:

CASE <variable>
WHEN condition **THEN** value| column| expression| query
<**WHEN** condition **THEN** value| column| expression| query>
<**ELSE** column| value| expression| query >
END

Tip: The ELSE clause is optional. If an ELSE clause is not included in your CASE expression, missing values will be used for all values not meeting any of the WHEN conditions in the CASE expression. The following note will be written to the SAS log:

```
NOTE: A CASE expression has no ELSE clause. Cases not
      accounted for by the  WHEN clauses will result
      in a missing value for the CASE expression.
```

Caution: If your query includes nested CASE expressions, it is easy to forget an ELSE clause.

The guidelines for CASE expressions are as follows:

- The keyword CASE starts the expression and the keyword END closes it.
- One or more conditions may be included in a CASE expression after a WHEN keyword.
- The ELSE keyword may be used to set the value of a column for every row that does not meet the conditions set out after the WHEN keyword.
- A column from an existing table, a constant value, expression, or subquery may be included after the WHEN or ELSE keywords.
- Subqueries included within CASE expressions must adhere to the standard guidelines.

Tip: Information on subqueries and an example of a CASE expression used in conjunction with a subquery are included in Chapter 5, "Working with Two or More Tables."

In the next example a CASE expression is used to format the book categories stored in the Bluesky *stock* table. The CASE expression presented in this example operates in the same manner as PROC FORMAT. Notice that there are six books for which there is no assigned category. The absence of an ELSE keyword and value results in a missing category unless an exact match to one of the WHEN conditions is found.

```
LIBNAME bluesky "C:\mydata\bluesky bookstore\";

SELECT    CASE category
          when 'general' then 'General Subjects'
          when  'arts' then 'Arts and Philosophy'
          when  'science' then 'General Science'
          when  'medicine' then 'Medicine and Pharmacology'
          when  'engineering' then 'Engineering'
          end "Book Category" ,
          category, count(prodcode)"Number of Books"
FROM      bluesky.stock
GROUP BY  category;
```

```
                                                      Number
Book Category                 category               of Books
-----------------------------------------------------------------
Arts and Philosophy           arts                          4
                              computer                      6
Engineering                   engineering                   4
General Subjects              general                       5
Medicine and Pharmacology     medicine                      6
General Science               science                       5
```

Tip: The order of the rows in the report in the previous example is controlled by the category value and not the book category label assigned to each category in the CASE expression. As a result, the blank book category is displayed after "Arts and Philosophy" because it has a category value of "computer."

An ELSE keyword and value of "Not Categorized" has been added to the CASE expression in the next example. All category values that do not match one of the WHEN values will be automatically set to the ELSE value.

```
LIBNAME bluesky "C:\mydata\bluesky bookstore\";

SELECT     CASE category
           when 'general' then 'General Subjects'
           when  'arts' then 'Arts and Philosophy'
           when  'science' then 'General Science'
           when  'medicine' then 'Medicine and Pharmacology'
           when  'engineering' then 'Engineering'
           else 'Not Categorized'
           end "Product Category" ,
           category, count(prodcode)"Number of Books"
FROM       bluesky.stock
GROUP BY   category;
```

Product Category	category	Number of Books
Arts and Philosophy	arts	4
Not Categorized	computer	6
Engineering	engineering	4
General Subjects	general	5
Medicine and Pharmacology	medicine	6
General Science	science	5

SAS/ACCESS and SQL Pass-Through facility users: Not all versions of databases allow CASE expressions in SQL. In some cases there is a similar function such as the DECODE function in Oracle. In others, the CASE expression is available in database-specific procedural languages based on SQL such as PL/SQL or TRANSACT/SQL.

FROM clause

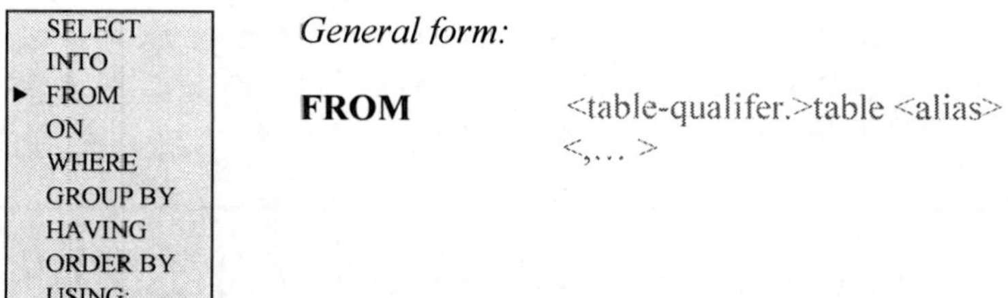

General form:

FROM <table-qualifer.>table <alias>
<,... >

The FROM clause indicates the table or tables from which columns are available for the SELECT statement. It is not necessary for all columns to be located in a single table because a WHERE or ON clause can link two or more tables together. But when columns of the same name appear in two or more of the tables, it is necessary to indicate the table serving as the source of the column.

Tip: Tables may also be joined or linked with a WHERE clause or through the use of an ON clause with a FROM clause. Joins are discussed in detail in Chapter 5, "Working with Two or More Tables."

Notice in the next example that the SAS library name is referenced only in the FROM clause. The prefix on each of the columns in the SELECT clause refers only to the table name. The inclusion of this prefix is only necessary if the same column exists in more than one table referenced in the FROM clause. In this situation a prefix is required to indicate which table is the source of the column. For example, the WHERE clause in the next example refers to a column called clientno which exists in both the *client* and *orders* tables. In order to distinguish between them, the column name is prefixed with a table qualifier.

```
LIBNAME bluesky "C:\mydata\bluesky bookstore\";

SELECT    orders.prodcode, orders.ord_date,
          orders.quantity, orders.totsale,
          client.cont_fst, client.cont_lst
FROM      bluesky.orders,
          bluesky.client
WHERE     orders.clientno = client.clientno
          and ord_date > '01JUL2004'd;
```

prod Code	ord_date	quantity	totsale	cont_fst	cont_lst
500168	20JUL04	335	11390	Emily	Baird
100601	23JUL04	590	15487.5	Marge	Wallace
400102	23JUL04	1500	82500	Emily	Baird
400178	23JUL04	10	657.5	Gary	Smith
500116	23JUL04	400	13600	Curtis	Jennings

Your PROC SQL statements are much easier to understand and simpler to write if you use table aliases instead. The next example contains the same SQL statement as the preceding example, but here we are using a simple one-letter alias for each of the tables.

```
LIBNAME bluesky "C:\mydata\bluesky bookstore\";

SELECT    o.prodcode, o.ord_date,
          o.quantity, o.totsale,
          c.cont_fst, c.cont_lst
FROM      bluesky.orders AS o,
          bluesky.client c
WHERE     o.clientno = c.clientno;
```

Although not strictly necessary, the use of the table alias as a prefix to every column rather than just the common columns can improve readability. This is especially true if information is drawn from more than two tables.

You can use either the full table name or its alias as a prefix to a column. However, if your SELECT clause lists many columns, the alias is preferred because the query length is kept to a minimum and it is easier to distinguish the column names from the table names.

The AS keyword is required in a SELECT clause when associating an alias with a column or expression. However, the AS keyword can be omitted in the FROM clause when specifying an alias. In the above example, the alias for the *orders* table is preceded by an AS keyword, but the *client* table alias is not; both are equally correct.

The most common mistake made in a FROM clause is the omission of a comma between table names when more than one table appears in a FROM clause.

Throughout this book, full tables names are routinely added to eliminate any confusion. However, when programming I consistently use just a table name and an alias of one or two characters and exclude the AS keyword. As a result, it is easy for me to quickly check a FROM clause for pairs of values followed by a comma:

```
FROM bluesky.stock s, bluesky.orders o, bluesky.client c,
bluesky.address a
```

A more detailed discussion of the WHERE clause is included in the next section of this chapter. The selection of data from two or more tables is covered in Chapter 5, "Working with Two or More Tables."

The guidelines for table alias names are as follows:

- A table alias is only active on the SELECT statement in which it is specified.
- Table aliases from an outer SELECT statement may be referenced from within a correlated subquery. More information on correlated subqueries is included in Chapter 5, "Working with Two or More Tables."
- An optional AS keyword may be included between the table name and its alias.
- SAS variable-naming conventions apply.
- Alias names are not case-sensitive.
- If an alias for a table is defined, it is still possible to use the table name as part of the column identification.
- Not all tables in the FROM clause must have an alias.
- If you have two or more tables with a common column name, a table alias is mandatory; it is required to distinguish which table the column is taken from.

WHERE clause

SELECT
INTO
FROM
ON
▸ WHERE
GROUP BY
HAVING
ORDER BY
USING;

General form:

WHERE <CALCULATED> alias | column | expression
COMPARISON OPERATOR
constant |<CALCULATED> alias
|column|expression|subquery
<LOGICAL OPERATOR condition…>

The WHERE clause determines which observations will be retrieved from one or more tables. In a simple PROC SQL query, the WHERE clause contains one or more conditions or criteria that column values must meet, or the row is excluded from the result set.

The WHERE clause can use any of the columns defined in the table(s) listed on the FROM clause as part of the criteria. It is not necessary to include columns that are part of the WHERE clause in the SELECT clause. The next example shows a SELECT statement with a simple WHERE clause. Notice that the criteria are built on the quantity of books ordered; however, only the product code (prodcode) and order date (ord_date) are included in the output.

```
LIBNAME bluesky "C:\mydata\bluesky bookstore\";

SELECT    prodcode, ord_date
FROM      bluesky.orders
WHERE     quantity >=500;
```

```
prod
Code     ord_date
-----------------
100340    09JAN03
100601    23JUL04
200145    12APR04
200345    10NOV03
200345    27SEP03
200678    12JUN04
300680    20OCT03
400102    23JUL04
400128    12APR04
400178    06MAY03
500120    06MAY03
500120    06SEP03
600125    05MAY04
```

Tip: The SQL Optimizer uses indexes when available to improve query performance when a WHERE clause is added to a SELECT statement. Information on the Optimizer is included in Chapter 6, "Creating and Managing Tables and Views."

A WHERE clause may also include an expression defined in a SELECT clause. Either the expression must be retyped in its entirety or the keyword CALCULATED together with the alias assigned to the expression in the SELECT clause can be used. The use of the CALCULATED keyword greatly simplifies the WHERE clause, and it is the recommended method.

Tip: The WHERE clause is processed before the SELECT clause so expressions included in the SELECT clause are unknown. The CALCULATED keyword is needed to direct the processor to the SELECT clause to resolve the alias.

The next example shows the use of the CALCULATED keyword with an expression in a WHERE clause.

```
LIBNAME bluesky "C:\mydata\bluesky bookstore\";

SELECT    title, stock*price as totprice
FROM      bluesky.stock
WHERE     CALCULATED totprice < 3000;
```

```
title                                                    totprice
-----------------------------------------------------------------

Democracy in America                                         1980
The Ultimate Philosophy                                       950
National Library of Medicine                              2301.25
Medications and Maintenance                                  2580
Computer: Beginners Guide                                    2350
The Maestro                                                   695
Mountaineering Skills                                        1100
```

Tip: The WHERE clause can include columns that are not contained in the SELECT clause. Columns may be taken from any of the tables listed in the FROM clause.

Comparison operators

Simple conditions can be constructed by comparing a column value to a numeric or character value or another column value using comparison operators. The comparison operators as summarized in the following table are similar to those used in the SAS language.

Comparison operators

Symbol	Mnemonic equivalent	Definition
=	EQ	equal to
^=	NE	not equal to
¬=	NE	not equal to
~=	NE	not equal to
<>	NE	not equal to
>	GT	greater than
<	LT	less than
>=	GE	greater than or equal to
<=	LE	less than or equal to

COMPARISON OPERATORS always take precedence over logical operators unless parentheses are used.

There are several possible symbols that can be used to represent “not,” which can be used in combinations such as NE or "not equal to." Each is equally correct, although not all of the symbols may be appropriate for your terminal or available on your keyboard. A complete listing of the symbols (logical operators) is included in the next section.

```
LIBNAME bluesky "C:\mydata\bluesky bookstore\";

SELECT   prodcode 'Product Code' , ord_date 'Date Ordered' format=date9.,
         quantity 'Quantity' format=comma8.0, totsale 'Order Total'
         format= comma10.2
FROM     bluesky.orders
WHERE    ord_date = '10MAR2004'd;
```

Product Code	Date Ordered	Quantity	Order Total
100345	10MAR2004	180	11,700.00
400100	10MAR2004	350	15,312.50
500500	10MAR2004	70	1,645.00
600125	10MAR2004	100	1,250.00

Tip: Those who are familiar with the SAS language may notice that the angle brackets (<>), which are normally used to indicate a MAX comparison between two values, are included here as a NE equivalent in a WHERE clause. Neither the MIN (><) nor MAX (<>) comparison operators are valid in PROC SQL.

The => and <= comparison operators for GE and LE, available in Base SAS for compatibility with previous releases, are not valid in PROC SQL. In PROC SQL, the equal sign must follow the greater than or less than sign as shown in the preceding table of comparison operators.

A new character comparison operator =: was introduced in SAS 9. It allows you to find instances where the first character of a string matches a specified character. This operator is not valid in PROC SQL. In PROC SQL, a substring (SUBSTR or SUBSTRN) function provides the same functionality. The next example provides a DATA step example with the =: operator and the equivalent PROC SQL statement.

```
LIBNAME bluesky "C:\mydata\bluesky bookstore\";

* The names data set would contain only those clients whose first name begins
  with A;

DATA names;
SET bluesky.client;
IF cont_fst =: 'A';
RUN;

* The following substring function would give the same results;

PROC SQL;

SELECT    *
FROM  bluesky.client
WHERE SUBSTR(cont_fst,1,1)  =  'A';
```

Tip: A new substring function, SUBSTRN was introduced in SAS 9. It handles nonpositive and missing length and position values differently than its predecessor, the SUBSTR function. The SUBSTR function continues to be available. More information on the features introduced in Version 9 is included in Chapter 8, "PROC SQL Enhancements in Version 9."

Logical (Boolean) operators

Logical or Boolean operators can be used to link a series of conditions together. There are two main operators, AND and OR, and each of these operators can be combined with a NOT operator. The operator symbols and their mnemonic equivalents are shown in the following table:

Symbol	Mnemonic equivalent
&	AND
|, !, ¦	OR
¬	NOT
^	NOT
~	NOT

Order of precedence for LOGICAL operators: NOT, AND, OR, unless parentheses are used.

These operators cause an expression to evaluate to TRUE or FALSE. When the AND operator is used to join two conditions, both conditions must be TRUE for that observation or row to be included in the report.

The next example shows a WHERE clause that limits the rows retrieved from the *orders* table. Both the conditions involving the quantity and order date must be met for a row to be reported in the SAS output.

```
LIBNAME bluesky "C:\mydata\bluesky bookstore\";

SELECT   prodcode 'Product Code',
         ord_date 'Date Ordered' format=date9.,
         quantity 'Quantity' format=comma8.0,
          totsale 'Order Total' format= comma10.2
FROM     bluesky.orders
WHERE    quantity > 200 and ord_date = '10MAR2004'd;
```

Product Code	Date Ordered	Quantity	Order Total
400100	10MAR2004	350	15,312.50

However, if two conditions are included in a WHERE clause linked by an OR operator, only one of the two conditions must be true. In the next example, either the quantity ordered must be greater than 1000 or the date the order was placed must be March 10, 2004.

```
LIBNAME  bluesky "C:\mydata\bluesky bookstore\";

SELECT   prodcode 'Product Code' ,
         ord_date 'Date Ordered' format=date9.,
         quantity 'Quantity' format=comma8.0,
         totsale 'Order Total' format= comma10.2
FROM     bluesky.orders
WHERE    quantity > 1000 or ord_date = '10MAR2004'd;
```

Product Code	Date Ordered	Quantity	Order Total
200345	10NOV2003	1,400	76,972.00
300680	20OCT2003	2,900	3,390.00
100345	10MAR2004	180	11,700.00
400100	10MAR2004	350	15,312.50
500500	10MAR2004	70	1,645.00
600125	10MAR2004	100	1,250.00
400128	12APR2004	1,230	41,820.00
200678	12JUN2004	5,000	225,000.00
400102	23JUL2004	1,500	82,500.00

The conditions joined by an AND operator are evaluated before those conditions that are joined by an OR operator. When parentheses are used, the expression(s) or condition(s) within the parentheses are evaluated first.

The use of logical operators joining more than two conditions can result in a very complex set of conditions. Especially when using an OR or NOT operator in a complex set of conditions, the query can be difficult to write correctly and the results can be hard to interpret. The use of parentheses is highly recommended in these situations in order to ensure the correct processing order of the conditions.

> **Tip:** If you are checking a column against several values, the IN operator described in the next section is a better choice than the OR operator.

The next two examples show how the SQL query results may differ with the use of parentheses. In the following example, rows must meet one of the following criteria to be included in the report:

1. Quantity is greater than 1000 and the order date is March 10, 2004.
2. Order date is July 23, 2004.

```
LIBNAME bluesky "C:\mydata\bluesky bookstore\";

SELECT    prodcode 'Product Code' ,
          ord_date 'Date Ordered' format=date9.,
          quantity 'Quantity' format=comma8.0,
          totsale 'Order Total' format= comma10.2
FROM      bluesky.orders
WHERE     quantity > 1000 and ord_date = '10MAR2004'd
          or ord_date = '23JUL2004'd;
```

Product Code	Date Ordered	Quantity	Order Total
100601	23JUL2004	590	15,487.50
400102	23JUL2004	1,500	82,500.00
400178	23JUL2004	10	657.50
500116	23JUL2004	400	13,600.00

With the addition of parentheses around the ord_date criteria, the processing order of the operators is overridden. In the next example, rows must meet BOTH of the following criteria to be included in the report:

1. Order date is either March 10, 2004, or July 23, 2004.
2. Quantity must be greater than 1000.

```
LIBNAME bluesky "C:\mydata\bluesky bookstore\";

SELECT    prodcode 'Product Code' ,
          ord_date 'Date Ordered' format=date9.,
          quantity 'Quantity' format=comma8.0,
           totsale 'Order Total' format= comma10.2
FROM      bluesky.orders
WHERE     quantity > 1000
          and (ord_date = '10MAR2004'd
          or ord_date = '23JUL2004'd);
```

```
Product        Date                    Order
Code        Ordered  Quantity          Total
________________________________________________

400102   23JUL2004      1,500      82,500.00
```

The next example shows an example of a problem that can occur. Notice that although the criteria set out in the WHERE clause were intended to limit the results to orders placed on only two dates, all rows were reported. The reason? The ord_date column name was omitted from one of the criteria in the WHERE clause.

Warning: Be careful when creating a WHERE clause using many OR operators for the same column. If you forget to include the column name, the value in the WHERE clause is evaluated as a character or numeric literal. Because this is always true, every row satisfies the condition.

To make matters worse, the SAS log will not record an error or warning message because the syntax of the statement is correct.

```
PROC SQL;
OPTIONS obs=10;
LIBNAME bluesky "C:\mydata\bluesky bookstore\";

SELECT  prodcode 'Product Code' ,
        ord_date 'Date Ordered' format=date9.,
        quantity 'Quantity' format=comma8.0,
         totsale 'Order Total' format=comma10.2
FROM    bluesky.orders
WHERE   quantity > 1000 and
        ord_date = '10MAR2004'd or '23JUL2004'd;

QUIT;
```

Product Code	Date Ordered	Quantity	Order Total
300456	07FEB2003	300	2,850.00
300680	06MAY2003	150	2,175.00
400178	06MAY2003	500	32,875.00
500120	06MAY2003	600	20,700.00
200345	10NOV2003	1,400	76,972.00
300680	20OCT2003	2,900	3,390.00
400100	15MAR2003	125	5,468.75
400128	11APR2003	200	6,800.00
400100	11APR2003	200	8,750.00
600125	24JUN2003	350	2,432.50

Tip: An OPTIONS OBS=10 statement was added in the above example to limit the results reported to 10 rows. This query returns every row in the *orders* table.

This option remains in effect for the entire SAS session, whether you are running PROC SQL or other DATA steps or procedures. To reset the option so that all rows are returned, add the statement OPTIONS OBS=MAX before the SELECT statement.

You might wonder why the first criterion of "quantity > 1000" was ignored. Recall that an AND operator is processed before an OR operator. The omission of the ord_date column name results in the evaluation of a literal ('23JUL2004'd). Because this condition is TRUE for every row and it is linked to the quantity criterion with an OR, every row is reported.

The next example shows a WHERE clause in which the column name has been omitted from one of the criteria. In this case, however, the order date criteria are enclosed within parentheses. Although a result of TRUE is still obtained from the criteria enclosed in parentheses for every row, the parentheses override the normal processing order of the AND and OR operators and only those rows that also meet the first condition are included in the report.

```
LIBNAME bluesky "C:\mydata\bluesky bookstore\";

SELECT   prodcode 'Product Code' ,
         ord_date 'Date Ordered' format=date9.,
         quantity 'Quantity' format=comma8.0,
         totsale 'Order Total' format= comma10.2
FROM     bluesky.orders
WHERE    quantity > 1000 AND
         (ord_date='10MAR2004'd OR '12JUN2004'd);
```

Product Code	Date Ordered	Quantity	Order Total
200345	10NOV2003	1,400	76,972.00
300680	20OCT2003	2,900	3,390.00
400128	12APR2004	1,230	41,820.00
200678	12JUN2004	5,000	225,000.00
400102	23JUL2004	1,500	82,500.00

IN operator

The IN comparison operator can save on typing and confusion. Consider the WHERE clause shown in the next example. The same condition can be written more simply with an IN operator as shown in the subsequent example

```
LIBNAME bluesky "C:\mydata\bluesky bookstore\";

SELECT   prodcode 'Product Code' ,
         ord_date 'Date Ordered' format=date9.,
         quantity 'Quantity' format=comma8.0,
         totsale 'Order Total' format= comma10.2
FROM     bluesky.orders
WHERE    quantity >= 1000 and
         (ord_date='10MAR2004'd or ord_date= '23JUL2004'd
         or ord_date= '12JUN2004'd or ord_date= '12APR2004'd
         or ord_date='12MAY2004'd);
```

```
LIBNAME bluesky "C:\mydata\bluesky bookstore\";

SELECT   prodcode 'Product Code' ,
         ord_date 'Date Ordered' format=date9.,
```

```
        quantity 'Quantity' format=comma8.0,
        totsale 'Order Total' format= comma10.2
FROM    bluesky.orders
WHERE   quantity >= 1000 and
        ord_date IN ('10MAR2004'D,'23JUL2004'd,
        '12JUN2004'd,'12APR2004'd,'12MAY2004'd);
```

```
Product       Date                    Order
Code        Ordered  Quantity         Total
-------------------------------------------

400128    12APR2004     1,230     41,820.00
200678    12JUN2004     5,000    225,000.00
400102    23JUL2004     1,500     82,500.00
```

Notice that the use of the IN operator has several advantages. First, the ord_date criteria are easier to write and understand. Second, we have eliminated the parentheses that were included in the first WHERE clause because of the logical operators joining the quantity and the ord_date conditions. Although not always possible, IN operator usage often results in a simpler WHERE clause overall.

The mnemonic NOT operator can be used in conjunction with the IN operator for added functionality. In the next example the WHERE clause has been re-written to exclude the order dates in the list enclosed in parentheses.

```
LIBNAME bluesky "C:\mydata\bluesky bookstore\";

SELECT   prodcode 'Product Code',
         ord_date 'Date Ordered' format=date9.,
         quantity 'Quantity' format=comma8.0,
         totsale 'Order Total' format= comma10.2
FROM     bluesky.orders
WHERE    quantity >= 1000 and
         (ord_date NOT IN('10MAR2004'D,'23JUL2004'd,'12JUN2004'd,
         '12APR2004'd,'12MAY2004'd));
```

```
Product       Date                    Order
Code        Ordered  Quantity         Total
-------------------------------------------

200345    10NOV2003     1,400     76,972.00
300680    20OCT2003     2,900      3,390.00
500120    06SEP2003     1,000     34,500.00
```

Single functions

Single functions such as SCAN and FLOOR that produce one value per row are allowed in a WHERE clause. The next example shows gives an example of the use of the SCAN function in the WHERE clause, limiting the reported books by ISBN number. The SCAN function separates the ISBN into "words" or segments, using the dash (-) as a delimiter. Only those books with a numeral two in the fourth segment, for example 1-7890-1209-2, are reported.

For more information on single functions, refer to Chapter 4, "Functions." In addition, comprehensive information on the use of functions is included in the *SAS Language Reference: Dictionary*.

```
LIBNAME bluesky "C:\mydata\bluesky bookstore\";

SELECT    title, category, stock
FROM      bluesky.stock
WHERE     scan(isbn,3) = '1209';
```

```
title                                              category                    stock
-----------------------------------------------------------------------------------
The Art of Computer Programming                    computer                     1600
```

Tip: Notice that the WHERE clause in the preceding example includes a column that is not listed in the SELECT clause. The SELECT clause specifies the columns to be reported or displayed, while the WHERE clause uses nondisplayed columns to limit the rows selected from the table. As with other SAS reporting procedures and tools, it is not necessary to include all of the variables used to manipulate or limit the output in the report.

BETWEEN-AND operator

Often a WHERE clause condition checks for values within a given range. This condition can be constructed with a combination of LESS THAN and GREATER THAN operators. However, it is often easier to use the BETWEEN–AND operator to establish the condition.

The following two WHERE clauses are equivalent:

WHERE variable >= value **AND** variable <= value

WHERE *variable* **BETWEEN** *value* **AND** *value*

The BETWEEN–AND operator defines an inclusive range. The report in the next example includes orders placed between February 1, 2003, and April 30, 2003, inclusive.

```
LIBNAME bluesky "C:\mydata\bluesky bookstore\";

SELECT     prodcode, ord_date,clientno
FROM       bluesky.orders
WHERE      ord_date between '01FEB2003'd and '30APR2003'd;
```

```
prod
Code      ord_date  clientNo
----------------------------
300456    07FEB03       1001
300456    07FEB03       3007
400100    15MAR03       4008
400100    11APR03       5005
400128    11APR03       7008
```

As with the GREATER THAN and LESS THAN operators, BETWEEN–AND can be combined with NOT. Again the range is inclusive, resulting in rows that are outside of the range. In the next example the NOT keyword has been added, generating a report of all orders before February 1, 2003, and after April 30, 2004. The number of rows in the report has been limited to 10 with an OBS=10 option.

```
PROC SQL;
OPTIONS OBS=10;
LIBNAME bluesky "C:\mydata\bluesky bookstore\";

SELECT     prodcode, ord_date,clientno
FROM       bluesky.orders
WHERE      ord_date NOT between '01FEB2003'd and '30APR2004'd;

QUIT;
```

```
prod
Code      ord_date   clientNo
------------------------------
300678    09JAN03        8003
100340    09JAN03        8003
600125    05MAY04        2010
500127    07JUN04        2010
500168    20JUL04        5005
400345    11MAY04        4008
100890    12MAY04        3007
100340    12JUN04        8003
200678    12JUN04        3007
300289    12JUN04        6090
```

Tip: Always put the lowest value first when using the BETWEEN–AND operator to increase readability.

IS NULL or IS MISSING operators

In each of the previous WHERE clause examples, columns are compared to other columns or they are compared to one or more numeric or character values. However, if the column value is missing or undefined, such a WHERE condition cannot be evaluated. The IS NULL operator is the ANSI standard method for checking for missing or undefined values. Its negated form, NOT IS NULL, is used to retrieve only those rows in which the column value has a nonmissing value.

In the next example, the IS NULL operator is used to find missing values in the numeric exchange rate (exchrate) column of the *currency* table.

```
LIBNAME bluesky "C:\mydata\bluesky bookstore\";

SELECT     *
FROM       bluesky.currency
WHERE      exchrate is null;
```

```
currency  cur_date   exchRate
------------------------------
AUD        01FEB03          .
EUR        01APR03          .
```

In PROC SQL, the IS MISSING operator can be substituted for the IS NULL operator to search for undefined character and numeric values. The IS MISSING and NOT IS MISSING operators can also be used to check for special missing values defined in SAS tables and data sets. Although appropriate for PROC SQL, the IS MISSING operator is not universally accepted in SQL queries.

Tip: NOT IS MISSING and NOT IS NULL can also be written as IS NOT MISSING and IS NOT NULL. I prefer to write these operators with NOT first so I can more easily distinguish the negated form of these operators.

The code in the next example checks for undefined character values in the fax column of the *client* table using the IS MISSING operator.

```
LIBNAME bluesky "C:\mydata\bluesky bookstore\";

SELECT    company,
          cont_fst||cont_lst "Contact Name",
          phone
FROM      bluesky.client
WHERE     fax is missing;
```

```
company                              Contact Name               phone
-------------------------------------------------------------------------
Chicago State University             Holee    Davis             312-756-789
National University of Singapore     John     Clements          874-2339
```

SAS/ACCESS or SQL Pass-Through facility users: The IS NULL and NOT IS NULL operators rather than IS MISSING and NOT IS MISSING must be used in queries passed to a relational database system for processing.

Warning: Not all databases will use available indexes when a WHERE clause includes an IS NULL or NOT IS NULL condition. Check the documentation for your database system for details on index usage and methods of checking the execution plan for your query.

LIKE operator

The LIKE operator is used to facilitate pattern-matching searches on columns containing character values. Wildcard symbols, as shown below, are used to indicate unknown characters in a string by position.

Wildcard symbols

%	any sequence of 0 or more characters
_	any single character

The LIKE operator guidelines are as follows:

- Characters that are included with the wildcard symbol must match the case of the value in the column.
- Characters within the quoted string are case-sensitive.
- All wildcard symbols are included inside the quotes along with the string.
- Wildcard symbols may be combined.
- To search for a wildcard symbol itself, an ESCAPE clause is added to the LIKE condition.

Tip: The escape character has been available since SAS Release 8.2. More information on the escape character is included later in this section.

Wildcard symbols allow more flexibility than the use of other pattern-matching functions such as SUBSTRN or SCAN. Both of those functions require some knowledge of the placement of the string within the column value. Wildcard symbols can be used to replace one or more valid characters including special characters in the column regardless of position.

The next example is of a search in the title column of the *stock* table for all book titles that include the word "Computer." Notice that the matching records include words both before and after the word "Computer." The inclusion of the percent (%) wildcard symbol both before and after the string "Computer" makes this possible.

```
LIBNAME bluesky "C:\mydata\bluesky bookstore\";

SELECT    isbn, title, prodcode
FROM      bluesky.stock
WHERE     title like '%Computer%';
```

ISBN	title	prod Code
1-7890-1209-0	The Art of Computer Programming	500120
1-7890-1378-x	New User's Guide to Computers	500127
1-7890-5634-9	Start a Business Using a Computer	500238
1-7890-2829-9	Computer: Beginners Guide	500500
1-7890-3473-6	Introduction to Computer_Science	500890

Tip: Indexes may be used when the LIKE and NOT LIKE operators are included in a WHERE clause, improving performance. Information on indexes and their usage is included in Chapter 6, "Creating and Managing Tables and Views."

The next example shows the same SELECT statement but with a single % wildcard symbol before the word "Computer." Notice that the resulting report includes only the one title in the *stock* table that has the word "Computer" as the last word. Furthermore, the title ending in "Computers" is also excluded because it has a single letter after the word "Computer".

```
LIBNAME bluesky "C:\mydata\bluesky bookstore\";

SELECT    isbn, title, prodcode
FROM      bluesky.stock
WHERE     title like '%Computer';
```

ISBN	title	prod Code
1-7890-5634-9	Start a Business Using a Computer	500238

Tip: There is a difference between %Computer' and '%computer.' The quoted string is case-sensitive, and a match is made only if the exact case and characters, including blanks, are matched.

In order to limit the unknown characters to just one letter, the underscore (_) wildcard symbol is used instead. The next example shows the use of the underscore wildcard symbol to find all delivery codes that are exactly 3 characters in length and start with "EX".

```
LIBNAME bluesky "C:\mydata\bluesky bookstore\";

SELECT    *
FROM      bluesky.shipping
WHERE     delcode like 'EX_';
```

```
del
Code  delType                           charge
________________________________________________

EXE   2 day Express shipping                15
EXP   express mail                          10
EXA   express air delivery                  15
```

Table columns that are declared as character types have values that are padded with trailing blanks if the value length is less than the declared length. For example, if you declare a character column with a length of 3 and subsequently place a value containing only 2 characters in the column, that value will include a single trailing blank. As blanks are considered to be valid characters, they will match a _ wildcard symbol.

The code in the next example contains a WHERE clause that gives an example using the title column of the *stock* table. The title column has a declared length of 50 to accommodate a variety of titles. As a result, a title ending in "Computer" rather than "Computers" also meets the criteria.

```
LIBNAME bluesky "C:\mydata\bluesky bookstore\";

SELECT    isbn, title, prodcode
FROM      bluesky.stock
WHERE     title like '%Computer_';
```

```
                                                                  prod
ISBN           title                                              Code
______________________________________________________________________

1-7890-1378-x  New User's Guide to Computers                      500127
1-7890-5634-9  Start a Business Using a Computer                  500238
```

In order to avoid this situation, the TRIM function is applied to the character column to eliminate all trailing blanks. The revised SELECT statement and the corresponding report are shown in the following example.

```
LIBNAME bluesky "C:\mydata\bluesky bookstore\";

SELECT   isbn, title, prodcode
FROM     bluesky.stock
WHERE    trim(title) like '%Computer_';
```

ISBN	title	prod Code
1-7890-1378-x	New User's Guide to Computers	500127

It is also possible to use several of the underscore wildcard symbols together to represent several unknown characters. The next example shows the use of several underscore symbols to indicate a precise number of characters before and after the value for which we are searching.

> **Tip:** An equivalent condition may have been written using a substring (SUBSTR or SUBSTRN) function. A full explanation of the substring function is included in Chapter 4, "Functions."

```
LIBNAME bluesky "C:\mydata\bluesky bookstore\";

SELECT   isbn, title, prodcode
FROM     bluesky.stock
WHERE    prodcode like '___1__';
```

ISBN	title	prod Code
1-7890-1290-2	Space Sciences	200145
1-7890-3891-x	Medical Education in School	400100
1-7890-7893-8	Unconventional treatments	400102
1-7890-5475-3	Tibetan Medicine	400128
1-7890-3479-5	National Library of Medicine	400178
1-7890-1209-0	The Art of Computer Programming	500120
1-7890-1378-x	New User's Guide to Computers	500127
1-7890-7648-x	Visual Basic for Beginners	500168
1-7890-4578-9	Risks in Life - % Gain or Loss?	600123
1-7890-3007-2	The Maestro	600125

Escape character

But what if you want to find entries that match or contain either the percent (%) or underscore (_) wildcard characters? An escape character forces the next character to be interpreted literally rather than as a wildcard. Any single character or an expression that evaluates to a single character can be assigned as an escape character in an escape clause added to the LIKE condition.

> **Tip:** The specified escape character is valid only for the LIKE condition with which it is associated. Each time an escape character is required, it must be specified in an escape clause. Escape clauses are commonly added to a WHERE or HAVING clause in a SELECT statement.

The next example includes a SELECT statement that searches for titles containing strings that contain the wildcard characters underscore (_) and percent (%). In the first LIKE condition, the asterisk is the defined escape symbol for this condition. It precedes the underscore forcing the conversion of the underscore from a wildcard to a simple character. Notice that this condition also includes a percent wildcard, which is not affected by the escape clause.

In the second LIKE condition, a search for titles containing the percent sign is used in conjunction with the percent wildcard symbol. Only the percent sign immediately preceded by the hash mark, the defined escape symbol for this condition, is interpreted literally. The first and last percent signs within the same set of quotes are treated as wildcards.

```
LIBNAME bluesky "C:\mydata\bluesky bookstore\";

SELECT     title
FROM       bluesky.stock
WHERE      title like '%Computer*_%' escape '*'
           or title like '%#%%' escape '#';
```

```
title
------------------------------------------------
The 10% Solution
Introduction to Computer_Science
Risks in Life - % Gain or Loss?
```

> **Tip:** Confusing? Select a standard escape character, such as an asterisk for all of your LIKE clauses rather than changing the escape character throughout your PROC SQL queries.

SAS/ACCESS and SQL Pass-Through facility users: Each relational database system has a default escape character. If you are passing your SELECT statement to a database for processing, the escape character specific to the database should be used and the escape clause excluded.

Both escape characters and escape clauses may be included in a SELECT statement issued against a database when a connection to the database is made through the LIBNAME statement.

String comparison operators

Comparisons between two strings of differing lengths can be accomplished with a truncated string comparison operator. The longer string is truncated to match the length of the shorter string before the comparison occurs. The table below summarizes the new comparison operators.

Comparison operator	Definition
EQT	equal to
GTT	greater than
LTT	less than
GET	greater than or equal to
LET	less than or equal to
NET	not equal to

In the new example, the EQT comparison operator is used to find book titles starting with the letters "Medi." Traditionally, this partial string comparison would be done using a substring function (SUBSTR or SUBSTRN) or a LIKE condition using wildcards.

```
LIBNAME bluesky "C:\mydata\bluesky bookstore\";

SELECT    title
FROM      bluesky.stock
WHERE     title EQT 'Medi';
```

```
title
______________________________________________

Medical Education in School
Medications and Maintenance
```

Tip: These comparison operators, available since SAS Release 8.2, can only be used for string-to-string comparisons.

SAS/ACCESS and SQL Pass-Through facility users: These comparison operators can be applied to tables residing in a database if a connection is made through the LIBNAME statement. However, as they are not ANSI standard operators, they cannot be used in inner SELECT statements passed to an RDBMS for processing using the SQL Pass-Through facility. Refer to Appendix C, "Information for Database Users," for more information on the use of PROC SQL with databases.

CONTAINS operator

The CONTAINS operator also allows for pattern matching; however, it does not include a positional element. Instead, the entire column value is searched for the given string. A column value is only retrieved if it contains an exact match to the complete given string.

Tip: The CONTAINS operator may be represented by a question mark (?) but it is non-intuitive. I always find myself struggling to remember if the question mark indicates something I need to recheck in my program.

A match is not made if the column value differs in case or if the column contains one or more blanks between characters in the matching string. In the next example, the WHERE clause criteria limit the returned rows from the *stock* table to those whose titles contain the string "Medi". Notice that the string may appear anywhere within the title. However, the first character must be capitalized.

```
LIBNAME bluesky "C:\mydata\bluesky bookstore\";

SELECT   isbn, title, prodcode
FROM     bluesky.stock
WHERE    title contains 'Medi';
```

ISBN	title	prod Code
1-7890-3891-x	Medical Education in School	400100
1-7890-5475-3	Tibetan Medicine	400128
1-7890-3479-5	National Library of Medicine	400178
1-7890-3467-1	Medications and Maintenance	400345

The SELECT statement in the next example has a CONTAINS operator in the WHERE clause to enable a search for the wildcard character underscore with the e-mail column of the *address* table.

```
LIBNAME bluesky "C:\mydata\bluesky bookstore\";

SELECT    clientno, email
FROM      bluesky.address
WHERE     email contains '_';
```

```
clientNo  email
----------------------------------------

    6090  g_smith@home.com
```

The CONTAINS operator also enables a search for the percent (%) character, another wildcard character. In the next example, the CONTAINS operator is used in the WHERE clause to retrieve a book entitled "The 10 % Solution" from the Bluesky Publishing Company *stock* table.

```
LIBNAME bluesky "C:\mydata\bluesky bookstore\";

SELECT    title
FROM      bluesky.stock
WHERE     title contains '%';
```

```
title
--------------------------------------------------

The 10% Solution
Risks in Life - % Gain or Loss?
```

SAS/ACCESS and SQL Pass-Through facility users: The CONTAINS operator can also be applied to tables residing in a database if a connection is made through the LIBNAME statement. However, because it is not an ANSI standard operator, it cannot be used in inner SELECT statements passed to an RDBMS for processing using the SQL Pass-Through facility. Refer to Appendix C, "Information for Database Users," for more information on the use of PROC SQL with databases.

SOUNDS-LIKE operator

The SOUNDS-LIKE operator (=*) can be helpful in retrieving values that may have slight spelling variations. It can only be applied to columns containing character strings. The Soundex algorithm is used to compare each value in a character defined column to a specified character string. Although it will not always return every variation, it can be a valuable tool especially when checking for misspelled column values.

The next example shows a search for author last names that sound like Johnson. Notice that the SQL query returns a similar sounding name, Jensen.

```
LIBNAME bluesky "C:\mydata\bluesky bookstore\";

SELECT    title, auth_lst, auth_fst
FROM      bluesky.stock
WHERE     auth_lst =* 'Johnson';
```

title	auth_lst	auth_fst
The Ultimate Philosophy	Johnson	Cory
Introduction to Computer_Science	Jensen	April

SAS/ACCESS and SQL Pass-Through facility users: The SOUNDS-LIKE operator can also be applied to tables residing in a database if a connection is made through the LIBNAME statement. However, because it is not an ANSI standard operator, it cannot be used in inner SELECT statements passed to an RDBMS for processing. Refer to Appendix C, "Information for Database Users," for more information on the use of PROC SQL with databases.

Complex queries

Complex PROC SQL queries can be built to retrieve information from two or more tables included in a FROM clause or combination of FROM-ON clauses. Criteria matching equivalent column values in two or more tables are added to the WHERE clause to join the tables. Alternatively, an ON clause can be used to make the join. Once the tables are joined, they are treated as one large table and columns from any of the tables can be referenced in the query.

Tip: Table joins are discussed in detail in Chapter 5, "Working with Two or More Tables."

Additional conditions using any combination of columns contained in the tables referenced in the FROM clause may be added to the WHERE clause. The next example shows gives an example of a complex query that includes columns from 4 tables. The WHERE clause specifies the join criteria for the tables and also restricts the book category and quantity sold. Notice that the quantity column, included in the criteria in the WHERE clause, is not part of the report.

```
LIBNAME bluesky "C:\mydata\bluesky bookstore\";

SELECT  s.title "Title" format=$25.,
        c.company "Customer" format=$35.,
        a.city "Location" format=$12.,
        o.totsale "Total Sale" format=dollar10.2
FROM    bluesky.orders o,
        bluesky.address a,
        bluesky.client c,
        bluesky.stock s
WHERE   o.clientno = a.clientno
        and a.clientno = c.clientno
        and o.prodcode=s.prodcode
        and s.category in ('arts', 'general')
        and o.quantity >=100;
```

Title	Customer	Location	Total Sale
The Ultimate Philosophy	University of Texas	Austin	$2,850.00
The Underground Economy	University of Texas	Austin	$2,175.00
The Underground Economy	Chicago State University	Chicago	$3,390.00
The Maestro	Chicago State University	Chicago	$8,580.00
The Maestro	Heffers Booksellers	Cambridge	$2,432.50
Women Writers	National University of Singapore	Singapore	$885.80
The Maestro	National University of Singapore	Singapore	$1,250.00
Decorative Arts	Lawrence Books	Vancouver	$4,661.25

SQL Pass-Through facility users: Although both the inner and outer SELECT statements can include a WHERE clause to subset the data when using SQL Pass-Through facility, subsetting should be done on the database side.

A WHERE clause in an inner SELECT statement limits the rows available in the SAS session. The criteria in the WHERE clause of the outer SELECT statement are applied to the database table rows that are returned to the SAS session by the inner SELECT statement. If your database is very large, this can result in poor performance.

ORDER BY clause

SELECT
INTO
FROM
ON
WHERE
GROUP BY
HAVING
▶ ORDER BY
USING;

General form:

ORDER BY column|expression|alias|position <ASC|DESC>
<,column|expression|alias|position <ASC|DESC>...>;

The ORDER BY clause is used to sort the rows retrieved by a SELECT statement.

The ORDER BY clause guidelines are as follows:

- One or more table columns can be specified in the clause; columns do not have to be included in a SELECT clause to be added to an ORDER BY clause.
- Aliases assigned to columns or expressions in the SELECT clause can be referenced.
- A positional reference to columns in the SELECT clause can be used instead of column or expression names or aliases.
- The sort order of each column or expression listed in the ORDER BY clause can be specified as ascending or descending.
- The default sort order is ascending.
- The SORTSEQ option can be set to control sorting. Either one of the available options, such as REVERSE, ASCII, and SPANISH, can be specified or users can create their own collating sequence using the TRANTAB procedure.

Tip: To change the sort order of data stored in a table in a native SAS data library choose either of the following sections:

- Use the OUT option in a PROC SORT statement, using the same name to overwrite the existing data set.
- Create a new table using a subquery that includes an **ORDER BY** clause.

```
CREATE  TABLE <newtable> as
(SELECT * FROM <original table> ORDER BY <col1,
                col2...coln)
```

For more information on the CREATE TABLE statement, refer to Chapter 6, "Creating and Managing Tables and Views."

PROC SQL query results are not always returned in the order stored in the table. There are many factors relating to storage and processing that may affect the default order. The ORDER BY clause allows you to sort your results by one or more columns or expressions. The code in the next example contains a SELECT statement that sorts the returned rows from the *client* table by the company column values.

```
LIBNAME   bluesky "C:\mydata\bluesky bookstore\";

SELECT    company "Company", phone "Phone",
          cont_fst "First Name", cont_lst "Last Name"
FROM      bluesky.client
ORDER BY company;
```

Company	Phone	First Name	Last Name
Chicago State University	312-756-7890	Holee	Davis
Cosmos 2000	33-14-362-1899	Curtis	Jennings
Heffers Booksellers	01223-568568	Marge	Wallace
Heymann's	49-30-8252573	Gary	Smith
Lawrence Books	604-261-3612	Alan	Caston
National University of Singapore	874-2339	John	Clements
University of Adelaide	61-8-8303-4402	Emily	Baird
University of Texas	512-495-4370	Alice	Eagleton

If you use an alias for a column or expression in your SELECT clause, you can refer to it in the ORDER BY clause. This can be particularly helpful if you are referring to a column that is part of a complex set of functions or mathematical calculations. Notice that in the next example, an alias was created for the concatenated last name and first name of the contact person at each company. The ORDER BY clause refers to that alias rather than the original column name.

```
LIBNAME   bluesky "C:\mydata\bluesky bookstore\";

SELECT    company "Company", phone "Phone",
          cont_fst||cont_lst as name "Contact Name"
FROM      bluesky.client
ORDER BY name;
```

```
Company                                 Phone                      Contact   Name
------------------------------------------------------------------------------------
Lawrence Books                          604-261-3612               Alan      Caston
University of Texas                     512-495-4370               Alice     Eagleton
Cosmos 2000                             33-14-362-1899             Curtis    Jennings
University of Adelaide                  61-8-8303-4402             Emily     Baird
Heymann's                               49-30-8252573              Gary      Smith
Chicago State University                312-756-7890               Holee     Davis
National University of Singapore        874-2339                   John      Clements
Heffers Booksellers                     01223-568568               Marge     Wallace
```

Tip: An ORDER BY clause is executed after the SELECT clause. As a result, aliases and the column order specified in the SELECT clause are known at the time the ORDER BY clause is processed. Only column names, aliases, or positional references can be included in an ORDER BY clause.

Caution: If a label or heading is enclosed in quotation marks and you refer to it in an ORDER BY clause, it is removed from the ORDER BY clause during processing. A warning message is printed to the SAS log, but processing of the query continues.

```
Warning:  At least one nonessential ordering column
          reference has been removed from an ORDER BY
          reference list.
```

An unquoted string in the ORDER BY clause that is not an alias or column name will generate an error message and processing of the query stops.

Alternatively, you can refer to the columns in your SELECT clause by their ordinal positions in that clause. The next example shows ordering by the concatenated contact name; but now the column is referenced by its position in the SELECT clause. It will produce the same result as shown in the preceding example.

```
LIBNAME  bluesky "C:\mydata\bluesky bookstore\";

SELECT   company "Company", phone "Phone",
         cont_fst||cont_lst as name "Contact Name"
FROM     bluesky.client
ORDER BY 3;
```

Company	Phone	Contact	Name
Lawrence Books	604-261-3612	Alan	Caston
University of Texas	512-495-4370	Alice	Eagleton
Cosmos 2000	33-14-362-1899	Curtis	Jennings
University of Adelaide	61-8-8303-4402	Emily	Baird
Heymann's	49-30-8252573	Gary	Smith
Chicago State University	312-756-7890	Holee	Davis
National University of Singapore	874-2339	John	Clements
Heffers Booksellers	01223-568568	Marge	Wallace

Tip: Although it can save typing, the positional reference can be a problem. It is not uncommon to make changes to a SELECT clause—adding columns and repositioning them—to fine-tune a report. More often than not, I forget to make the corresponding changes to the ORDER BY clause.

Any number of columns or expressions can be listed in the ORDER BY clause, including those not listed in the SELECT clause. If the sort order is not indicated, the results will be sorted in ascending order by the first column or expression, then by the next column, continuing on until all of the columns listed in the ORDER BY clause are sorted.

Tip: Although it may seem counter-intuitive to sort your report by absent columns, it can provide added flexibility when working with interactive applications. For example, you might want to allow a user to review and edit all entries made today. The query could return the appropriate rows in descending order, starting with the most recent transaction. Although a timestamp is used to retrieve and sort the results, it would not be displayed on the screen.

It is also possible to sort each of the columns in an ORDER BY clause differently. The next example shows a complex ORDER BY clause. There are several columns included here and each is sorted differently. The sorting sequence can be described as follows:

1. The output is first sorted in descending order by the order date.
2. If several clients placed orders on the same order date, they are then listed in the report in ascending order. For example, on July 23, 2004, book orders were received from four clients. The lowest client number appears first and the highest appears last.
3. If a single client placed several orders on the same date, their orders are listed in the report in descending order by quantity. For example, client 2010 placed 2 orders on April 12, 2004. The quantity of books the client purchased are shown from highest (1230 books) to lowest (700 books).

```
LIBNAME bluesky "C:\mydata\bluesky bookstore\";

SELECT    ord_date, clientno, prodcode, quantity
FROM      bluesky.orders
WHERE     ord_date > '01APR2004'd
ORDER BY  ord_date desc, clientno asc, quantity desc;
```

ord_date	clientNo	prod Code	quantity
23JUL04	3007	100601	590
23JUL04	5005	400102	1500
23JUL04	6090	400178	10
23JUL04	7008	500116	400
20JUL04	5005	500168	335
12JUN04	3007	200678	5000
12JUN04	6090	300289	30
12JUN04	8003	100340	20
07JUN04	2010	500127	324
12MAY04	3007	100890	260
11MAY04	4008	400345	25
05MAY04	2010	600125	600
12APR04	2010	400128	1230
12APR04	2010	200145	700
12APR04	5005	500238	200
12APR04	7008	600489	25
10APR04	6090	300456	55
08APR04	4008	200507	20

Tip: The DESC or ASC keywords can be added after each column in an ORDER BY clause to sort that column in descending or ascending order.

The default sort order is ascending. As a result, it is not necessary to add the ASC keyword after a column that is to be sorted in ascending order. In the previous example, ASC was indicated for the clientNo column for clarity only.

The default sort sequence used by the ORDER BY clause can be overridden by specifying a SORTSEQ option in the PROC SQL statement or an OPTIONS statement.

Null or missing values are always included at the beginning of a list sorted in ascending order and at the end of the sorted results in descending order. If the SQL Pass-Through facility is used, the treatment of null or missing values in the sort process varies depending on the RDBMS. Null values may be placed at either the beginning or end of the sorted results.

> **Tip:** Many people have difficulty remembering where NULL values occur in a sorted sequence. It might help to think of a NULL value as negative infinity. Although not completely accurate, it applies to most areas of SAS.

GROUP BY clause

SELECT
INTO
FROM
ON
WHERE
► GROUP BY
HAVING
ORDER BY
USING;

General form:

GROUP BY column | expression | alias
<, ...>

The GROUP BY clause allows for the calculation of summary statistics for categories or groups of data retrieved in a SELECT statement. Summary statistics produce a single value for an entire column of data. Examples of summary statistics include SUM, AVG, MIN, and MAX.

The addition of the GROUP BY clause to a SELECT statement gives results that are similar to SAS MEANS and UNIVARIATE procedures with BY statements or PROC SUMMARY and PROC TABULATE class variables. A GROUP BY clause causes the results of a SELECT statement to be rolled-up or summarized by each distinct occurrence of the variable or variables listed in the clause.

A GROUP BY clause is only added to a SELECT statement if one or more summary functions are included in the SELECT or HAVING clause. An example of a GROUP BY clause is shown in the next example. Here a count of the number of orders for each date together with the average quantity ordered is shown.

> **SAS/ACCESS of SQL Pass-Through facility users:** Some DBMSs require that every column listed in a SELECT clause that is not associated with a summary function must be included in the GROUP BY clause.

```
LIBNAME bluesky "C:\mydata\bluesky bookstore\";

SELECT     ord_date "Date",
           count(prodcode) "Count",
           mean(quantity) "Avg Quantity" format=6.1
FROM       bluesky.orders
WHERE      ord_date > '01JAN2004'd
GROUP BY   ord_date;
```

Date	Count	Avg Quantity
01FEB04	2	57.5
07MAR04	1	45.0
10MAR04	4	175.0
08APR04	1	20.0
10APR04	1	55.0
12APR04	4	538.8
05MAY04	1	600.0
11MAY04	1	25.0
12MAY04	1	260.0
07JUN04	1	324.0
12JUN04	3	1683.3
20JUL04	1	335.0
23JUL04	4	625.0

If you do not specify at least one summary function in your SELECT or HAVING clause, PROC SQL will interpret the GROUP BY clause as an ORDER BY clause. A message informing you of this transformation is written to the SAS log. An example of such a SELECT clause and the accompanying SAS log message is shown in the next example.

```
LIBNAME    bluesky "C:\mydata\bluesky bookstore\";

SELECT     ord_date, clientno, prodcode, quantity
FROM       bluesky.orders
GROUP BY   ord_date, clientno;
```

SAS log:

```
WARNING:  A GROUP BY clause has been transformed into an ORDER BY
clause because neither the SELECT clause nor the optional HAVING
clause of the associated table-expression referenced a summary
function.
```

Single function expressions defined in a SELECT clause can be used in GROUP BY clauses, but they must be referenced by an alias if the goal is to summarize by the results of the function. When a single function or the column on which it operates rather than an alias is included in a GROUP BY clause, the report does not always generate the expected results.

> **Tip:** A GROUP BY clause may include the alias of a single function expression included in a SELECT clause. Summary functions, on the other hand, may not be included in a GROUP BY clause.

The following example shows a portion of the *orders* table for the Bluesky Publishing Company. There are orders associated with four distinct months within the period of January 1, 2004, and May 31, 2004, in the *orders* table.

ord_date	clientNo	prod Code	quantity
01FEB04	8003	600125	12
01FEB04	4008	600780	103
07MAR04	3007	100406	45
10MAR04	7008	100345	180
10MAR04	8003	400100	350
10MAR04	8003	500500	70
10MAR04	4008	600125	100
08APR04	4008	200507	20
10APR04	6090	300456	55
12APR04	2010	200145	700
12APR04	2010	400128	1230
12APR04	5005	500238	200
12APR04	7008	600489	25
05MAY04	2010	600125	600
11MAY04	4008	400345	25
12MAY04	3007	100890	260

In the next example the month is extracted from the order date using the month function in the SELECT clause, and an alias order_months is defined for the expression. A format created in PROC FORMAT is assigned providing a label for each resulting numeric month value. The order_months alias is included in the GROUP BY clause, resulting in a report of total sales and average quantity for each month in the *orders* table.

```
/* Create a format to assign names to each month in the report*/

PROC FORMAT;
      value monthChar
      1='January'
      2='February'
      3='March'
      4 ='April'
      5 = 'May'
      ;

/* Run the query*/
TITLE1     'Average Monthly quantity sold and total sales';
TITLE2     'Between Jan 1, 2004 and May 31, 2004';


LIBNAME bluesky "C:\mydata\bluesky bookstore\";

SELECT    month(ord_date) as month "Month" format monthChar.,
          sum(totsale) format= comma10.2 "Total Sale" as total,
          mean(quantity) format= comma10.2 "Avg Quantity" as avgqty
FROM      bluesky.orders
WHERE     ord_date between '01JAN2004'd and '31MAY2004'd
GROUP BY month;
```

```
           Average Monthly quantity sold and total sales
              Between Jan 1, 2004 and May 31, 2004

                                          Avg
                  Month  Total Sale   Quantity
               ________________________________

               February      969.20      57.50
               March      30,582.50     149.00
               April      88,070.00     371.67
               May        28,670.00     295.00
```

Tip: The previous example shows a report generated through a SAS remerging operation. If you check the SAS log, you will find a note indicating that remerging has occurred:

```
NOTE: The query requires remerging summary statistics
      back with the original data.
```

Remerging is executed automatically in situations where two passes are required through a table or view. Summary functions by the specified group, or for the entire table or view are calculated in the first pass and stored. These values are then merged back to the original table or view in the second pass. More information on remerging is included later in this chapter.

The following example shows the inclusion of a single function in a GROUP BY clause. Although the function is correctly written and an identical function is included in the SELECT clause, the results are not as expected. The average quantity and total sale values for each month are repeated for each row in the table that has the corresponding order month. If you compare this report to the original data in the Bluesky Publishing Company partial *orders* table shown earlier, you will find that the average quantity and total sale values are correct for each month.

```
TITLE1'Average Monthly quantity sold and total sales';
TITLE2 'Between Jan 1, 2004 and May 31, 2004';

LIBNAME bluesky "C:\mydata\bluesky bookstore\";

SELECT   month(ord_date) as month "Month" format monthChar.,
         sum(totsale) format= comma10.2 "Total Sale" as total,
         mean(quantity) format= comma10.2 "Avg Quantity" as avgqty
FROM     bluesky.orders
WHERE    ord_date between '01JAN2004'd and '31MAY2004'd
GROUP BY month(ord_date);
```

```
   Average Monthly quantity sold and total sales
        Between Jun 1, 2004 and May 31,20004
                                          Avg
            Month   Total Sale       Quantity
         ------------------------------------
         February       969.20          57.50
         February       969.20          57.50
         March       30,582.50         149.00
         March       30,582.50         149.00
         March       30,582.50         149.00
         March       30,582.50         149.00
         March       30,582.50         149.00
         April       88,070.00         371.67
         April       88,070.00         371.67
         April       88,070.00         371.67
         April       88,070.00         371.67
         April       88,070.00         371.67
         April       88,070.00         371.67
         May         28,670.00         295.00
         May         28,670.00         295.00
         May         28,670.00         295.00
```

Tip: The format *monthChar* assigning a label to each numeric month value was created in the PROC FORMAT statement in the example on page 62. However, formats defined using PROC FORMAT cannot be specified in a GROUP BY clause, nor does the GROUP BY clause acknowledge the formatted values.

One option is to create a small look-up table that associates each numeric month value with a label and join this table to the *orders* table. Joins are discussed in Chapter 5, "Working with Two or More Tables."

The next example shows the order date (ord_date) column included in the GROUP BY clause. In this case, the report generates a single line for each distinct order date in the table. The month function in the SELECT clause has the effect of modifying the display of the order date in the report only. The report is difficult if not impossible to interpret because the grouping is not evident.

```
TITLE1 'Average Monthly quantity sold and total sales';
TITLE2 'Between Jan 1, 2004 and May 31, 2004';

LIBNAME bluesky "C:\mydata\bluesky bookstore\";

SELECT   month(ord_date) as months "Month" format monthChar.,
         sum(totsale) format= comma10.2 "Total Sale" as total,
         mean(quantity) format= comma10.2 "Avg Quantity" as avgqty
FROM     bluesky.orders
WHERE    ord_date between '01JAN2004'd and '31MAY2004'd
GROUP BY ord_date;
```

Average Monthly quantity sold and total sales
Between Jan 1, 2004 and May 31, 2004

Month	Total Sale	Avg Quantity
February	969.20	57.50
March	675.00	45.00
March	29,907.50	175.00
April	1,490.00	20.00
April	797.50	55.00
April	85,782.50	538.75
May	8,580.00	600.00
May	2,150.00	25.00
May	17,940.00	260.00

Tip: It is possible to add columns to your GROUP BY clause that are not included in your SELECT clause; however, the SELECT statement and its results are less readily understood.

Other problems arise when columns in a SELECT clause are not consistent with the columns in a GROUP BY clause. Take a close look at the report in in the next example. You will notice that there are now several values shown for the count and average quantity repeated many times for certain dates such as February 1, 2004. However, unless you carefully checked the SELECT statement you might not realize that there is an extra level of subgrouping in this report compared to the previous one. The GROUP BY clause in this example contains an extra column—clientno—that is not included in the SELECT statement. Here we are counting clients for each date and calculating the average quantity of books ordered for each client. The report, however, does not provide enough detail for an accurate interpretation.

```
LIBNAME bluesky "C:\mydata\bluesky bookstore\";

SELECT    ord_date "Date",
          count(prodcode) "Count",
          mean(quantity) format= comma8.2 "Avg Quantity"
FROM      bluesky.orders
WHERE     ord_date between '01JAN2004'd and '31MAY2004'd
GROUP BY ord_date, clientno;
```

```
                              Avg
Date          Count   Quantity
_________________________________

01FEB04           1     103.00
01FEB04           1      12.00
07MAR04           1      45.00
10MAR04           1     100.00
10MAR04           1     180.00
10MAR04           2     210.00
08APR04           1      20.00
10APR04           1      55.00
12APR04           2     965.00
12APR04           1     200.00
12APR04           1      25.00
05MAY04           1     600.00
11MAY04           1      25.00
12MAY04           1     260.00
```

If we modify the SELECT statement slightly, we can more easily interpret the report. The modified SELECT statement is shown in the next example together with the new report.

```
LIBNAME bluesky "C:\mydata\bluesky bookstore\";

SELECT    ord_date "Date", clientno "Client",
          count(prodcode) "Count",
          mean(quantity) format= comma8.2 "Avg
          Quantity"
FROM      bluesky.orders
WHERE     ord_date between '01JAN2004'd and '31MAY2004'd
GROUP BY  ord_date, clientno;
```

Date	Client	Count	Avg Quantity
01FEB04	4008	1	103.00
01FEB04	8003	1	12.00
07MAR04	3007	1	45.00
10MAR04	4008	1	100.00
10MAR04	7008	1	180.00
10MAR04	8003	2	210.00
08APR04	4008	1	20.00
10APR04	6090	1	55.00
12APR04	2010	2	965.00
12APR04	5005	1	200.00
12APR04	7008	1	25.00
05MAY04	2010	1	600.00
11MAY04	4008	1	25.00
12MAY04	3007	1	260.00

Confusing results can arise from the exclusion of columns on a GROUP BY clause that are included in the SELECT clause, but are not associated with summary functions. As with the example shown just above, the resulting report includes both detail and summary information. The summary statistics are calculated for the groups listed on the GROUP BY clause, but a separate entry in the report appears for each row in the table.

Compare two SELECT statement examples that differ only in the make-up of the GROUP BY clause. The GROUP BY clause in the second SELECT statement includes a single column and the order date (ord_date). As a result, the total sale and average quantity values are calculated for each order date. However, the report also includes detailed information for each order retrieved by the SELECT statement.

```
LIBNAME  bluesky "C:\mydata\bluesky bookstore\";

SELECT   ord_date "Date" ,clientno "Client",
         currency "Currency",
         sum(totsale) format= comma10.2 "Total Sale" as total,
         mean(quantity) format= comma10.2 "Avg Quantity" as
         avgqty
FROM     bluesky.orders
WHERE    ord_date between '01JAN2004'd and '31MAY2004'd
GROUP BY ord_date;
```

Date	Client	Currency	Total Sale	Avg Quantity
01FEB04	4008	SGD	969.20	57.50
01FEB04	8003	CAD	969.20	57.50
07MAR04	3007	EUR	675.00	45.00
10MAR04	8003	USD	29,907.50	175.00
10MAR04	4008	SGD	29,907.50	175.00
10MAR04	8003	CAD	29,907.50	175.00
10MAR04	7008	EUR	29,907.50	175.00
08APR04	4008	SGD	1,490.00	20.00
10APR04	6090	EUR	797.50	55.00
12APR04	7008	EUR	85,782.50	538.75
12APR04	5005	AUD	85,782.50	538.75
12APR04	2010	USD	85,782.50	538.75
12APR04	2010	USD	85,782.50	538.75
05MAY04	2010	USD	8,580.00	600.00
11MAY04	4008	SGD	2,150.00	25.00
12MAY04	3007	EUR	17,940.00	260.00

The SELECT statement in the next example is exactly the same as the one shown in the preceding example except that several columns are now included in the GROUP BY clause. Notice that in this report a separate set of summary statistics are calculated for each client and currency on a given order date.

```
LIBNAME bluesky "C:\mydata\bluesky bookstore\";

SELECT   ord_date "Date", clientno "Client",
         currency "Currency",
         sum(totsale) format= comma10.2 "Total Sale" as total,
         mean(quantity) format= comma10.2 "Avg Quantity" as
         avgqty
FROM     bluesky.orders
WHERE    ord_date between '01JAN2004'd and '31MAY2004'd
GROUP BY ord_date, clientno, currency;
```

Date	Client	Currency	Total Sale	Avg Quantity
01FEB04	4008	SGD	885.80	103.00
01FEB04	8003	CAD	83.40	12.00
07MAR04	3007	EUR	675.00	45.00
10MAR04	4008	SGD	1,250.00	100.00
10MAR04	7008	EUR	11,700.00	180.00
10MAR04	8003	CAD	15,312.50	350.00
10MAR04	8003	USD	1,645.00	70.00
08APR04	4008	SGD	1,490.00	20.00
10APR04	6090	EUR	797.50	55.00
12APR04	2010	USD	81,195.00	965.00
12APR04	5005	AUD	4,450.00	200.00
12APR04	7008	EUR	137.50	25.00
05MAY04	2010	USD	8,580.00	600.00
11MAY04	4008	SGD	2,150.00	25.00
12MAY04	3007	EUR	17,940.00	260.00

In several of the previous examples, a WHERE clause was added to the SELECT statement limiting the order dates to those between January 1, 2004, and May 31, 2004. Each row or record in the table must first meet the criteria specified in the WHERE clause before it is passed to the GROUP BY clause for processing. Only those rows meeting the WHERE clause criteria are included in the summary statistic calculation for the GROUP BY clause.

However, to subject the group value to a criterion, a HAVING clause must be added. A HAVING clause is processed after the GROUP BY clause and only those groups that meet the criteria set out in the HAVING clause are included in the report. The next example expands on the previous SQL query by limiting the report to those groups or combinations of order date, client number, and currency dates with an average quantity of more than 200 and a total sale value of more than 10000. The HAVING clause is covered in more detail in the next section.

> **Tip:** A WHERE clause is processed before a GROUP BY clause and a HAVING clause is processed after. Rows not meeting the WHERE clause criteria are eliminated before the aggregation specified in the GROUP BY clause. After the rows are aggregated and the summary functions are calculated, the criteria in the HAVING clause are checked. The group is removed from the final report if it does not meet the criteria.

```
LIBNAME   bluesky "C:\mydata\bluesky bookstore\";

SELECT    ord_date "Date" ,clientno "Client",
          currency "Currency",
          sum(totsale) format= comma10.2 "Total Sale" as total,
          mean(quantity) format= comma10.2 "Avg Quantity" as avgqty
FROM      bluesky.orders
WHERE     clientno NE 4008
          and ord_date between '01JAN2004'D and '31MAY2004'D
GROUP BY ord_date, clientno, currency
HAVING    avgqty > 200 and total > 10000;
```

Date	Client	Currency	Total Sale	Avg Quantity
10MAR04	8003	CAD	15,312.50	350.00
12APR04	2010	USD	81,195.00	965.00
12MAY04	3007	EUR	17,940.00	260.00

When the GROUP BY clause is processed, the SQL Optimizer chooses to either execute a sort or a hash operation to faciliate the grouping of the data. If a sort operation occurs, results are sorted in ascending order by the first column listed, then by each additional column from left to right. In the two preceding examples, the reports are sorted in ascending order by their position in the GROUP BY clause. The results are sorted by the column ord_date, then by clientno, and finally by currency. However, if the SQL Optimizer executes a hash operation, the sort order of the resuls may not be as expected.

Tip: A GROUP BY clause may or may not generate results reported in ascending order by the columns on the GROUP BY clause. The sort order of the results after the GROUP BY clause is processed depends on the execution method selected by the SQL Optimizer. The Optimizer may not complete a sort operation before processing the GROUP BY clause. I recommend that an ORDER BY clause always be used if a particular sort order is required for the report.

Information on the SQL Optimizer is included in Chapter 6, "Creating and Managing Tables and Views."

An ORDER BY clause must be included in the SELECT statement to ensure that the results of the GROUP BY clause are sorted as required. The next example shows a SELECT statement that includes both a GROUP BY and an ORDER BY clause, with a descending sort order specified. The results without the ORDER BY clause are also included for comparison.

```
LIBNAME  bluesky "C:\mydata\bluesky bookstore\";

SELECT   ord_date "Date" ,
         count(prodcode) "Number of Products",
         mean(quantity) format= comma8.2 "Avg Quantity" as avgqty
FROM     bluesky.orders
WHERE    ord_date between '01JAN2004'd and '31MAY2004'd
GROUP BY ord_date;
```

```
                  Number
                      of       Avg
            Date  Products  Quantity
         ___________________________

         01FEB04         2     57.50
         07MAR04         1     45.00
         10MAR04         4    175.00
         08APR04         1     20.00
         10APR04         1     55.00
         12APR04         4    538.75
         05MAY04         1    600.00
         11MAY04         1     25.00
         12MAY04         1    260.00
```

```
LIBNAME bluesky "C:\mydata\bluesky bookstore\";

SELECT   ord_date "Date" ,
         count(prodcode) "Number of Products",
         mean(quantity) format= comma8.2 "Avg Quantity" as avgqty
FROM     bluesky.orders
WHERE    ord_date between '01JAN2004'd and '31MAY2004'd
GROUP BY ord_date
ORDER BY avgqty desc;
```

```
                 Number
                     of        Avg
     Date      Products   Quantity
-----------------------------------
05MAY04               1     600.00
12APR04               4     538.75
12MAY04               1     260.00
10MAR04               4     175.00
01FEB04               2      57.50
10APR04               1      55.00
07MAR04               1      45.00
11MAY04               1      25.00
08APR04               1      20.00
```

HAVING clause

SELECT
INTO
FROM
ON
WHERE
GROUP BY
► HAVING
ORDER BY
USING;

General form:

HAVING alias | column | expression COMPARISON OPERATOR
constant | alias | column | expression
<LOGICAL OPERATOR condition...>

The HAVING clause, like the WHERE clause, determines which rows from one or more tables will be reported. However, the HAVING clause criteria are applied to groups of data whereas the WHERE clause is applied to each row of data before grouping occurs. The WHERE clause is processed first, determining which rows will be passed to the GROUP BY clause for further processing. The rows are then grouped according to the specifications in the GROUP BY clause.

For each group, the summary functions indicated in the HAVING clause are then calculated and evaluated against the criteria. Only those groups that meet the criteria set out in the HAVING clause are included in the report or result set.

Tip: A single function is allowed in a HAVING clause only if it is part of a summary function. For example:

```
HAVING max(round(salary))
```

In this example, the ROUND function, a single function, is applied first and the results are passed to the summary function MAX.

The following would not be allowed however:

```
HAVING round(salary)
```

A comparison of the WHERE and HAVING clauses is shown in the following table.

Feature	WHERE clause	HAVING clause
Operators used with numeric variables	Comparison operators, Boolean operators, in, between, is null, is missing	Comparison operators, Boolean operators, IN, BETWEEN, IS NULL, IS MISSING.
Operators used with character variables	like, sounds like, contains	Only available if used in conjunction with a summary function.
Single functions	Allowed.	Single functions may only be included when they are used in conjunction with a summary function.
Summary functions	Not allowed.	Allowed.
Alias	Can be included only if preceded by CALCULATED keyword.	Can be referenced in the same fashion as columns in the table.

Tip: Why is an alias without the CALCULATED keyword allowed in a HAVING clause and not in the WHERE clause? A GROUP BY clause is linked to a SELECT clause; it takes its group columns and summary functions from the SELECT clause. It is processed after the SELECT clause and all aliases, functions, and expressions assigned in the SELECT clause are known.

On the other hand, a WHERE clause is processed before the SELECT clause using only the tables listed in the FROM and FROM-ON clauses. As a result, at the time the WHERE clause is processed, it is unaware of aliases assigned in the SELECT clause unless the CALCULATED keyword is included, directing it to the SELECT clause.

Although it is possible to apply a HAVING clause to any SELECT statement containing summary functions, it is generally coupled with a GROUP BY clause. If a HAVING clause is included without a GROUP BY clause, the data is treated as a single group and evaluated against the criteria in the HAVING clause. The summary function result for the single group is compared to the conditions included in the HAVING clause. If the group meets the condition(s), it is included in the output; otherwise, the entire group is excluded and a report is not generated.

SAS/ACCESS and SQL Pass-Through facility users: Not all RDBMS SQL languages allow a GROUP BY without a HAVING clause. In addition, aliases may or may not be permitted in the GROUP BY clause.

The SELECT statement contained in the example below calculates the total sale amount (totsale) and the average quantity (quantity) for each date in the Bluesky Publishing *orders* table.

```
LIBNAME bluesky "C:\mydata\bluesky bookstore\";

SELECT    ord_date "Date",
          sum(totsale) format= comma10.2 "Total Sale" as total,
          mean(quantity) format= comma10.1 "Avg Quantity" as
          avgqty
FROM      bluesky.orders
GROUP BY ord_date;
```

Date	Total Sale	Avg Quantity
09JAN03	19,061.25	537.5
07FEB03	3,325.00	175.0
15MAR03	5,468.75	125.0
11APR03	15,550.00	200.0
06MAY03	55,750.00	416.7
24JUN03	2,432.50	350.0
06SEP03	34,500.00	1,000.0
27SEP03	27,490.00	500.0
20OCT03	3,390.00	2,900.0
10NOV03	76,972.00	1,400.0
01FEB04	969.20	57.5
07MAR04	675.00	45.0
10MAR04	29,907.50	175.0
08APR04	1,490.00	20.0
10APR04	797.50	55.0
12APR04	85,782.50	538.8
05MAY04	8,580.00	600.0
11MAY04	2,150.00	25.0
12MAY04	17,940.00	260.0
07JUN04	8,505.00	324.0
12JUN04	226,440.00	1,683.3
20JUL04	11,390.00	335.0
23JUL04	112,245.00	625.0

In the next example the SELECT statement from the previous example has been modified to include a HAVING clause. The average quantity and total sale amount for each order date is evaluated against the criteria in the HAVING clause. Only those order dates with average quantities of more than 600 and total sales of more $10,000 will be included in the report.

```
LIBNAME  bluesky "C:\mydata\bluesky bookstore\";

SELECT   ord_date "Date",
         sum(totsale) format= comma10.2 "Total Sale" as total,
         mean(quantity) format= comma10.1 "Avg Quantity" as avgqty
FROM     bluesky.orders
GROUP BY ord_date
HAVING   avgqty > 600 and total > 10000;
```

```
                                    Avg
     Date  Total Sale          Quantity
----------------------------------------
  06SEP03   34,500.00           1,000.0
  10NOV03   76,972.00           1,400.0
  12JUN04  226,440.00           1,683.3
  23JUL04  112,245.00             625.0
```

One final comparison is helpful. If we use a WHERE clause in the SELECT statement shown in the preceding example in addition to a HAVING clause, we get yet another set of results. The HAVING clause in the next example applies the same criteria as the previous example, but now an additional criterion is applied to every row prior to the summary function calculation. In this case, the orders made by client number 3007 are excluded from the average and total calculations. As a result, there are fewer dates in the report and fewer orders contributing to the average calculation. Notice that June 12, 2004, is missing from this report and the total sale and average quantity values for July 23, 2004, differ from the previous report.

```
LIBNAME  bluesky "C:\mydata\bluesky bookstore\";

SELECT   ord_date "Date",
         sum(totsale) format =comma10.2 "Total Sale" as total,
         mean(quantity) format= comma10.1 "Avg Quantity" as avgqty
FROM     bluesky.orders
WHERE    clientno ne 3007
GROUP BY ord_date
HAVING   avgqty > 600 and total > 10000;
```

```
                                    Avg
     Date  Total Sale          Quantity
----------------------------------------
  06SEP03   34,500.00           1,000.0
  10NOV03   76,972.00           1,400.0
  23JUL04   96,757.50             636.7
```

As mentioned above, it is possible to include a HAVING clause in SELECT statements without a GROUP BY clause. In this type of query, all of the rows contribute to a single group for which a single set of summary function values is calculated. If the group summary results meet the criteria set out in the HAVING clause, all of the rows in the table are reported. However, if the result does not meet the criteria, none of the rows in the table is reported.

This "all or nothing" approach is useful for some forms of reports. For example, you might want to exclude an entire month of sales data from a report if the average sales were below a particular threshold value. Generally, these forms of reports use macro variables or other forms of variable input that allow the user to interactively generate the WHERE or HAVING clause criteria.

In the next example, a query generating a list of the orders from the most recent order date is shown. The detail of each order is required, so a GROUP BY clause has not been included. Rather, the maximum order date is calculated for the entire group, including all rows in the *orders* table. The HAVING clause criterion compares the order date for each row in the table to the group maximum to determine whether the row should be included in the report.

```
TITLE1    'Details on most recent sales date';
LIBNAME bluesky "C:\mydata\bluesky bookstore\";

SELECT    ord_date "Date",
          clientno "Client No.",
          totsale format= comma10.2 "Total Sale" ,
          quantity format= comma10.2 "Quantity Ordered",
          prodcode "Product code"
FROM      bluesky.orders
HAVING    ord_date = max(ord_date);
```

Details on most recent sales date

Date	Client No.	Total Sale	Quantity Ordered	Product code
23JUL04	3007	15,487.50	590.00	100601
23JUL04	5005	82,500.00	1,500.00	400102
23JUL04	6090	657.50	10.00	400178
23JUL04	7008	13,600.00	400.00	500116

Tip: The SELECT clause does not have to include summary functions despite the inclusion of a HAVING clause in the query. The HAVING clause must include summary functions in its criteria; however, these same summary functions do not have to be included in the SELECT clause. The HAVING clause limits the rows in the result set; the SELECT clause determines the columns included in the result set.

A GROUP BY clause has not been included in this SELECT statement. The HAVING clause operates on a single group, which in this case includes all of the rows in the *orders* table.

Remerging summary statistics

SQL queries that contain a GROUP BY and HAVING clause may have to complete at least two passes through a table. Remerging occurs any time a summary function result must be compared to or reported with columns that are not part of the GROUP BY clause.

In the first pass, the summary statistic for each group is calculated. The table is then processed a second time with a column value for each row in a group compared to the summary statistic. Essentially an extra column containing the summary statistic is merged with the table. As a result, a message is written to your SAS log indicating that the summary statistics were remerged with the original data. More detailed information on the remerging process is contained in Chapter 4, "Functions."

Tip: Often remerging occurs by accident when an SQL statement has an incomplete or incorrect GROUP BY or HAVING clause. It is important to review the SAS log for the following remerging message when working with these clauses:

```
NOTE: The query requires remerging summary statistics
      back with the original data.
```

The next example shows a SELECT statement that would require remerging summary data with each row in the Bluesky Publishing Company *orders* table. We want to generate a report includes the sale amount (totsale) and quantity ordered by each client on a particular date together with the sale and quantity as a percentage of the total sale amount and quantity for all orders.

```
TITLE1 'Orders as percentage of total sales and quantity';

LIBNAME bluesky "C:\mydata\bluesky bookstore\";
SELECT  Ord_date "Date", clientno "Client No.",
        totsale "Total sale", quantity "Quantity",
        totsale/sum(totsale) format= percent10.
        "Sale as % of total sales ",
        quantity/sum(quantity) format= percent10.
        "Quantity as % of total quantity"

FROM    bluesky.orders
WHERE   ord_date between '01JAN2004'd and '31MAY2004'd ;
```

The query is designed to report a number of measures for each row of the *orders* table that meets the WHERE clause criteria, not a combined set of measures. Moreover, the calculations in the SELECT clause require the sale and quantity amount for each row to be divided by the table totals for these variables. As a result, SAS takes the summary statistic result and remerges it with the original table data. Each row in the table now has both detail and summary information allowing the percentage calculations to be made. The next example shows the output of the query.

Orders as percentage of total sales and quantity

Date	Client No.	Total sale	Quantity	Sale as % of total sales	Quantity as % of total quantity
01FEB04	8003	83.4	12	0%	0%
01FEB04	4008	885.8	103	1%	3%
07MAR04	3007	675	45	0%	1%
10MAR04	7008	11700	180	8%	5%
10MAR04	8003	15312.5	350	10%	9%
10MAR04	8003	1645	70	1%	2%
10MAR04	4008	1250	100	1%	3%
08APR04	4008	1490	20	1%	1%
10APR04	6090	797.5	55	1%	1%
12APR04	2010	39375	700	27%	18%
12APR04	2010	41820	1230	28%	31%
12APR04	5005	4450	200	3%	5%
12APR04	7008	137.5	25	0%	1%
05MAY04	2010	8580	600	6%	15%
11MAY04	4008	2150	25	1%	1%
12MAY04	3007	17940	260	12%	7%

Tip: Remerging occurs automatically if one or more columns in the SELECT clause is neither a summary function nor part of a GROUP BY clause. More information on remerging is included in Chapter 4, "Functions."

ON Clause

SELECT
INTO
▸ FROM
▸ ON
WHERE
GROUP BY
HAVING
ORDER BY
USING;

General form:

FROM <libref.>table <alias >
<LEFT JOIN|RIGHT JOIN|FULL JOIN|<INNER>JOIN>
<libref.>table <alias> ...

ON table.column = table.column
<LOGICAL OPERATOR condition>

The ON clause is similar to a WHERE or HAVING clause because it includes one or more conditions that a row must meet in order to be included in the output. However, it is only used when an SQL statement requires a join between two or more tables. The joining process matches values in the column of one table with values stored in the column of another. When a match is found, the rows from each of the tables are combined to form a single row. Joins are covered in detail in Chapter 5, "Working with Two or More Tables."

The FROM clause must include a JOIN keyword for an ON clause to be added to the SELECT statement. The ON clause specifies the table columns that are to be compared in order to match or join rows in one table with another table.

Tip: Both a WHERE clause and an ON clause can be used to specify inner join conditions between two or more tables. However, the ON clause is required when specifying outer joins. When an ON clause is included in a SELECT statement, the FROM clause must include a JOIN keyword.

The next example shows an SQL query that uses the values from one table to determine the rows that are reported from another table. Both the *stock* and the *orders* tables have a column containing a product code (prodcode). Notice that the SELECT clause contains a JOIN keyword between two different table names. The first line of the ON clause indicates that the join should be made between rows with the same product code in each table. The next line of the ON clause contains a criterion based on the order date from the *orders* table. It serves to limit the rows that will be joined together. In this example, only those rows in the *orders* table that have dates between January 1, 2004, and May 31, 2004, will be joined to rows with matching product code values in the *stock* table. The DISTINCT keyword in the SELECT clause prevents duplicate information from appearing in the final report. Finally, an ORDER BY clause has been added to sort the report by the title in the *stock* table.

```
TITLE1    'Books in inventory that were sold between January 1 and
          May 31, 2004';
LIBNAME   bluesky "C:\mydata\bluesky bookstore\";

SELECT    DISTINCT isbn, title, category
FROM      bluesky.stock
          JOIN  bluesky.orders
ON        stock.prodcode = orders.prodcode
          and orders.ord_date between '01JAN2004'd and '31MAY2004'd
ORDER BY stock.title;
```

```
Books in inventory that were sold between January 1 and May 31, 2004

isbn           title                                                    category
--------------------------------------------------------------------------------------
1-7890-4567-3  Book of Science and Nature                               science
1-7890-2829-9  Computer: Beginners Guide                                computer
1-7890-1267-8  Materials Science                                        engineering
1-7890-3891-x  Medical Education in School                              medicine
1-7890-3467-1  Medications and Maintenance                              medicine
1-7890-3278-4  Mountaineering Skills                                    general
1-7890-1280-5  Science and Technology                                   science
1-7890-5678-0  Science of Biology                                       science
1-7890-1290-2  Space Sciences                                           engineering
1-7890-5634-9  Start a Business Using a Computer                        computer
1-7890-3007-2  The Maestro                                              general
1-7890-2878-7  The Ultimate Philosophy                                  arts
1-7890-5475-3  Tibetan Medicine                                         medicine
1-7890-3468-x  Women Writers                                            general
```

The ON clause has the same options and restrictions as a WHERE clause. The most important restriction to note is that summary functions cannot be included in an ON clause. However, it is possible to add both a GROUP BY and HAVING clause to a query containing an ON clause. The next example shows a query that reports on the number of orders by book category using information in the *orders* table to limit the rows included in the report. The criteria based on the summary count function are indicated in the HAVING clause rather than the ON clause. Notice that the query in the following example also contains an ORDER BY clause that sorts the reported rows in descending order by category. A WHERE clause may also be included.

```
LIBNAME   bluesky "C:\mydata\bluesky bookstore\";

SELECT    count(isbn) as orders "No. of Orders",
          category "Category"
FROM      bluesky.stock JOIN bluesky.orders
ON        stock.prodcode = orders.prodcode
          and orders.ord_date between '01JAN2004'd and '31MAY2004'd
GROUP BY  category
HAVING    orders > 1
ORDER BY  category desc;
```

```
No. of
Orders  Category
______________________________

  3   science
  3   medicine
  5   general
  2   engineering
  2   computer
```

Tip: Joins are covered in detail in Chapter 5, "Working with Two or More Tables."

USING clause

SELECT
INTO
FROM
ON
WHERE
GROUP BY
HAVING
ORDER BY
▶ USING;

General form:

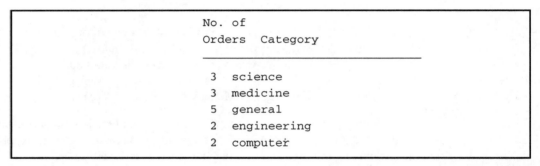

USING LIBNAME <libref> 'directory-path'
| RDBMS <connection parameters> ;

Tip: The USING clause was introduced in SAS 8. It allows a view to be permanently associated with a libref in which the tables used to create the view are stored. Views are discussed in detail in Chapter 6, "Creating and Managing Tables and Views."

The USING clause can be added to a SELECT statement that retrieves data as part of the creation of a view. It allows the LIBNAME to be permanently stored with the view, allowing for automatic update of the view data without the reassignment of the library.

If a database rather than a disk location is specified in the LIBNAME statement a connection with the database is made, enabling the view to retrieve rows and columns from tables stored in a database. Connection parameters appropriate to the specific database are specified in the USING clause.

When the LIBNAME statement is embedded into a CREATE VIEW statement, the libref association is local to that statement. Once the view is created, the library reference is de-assigned and any database connections terminated.

Tip: A complete discussion of the LIBNAME statement options is included in Chapter 2, "Working with PROC SQL." Information on using the SAS/ACCESS LIBNAME statement to connect to a database covered in Appendix C, "Information for Database Users." Views are discussed in Chapter 6, "Creating and Managing Tables and Views."

The next example shows the creation of a view using an Oracle table as the source for the view data. A view may contain some or all of the columns in one or more tables. Further conditions may be imposed limiting the actual rows retrieved.

```
CREATE view address AS
      SELECT *
      FROM   oralib.address
      USING  LIBNAME oralib oracle
             user=scott password=tiger path=master schema=bluesky;
```

Tip: The LIBNAME reference embedded in the CREATE VIEW statement is local to that statement. The same LIBNAME reference can be used in your SAS session without conflict.

INTO Clause

SELECT
▸ INTO
FROM
ON
WHERE
GROUP BY
HAVING
ORDER BY
USING;

General form:

INTO :macro-variable <, :macro-variable ...>

The INTO clause enables you to pass either a column value or the result of a calculated expression into a macro variable. Selection criteria can be set using WHERE and HAVING clauses in your query. If the macro variable named in the INTO clause does not exist, it is created at the time the SQL query is run.

There are limitations:

- The INTO clause cannot be part of a CREATE TABLE or CREATE VIEW statement. The INTO clause cannot be included in a subquery. (Refer to Chapter 5, "Working with Two or More Tables," for more information on subqueries.) In addition, it cannot be included in an SQL Pass-Through facility inner SELECT statement.
- Macro variables are limited to a length of 64K. If you are working in SAS 6, macros are limited to a length of 32K.

If you refer to more macro variables in the INTO clause than there are retrieved columns, there will be unassigned macro variables. A warning message is written to the SAS log indicating that the unassigned or surplus macro variables will not be created. More information on macros and the use of the INTO clause is provided in Chapter 7, "Building Interactive Applications."

Tip: If the number of variables in your SELECT clause differs from the number of macro variables on the INTO clause, the following warning will appear in the SAS log:

```
WARNING: INTO clause specifies more host variables than columns
         listed in the SELECT clause.  Surplus host variables
         will not be set.
```

Putting it all together

The SELECT statement in the example below includes most of the commonly used clauses discussed in this chapter. The SELECT clause includes columns from the *client*, *orders*, and *stock* tables, each of which is listed in the FROM clause together with a one-letter alias. Two expressions are included in the SELECT clause, calculating the total sale and quantity of books sold using the SUM function. Labels and formatting have been applied to each column and expression, and aliases have been specified for the expressions.

The WHERE clause specifies the join conditions for the tables, using columns of common data type to link or match common values in the tables. It also limits the retrieved rows to those books in the Arts, Engineering, and Medicine categories ordered between January 1, 2004, and June 30, 2004. The information is grouped by the book title and customer with a total sale value and total quantity calculated for each group. The HAVING clause filters each group, limiting the report to those groups with a total quantity of more than 100 and a total sale value of more than 1000. Finally, the report is sorted in descending order by the total sale value.

```
LIBNAME bluesky "C:\mydata\bluesky bookstore\";

TITLE1    "Arts, Engineering and Medical book orders";
TITLE2    "Quantity > 100 and Total Sale > $1000";
TITLE3    "January 1, 2004 to June 30, 2004";

SELECT    s.title "Title" format=$30.,
          c.company "Customer" format=$35.,
          sum(o.totsale) as total "Total Sale" format=dollar15.2,
          sum(o.quantity) as qty "Total Qty" format=comma8.

FROM      bluesky.orders o,
          bluesky.client c,
          bluesky.stock s

WHERE     o.clientno = c.clientno
          and o.prodcode=s.prodcode
          and s.category in ('arts', 'engineering','medicine')
          and o.ord_date between '01JAN2004'd and '30JUN2004'd

GROUP BY  s.title, c.company
HAVING    qty > 100 and total > 1000
ORDER BY  total desc;
```

```
Arts, Engineering and Medical book orders
Quantity > 100 and Total Sale > $1000
January 1, 2004 to June 30, 2004


Total
Title                          Customer                   Total Sale      Qty
-------------------------------------------------------------------------------
Managing Water Resources       Heffers Booksellers        $225,000.00    5,000
Tibetan Medicine               Chicago State University    $41,820.00    1,230
Space Sciences                 Chicago State University    $39,375.00      700
Medical Education in School    Lawrence Books              $15,312.50      350
```

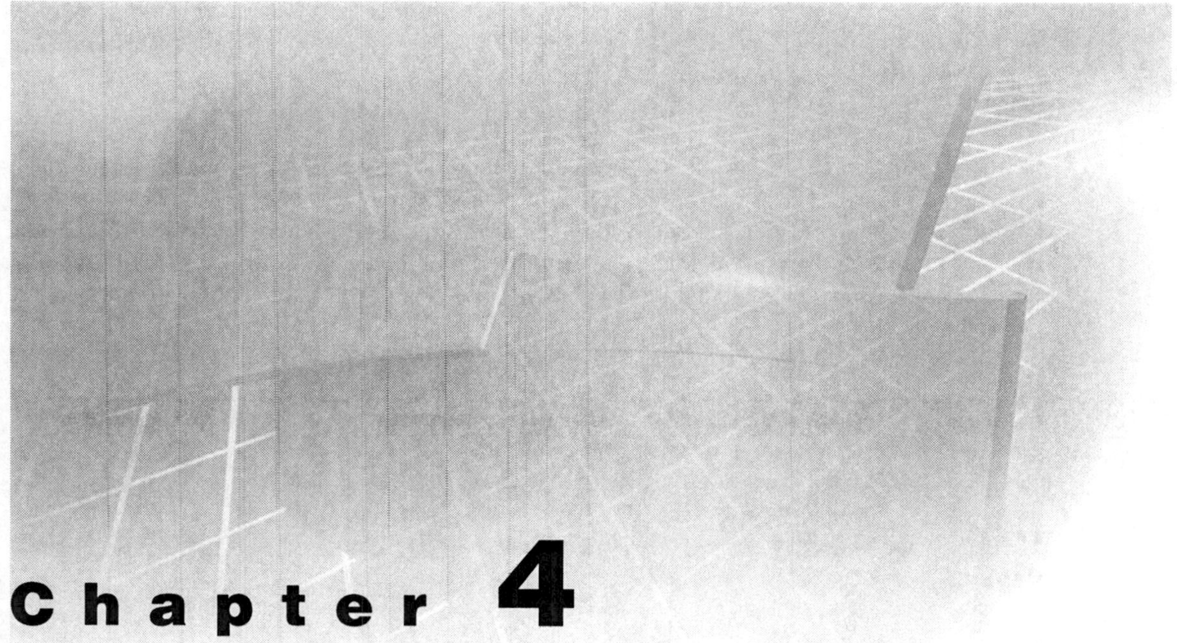

Chapter 4

Functions

SAS functions and PROC SQL

PROC SQL supports almost all of the SAS DATA step functions giving the SAS SQL language a distinct advantage over other database-specific SQL products. A detailed description of each function is contained in *SAS Language Reference: Dictionary.*

PROC SQL functions are divided into two categories based on the number of rows on which they operate. The first category covers single functions that return one value for each row in a table. The second category covers summary functions that return one value for a number of rows in a table. In addition there are several categories of SAS functions that are available for use within PROC SQL. The table following summarizes their usage.

Function category	Single function	Summary function	Not available
Arithmetic	√	MAX, MIN	
Array			√
Character	√		
Date and time	√		
Financial	√		
Mathematical	√		
Probability	√		
Quantile	√		
Random number	√		
Sample statistics	KURTOSIS, SKEWNESS	All except those mentioned under single functions *	
Special functions	SYMGET, INPUT, PUT, SOUNDEX		DIF, LAG
PROC SQL only	COALESCE		

* SUMWGT limited to weighting of 1 for each row

SAS/ACCESS and SQL Pass-Through Facility users: The inner SELECT statement of a PROC SQL query that is passed to an RDBMS for processing may include any functions that are valid in the SQL language of that database. For example, DECODE and NVL are available when using the SQL Pass-Through Facility with Oracle.

Some of the functions discussed in this chapter cannot be included in the inner SELECT statement of a PROC SQL query because they are unknown in many of the database-specific SQL languages.

It is possible, however, to use these functions when referencing a table stored in a database through a LIBNAME statement, available since SAS Version 8. In this case, SAS-specific functions are processed within the SAS session.

SAS functions introduced in SAS Versions 8 and 9

In SAS Versions 8 and 9, several new functions have been added and changes have been made to existing functions. A full description of each function can be obtained in the *SAS Language Reference: Dictionary*. A brief summary of new and modified functions often used in SQL statements is contained in the following table.

Function name	New/modified (release version)	Description
BTRIM	New (8.2)	Trims a single character from the beginning, end or both ends of a string.
FOLD	New (8.2)	Changes the case of the argument.
PUT	Modified	Now allows for the alignment of values with formats.
SCAN	Modified	Expressions can now be scanned from right to left as well as left to right.
SUBSTRN	New (9.0)	Provides the same functionality as the SUBSTR function; however, it allows a result with a length of zero. The SUBSTR function continues to be available.

SAS/ACCESS and SQL Pass-Through Facility users: When using the SAS/ACCESS LIBNAME statement, you can automatically convert some SAS functions to database-specific functions. As a result, the processing of these functions is handled by the RDBMS and performance may be significantly improved. SQL Pass-Through Facility inner SELECT statements must use functions supported by the RDBMS. Refer to the RBDMS documentation for functions available in your database system.

Options SASTRACE and SASTRACELOC can be set in the PROC SQL statement to obtain details about the statement submitted to the database. If SASLOG is set for SASTRACELOC, information is written to the SAS log. Alternatively a directory path and file name can be specified to direct the trace information to an external file.

```
PROC SQL;
OPTIONS SASTRACE='...D' SASTRACELOC=SASLOG;
```

PROC SQL function names

There are several SAS DATA step functions that can be referenced by other names when used in PROC SQL. The ANSI SQL naming standard for some functions differs from that of the SAS DATA step functions. As a result, certain functions can be referenced within an SQL query by either the SAS DATA step function name or by the ANSI SQL standard.

The following table provides the SAS DATA step and ANSI SQL standard names for the affected functions.

Function names		Usage in PROC SQL	Function description
SAS DATA step	ANSI SQL		
MEAN	AVG	MEAN, AVG	Arithmetic mean
N, FREQ	COUNT	N, COUNT, FREQ	Number of nonmissing values

SAS functions operating as single and summary functions

Summary functions can operate as either single or summary functions. These include most of the sample statistical functions such as MAX, MIN, and MEAN.

If the arguments for these functions consist of two or more columns, they behave as single functions. The column values in each row are used to generate a result for that row.

If a single column is furnished as an argument for the function, then the function operates as a summary function. The value for that column in every selected row of the group is used to generate one result.

SAS functions unavailable in PROC SQL

There are several SAS DATA step functions that are not available to PROC SQL users. PROC SQL does not process records in the same fashion as the SAS DATA step. It is therefore impossible to refer to the previous or to the *n*th previous record retrieved by a SELECT statement. As a result, the DIF and LAG functions cannot be implemented in PROC SQL.

Array processing is also handled differently by PROC SQL from the SAS DATA step. As a result, the DIM, HBOUND, and LBOUND array functions are not available in an SQL query.

The SYMGET function, which returns the value of a macro variable during DATA step processing, cannot be added to an SQL statement. There are PROC SQL alternatives to this function that are discussed in detail in Chapter 7, "Building Interactive Applications."

A function available only in PROC SQL

The COALESCE function is an ANSI SQL function that is not available in the SAS language but that can be used with PROC SQL. It is a single function that reports the first nonmissing value encountered in the columns included in its argument list for each row. More information on this function is provided in the next section of this chapter.

Single functions

A single function is one that returns one value per row computed from the argument of the function. When a function is used in a SELECT statement, it essentially results in the creation of a new variable. Without the application of an alias or label, the report will not provide a heading. In addition, although it is possible to include the complete function as part of a criterion for row selection in a WHERE clause, this can become cumbersome.

> **Tip:** Single function arguments can be table columns, expressions, or other functions.

The example below shows a simple single function that is included in both a SELECT and WHERE clause. Neither an alias nor a heading have been applied to the function in the SELECT clause. As a result, the complete function must be entered in the WHERE clause, and the report does not include a column heading for the new values.

```
LIBNAME bluesky "C:\mydata\bluesky bookstore\";

SELECT title, round(stock*price)
FROM   bluesky.stock
WHERE  round(stock*price) < 3000;
```

```
title
------------------------------------------------------------
Democracy in America                                    1980
The Ultimate Philosophy                                  950
National Library of Medicine                            2301
Medications and Maintenance                             2580
Computer: Beginners Guide                               2350
The Maestro                                              695
Mountaineering Skills                                   1100
```

Compare the previous SELECT statement to the one shown in the next example. Here an alias is applied to the function. Notice that the WHERE clause has been modified to include a reference to the alias instead of repeating the function. The keyword CALCULATED indicates to SAS that an alias for a derived column rather than a column name is referenced. The alias also provides a heading for the column in the resulting report.

```
LIBNAME bluesky "C:\mydata\bluesky bookstore\";

SELECT title , round(stock*price) as totprice
FROM   bluesky.stock
WHERE  CALCULATED totprice < 3000;
```

```
title                                               totprice
------------------------------------------------------------
Democracy in America                                    1980
The Ultimate Philosophy                                  950
National Library of Medicine                            2301
Medications and Maintenance                             2580
Computer: Beginners Guide                               2350
The Maestro                                              695
Mountaineering Skills                                   1100
```

Single functions can be included in an ORDER BY clause. As with the WHERE clause, the use of an alias can provide for clearer, easier inclusion of a function. The next example shows an ORDER BY clause using a function. Notice that although the CALCULATED keyword is required in a WHERE clause before referencing a function generated value, it is not required in an ORDER BY clause. The ORDER BY clause is processed last, and as such it has knowledge of all expressions used throughout a SELECT statement.

```
LIBNAME  bluesky "C:\mydata\bluesky bookstore\";

SELECT   title,round(stock*price) as totprice
FROM     bluesky.stock
WHERE    CALCULATED totprice < 3000
ORDER BY totprice;
```

title	totprice
The Maestro	695
The Ultimate Philosophy	950
Mountaineering Skills	1100
Democracy in America	1980
National Library of Medicine	2301
Computer: Beginners Guide	2350
Medications and Maintenance	2580

A single function may also be included in a GROUP BY clause. The inclusion of a function in a GROUP BY clause requires an alias, but it does not require the CALCULATED keyword. The next example illustrates a GROUP BY clause that references a SUBSTR function value from the SELECT statement using an alias. Notice that only the WHERE clause includes the CALCULATED keyword. The COUNT function is a summary function, producing a count of the number of occurrences of a product code (prodcode) value for each group. Summary functions are discussed in the next section of this chapter.

Why is an alias allowed in a GROUP BY clause but not in a WHERE clause? It has to do with the way a SELECT statement is processed. The FROM clause is processed first, identifying the tables from which data is to be drawn for the query. Processing then passes to the WHERE clause, with each row from the table(s) checked against the criteria to determine which rows will be passed to other clauses in the query. The WHERE clause is processed without reference to the SELECT clause unless a CALCULATED keyword is encountered. As result, functions and their aliases are not known to the WHERE clause at the time of processing.

The GROUP BY clause, on the other hand, is linked to the functions in the SELECT clause. When processing is passed to a GROUP BY clause from the WHERE clause, the rows are first sorted by values in the GROUP BY columns. Next the summary functions in the SELECT clause are processed for each group of distinct values in the GROUP BY columns. This link between the SELECT and GROUP BY clauses means that functions and their aliases are known to the GROUP BY clause.

```
LIBNAME bluesky "C:\mydata\bluesky bookstore\";

SELECT    SUBSTR(auth_lst,1,1) as lastinit format= $10.,
          count(prodcode) "Count"
FROM      bluesky.stock
WHERE     CALCULATED lastinit IN ('B','C','D','E','F')
GROUP BY lastinit;
```

lastinit	Count
B	3
C	1
D	2
E	1
F	2

If you accidentally include a function rather than an alias in a GROUP BY clause, you will not receive an error message in your SAS log; however, you may receive a note indicating that remerging was required. The next example shows the same SQL query as contained in the previous example but without an alias in the GROUP BY clause. Notice that the count values are correct for each group of last initial; however, there is an entry for every row in the *stock* table that meets the WHERE clause criteria. The GROUP BY clause is executed to generate the count for each unique last initial, but these results are then matched to each row in the stock table with that last initial.

```
LIBNAME   bluesky "C:\mydata\bluesky bookstore\";

SELECT    SUBSTR(auth_lst,1,1) as lastinit format= $10.,
          count(prodcode) "Count"
FROM      bluesky.stock
WHERE     CALCULATED lastinit IN ('B','C','D','E','F')
GROUP BY SUBSTR(auth_lst,1,1);
```

```
lastinit        Count
_____________________

B                   3
B                   3
B                   3
C                   1
D                   2
D                   2
E                   1
F                   2
F                   2
```

Tip: The DISTINCT keyword can be added to the SELECT clause to clean up the query results in the preceding example. However, query performance will be compromised. The remerging operation that takes place because of the incorrect GROUP BY clause is not eliminated if a DISTINCT keyword is added.

```
LIBNAME bluesky "C:\mydata\bluesky bookstore\";

SELECT  DISTINCT SUBSTR(auth_lst,1,1) as lastinit format= $10.,
        count(prodcode) "Count"
FROM    bluesky.stock
WHERE   CALCULATED lastinit IN ('B','C','D','E','F');
```

```
lastinit        Count
_____________________

B                   9
C                   9
D                   9
E                   9
F                   9
```

New users sometimes confuse the functionality of the DISTINCT keyword and the GROUP BY clause. Let's examine the query just above and the query at the top of page 138.

The DISTINCT keyword provides a list of unique last initials from all rows that meet the WHERE clause criteria; the rows are treated as a single group, and a count of the number of product codes for the entire group is calculated. The number of product codes for the group remains static; it is reported for each of the unique initials as shown in the preceding example.

The GROUP BY clause is executed immediately after the WHERE clause. It groups or segments the rows that meet the WHERE clause criteria by the columns or expressions set out in the GROUP BY clause. Essentially, it creates a list of distinct or unique values just as the DISTINCT keyword does. However, as seen in the earlier example, a count of the number of product codes is calculated for each unique last initial or group. The number of product codes for each group may be different as is seen in the report included in the example.

Single function arguments

Many single functions require only one argument while others require multiple arguments. An argument may take several forms as described below.

Single column value

In the simplest case, the function operates on the column value for each row in the table. For each row in the table, the query will calculate a value for the function. The next example shows a function that returns the length of each value stored in the state column of the *address* table. Notice that the rows for which the state is missing still return a value for the function; a value of one is reported for missing character strings.

```
LIBNAME bluesky "C:\mydata\bluesky bookstore\";

SELECT  state, length(state) as length
FROM    bluesky.address;
```

state	length
TX	2
IL	2
	1
	1
	1
	1
	1
BC	2

Expression based on one or more columns

It is possible to first apply a mathematical calculation to a column before it is passed as an argument to the function. For example, to obtain an estimate of prices in another currency, you might multiply each book price by a currency conversion factor before applying the ROUND function as shown in the next example.

```
LIBNAME bluesky "C:\mydata\bluesky bookstore\";

SELECT  title, ROUND(price * 1.33) "CDN price" format= comma10.2
FROM    bluesky.stock
WHERE   category = 'science';
```

title	CDN price
Book of Science and Nature	92.00
Free Thinking in Mathematics	35.00
Science and Technology	20.00
Science of Biology	86.00
Geology: Volcanos	24.00

In this next example the Canadian price for each book is multiplied by an exchange rate stored in a column in a different table. This is a complex query using a Cartesian join, but it is used here to show that an expression may consist of columns in one or more tables. Joins are covered in detail in Chapter 5, "Working with Two or More Tables."

```
LIBNAME bluesky "C:\mydata\bluesky bookstore\";

SELECT  title, price format=comma10.2, currency.exchrate,
        ROUND(price * currency.exchrate) "CDN price" format=
        comma10.2
FROM    bluesky.stock, bluesky.currency
WHERE   currency.cur_date = '01FEB04'd and currency.currency =
        'CAD'
        and stock.category = 'science';
```

title	price	exchRate	CDN price
Book of Science and Nature	69.00	1.32906	92.00
Free Thinking in Mathematics	26.25	1.32906	35.00
Science and Technology	15.00	1.32906	20.00
Science of Biology	65.00	1.32906	86.00
Geology: Volcanos	18.00	1.32906	24.00

Tip: Cartesian joins generate a complete set of combinations of rows in two or more tables. Each row in one table is joined to every row in a second table and so on. If a WHERE clause is included in the query, only those rows that meet the criteria are included in the joining process. Cartesian joins are covered in more detail in Chapter 5, "Working with Two or More Tables."

Two or more column or expression arguments

Some functions require more than one argument, although they still calculate a single value for the row. The arguments may be columns, expression, character, or numeric values.

The next example illustrates the SCAN function being used to extract the title identification portion of the ISBN value stored in the *stock* table. The arguments for the SCAN function consist of a column, a user-supplied numeric value, and a character value that appear as delimiters or separators in the column value. In this specific example, the ISBN value contains hyphens separating the various "words" in the ISBN. The function returns the third word in the ISBN, which is the title identifier.

```
LIBNAME bluesky "C:\mydata\bluesky bookstore\";

SELECT  title format= $30., ISBN format= $15.,
        scan (isbn, 3, '-') "Title Identifier" format =$10.
FROM    bluesky.stock
WHERE   category = 'general';
```

title	ISBN	Title Identifier
Risks in Life - % Gain or Loss	1-7890-4578-9	4578
The Maestro	1-7890-3007-2	3007
Greece and Beyond	1-7890-2390-4	2390
Mountaineering Skills	1-7890-3278-4	3278
Women Writers	1-7890-3468-x	3468

The next example shows a function that has as its arguments two columns in a table. The RANGE function is used here to determine the quantity range of stocked books and reprint cutoff levels. A join is made between the *stock* and *reprint* tables to obtain the numeric cutoff values associated with the cutoff alpha code in the *stock* table. Table joins are covered in detail in Chapter 5, "Working with Two or More Tables."

Tip: The two columns used as arguments in a RANGE function can be taken from different tables.

SAS/ACCESS and SQL Pass-Through Facility users: One or both of the tables referenced in a RANGE function can reside in a DBMS.

```
LIBNAME bluesky "C:\mydata\bluesky bookstore\";

TITLE1  "Stock to Cutoff Range for Arts Books";

SELECT  title 'Title', RANGE(stock,r.cutoff ) 'Range'
FROM    bluesky.stock s, bluesky.reprint r
WHERE   category = 'arts' and s.reprint=r.reprint;
```

Stock to Cutoff Range for Arts Books

Title	Range
Decorative Arts	1000
The Ultimate Philosophy	50
Democracy in America	5
The Underground Economy	500

The RANGE function is an example of a function that can operate as either a single or summary function. When the RANGE function is used to calculate the difference between two columns, it is a single function. However, if a single column is used as an argument, the RANGE function results in a single value for all of the rows in the table. More information on summary functions is contained in the next section.

When the RANGE function is applied to two columns, it is considered a single function; a GROUP BY clause cannot be added to the previous example. However, if the argument consists of a single column, the RANGE function is considered a summary function and a GROUP BY clause can be added to the SELECT statement.

Arguments may also consist of a column or expression and a user-supplied character expression. In the next example the VERIFY function is used to check that each reprint code in the *stock* table is valid. The VERIFY function will check the column characters against the characters contained within quotes in the second argument or excerpt. The first position within the column value that does not match one of the characters listed in the excerpt is returned. If every character in the column value is included in the characters listed in the excerpt, the function returns a 0. An alias is applied to the function to allow for an easy method of incorporating the function into the WHERE clause criteria.

```
LIBNAME bluesky "C:\mydata\bluesky bookstore\";

SELECT  verify(reprint, 'ABCDEF')as check
FROM    bluesky.stock
WHERE   calculated check > 0;
```

If all reprint codes have been correctly entered into the *stock* table, then the SAS log would report the following:

```
NOTE: No rows were selected.
```

> **Tip:** Foreign key relationships force column values in one table to exist in a second table. If a foreign key relationship is established between the reprint code columns in the *stock* and *reprint* tables, only reprint codes existing in the *reprint* table can be entered into the *stock* table.

Nested functions

Complex calculations based on functions can be achieved through the incorporation of a function as an argument to another function. This nesting of functions adds a powerful flexibility to PROC SQL queries and SAS in general. When functions are nested, the innermost function is evaluated first. The result of that function is passed to the next function moving outward.

The next example is based on an earlier query shown in this chapter. In this case the SCAN function is used as an argument for a SUBSTR function. For clarity, the SCAN function as well as the original ISBN column is included in the SELECT clause. The SCAN function is applied first to the ISBN values shown in the column labeled "ISBN argument for scan function." The results of the SCAN function are included in the column labeled "Result of inner scan function." The SCAN function returns the "word" in the third position, with each word separated by a dash (-) delimiter. The function result becomes the first argument for the SUBSTR function resulting in the values shown in the column labeled "First 2 characters of Title Identifier."

```
LIBNAME bluesky "C:\mydata\bluesky bookstore\";

SELECT   ISBN format= $15. "ISBN argument for scan function",
         scan(isbn,3,'-') "Result of inner scan function"
         format= $10.,
         SUBSTR(scan(isbn, 3, '-'),1,2)
         "First 2 characters of Title Identifier" format= $10.
FROM     bluesky.stock
WHERE    category = 'general';
```

ISBN argument for scan function	Result of inner scan function	First 2 characters of Title Identifier
1-7890-4578-9	4578	45
1-7890-3007-2	3007	30
1-7890-2390-4	2390	23
1-7890-3278-4	3278	32
1-7890-3468-x	3468	34

Tip: SAS/ACCESS and SQL Pass-Through Facility users: SAS functions not recognized by an RDBMS can be added to the outer query when using the SQL Pass-Through facility. If a SAS/ACCESS LIBNAME statement is used, SAS functions can be included in the SELECT statement because SAS processes the query using data stored in the database tables.

Any number of functions can be nested. However, care needs to be taken to ensure that the correct type of argument is being passed from one function to another. For example, a function requiring a character argument should be nested with a function that generates a character argument.

The next example shows a SELECT statement that contains a character function LENGTH and a numeric function INT. In each case, the function argument is of the wrong data type. The PUT function, which converts numeric data into character form, is nested with the LENGTH function. A LEFT function is added to the character version of the stock value to left justify the values in the report. The INPUT function, which converts character data into numeric form, is nested with the INT function. The SELECT statement contains columns that provide intermediate information in the process. Notice that a COMPRESS function is required to ensure that all leading blanks are eliminated before evaluating the LENGTH function. A PUT function will pad all numeric values with blanks to the length of the supplied character format. In this example, the stock value is converted to a character string with a length of 10.

```
LIBNAME bluesky "C:\mydata\bluesky bookstore\";

SELECT    stock "Numeric Stock value",
          left(put(stock,10.)) "Text Stock value" format=$7.,
          length(put(stock,10.)) "Length of Stock value w/o
          compression",
          length(compress(put(stock,10.),' ')) "Length of Stock
          value",
          scan(isbn,3,'-') "Part of Text ISBN" format= $10. ,
          input(scan(isbn,3,'-'),4.2) "Numeric ISBN",
          int(input(scan(isbn,3,'-'),4.2)) "Integer portion of
ISBN"
FROM      bluesky.stock
WHERE     category = 'general';
```

Numeric Stock value	Text Stock value	Length of Stock value w/o compression	Length of Stock value	Part of Text ISBN	Numeric ISBN	Integer portion of ISBN
1000	1000	10	4	4578	45.78	45
1000	1000	10	4	3468	34.68	34
398	398	10	3	2390	23.9	23
200	200	10	3	3278	32.78	32
100	100	10	3	3007	30.07	30

PROC SQL does not perform an implicit conversion of function arguments. Two special functions are available to assist in the conversion of variables from character to numeric and vice versa.

Function	Description	General Form
INPUT	Character to numeric conversion	INPUT(character variable, informat)
PUT	Numeric to character conversion	PUT(numeric variable, format)

Another potential problem arises when null values are passed to a second function. In many cases, a null value will still allow the function to be evaluated without the generation of error messages. Consider this example that we examined earlier in this chapter.

```
LIBNAME bluesky "C:\mydata\bluesky bookstore\";

SELECT  state, length(state) as length
FROM    bluesky.address;
```

```
state    length
---------------
TX            2
IL            2
              1
              1
              1
              1
              1
BC            2
```

In this case, a value of 1 is returned when the LENGTH function is evaluated for null values contained in the state column of the *client* table. In other functions such as the AVG, SUM, and MAX null values are excluded from the calculation.

Without knowledge of the null values in a table, it can be difficult to determine whether the reported results are correct. This is especially true if a complex set of nested functions is incorporated into the SELECT statement. It is not feasible to check each value to ensure it is correct when retrieving a large number of rows from a table. Consider the following suggestions:

- Write a query that checks for null values in table columns that are to be used as arguments before applying the functions.

- Print the contents of each column used as an argument in the nested function query. After you have checked the results, you can rerun the query without the extra columns.
- Determine the range of values that should be returned by the nested function.

Special single functions

Coalesce function

The SAS COALESCE function is unique to the SAS SQL procedure. The COALESCE function returns the first nonmissing value found in a column that is included its argument list. It accepts any number of columns or expressions as arguments, but each must be of the same data type. It has the following general form:

SELECT COALESCE(*argument1*, *argument2* <,*argument3…*>)

The next example shows a COALESCE function applied to several columns in the *address* table.

```
LIBNAME bluesky "C:\mydata\bluesky bookstore\";

SELECT  city "City", state "State", country "Country",
        coalesce(city, state, country) "Coalesce result"
FROM    bluesky.address;
```

City	State	Country	Coalesce result
Austin	TX	USA	Austin
Chicago	IL	USA	Chicago
Cambridge		UK	Cambridge
Singapore		Singapore	Singapore
Adelaide		Australia	Adelaide
Berlin		Germany	Berlin
Paris		France	Paris
Vancouver	BC	Canada	Vancouver

Tip: If all of the column or expression values are SAS missing values, the COALESCE function returns a null or missing value.

The COALESCE function can be invaluable when trying to merge nonmissing values collected from a variety of sources into a single column. For example, in a data warehouse your client information may be derived from more than one source or table. The COALESCE function used in conjunction with table joins can be used to retrieve the information from the sources using a priority source condition.

In the next example the COALESCE function is used to retrieve the earliest order date for each client. Orders placed with the Bluesky Publishing Company over a two-year period prior to January 1, 2003, have been stored in a separate table called *order_2001_2002*. The current *orders* table includes orders placed by both new and existing clients. If we want to report the earliest order date for each client, the tables must be joined. The COALESCE function is used to pull the first nonmissing value from the *orders* tables. If the client is in both tables, the earlier *order_2001_2002* table takes precedence.

> **Tip:** More information on joins is included in Chapter 5, "Working with Two or More Tables."

```
LIBNAME bluesky "C:\mydata\bluesky bookstore\";

SELECT  coalesce(order_2001_2002.clientno, orders.clientno) as
        combine "Clients",
        coalesce(min(order_2001_2002.ord_date),
        min(orders.ord_date)) format=date9."Earliest order date"
FROM    bluesky.order_2001_2002 FULL JOIN bluesky.orders
ON      orders.clientno = order_2001_2002.clientno
```

Clients	Earliest order date
1001	05JAN2001
2010	20OCT2003
3007	28FEB2002
4008	15MAR2003
5005	13JUL2002
6090	20APR2001
7008	16JAN2001
8003	09MAR2001

The COALESCE function allows you to set the priority for a variable that is available from more than one table. The tables are joined and the columns listed as arguments to the COALESCE function parentheses is in the order of precedence. This can be an invaluable tool when working with a data warehouse.

Summary functions

A summary function generates a single value. It uses all of the values retrieved for the argument from rows in the table that meets the selection criteria set out in the WHERE clause. If the DISTINCT keyword is added to the argument, only unique column values from rows meeting the selection criteria are included in the evaluation of the summary function. The SELECT statement in the next example illustrates the use of the DISTINCT keyword with the COUNT function. Notice that the DISTINCT keyword can be applied to different function arguments.

The argument of a summary function can be a single column, expression, or a single function. In addition, the DISTINCT keyword can be added to eliminate duplicate values of the argument.

```
LIBNAME bluesky "C:\mydata\bluesky bookstore\";

SELECT  count (distinct category) "Count of unique categories",
        count(distinct auth_lst) "Count of unique author names",
        count(prodcode) "Count of number of products"
FROM    bluesky.stock;
```

```
                Count of  Count of
    Count of      unique    number
      unique      author        of
  categories       names  products
  --------------------------------

           6          30        30
```

When a summary function is used together with a GROUP BY clause in an SQL query, a function result is generated for each group defined by the GROUP BY clause. In the next example a MIN and MAX price for each book category is generated using the GROUP BY clause.

```
LIBNAME  bluesky "C:\mydata\bluesky bookstore\";

SELECT   category "Category",
         min(price) "Minimum Price" format= comma10.2,
         max(price) "Maximum Price" format= comma10.2
FROM     bluesky.stock
GROUP BY category;
```

Category	Minimum Price	Maximum Price
arts	9.50	36.00
computer	22.25	34.50
engineering	45.00	74.50
general	5.50	14.30
medicine	34.00	86.00
science	15.00	69.00

A summary function cannot be referenced in a WHERE clause; a WHERE clause may only limit the rows used in the calculation of a summary function. PROC SQL will incorporate the argument values from all rows that meet the criteria set out in the WHERE clause before it evaluates the summary function. The code in the next example repeats the previous SQL query in the above output with the addition of a WHERE clause that limits the scope of the query. Notice that the MIN function results are different for the arts and science categories and the general category is excluded.

```
LIBNAME  bluesky "C:\mydata\bluesky bookstore\";

SELECT   category "Category",
         min(price) "Minimum Price" format =comma10.2,
         max(price) "Maximum Price" format= comma10.2
FROM     bluesky.stock
WHERE    price > 15
GROUP BY category;
```

Category	Minimum Price	Maximum Price
arts	16.95	36.00
computer	22.25	34.50
engineering	45.00	74.50
medicine	34.00	86.00
science	18.00	69.00

Although summary functions cannot be used in a WHERE clause in a SELECT statement, they can appear in a WHERE clause criterion built on a subquery. The next example shows a simple example of a summary function within a subquery in a WHERE clause. In this example, only those books that are priced higher than the average price for all books sold by Bluesky Publishing are passed to the summary functions.

```
LIBNAME  bluesky "C:\mydata\bluesky bookstore\";

SELECT   category "Category",
         min(price) "Minimum Price" format= comma10.2,
         max(price) "Maximum Price" format= comma10.2
FROM     bluesky.stock
WHERE    price > (SELECT mean(price)
                  FROM bluesky.stock)
GROUP BY category;
```

Category	Minimum Price	Maximum Price
engineering	45.00	74.50
medicine	43.75	86.00
science	65.00	69.00

Tip: Subqueries are SELECT statements within other SELECT statements. They are often used to retrieve single or multiple values that become part of WHERE criteria. Subqueries are covered in detail in Chapter 5, "Working with Two or More Tables."

In order to apply a criterion to a summary function result, you must use a HAVING clause. The full function can be repeated in the HAVING clause, but the use of an alias can simplify the clause. The next example repeats the SQL query in that we considered earlier, but includes a criterion similar to the previous example in a HAVING clause. Notice that an alias has been applied to the MIN function to allow for easier reference in the HAVING clause. The results here are different from those generated by the previous two queries. In this example, the arts, science, and general categories have been excluded because the MIN function evaluates to a value of 15 or less.

```
LIBNAME  bluesky "C:\mydata\bluesky bookstore\";

SELECT   category "Category",
         min(price) as minpr "Minimum Price" format= comma10.2,
         max(price) "Maximum Price" format= comma10.2
FROM     bluesky.stock
GROUP BY category
HAVING   minpr > 15;
```

Category	Minimum Price	Maximum Price
computer	22.25	34.50
engineering	45.00	74.50
medicine	34.00	86.00

A summary function may be referenced in an ORDER BY clause by alias only. The next example illustrates this function.

> **Tip:** Alias or label? An alias is always preceded by the AS keyword, but a label is enclosed in quotes.

```
LIBNAME  bluesky "C:\mydata\bluesky bookstore\";

SELECT   category "Category",
         min(price) as minpr "Minimum Price" format= comma10.2,
         max(price) "Maximum Price" format= comma10.2
FROM     bluesky.STOCK
GROUP BY category
ORDER BY minpr;
```

Category	Minimum Price	Maximum Price
general	5.50	14.30
arts	9.50	36.00
science	15.00	69.00
computer	22.25	34.50
medicine	34.00	86.00
engineering	45.00	74.50

Tip: An alternative to the use of the Min(price) alias minpr in the ORDER BY clause is to reference the column by position. In the previous example the ORDER BY clause can also be written as ORDER BY 2.

Summary functions cannot be included in an ON clause. An ON clause provides a criterion that affects the rows that can be joined in two or more tables. As a result, the ON clause criteria must be evaluated for each row; an aggregate or summary value is not appropriate in this case. More information on the ON clause is provided in Chapter 3, "Understanding the SELECT Statement." A detailed examination of joining tables is contained in Chapter 5, "Working with Two or More Tables."

Summary function arguments

Summary functions summarize or aggregate all of the values for an argument taken from the selected rows. An argument may take several forms as described below.

Single column value

In the simplest case, the summary function generates a value from the values stored in each row in the table for the column argument. The next example shows a SELECT statement that contains three summary functions based on the total sale (totsale) column in the *order* table. The query generates a single value for each function based on all of the rows in the table.

```
LIBNAME bluesky "C:\mydata\bluesky bookstore\";

SELECT  mean(totsale) "Average sale" format= comma10.2,
        min(totsale) "Minimum sale" format= comma10.2,
        max(totsale) "Maximum sale" format= comma10.2
FROM    bluesky.orders;
```

```
         Average      Minimum      Maximum
            sale         sale         sale
      ------------------------------------
       18,770.28        83.40   225,000.00
```

Expression based on one or more columns

It is possible to first apply a mathematical calculation to a column before it is passed as an argument to the function. In the next example the code has the total sale price divided by the order size as an argument in the MEAN function.

```
LIBNAME bluesky "C:\mydata\bluesky bookstore\";

SELECT  mean(totsale/quantity) "Average book price per order"
        format=10.2
FROM    bluesky.orders;
```

```
Average
book price
per order
-----------
33.37
```

In the next example the code also builds an expression on more than one column in the *stock* table. In this query, the ratio of engineering books to computer books is calculated. The stock amount is multiplied by 1 if the condition enclosed in parenthesis is TRUE, or 0 if the condition is FALSE. This value is then passed to the SUM function.

```
LIBNAME bluesky "C:\mydata\bluesky bookstore\";

SELECT sum(stock*(category='engineering'))/sum(stock*
          (category='computer')) format=percent10.
          'Engineering to Computer'
FROM      bluesky.stock;
```

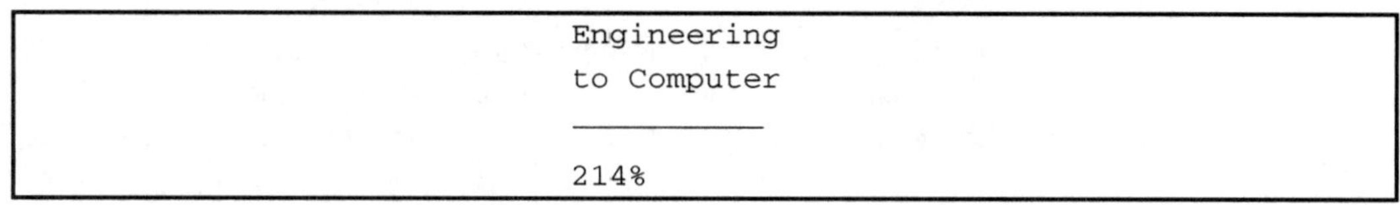

```
Engineering
to Computer
-----------
214%
```

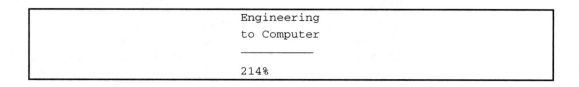

Nested functions

Summary functions can be nested with single functions for added versatility. The innermost single function is evaluated for the column value in a row first. The single function result is then passed to the summary function for calculation. In the next example a RANGE function has a ROUND function as part of the argument.

```
LIBNAME  bluesky "C:\mydata\bluesky bookstore\";

SELECT   category, range(round(price)) "PRICE"
FROM     bluesky.stock
GROUP BY category;
```

category	PRICE
arts	26
computer	13
engineering	30
general	8
medicine	52
science	54

There are some interesting results when missing values are involved with summary functions. If you include a restrictive WHERE clause that eliminates all rows in your table, for example, the summary function will return a zero value for the COUNT or NMISS functions. However, for all other functions a missing value is returned.

Tip: Functions such as MEAN or AVG will calculate a value based on nonmissing values only. As a result, it is always a good idea to include a count of the nonmissing values in a column in which such a function is applied.

Remerging summary function results

What if you want to compare the value of a column in every row to a summary function value? For example, you might want to compare the price for every arts and science category book in your inventory to the average price of these books.

Most of us would approach this problem stepwise. First, an average price can be calculated from the *stock* table and stored in a new table called average. This first step together with the contents of the new table is shown in the next example.

```
LIBNAME bluesky "C:\mydata\bluesky bookstore\";

CREATE table average
AS     SELECT avg(price) as avgprice
       FROM bluesky.stock
       WHERE category in ('arts','science');

       SELECT *
       FROM   average;
```

```
avgprice
________

30.02222
```

Next each price from the *stock* table is divided by the average price from the average table. There is a special procedure happening behind the scenes here called a Cartesian join. A Cartesian join allows the single value from the *average* table to become part of every row in the *price* table. SAS will execute a Cartesian join without instruction from the user, and it will report the action in the SAS log. The SQL query and the output and SAS log message produced from it are shown in the following example.

Tip: Cartesian and other joins are covered in detail in Chapter 5, "Working with Two or More Tables."

```
LIBNAME bluesky "C:\mydata\bluesky bookstore\";

SELECT  title "Title" , category "Category" ,
        price/avgprice "Price/Avg. Price" format= 6.2
FROM    bluesky.stock, average
WHERE   category IN ('arts','science');
```

SAS log:

```
NOTE: The execution of this query involves performing one or more Cartesian
product joins that cannot be optimized.

                                                                   Price/Avg.
Title                                              Category        Price
------------------------------------------------------------------------------
Decorative Arts                                    arts              0.56
The Ultimate Philosophy                            arts              0.32
Democracy in America                               arts              1.20
The Underground Economy                            arts              0.48
Book of Science and Nature                         science           2.30
Free Thinking in Mathematics                       science           0.87
Science and Technology                             science           0.50
Science of Biology                                 science           2.17
Geology: Volcanos                                  science           0.60
```

Tip: As an alternative to remerging, one or more subqueries can be added to the SELECT statement. Information on subqueries is included in Chapter 5, "Working with Two or More Tables."

SAS/ACCESS and SQL Pass-Through Facility users: The remerging process is a unique SAS functionality not found in native database SQL. Consider using subqueries in your inner SELECT statements when using the SQL Pass-Through facility.

Although it might be easiest to understand each step if it is taken separately, this is not the most efficient way to accomplish the task. If we include both steps in the same query, SAS will take two passes through the data and join the summary function results with the original data. This logical process is referred to as remerging.

The next example shows the SELECT statement that completes both of the previous steps. Notice that the results are identical to the previous example. SAS automatically completes two passes through the data and remerges the results with the original table. A message confirming that a remerging process has occurred is reported in the SAS log as shown in the example.

```
LIBNAME bluesky "C:\mydata\bluesky bookstore\";

SELECT  title "Title" , category "Category" ,
        price/(avg(price)) "Price/Avg. Price" format= 6.2
FROM    bluesky.stock
WHERE   category IN ('arts','science');
```

Title	Category	Price/Avg. Price
Geology: Volcanos	science	0.60
Science of Biology	science	2.17
Science and Technology	science	0.50
Free Thinking in Mathematics	science	0.87
Book of Science and Nature	science	2.30
Democracy in America	arts	1.20
The Ultimate Philosophy	arts	0.32
Decorative Arts	arts	0.56
The Underground Economy	arts	0.48

SAS log:

```
NOTE: The query requires remerging summary statistics back with the
original data.
```

One final comment on the remerging process: Due to the complex nature of queries involving single and summary functions, remerging sometimes occurs by accident. It is a good idea to always check your log for messages regarding remerging or Cartesian joins. If SAS executes one of these processes unexpectedly, it often indicates an inappropriate combination of single and summary functions.

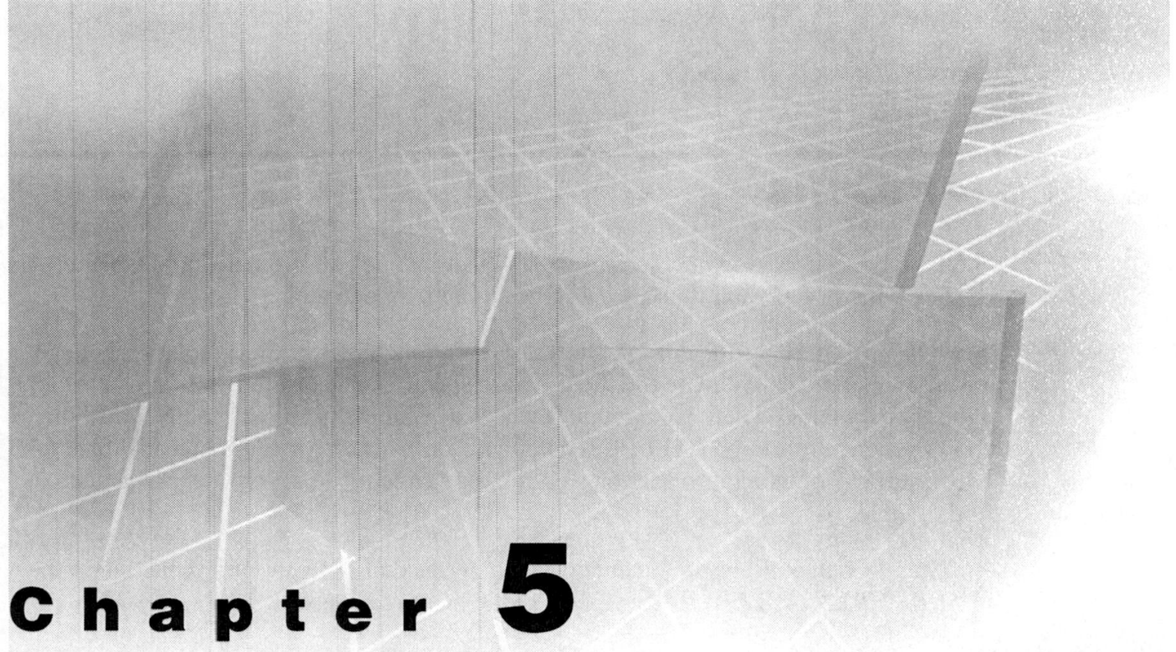

Chapter 5

Working with Two or More Tables

Join operations

So far we have discussed how to retrieve and manipulate data from a single table or data set. But what if you want to draw data from more than one table?

The SQL procedure join operation allows two or more tables, views, or data sets to be treated as a single entity. The SELECT clause specifies one or more columns from any of the joined tables. There is no requirement that columns from each table contribute to reports generated through a SELECT statement. Joins can be made between tables solely for the purpose of using information stored in one table to subset or manipulate data in another table.

> **Tip:** Join operations do not create a new permanent or temporary table unless the CREATE TABLE AS SELECT statement is issued.

The simplest form of join can be accomplished using a FROM clause listing several tables from which the SELECT clause columns are drawn. An optional ON or WHERE clause can be added to construct more complex or restrictive joins.

> **Tip:** Joins can be added to any SQL statement that includes a query such as SELECT, CREATE, UPDATE, and INSERT statements.

> **SAS/ACCESS and SQL Pass-Through Facility users:** Joins between tables stored in one or more databases and tables or data sets created in a SAS session can be joined. Database specific examples are included in Appendix C, "Information for Database Users."

If you've ever used the MERGE statement in the SAS DATA step you already understand the concepts of joining tables or data sets. Unlike the SAS DATA step merging process however, the columns do not have to be sorted using PROC SORT prior to the merge. Nor does each table need to be joined by the same set of commonly named columns.

> **Note:** Throughout this book, the term *table* is used to refer to tables, views, or data sets. The word *column* is used to refer to columns or expressions.

Guidelines

Several guidelines apply to all forms of joins:

- Each of the tables from which data will be drawn must be included in the FROM clause or combination of FROM and ON clauses.
- Tables may include those stored in a database, views, PROC SQL-generated tables, and SAS data sets generated through Base SAS and SAS procedures.

- The WHERE clause can be used to include restrictive criteria, regardless of the type of join.
- Other optional clauses such as ORDER BY, GROUP BY, and HAVING can be included.
- Table aliases, assigned in a FROM clause, are allowed on any of the clauses in the SQL query.
- If a column exists in more than one table, the column name must be prefixed with the table name or its alias. Other columns referenced in the SELECT statement may also have a table name or alias prefix.
- A maximum of thirty-two tables or views may be joined in a single SQL query.

Tip: When many very large tables are joined, the high number of variables can increase processing time. Performance can be improved by limiting the variables to those that are needed rather than using the asterisk. The maximum number of variables allowed in a single query is 32,767.

Keep in mind that files are created in the Work library by the SAS processor to facilitate the join. These files may be very large; if you run out of space in the Work library, consider breaking the query up into several steps.

SAS/ACCESS and SQL Pass-Through Facility users: Whenever possible, PROC SQL passes joins to the DBMS rather than performing the joins itself, thereby enhancing performance. For information on when joins are passed to a DBMS, refer to Appendix C, "Information for Database Users."

There are several types of joins broadly categorized as inner and outer joins, discussed in detail in this chapter. For all joins except for cross joins, join criteria are included in the SQL statement specifying which columns in each of the tables is to be joined and how the column contents should be matched. Join criteria can be specified in an ON or WHERE clause for inner joins whereas outer join criteria can only be specified in an ON clause in PROC SQL. Cross joins, or Cartesian products, are an exception. They are a form of inner join created through the FROM clause alone without the specification of join criteria.

Tip: The role of the SQL optimizer in join processing is covered in Chapter 6, "Creating and Managing Tables and Views," together with information on the use of indexes to optimize performance.

FROM-ON clause joins versus WHERE clause joins

ON clause joins are processed in exactly the same manner as joins that specify the joining criteria in the WHERE clause. As the WHERE clause is limited to inner joins, you might wonder why you should learn WHERE clause join syntax and when you might select the WHERE clause over the ON clause.

Some SQL languages associated with RDBMS systems do not support the ON clause. It was introduced with the SQL-92 standard language primarily to support outer joins. However, not all commercial SQL products shipped with database systems are fully SQL-92 compliant. For example, Oracle Versions 8 and 8i and Sybase Version 11 do not support the ON clause; however, the ON clause is supported by DB2 Version 7.1, Microsoft SQL Server 2000, and Oracle Version 9i. As a result, if you are working with SQL Pass-Through Facility, the WHERE clause may be your only choice.

Many users find the WHERE clause more intuitive and easier to use when joining more than two tables. However, other users find specifying their join criteria in the ON clause and setting out other criteria in the WHERE clause more logical. The choice of which join form to use for inner joins is entirely yours in PROC SQL. If you are also expecting to work in database-specific SQL, it is best to choose the form that is consistent with your database.

Both forms of join are shown throughout this chapter. However, more WHERE clause joins are used throughout the book as a whole. I use the WHERE clause for joins whenever possible because I find them easier to construct when joining more than two tables. Moreover, almost every query I write already has a WHERE clause, so all of my criteria—including my join criteria—are contained in a single clause.

One final word: It helps if you become familiar with the nuances and tricks of one form or the other in order to prevent errors. Choose between the WHERE and ON clauses based on which syntactical form seems most intuitive to you and meets most of your programming needs. Then use it consistently.

Inner joins

Inner joins match rows in one table against rows in one or more other tables. During processing, the combined rows are stored in a temporary table, and the SELECT statement can list columns from any of the original tables. You use an optional join expression set out in a WHERE or ON clause to specify how the rows in the tables should be matched. The report can be limited to specific rows through the inclusion of criteria in a WHERE clause.

> **Tip:** Inner joins, with the exception of cross joins, require the same data type in each of the columns used to construct the join. Use the PUT and INPUT functions to make any necessary data type conversions. The column name, length of character data, and the number of decimal places declared for numeric data do not have to match.

Cross-join

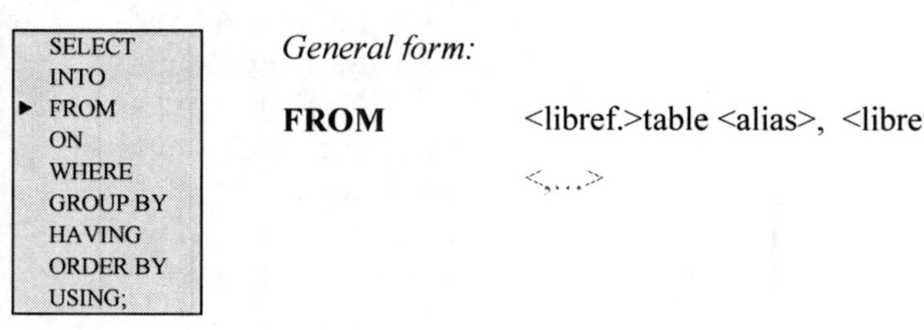

General form:

FROM <libref.>table <alias>, <libref.>table <alias>

<,...>

The simplest form of join is a cross join. A cross join is achieved through the inclusion of two or more tables in a FROM clause within a SELECT statement. A result set is created that matches all of the rows in one table with each row in one or more additional tables named in the FROM clause. This type of result is referred to as a Cartesian product because every possible combination of rows contributed from each of the tables is generated.

> **Tip:** Not all authors consider a cross join to be an actual join because the cross join produces a Cartesian product. I have elected to treat the cross join as a join because it does function as an inner join in that it matches columns in one table with those of another. However, unlike other joins, a join criterion is not set for a cross join.

A simple example of a cross join is shown in the next example. The SELECT statement retrieves rows from both the *client* and *address* tables for addresses located in the United States. If you look closely at the resulting output, you will notice that each record retrieved from the *client* table is repeated for each record in the *address* table with a United States address.

```
LIBNAME bluesky "C:\mydata\bluesky bookstore\";

SELECT  company, address
FROM    bluesky.client, bluesky.address
WHERE   country = 'USA';
```

```
company                                     address
-----------------------------------------------------------------
University of Texas                         6015 Pine Street
Chicago State University                    6015 Pine Street
Heffers Booksellers                         6015 Pine Street
National University of Singapore            6015 Pine Street
University of Adelaide                      6015 Pine Street
Heymann's                                   6015 Pine Street
Cosmos 2000                                 6015 Pine Street
Lawrence Books                              6015 Pine Street
University of Texas                         951 South King Drive
Chicago State University                    951 South King Drive
Heffers Booksellers                         951 South King Drive
National University of Singapore            951 South King Drive
University of Adelaide                      951 South King Drive
Heymann's                                   951 South King Drive
Cosmos 2000                                 951 South King Drive
Lawrence Books                              951 South King Drive
```

Tip: The SQL Optimizer is not used in cross joins. A message confirming that your query cannot be optimized is written to the SAS log:

```
NOTE:  The execution of this query involves performing
       one or more Cartesian product joins that cannot
       be optimized.
```

You may be able to improve performance of your cross joins or Cartesian product joins by increasing the BUFSIZE option. Information on options available when working in PROC SQL is included in Chapter 2, "Working with PROC SQL."

The next figure provides a few records from each of the *company* and *address* tables to help illustrate the Cartesian product result shown above. The WHERE clause limits the rows selected from the *address* table to the two highlighted rows. The query does not restrict the rows retrieved from the *company* table; therefore, every row in that table becomes part of the report. Each row in the *company* table is listed twice in the report shown above, once for each of the rows retrieved from the *address* table.

Tip: How do you create tables such as these with the same client number in each table? Information on the creation of tables, insertion of data, and foreign-to-primary-key relationships is included in Chapter 6, "Creating and Managing Tables and Views."

Table name: COMPANY	
clientno	**company**
1001	University of Texas
2010	Chicago State University
3007	Heffers Booksellers
4008	National University of Singapore
5005	University of Adelaide
6090	Heymann's
7008	Cosmos 2000
8003	Lawrence Books

Table name: ADDRESS		
clientno	**address**	**country**
1001	6015 Pine Street	USA
2010	951 South King Drive	USA
3007	200 Trinity St.	UK
4008	6D Lor Ampas	Singapore
5005	102S North Terrace	Australia
6090	Flemmingstr. 270	Germany
7008	190 rue de l'Arc de Triomphe	France
8003	359 T 41st at Dunbar	Canada

Tip: Rows returned by a SELECT statement are not reported in any specific order. They are generally reported in the order in which they are retrieved by the SQL processor. Use an ORDER BY clause to control the sort order of your report.

FROM clause restrictions

A Cartesian product or cross join does not use a JOIN keyword in the FROM clause. An ON clause is necessary if a JOIN keyword is included between two tables in the FROM clause. However, a cross join does not compare column values in two tables; therefore, an ON clause is not applicable.

The next example shows a simple SELECT statement that attempts to achieve a cross join between the *client* and *address* tables using an INNER JOIN keyword in the FROM clause. The SAS error message generated by the statement is included in the example.

```
LIBNAME bluesky "C:\mydata\bluesky bookstore\";

SELECT  company, address
FROM    bluesky.client INNER JOIN bluesky.address
WHERE   country = 'USA';
```

SAS log:

```
PROC SQL;

SELECT  company, address
FROM    bluesky.client INNER JOIN bluesky.address
WHERE   country = 'USA';
-----
22
76
ERROR 22-322: Syntax error, expecting one of the following: a name, (, AS, ON.

ERROR 76-322: Syntax error, statement will be ignored.
```

Tip: Although sometimes a Cartesian product is desirable, it is often generated by an invalid WHERE or ON clause or a missing WHERE clause. Consider using the LOOPS option to limit the number of rows processed by a SELECT statement when testing your queries. In this way, the accidental generation of large Cartesian products can be caught before hundreds of rows are retrieved.

```
PROC sql loops = 50;
SELECT *
FROM   bluesky.stock,
       bluesky.order;

NOTE: The execution of this query involves performing one
or more Cartesian product joins that can not be optimized.
NOTE: PROC SQL statement interrupted by LOOPS=50 option.
```

Caution: If you set too low a value for loops, you might impede the join process. For example, if you set loops=50 and a matching entry for the join variable is not present in those first 50 rows, the join will fail.

Equijoins (simple joins)

Equijoins provide control over how the rows in two or more tables are combined through the specification of join criteria in either a WHERE clause or an ON clause. The join criteria indicate which column or expression occurring in one table is to be joined to a column or expression in another table. SAS checks for an exact match between values in the two columns in which the join is indicated. If a match is found, the two rows are combined or joined together allowing values from columns in either table to be retrieved.

> **SAS/ACCESS and SQL Pass-Through Facility users:** Equijoins are commonly used to join tables using primary and foreign keys. A foreign key relationship is commonly constructed between the primary key of a parent table and the foreign key of a child table; only those values stored in the primary key column of the parent table can occur in the foreign key column child table. As a result, equijoins built on these key columns produce a match between all rows in the two tables.

FROM-WHERE clause equijoins

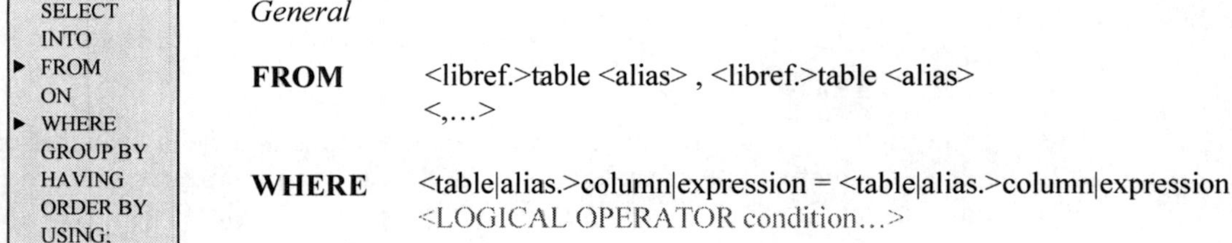

SELECT
INTO
▶ FROM
ON
▶ WHERE
GROUP BY
HAVING
ORDER BY
USING;

General

FROM <libref.>table <alias> , <libref.>table <alias>
<,...>

WHERE <table|alias.>column|expression = <table|alias.>column|expression
<LOGICAL OPERATOR condition...>

A simple equijoin is included in the SELECT statement shown in the next example. In this example, the *client* and *orders* tables are joined using the values in the clientno column to forge a link between the tables and all orders placed in April.

```
LIBNAME bluesky "C:\mydata\bluesky bookstore\";

TITLE1  "Product orders by company";
SELECT  o.prodcode "Product Code", o.ord_date "Date Ordered",
        c.company "Company"
FROM    bluesky.client c, bluesky.order o
WHERE   c.clientno = o.clientno
        and month(o.ord_date) = 4;
```

> **Tip:** Criteria other than those required for the joining process can be added to the WHERE clause. The link between join criteria and other criteria is made with an AND logical operator.

Notice that in the above example an alias has been assigned to each of the tables listed in the FROM clause and each of the columns are prefixed by the appropriate alias. Columns that appear in more than one table must include a qualifier that identifies the source table either by name or alias. This query also includes qualifiers for each of the columns in the SELECT clause, although none of these columns is present in both the *orders* and *client* tables. The qualifers have been added to improve query readability; it makes it clear that the product code and order date columns are stored in the *orders* table and the company is stored in the *client* table.

Tip: Columns with the same name that occur in more than one table must be qualified. Either an alias or table name referencing the source table for the column is added as a prefix to the column name. Otherwise an error message similar to this one will be written to your SAS log:

```
ERROR: Ambiguous reference, column prodcode is in more
than one table.
```

Although they are not strictly necessary, you should include the table names or aliases as a prefix for every column in an SQL query containing two or more joined tables. It makes for a more readable query that is easier to debug. Pick a simple one- or two-character alias for each table to make the statement easy to read and to minimize typing.

The next example gives a graphical representation of the processing steps of the SELECT statement shown in the previous example. Selected columns in the *orders* table are shown with details for orders placed in April sorted by product code (prodcode). The client number (clientno) and company columns from the *client* table for every client are also included in the figure. When a join is constructed on the values in the clientno column in the *orders* and *client* tables, the rows are joined together as shown.

Tip: Although the column name clientno is the same in the *orders* and *client* tables, this is not required to join the tables. Joined columns must have the same data type but their name and other column modifiers can differ. In addition, functions such as SUBSTR or MAX can be applied to one or more of the join columns. Information on functions is included in Chapter 4, "Functions."

Table name: ADDRESS		
clientno	**address**	**country**
1001	6015 Pine Street	USA
2010	951 South King Drive	USA
3007	200 Trinity St.	UK
4008	6D Lor Ampas	Singapore
5005	102S North Terrace	Australia
6090	Flemmingstr. 270	Germany
7008	190 rue do l'Arc de Triomphe	France
8003	359 T 41st at Dunbar	Canada

Table name: CLIENT	
clientno	**company**
1001	University of Texas
2010	Chicago State University
3007	Heffers Booksellers
4008	National University of Sydney
5005	University of Adelaide
6090	Heymann's
7008	Cosmos 2000
8003	Lawrence Books

	Cartesian product or cross-join is generated			
	clientno	**company**	**country**	**address**
First Result Set	1001	University of Texas	USA	6015 Pine Street
	2010	Chicago State University	USA	951 South King Drive
Second Result Set	1001	University of Texas	USA	200 Trinity St.
	2010	Chicago State University	USA	200 Trinity St.
	3007	Heffers Booksellers	UK	200 Trinity St.
	4008	National University of Sydney	Singapore	200 Trinity St.
	5005	University of Adelaide	Australia	200 Trinity St.
	6090	Heymann's	Germany	200 Trinity St.
	7008	Cosmos 2000	France	200 Trinity St.
	8003	Lawrence Books	Canada	200 Trinity St.

Tip: The join product is generally sorted on the column or columns upon which the join is built. Use the ORDER BY clause to control sorting in your report.

It is possible for more than one row in a table to match or join with a row in another table. If you review the highlighted rows in the example, you will notice that there are two rows in the *orders* table that have a value of 5005 for the client number (clientno). When the tables are joined on the clientno column, each of these rows is combined with the row in the *client* table with the same value. The results of the SQL query are shown in the next example.

```
Product orders by company

Product     Date
Code      Ordered  Company
--------------------------------------------------------------

200145    12APR04  Chicago State University
400128    12APR04  Chicago State University
200507    08APR04  National University of Singapore
400100    11APR03  University of Adelaide
500238    12APR04  University of Adelaide
300456    10APR04  Heymann's
400128    11APR03  Cosmos 2000
600489    12APR04  Cosmos 2000
```

Tip: The column or expression used to construct the join does not have to be included in the report. In the above example, the client number (clientno) column was used to join the tables, but the company name is included in the report instead of the client number. This technique can also be used to associate formatting labels or other details stored in one table with values or codes in another.

Snowflake and star schemas deployed in data warehouses often translate codes in the fact table with a join to the dimension table. Fact tables hold measures grouped by one or more codes or dimensions. A field description of the code is stored in a dimension table.

In a SAS DATA step, a BY statement used in conjunction with a MERGE statement will produce the same result.

The next example gives a comparable DATA step that will achieve the same equijoin presented above. The processing of these statements differs from the SELECT statement above. The data in each of the tables is first sorted by the join column clientno using PROC SORT. In the DATA step, all rows with the same client number in each table are joined or merged. An IF statement is then used to limit the records in the dataset to those with an order in April.

Tip: PROC SQL joins may outperform the DATA step merge operation when the table is not presorted. The SQL optimizer has a hash join option which uses an algorithm that eliminates the need to sort the tables prior to the join operation. More information on optimizing your query performance is included in Chapter 6, "Creating and Managing Tables and Views."

```
LIBNAME bluesky "C:\mydata\bluesky bookstore\";

PROC SORT data=bluesky.client;
          by clientno;

PROC SORT data=bluesky.order;
          by clientno;

DATA MERGEALL;
   MERGE   bluesky.client
           bluesky.order;
           BY clientno;

if month(ord_date) =4;

LABEL      prodcode= 'Product Code'
           company = 'Company'
           ord_date='Date Ordered';

PROC PRINT noobs label;
           var prodcode ord_date company;
run;
```

```
Product orders by company

Product     Date
 Code      Ordered     Company

200145     12APR04     Chicago State University
400128     12APR04     Chicago State University
200507     08APR04     National University of Singapore
400100     11APR03     University of Adelaide
500238     12APR04     University of Adelaide
300456     10APR04     Heymann's
400128     11APR03     Cosmos 2000
600489     12APR04     Cosmos 2000
```

The AND operator was used in the above examples to limit the results to rows with matching client numbers in both tables and orders placed in April. But what if an OR operator is used instead?

In the next example a join criterion is coupled with a subsetting criterion that includes an OR operator. You might expect to see only the matching rows (client number in the *client* table matches client number in the *address* table) for clients residing in the United States or the United Kingdom. Instead, the query generates a Cartesian product for each client in the *client* table with each US or UK address from the *address* table.

> **Caution:** The inclusion of an OR logical operator in a WHERE clause that contains a join criterion can produce unexpected results. Unless carefully constructed, a Cartesian product is generated between the rows that meet either of the criteria.

```
LIBNAME bluesky "C:\mydata\bluesky bookstore\";

SELECT  c.company, a.address
FROM    bluesky.client c, bluesky.address a
WHERE   c.clientno = a.clientno
        and country='USA' or country = 'UK';
```

company	address
University of Texas	6015 Pine Street
University of Texas	200 Trinity St.
Chicago State University	951 South King Drive
Chicago State University	200 Trinity St.
Heffers Booksellers	200 Trinity St.
National University of Singapore	200 Trinity St.
University of Adelaide	200 Trinity St.
Heymann's	200 Trinity St.
Cosmos 2000	200 Trinity St.
Lawrence Books	200 Trinity St.

The above query processes two table joins when generating the results in the above example. Rows in the address and client tables with matching client numbers are joined and those clients in the United States are selected. However, all of the rows in the client table are then joined to the single address in the United Kingdom, generating a Cartesian product of all possible unique combinations.

Table name: ADDRESS		
clientno	**address**	**country**
1001	6015 Pine Street	USA
2010	951 South King Drive	USA
3007	200 Trinity St.	UK
4008	6D Lor Ampas	Singapore
5005	102S North Terrace	Australia
6090	Flemmingstr. 270	Germany
7008	190 rue do l'Arc de Triomphe	France
8003	359 T 41st at Dunbar	Canada

Table name: CLIENT	
clientno	**company**
1001	University of Texas
2010	Chicago State University
3007	Heffers Booksellers
4008	National University of Singapore
5005	University of Adelaide
6090	Heymann's
7008	Cosmos 2000
8003	Lawrence Books

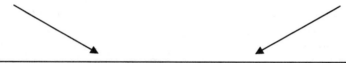

	Cartesian product or cross-join is generated			
	clientno	**company**	**country**	**address**
First Result Set	1001	University of Texas	USA	6015 Pine Street
	2010	Chicago State University	USA	951 South King Drive
Second Result Set	1001	University of Texas	USA	200 Trinity St.
	2010	Chicago State University	USA	200 Trinity St.
	3007	Heffers Booksellers	UK	200 Trinity St.
	4008	National University of Singapore	Singapore	200 Trinity St.
	5005	University of Adelaide	Australia	200 Trinity St.
	6090	Heymann's	Germany	200 Trinity St.
	7008	Cosmos 2000	France	200 Trinity St.
	8003	Lawrence Books	Canada	200 Trinity St.

If the query is rewritten in one of two ways as shown in the next example, only three rows are reported when the query is run.

```
LIBNAME bluesky "C:\mydata\bluesky bookstore\";

SELECT  c.company, a.address
FROM    bluesky.client c, bluesky.address a
WHERE   c.clientno = a.clientno and country ='USA'
        or c.clientno=a.clientno and country ='UK';


SELECT  c.company, a.address
FROM    bluesky.client c, bluesky.address a
WHERE   c.clientno = a.clientno and (country ='USA' or country ='UK');
```

company	address
University of Texas	6015 Pine Street
Chicago State University	951 South King Drive
Heffers Booksellers	200 Trinity St.

For comparison, the query has also been rewritten as a DATA step in the next example.

```
LIBNAME  bluesky "C:\mydata\bluesky bookstore\";
PROC sort data=bluesky.address;
by clientno;

DATA MERGEALL;
   MERGE bluesky.client (in=in1)
         bluesky.address (in=in2);
         BY clientno;
if (country='USA' or country='UK')and (in1 and in2);

PROC print noobs ;
var company address;
RUN;
```

The next example illustrates an equijoin. The WHERE clause contains a join expression linking the product code column in the *stock* table to the product code column in the *orders* table. In this query, another criterion is added to the WHERE clause, restricting the retrieved rows to those with a category of arts or general. The report includes repeated books because product codes in the *stock* table may be repeated for different dates or clients in the *orders* table.

```
LIBNAME    bluesky "C:\mydata\bluesky bookstore\";

TITLE1     "All general and arts books for which there are orders";

SELECT     orders.prodcode "Product Code" format= $15.,
           stock.category "Category" format= $10.,
           stock.title "Title" format= $40.
FROM       bluesky.stock, bluesky.orders
WHERE      stock.prodcode = orders.prodcode
           AND stock.category IN ('arts', 'general')
ORDER BY   stock.category, stock.title;
```

All general and arts books for which there are orders

Product Code	Category	Title
300678	arts	Decorative Arts
300289	arts	Democracy in America
300456	arts	The Ultimate Philosophy
300456	arts	The Ultimate Philosophy
300456	arts	The Ultimate Philosophy
300680	arts	The Underground Economy
300680	arts	The Underground Economy
600489	general	Mountaineering Skills
600125	general	The Maestro
600125	general	The Maestro
600125	general	The Maestro
600125	general	The Maestro
600780	general	Women Writers

Tip: GROUP BY, HAVING, INTO, and ORDER BY clauses are all allowed in queries that include table joins.

In the following example we have the same query, but with a slightly different format. In this SELECT statement, aliases have been assigned to each table listed in the FROM clause. The use of aliases is optional, but it can make for an easier query to write. Notice that our WHERE clause is using an OR logical operator to construct the category criterion. The SELECT clause has been modified to include the DISTINCT keyword so that books ordered more than once will be included in the result set only once. Finally, the positional form of the ORDER BY clause has been included rather than the column name.

```
LIBNAME  bluesky "C:\mydata\bluesky bookstore\";

TITLE1   'All general and arts books for which there are orders';

SELECT   DISTINCT o.prodcode "Product Code" format= $15.,
         s.category "Category" format= $10.,
         s.title "Title" format= $40.
FROM     bluesky.stock s, bluesky.orders o
WHERE    s.prodcode = o.prodcode
         AND (s.category ='arts' OR s.category= 'general')
ORDER BY 2,3;
```

```
All general and arts books for which there are orders

Product Code      Category     Title
--------------------------------------------------------------------

300678            arts         Decorative Arts
300289            arts         Democracy in America
300456            arts         The Ultimate Philosophy
300680            arts         The Underground Economy
600489            general      Mountaineering Skills
600125            general      The Maestro
600780            general      Women Writers
```

Tip: The use of parentheses is recommended when there are both join expressions and other criteria in a WHERE clause. This is especially true when combinations of AND and OR logical operators are part of the criteria.

In each of the above examples, only two tables have been joined. Both PROC SQL and the DATA step MERGE statement allow for multiple table joins. However, several DATA steps would be required to create such a statement, each preceded by an appropriate PROC SORT.

The next example shows an equijoin between four tables in PROC SQL. Take careful notice of the join criteria. Two columns of the *orders* table are used in the joins. The *stock* and *orders* tables are joined by product code (prodcode) and the *orders* and *client* tables are joined by the client number (clientno) in the same statement.

```
LIBNAME  bluesky "C:\mydata\bluesky bookstore\";

TITLE1   'Book Orders - First Quarter 2004';

SELECT   client.company "Company" format= $30.,
         address.city "City" format= $15.,
         order.ord_date "Order Date",
         stock.title "Title" format= $30.

FROM     bluesky.client, bluesky.address,
         bluesky.order, bluesky.stock

WHERE    stock.prodcode=order.prodcode
         AND client.clientno=address.clientno
         AND order.clientno=client.clientno
         AND ord_date between '01JAN2004'd and '30MAR2004'd

ORDER BY client.company, order.ord_date;
```

```
Book Orders - First Quarter 2004

                                                    Order
Company                          City                Date  Title
------------------------------------------------------------------------------------
Cosmos 2000                      Paris            10MAR04  Science of Biology
Heffers Booksellers              Cambridge        07MAR04  Science and Technology
Lawrence Books                   Vancouver        01FEB04  The Maestro
Lawrence Books                   Vancouver        10MAR04  Medical Education in
School
Lawrence Books                   Vancouver        10MAR04  Computer: Beginners Guide
National University of Singapo   Singapore        01FEB04  Women Writers
National University of Singapo   Singapore        10MAR04  The Maestro
```

Tip: Complex queries can be easier to understand if space is included between SELECT statement clauses.

Compare the PROC SQL example above with the DATA step statements and procedures required to accomplish the same task shown in the next example.

```
LIBNAME bluesky "C:\mydata\bluesky bookstore\";

PROC sort data=bluesky.client;
  by clientno;

PROC sort data=bluesky.address;
  by clientno;

DATA clntadd (keep=clientno company city);
   MERGE bluesky.client (in=in1)
         bluesky.address (in=in2);
         BY clientno;
   if in1 and in2;

PROC SORT data=bluesky.stock;
  by prodcode;

PROC SORT data=bluesky.order;
  by prodcode;

DATA stkorder(keep=ord_date clientno title);
  MERGE  bluesky.stock (in=in1)
         bluesky.order (in=in2);
         BY prodcode;
  if in1 and in2;
  if ord_date >= '01JAN2004'd and ord_date <='30MAR2004'd;

PROC SORT data=stkorder;
  by clientno;

PROC SORT data=clntadd;
  by clientno;

DATA final;
  MERGE  stkorder (in=in1)
         clntadd (in=in2);
         BY clientno;
  if in1 and in2;

PROC SORT data=final;
  by company ord_date;

PROC print noobs ;
  var company city ord_date title;
RUN;
```

Let's take a closer look at the mechanics of the join shown in the above example. The tables shown in the following figure represent selected portions of each of the tables that are used in the join. The client number (clientno) is common to the *orders*, *client,* and *address* tables and can be used to join those tables. The product code (prodcode), common to the *orders* and *stock* tables, is used to join the *orders* and *stock* tables. Notice that the *orders* table is joined twice, using two different columns, prodcode, and clientno to link the *orders* table to the *stock* and *client* tables.

The SQL optimizer determines an execution plan for the query which sets out the order in which the joins are processed and the method used for each join based on cost-efficiency. The following occurs in the join process; however, the order in which the SQL optimizer elects to process them may differ from that described:

- Each value in the clientno column of the *client* table is checked against the values in the clientno column of the *address* table. Matching rows are combined to form a single internal table with columns from both the *address* and *client* tables. In the tables below, only the rows for client numbers 2010, 3007, and 4008 are linked.
- Each value in the clientno column of the *orders* table is checked against the values in the clientno column of the *client* table. Matching rows are combined to form a single internal table with columns from both the *client* and *orders* tables. In the tables below, only the rows for client numbers 4008 and 3007 are linked.
- The prodcode column values in the *orders* table are compared to each prodcode value in the *stock* table, joining rows with matching values together. In the tables below, only the rows for product code numbers 100345 and 100406 are linked.
- Finally, the combined *stock-orders* table and the combined *client-orders-address* table are compared, linking rows with matching clientno values. Only those rows from all tables that meet all of the join conditions are reported. In the tables below, only a single row meets all of the join conditions: clientno 3007, Heffers Booksellers in Cambridge, ordering product 100406.

The SQL optimizer evaluates whether a MERGE, INDEX, or HASH join method provides the best performance for each join. An execution plan, specifying the order of the joins, join method, and other aspects of the join process is developed by the optimizer. To view the execution plan, invoke PROC SQL with the _METHOD option. Information on the SQL optimizer and the interpretation of execution plans is included in Chapter 6, "Creating and Managing Tables and Views."

Table name: ORDERS		
prodcode	**ord_date**	**clientno**
600125	01FEB04	8003
600780	01FEB04	4008
100406	07MAR04	3007
100345	10MAR04	7008

Table name: CLIENT	
clientno	**company**
1001	University of Texas
2010	Chicago State University
3007	Heffers Booksellers
4008	National University of Singapore

Table name: STOCK	
prodcode	**title**
100340	Geology: Volcanos
100345	Science of Biology
100406	Science and Technology
100601	Free Thinking in Mathematics

Table name: ADDRESS	
clientno	**city**
2010	Chicago
3007	Cambridge
4008	Singapore
5005	Adelaide

Tip: The number of expressions required in a WHERE clause to form an equijoin between *n* tables is *n-1*.

FROM-ON clause equijoins

SELECT
INTO
► FROM
► ON
WHERE
GROUP BY
HAVING
ORDER BY
USING;

General form:

FROM <libref.>table <alias> <INNER>JOIN <libref.>table <alias>

ON <table|alias.>column | expression = <table|alias.>column | expression
<, table JOIN KEYWORD table ON join condition…>
<LOGICAL OPERATOR condition…>

An equijoin can also be constructed using the FROM and ON clauses. Both of the tables are listed on the FROM clause, but they are separated by a JOIN keyword rather than the usual comma. The JOIN expression is immediately followed by an ON clause that indicates the columns to be linked or matched.

The next example shows a query that joins the *stock* and *orders* tables using an INNER JOIN keyword and an ON clause. A WHERE clause has also been added to the query, limiting the categories of books selected to those in the arts and general categories. The DISTINCT keyword is added to eliminate duplicate books from the result set; duplicates occur if a book has been ordered more than once. The query shown in the next example produces the same output as those in the example above.

```
TITLE1     "All general and arts books for which there are orders";

LIBNAME    bluesky "C:\mydata\bluesky bookstore\";

SELECT     distinct orders.prodcode "Product Code" format= $15.,
           stock.category "Category" format= $10.,
           stock.title "Title" format= $40.

FROM       bluesky.stock INNER JOIN bluesky.orders
           ON stock.prodcode=orders.prodcode

WHERE      stock.category = 'arts' OR stock.category = 'general'
ORDER BY   2,3;
```

All general and arts books for which there are orders

Product Code	Category	Title
300678	arts	Decorative Arts
300289	arts	Democracy in America
300456	arts	The Ultimate Philosophy
300680	arts	The Underground Economy
600489	general	Mountaineering Skills
600125	general	The Maestro
600780	general	Women Writers

Tip: There are two important rules to remember when using the ON clause:

- The ON clause is only allowed if a form of the JOIN keyword is included between two tables in a FROM clause.
- There must be one ON join criterion for every two tables linked by a JOIN keyword.

As with the WHERE clause version of a join, aliases can be used with the ON clause format. The next example contains a variation of the above SQL query, rewritten with aliases in place.

```
LIBNAME  bluesky "C:\mydata\bluesky bookstore\";

TITLE1  'All general and arts books';

SELECT    o.prodcode "Product Code" format= $15.,
          s.category "Category" format= $10.,
          s.title "Title" format= $40.


FROM      bluesky.stock s JOIN bluesky.orders o
          ON s.prodcode = o.prodcode

WHERE     s.category IN ('arts','general')
ORDER BY  2;
```

```
All general and arts books

Product Code     Category    Title
------------------------------------------------------------------

300680           arts        The Underground Economy
300678           arts        Decorative Arts
300456           arts        The Ultimate Philosophy
300680           arts        The Underground Economy
300456           arts        The Ultimate Philosophy
300289           arts        Democracy in America
300456           arts        The Ultimate Philosophy
600780           general     Women Writers
600489           general     Mountaineering Skills
600125           general     The Maestro
600125           general     The Maestro
600125           general     The Maestro
600125           general     The Maestro
```

The next example presents a simple SELECT statement that includes an equijoin based on an ON clause. The ON clause stipulates that the clientno column in the *orders* and *client* tables will be used to construct the join.

```
LIBNAME  bluesky "C:\mydata\bluesky bookstore\";

TITLE1  'Product orders by company';

SELECT    orders.prodcode label="Product Code" format= $8.,
          orders.ord_date "Date Ordered" format= date9.,
          client.company "Company" format= $40.

FROM      bluesky.orders JOIN bluesky.client
          ON orders.clientno = client.clientno
WHERE     month(ord_date)=4
ORDER BY  1;
```

```
Product orders by company

Product        Date
Code        Ordered  Company
------------------------------------------------------------------

200145    12APR2004  Chicago State University
200507    08APR2004  National University of Singapore
300456    10APR2004  Heymann's
400100    11APR2003  University of Adelaide
400128    11APR2003  Cosmos 2000
400128    12APR2004  Chicago State University
500238    12APR2004  University of Adelaide
600489    12APR2004  Cosmos 2000
```

Tip: The keywords JOIN and INNER JOIN are synonymous; most programmers find the JOIN keyword sufficient.

When multiple tables are joined through an ON clause, special care must be taken. Recall that only two tables can be referenced in a FROM clause join expression, and the ON clause must immediately follow. Additional criteria must be added to one or more of the ON clauses to ensure that the joined tables from each step are joined together.

The next example shows a three-table join using the ON clause. In this example, the *stock* and *orders* tables are joined using the product code (prodcode) column. The *client* table and the *orders* tables are then joined using the client number (clientno) column. The results of the query are included in the example.

Notice that the second ON clause adds another join criterion to link the *orders* table in the second join to the *orders* table in the first join on both the prodcode and clientno columns. The *orders* table is assigned two different aliases because it is referenced more than once in the clause.

> **Tip:** All ON clause alias and table references must occur AFTER the table has appeared in a FROM clause. In the next example the additional criteria linking the prodcode column in order1 to prodcode in order2 cannot be included on the first ON clause because the order2 alias has not yet been created.

```
LIBNAME bluesky "C:\mydata\bluesky bookstore\";

TITLE1 'All General Book Orders - Order, Stock and Client tables';

SELECT  client.company "Company" format= $20.,
        order2.clientno "Client #" format= 10.,
        order1.prodcode "Product Code" format= $15.,
        stock.title "Title" format= $20.

FROM    bluesky.stock JOIN bluesky.orders order1
        ON stock.prodcode=order1.prodcode,

        bluesky.client JOIN bluesky.orders order2
        ON order2.clientno = client.clientno
        AND order1.prodcode = order2.prodcode
        AND order1.clientno = order2.clientno

WHERE   stock.category = 'general';
```

All General Book Orders - Order, Stock and Client tables

Company	Client #	Product Code	Title
Heffers Booksellers	3007	600125	The Maestro
Lawrence Books	8003	600125	The Maestro
National University	4008	600125	The Maestro
Chicago State Univer	2010	600125	The Maestro
Cosmos 2000	7008	600489	Mountaineering Skill
National University	4008	600780	Women Writers

Tip: A JOIN expression must be immediately followed by an ON clause related to the expression. An implicit AND does not exist between FROM-ON join expressions, so additional criteria must be added to link the results of each join expression.

When more than two tables are joined, a *comma* is added to the end of the first ON clause, and the next two tables linked by a JOIN keyword are added with another ON clause.

A multitable join constructed using an ON clause is difficult both to write and understand. Specifying your join conditions for two or more tables in a WHERE clause results in a superior query for readability. You are also less likely to make an error in the construction of your joins.

In the next example the same query as above is presented using the WHERE clause to construct the join. It is both easier to understand and write. All of the tables from which data is drawn are included in a single FROM clause. Moreover, the set of criteria required to construct the joins are together in the WHERE clause, and each table is referenced only once.

```
LIBNAME  bluesky "C:\mydata\bluesky bookstore\";

SELECT   client.company "Company" format= $20.,
         orders.clientno "Client #" format= 10.,
         orders.prodcode "Product Code" format= $15.,
         stock.title "Title" format= $20.

FROM     bluesky.stock, bluesky.orders ,
         bluesky.client

WHERE    orders.clientno = client.clientno
         and stock.prodcode=orders.prodcode
         and stock.category = 'general';
```

```
Company                 Client #   Product Code   Title
-------------------------------------------------------------------

Chicago State Univer        2010   600125         The Maestro
Cosmos 2000                 7008   600489         Mountaineering Skill
Heffers Booksellers         3007   600125         The Maestro
Lawrence Books              8003   600125         The Maestro
National University         4008   600125         The Maestro
National University         4008   600780         Women Writers
```

The next example illustrates an equijoin between the *orders* and *stock* tables stored in an Oracle database called *master* using the SQL Pass-Through Facility. The criteria in a WHERE clause in an inner Pass-Through SQL statement joins the tables and restricts the rows retrieved from the database tables referenced in the FROM clause. These rows are then passed to the SAS session for processing by the outer SELECT statement.

There are several important differences between the inner database-specific SELECT statement and the outer SELECT statement interpreted by SAS. Notice that the dates in the WHERE clause are presented in a format understood by Oracle and not SAS. In addition, SAS formatting options for the report are included in the outer SELECT statement rather than the inner statement.

SQL Pass-Through Facility users: Although both the inner and outer SELECT statements can include a WHERE clause to subset the data when using SQL Pass-Through Facility, subsetting should be done on the database side.

A WHERE clause in an inner SELECT statement limits the rows available in the SAS session. The criteria in the WHERE clause of the outer SELECT statement are applied to the database table rows returned to the SAS session by the inner SELECT statement. If your database is very large, this can result in a large resource requirement for your SAS session and poor performance.

```
PROC SQL;

CONNECT to oracle (user=scott password=tiger path=master);

TITLE1  "Sales Information by Product Code and Author";
TITLE2  "January 1, 2004 to May 31, 2004";

SELECT     prodcode "Product Code" format=$15.,
           auth_lst "Author" format=$15.,
           mnqty "Average Quantity" format=comma8.,
           mnprice "Average Price" format= comma10.2,
           smprice "Quantity * Price" format= comma10.2
FROM       connection to oracle /* determines records returned to the
                                   SAS session*/

(SELECT    stock.prodcode  ,
           stock.auth_lst ,
           avg(orders.quantity) as mnqty ,
           avg(stock.price) as mnprice,
           sum(orders.quantity*stock.price) as smprice
FROM       bluesky.orders, bluesky.stock
WHERE      orders.ord_date between '01-JAN-2004' and '31-MAY-2004'
           and stock.prodcode = orders.prodcode
```

```
GROUP BY stock.prodcode, stock.auth_lst
ORDER BY stock.auth_lst);

DISCONNECT from oracle;
QUIT;
```

Tip: You will notice that the syntax in the inner SELECT statement differs from the PROC SQL SELECT statement syntax shown in the next example . The query passed to the DBMS must be consistent with the SQL that is native to that DBMS. In many cases the differences are slight; if you receive an error message, check that you used the correct syntax.

In the next example the same query shown in the SQL Pass-Through Facility example above is shown using the SAS/ACCESS LIBNAME statement.

```
LIBNAME oralib ORACLE
          user=scott password=tiger path=master schema=bluesky;

TITLE1   "Sales Information by Product Code and Author";
TITLE2   "January 1, 2004 to May 31, 2004";

SELECT   stock.prodcode "Product Code" format=$15.,
         stock.auth_lst "Author" format=$15.,
         avg(orders.quantity) as mnqty "Average Quantity"
             format=comma8.,

         avg(stock.price) as mnprice "Average Price" format=
             comma10.2,
         sum(orders.quantity*stock.price) as smprice "Quantity *
             Price" format= comma10.2
FROM     oralib.orders, oralib.stock
WHERE    orders.ord_date between '01JAN2004'd and '31MAY2004'd
         and stock.prodcode = orders.prodcode
GROUP BY stock.prodcode, stock.auth_lst
ORDER BY stock.auth_lst;
```

Tip: Compare this query to the last example. Notice that the dates in the WHERE clause are now presented in SAS format and SAS formatting options for the report are included in the SELECT statement. Although the data is retrieved from two tables stored in an Oracle database, the query itself is interpreted and processed by SAS.

The LIBNAME statement offers flexibility when joining tables stored in different locations. In the next example, the *stock* table stored in a native SAS library is joined to the current *orders* table in an Oracle database and an archive *orders* table stored in a

Microsoft SQL Server database. The LIBNAME statements for the Oracle and SQL Server databases include connection parameters appropriate for each database system. The SELECT statement uses the libref assigned in each LIBNAME statement to indicate the location of the table in the FROM clause.

```
LIBNAME orablue ORACLE
         user=scott password=tiger path=master schema=bluesky;

LIBNAME bluesky "C:\mydata\bluesky bookstore\";

LIBNAME sqlsrvr ODBC
         datasrc='bluesky' user=wayne password=john;


TITLE1   "Sales Information by Product Code and Author";
TITLE2   "January 1, 2004 to May 31, 2004";
TITLE3   "Compared to same period in 2002";

SELECT   stock.prodcode "Product Code" format=$15.,
         stock.auth_lst "Author" format=$15.,
         avg(orders.quantity) as mnqty2004
         "Average Quantity (2004)" format=comma8.,
         avg(order_2001_2002.quantity) as mnqty2002
         "Average Quantity (2002)" format=comma8.,
         avg(stock.price) as mnprice "Average Price" format=
             comma10.2,
         sum(orders.quantity*stock.price) as smprice2004
         "Quantity * Price (2004)" format= comma10.2,
         sum(order_2001_2002.quantity*stock.price) as smprice2002
         "Quantity * Price (2002)" format= comma10.2

FROM     orablue.orders, bluesky.stock, sqlsrvr.order_2001_2002
WHERE    orders.ord_date between '01JAN2004'd and '31MAY2004'd
         and order_2001_2002.ord_date between '01JAN2002'd and
             '31MAY2002'd
         and stock.prodcode = orders.prodcode
         and stock.prodcode=order_2001_2002.prodcode

GROUP BY stock.prodcode, stock.auth_lst
ORDER BY stock.auth_lst;
```

```
Sales Information by Product Code and Author
January 1, 2004 to May 31, 2004
Compared to same period in 2002

                              Average   Average              Quantity   Quantity
                              Quantity  Quantity    Average  * Price    * Price
Product Code      Author       (2004)    (2002)      Price     (2004)     (2002)
--------------------------------------------------------------------------------
200145            Bishop          700       363      56.25  78,750.00  40,781.25
600125            Dixon           237       100       6.95   4,948.40   2,085.00
600780            Paul            103       100       8.60     885.80     860.00
```

Tip: Each of the joins discussed in this chapter can be applied to tables that are stored in a database as well as tables stored in a SAS native library. Details on joining tables stored in one or more databases is covered in more detail in Appendix C, "Information for Database Users."

Non-equijoin

It is possible to join two tables using a comparison process rather than linking equal values. These types of joins are referred to a non-equijoins because they use mathematical or comparison operators other than an equal sign.

Caution: The SQL optimizer works best on equijoins. When using non-equijoins you will find your processing time generally increases. Consider using subqueries, covered later in this chapter, instead.

Both the WHERE clause and the ON clause can be used in conjunction with the FROM clause to construct a non-equijoin.

FROM-WHERE clause non-equijoins

SELECT
INTO
▸ FROM
ON
▸ WHERE
GROUP BY
HAVING
ORDER BY
USING;

General form:

FROM <libref.>table <alias> , <libref.>table <alias>
<,<libref.>table <alias>…>

WHERE <table|alias.>column|expression
OPERATOR <table|alias.>column|expression
<LOGICAL OPERATOR condition…>

The next example illustrates a simple non-equijoin. In this query, all of the rows in one table that have a stock quantity (stock) less than or equal to the cutoff values for the reprint category (cutoff) for that product are retrieved. In addition to the non-equijoin, an equijoin has been included in the WHERE clause. The equijoin is used to match the reprint codes in the two tables together to determine the reprint cutoff value for a specific book. The current stock quantity (stock) in the *stock* table is then compared to the reprint cutoff value (cutoff) in the *reprint* table.

```
LIBNAME bluesky "C:\mydata\bluesky bookstore\";

TITLE1  'Book Titles to be Reprinted';

SELECT  stock.title "Title" format= $40.
FROM    bluesky.stock, bluesky.reprint
WHERE   stock.reprint = reprint.reprint
        AND stock.stock LE reprint.cutoff;
```

```
             Book Titles to be Reprinted

             Title
             ________________________________________

             Book of Science and Nature
             Materials Science
             Start a Business Using a Computer
             Computer: Beginners Guide
             Risks in Life - % Gain or Loss?
```

The following figure shows a portion of the *stock* table and the entire *reprint* table to illustrate the mechanics of a non-equijoin. The first join expression in the WHERE clause matches the reprint column values in the two tables. The stock value is then compared to the cutoff value to determine which rows will be included in the report. Only the four rows indicated in the portion of the *stock* table shown below meet the conditions of the non-equijoin. In each case, their stock amounts are less than or equal to the cutoff values for that reprint category.

	Table name: STOCK		
	stock	**reprint**	**title**
	1500	E	Decorative Arts
⇨	100	D	Computer: Beginners Guide
⇨	1000	F	Book of Science and Nature
	100	C	The Ultimate Philosophy
⇨	50	C	Materials Science
⇨	1000	F	Risks in Life - % Gain or Loss?

Table name: REPRINT	
reprint	**cutoff**
A	0
B	10
C	50
D	100
E	500
F	1000

Compare the results of the previous example with the output generated by PROC FREQ. In the next example the product format has again been associated with the prodcode column of the *stock* table. The report groups the book counts by the product categories because the *order=formatted* option has been included.

```
LIBNAME   bluesky "C:\mydata\bluesky bookstore\";

PROC FREQ data=bluesky.stock order=formatted;
TABLES    prodcode ;
FORMAT    prodcode $product.;
RUN;
```

```
The FREQ Procedure

                                                      Cumulative    Cumulative
prodCode                  Frequency     Percent      Frequency       Percent
--------------------------------------------------------------------------------
Engineering                       4       13.33              4         13.33
General Arts                      4       13.33              8         26.67
General Interest                  5       16.67             13         43.33
General Science                   5       16.67             18         60.00
Information Technology            6       20.00             24         80.00
Medicine                          6       20.00             30        100.00
```

Such formatting may be applied in PROC SQL through table joins. In the next example a new table called *prodlabel* stores the labels associated with each product code range. The count and percentages are calculated in the SELECT statement in the generating part of the PROC FREQ output above. Two non-equijoins are constructed between the product code in the *orders* table and the columns representing the low and high value of each product code range, prodcode_low, and prodcode_high respectively in the *prodlabel* table. The joins retrieve the appropriate label for each product code in the *stock* table.

An INPUT function has been included in the WHERE clause to convert the product code in the *stock* table, a character field into a numeric value. Automatic data conversion does not occur in PROC SQL and columns involved in a join must have the same data type. The join between the columns is processed after the results of the function are returned.

> **Tip:** Columns involved in a join may include functions. If you recall from Chapter 4, "Functions," data conversion does not occur automatically in PROC SQL. Joins require columns of the same data type, so an INPUT or PUT function must be added to columns if required.

```
PROC SQL;

LIBNAME bluesky "C:\mydata\bluesky bookstore\";

CREATE  table bluesky.prodlabel
          (prodcode_low num,
         prodcode_high num,
         description          char (25)
         );

INSERT into bluesky.prodlabel
  values (100000,200000,'General Science')
  values (200000,300000,'Engineering')
  values (300000,400000,'General Arts')
  values (400000,500000,'Medicine')
  values (500000,600000,'Information Technology')
  values (600000,700000,'General Interest');

SELECT   description, count(prodcode) as Frequency,
         count(prodcode)/(select count(prodcode) from
         bluesky.stock)as Percent
         format=percent8.2
FROM     bluesky.stock, bluesky.prodlabel
WHERE    input(prodcode,6.) >= prodcode_low and
         input(prodcode,6.) < prodcode_high
GROUP BY description;

QUIT;
```

```
description                  Frequency   Percent
------------------------------------------------
Engineering                          4    13.33%
General Arts                         4    13.33%
General Interest                     5    16.67%
General Science                      5    16.67%
Information Technology               6    20.00%
Medicine                             6    20.00%
```

Tip: The SELECT statement used in this example includes several concepts discussed later in this chapter and in Chapter 6, "Creating and Managing Tables and Views."

- The CREATE and INSERT statements used to create and populate the look-up table are discussed in Chapter 6.
- The SELECT clause includes a subquery that retrieves the total count for the calculation of the percentage. Additional subqueries can be added to calculate the cumulative frequency and percent. Information on subqueries is included later in this chapter.

FROM-ON clause joins

SELECT
INTO
► FROM
► ON
WHERE
GROUP BY
HAVING
ORDER BY
USING;

General form:

FROM <libref.>table <alias> <INNER>JOIN <libref.>table <alias>

ON <table|alias.>column | expression
OPERATOR <table|alias.>column | expression
<, table JOIN KEYWORD table ON join condition…>
<LOGICAL OPERATOR condition…>

The next example shows the same join, but this time it is created by using the on clause.

```
LIBNAME bluesky "C:\mydata\bluesky bookstore\";

TITLE1 'Book Titles to be Reprinted';

SELECT   stock.title "Title" format= $40.
FROM     bluesky.stock JOIN bluesky.reprint
         ON stock.stock LE reprint.cutoff
         AND stock.reprint = reprint.reprint ;
```

```
                 Book Titles to be Reprinted

                 Title
                 __________________________________________

                 Book of Science and Nature
                 Materials Science
                 Start a Business Using a Computer
                 Computer: Beginners Guide
                 Risks in Life - % Gain or Loss?
```

Just as an equijoin may be used in conjunction with a non-equijoin, multiple non-equijoins may be included in a SELECT statement by joining each non-equijoin with an AND or an OR operator.

In the next example there are two non-equijoins that are used to report books that must be reprinted. The two non-equijoins set out the conditions under which the books must be reprinted. The *reprint* and *stock* tables are joined in the reprint code column. The join condition is met only by those rows in the *stock* table with an actual or slightly reduced stock quantity (90%) that is less than or equal to the cutoff value associated with the reprint code. Notice that the expression used to reduce the actual stock quantity to 90% of the quantity is included in the ON clause. The report generated by the query is included in the example.

> **Tip:** Expressions as well as columns can be used in join expressions in the ON or WHERE clauses for all types of joins.

```
LIBNAME bluesky "C:\mydata\bluesky bookstore\";

TITLE1  'Book Titles to be Reprinted';

SELECT  stock.title "Title" format= $40.,
        stock.stock "Stock On-hand" format= 6.,
        round(stock.stock*.9) "Stock On-hand less 10%" format= 6.,
        reprint.cutoff "Reprint Cutoff" format= 6.

FROM    bluesky.stock JOIN bluesky.reprint

        ON (stock.stock LE reprint.cutoff
        OR round(stock.stock*.9) le reprint.cutoff)
        AND stock.reprint = reprint.reprint;
```

Book Titles to be Reprinted

Title	Stock On-hand	Stock On-hand less 10%	Reprint Cutoff
Book of Science and Nature	1000	900	1000
Materials Science	50	45	50
Democracy in America	55	50	50
Start a Business Using a Computer	1000	900	1000
Computer: Beginners Guide	100	90	100
Risks in Life - % Gain or Loss?	1000	900	1000

Tip: You may find it much easier to both create and read non-equijoins in a WHERE clause. Even with just two tables, the ON clause in the above example is difficult to read.

Self-joins

It is also possible to join a table to itself. This kind of join is known as a self-join or reflexive join. It allows you to search the table a second time using information selected from the first pass through the table. Self-joins are closely related to subqueries in the way that they operate. Subqueries are often easier to work with, and they can accomplish many of the same tasks. They are covered in detail later in this chapter.

In the table below, a client may be either an individual or a company. Many clients are associated with the same company. If you look closely at the table, you will notice that the values in the company column refer back to the client number. This creates a recursive relationship.

Table: CONTACTS			
Clientno	**Name**	**Department**	**Company**
100	John Stuart	Book Store	204
101	Randy Hycal	Law Library	203
102	Marissa Stone	Medical Library	203
203	University of Adelaide	Purchasing	203
103	Michael Masters	Law Library	204
204	University of Texas	Purchasing	204

When you select rows from a table with a recursive relationship, the table is accessed twice. If a self-join is used, the table is listed in the FROM clause twice with a different alias applied each time. The query below is designed to generate the names and departments for all clients within each university together with the name of the university. However, it excludes the university as a client.

```
SELECT      b.name 'Client' , a.name 'Contact', a.department
            'Department'
FROM          contacts a, contacts b
WHERE        a.company = b.company
                    AND b.clientno = b.company
                    AND a.clientno <> b.company
ORDER BY    b.name;
```

```
Client                          Contact                    Department
------------------------------------------------------------------------
University of Adelaide        Marissa Stone               Medical Library
University of Adelaide        Randy Hycal                 Law Library
University of Texas           John Stuart                 Book Store
University of Texas           Michael Masters             Law Library
```

SAS/ACCESS and SQL Pass-Through Facility users: Self-joins and subqueries are often applied to database tables that are designed with a recursive relationship.

FROM-WHERE clause self-joins

SELECT
INTO
▶ FROM
ON
▶ WHERE
GROUP BY
HAVING
ORDER BY
USING;

General form:

FROM <libref.>table alias , <libref.>table alias <,<libref.>table alias…>

WHERE table|alias.column|expression = table|alias.column|expression <LOGICAL OPERATOR condition…>

In a query that uses a self-join, the FROM clause references the table twice. To distinguish between these two references, assign a different alias to each of them.

Tip: Although aliases are normally optional, they are mandatory with a self-join.

Consider the task of generating a report on all books that have been ordered by more than one client. One option is the use of BY GROUP processing. Following is an example of the SAS program that would determine whether a combination of product code and client number is unique.

```
LIBNAME bluesky "C:\mydata\bluesky bookstore\";

PROC SORT data=bluesky.orders;
  by prodcode clientno;

* Use By variable processing of prodcode and clientno in the
  orders table;
DATA temp ;
  SET bluesky.orders;
  BY prodcode clientno;

  * Delete those records for which there is a single entry ie only
    one client order;

  if first.prodcode and last.prodcode
    then delete;

  * If the same client ordered the book delete the record;
```

```
  if first.clientno and not last.clientno
    then delete;

  if last.clientno and not first.clientno
    then delete;

  * Count the number of clients per prodcode;

  if first.prodcode then count=0;
  count+1;

  * Output the last product code record to obtain the highest
    count;

  if last.prodcode then output;

* Eliminate duplicate product codes;

PROC sort nodupkey data=temp;
  by prodcode;

* Print the results;

PROC print data=temp;
  var prodcode count;
RUN;
```

Obs	prod Code	count
1	200345	2
2	300456	3
3	300680	2
4	400100	3
5	400128	2
6	400178	2
7	600125	4

Now consider how the task might be accomplished using the SQL procedures. In a standard SQL query, each row of the table is checked against the WHERE criteria. Those rows that pass are included in the report. SQL processing does not provide for value comparisons between one row and the row immediately before or after that row.

One possible solution involves the use of a GROUP BY clause and HAVING clause. In the next example the GROUP BY clause generates a count of the number of unique client numbers associated with each product code in the *orders* table. Each group is checked and only those books ordered by more than one client are selected. SAS will remerge the summary counts back with the original data automatically, in order to determine which groups meet the criteria set out in the HAVING clause.

```
PROC SQL;
LIBNAME  bluesky "C:\mydata\bluesky bookstore\";

TITLE1   'Books ordered by multiple clients';
TITLE2   'With Group by clause';
SELECT   prodcode,
         count(distinct clientno) as clients "Number of clients"
FROM     bluesky.orders
GROUP BY prodcode
HAVING   clients > 1;
```

```
                   Books ordered by multiple clients
                   With Group by clause



                                  Number
                      Product         of
                      Code       clients
                      ------------------

                      200345           2
                      300456           3
                     300680          2
                      400100           3
                      400128           2
                      400178           2
                      600125           4
```

The next example gives a query containing a self-join that generates the same result as shown above. Notice that the FROM statement lists the *orders* table twice, each time with a different alias. This allows us to essentially do a side-by-side comparison of each row in the table. Because each column in the *orders* table now occurs twice, an alias is required as a prefix to each column contained in the SELECT clause.

Tip: A reflexive or self-join allows you to take one or more copies of a table and treat each as though it is a separate table. Each copy must be assigned a unique alias.

```
LIBNAME bluesky "C:\mydata\bluesky bookstore\";

TITLE1    'Books ordered by multiple clients';

SELECT    order1.prodcode "Product Code",
          count(distinct order1.clientno)  "Clients"
FROM      bluesky.orders order1,
          bluesky.orders order2
WHERE     order1.prodcode = order2.prodcode
          AND order1.clientno NE order2.clientno
GROUP BY order1.prodcode;
```

```
                  Books ordered by multiple clients

                        Product
                        Code       Clients
                        __________________

                        200345           2
                        300456           3
                        300680           2
                        400100           3
                        400128           2
                        400178           2
                        600125           4
```

Tip: A self-join can be constructed in an equijoin, a non-equijoin, or a combination of these joins. Other joins can also be included in a query with one or more self-joins.

The next figure provides a portion of the *orders* table to show how the SELECT statement is processed. The order date has been included for clarity. If you examine the tables, you will notice that there are three orders for product code 300456 by different clients. When the tables are compared side-by-side, each of these rows meets the criteria specified in the WHERE clause above. They have the same product code (prodcode) values, but different client numbers (clientno). Without the DISTINCT keyword added to the count function 6 clients, all of the rows that meet the criteria set out in the WHERE clause would be reported.

Table name: ORDERS, alias order1		
ord_date	**prodcode**	**clientno**
09JAN03	100340	8003
07FEB03	300456	1001
07FEB03	300456	3007
10APR04	300456	6090
12JUN04	100340	8003

Table name: ORDERS, alias order2		
ord_date	**prodcode**	**clientno**
09JAN03	100340	8003
07FEB03	300456	1001
07FEB03	300456	3007
10APR04	300456	6090
12JUN04	100340	8003

FROM-ON clause self-joins

SELECT
INTO
▶ FROM
▶ ON
WHERE
GROUP BY
HAVING
ORDER BY
USING;

General form:

FROM <libref.>table <alias> <INNER>JOIN <libref.>table <alias>

ON table|alias.column | expression
OPERATOR table|alias.column | expression
<, table JOIN KEYWORD table ON join condition…>
<LOGICAL OPERATOR condition…>

The ON clause can also be used to construct a self-join. The following example provides the above query with both an equijoin and a non-equijoin specified in an ON clause. Aliases are also required here because the same table is referenced twice in the FROM and ON clauses.

```
LIBNAME bluesky "C:\mydata\bluesky bookstore\";

TITLE1    'Books ordered by multiple clients - ON clause';

SELECT    order1.prodcode "Product Code",
          count(distinct order1.clientno)  "Clients"
FROM      bluesky.orders order1 JOIN bluesky.orders order2

          ON order1.prodcode=order2.prodcode
          AND order1.clientno NE order2.clientno
GROUP BY order1.prodcode;
```

```
Books ordered by multiple clients - ON clause
Product
Code       Clients
_________________

200345           2
300456           3
300680           2
400100           3
400128           2
400178           2
600125           4
```

Tip: If a self-join is the only join in your query, the WHERE and FROM-ON clauses are more or less the same in terms of readability. You should choose the form with which you are most comfortable.

Outer joins

An outer join allows rows from one table that do not have a corresponding value in another table to be reported. All of the rows from one table are retrieved together with matching rows from another table. These types of joins require that one or both of the tables be augmented with rows that do not match the other table during processing.

Tip: Outer joins require the same data type in each of the columns used to construct the join. Neither the name, length of character data, nor number of decimal places declared for numeric data types have to match. Remember, the INPUT and PUT functions can be used to convert the data type of a column.

Three forms of outer joins are available: right, left and full outer joins. The left and right keywords refer to the position of a table name relative to the JOIN keyword. Outer joins in the SQL procedure must be constructed using the FROM and ON clauses.

Tip: Outer joins cannot be constructed using the WHERE clause in PROC SQL.

SAS/ACCESS and SQL Pass-Through Facility users: The SQL products associated with many databases support outer join criteria in the WHERE clause. Refer to the documentation relating to your RDBMS for more information.

Left and right outer joins

SELECT INTO ▸ FROM ▸ ON WHERE GROUP BY HAVING ORDER BY USING;

General form:

FROM <libref.>table <alias> LEFT JOIN | RIGHT JOIN
<libref.>table <alias>

ON <table|alias.>column | expression
OPERATOR <table|alias.>column | expression
<, table|alias JOIN KEYWORD table|alias ON join condition…>
<LOGICAL OPERATOR condition…>

If a left or right join is specified, all records in one table will be retrieved. This is true regardless of whether a matching value for that record exists in the table to which it is joined. If a left join is specified, all rows in the table to the left of join keyword will be retrieved; if a right join is specified, all rows in the table to the right of the join keyword will be retrieved.

> **Tip:** What's the difference between a left join and a right join? They both retrieve rows that would otherwise be excluded from an equijoin. Rows in one table are retrieved even if there is not a corresponding entry in the second table.
>
> The LEFT and RIGHT keywords indicate the position of the table from which all rows are to be retrieved, relative to the join keyword.

The next example shows a standard equijoin between the *stock* and *orders* tables of the Bluesky Publishing Company. The query limits the report to the Bluesky Publishing Company and to the general category of book titles for which orders have been placed by clients. The report includes details on the number of books sold and the total sale price.

```
LIBNAME bluesky "C:\mydata\bluesky bookstore\";

TITLE1    'Sales of General Category Books';

SELECT    stock.title "Title" format $40., sum(orders.quantity) "#
          Sold" format 8.0,
          sum(orders.totsale) "Total Sale" format Dollar10.2

FROM      bluesky.stock INNER join bluesky.orders
          ON stock.prodcode = orders.prodcode

WHERE     stock.category='general'

GROUP BY  stock.title;
```

```
Sales of General Category Books

Title                                        # Sold  Total Sale
_______________________________________________________________

Mountaineering Skills                            25     $137.50
The Maestro                                    1062  $12,345.90
Women Writers                                   103     $885.80
```

But what if you want your report to include all general category books, including those for which orders have not been placed? The equijoin in the previous example excludes all rows in the *stock* table that do not have a corresponding entry in the *orders* table. The equijoin criterion specifies that books must occur at least once in the *orders* table or they are not retrieved.

The general category books in the *stock* table are shown below together with a portion of the *orders* table showing the orders placed for general books. The highlighted rows in the *stock* table are book entries that do not have a corresponding entry in the *orders* table. As a result, they have not been included in the report shown in the preceding example. To correctly retrieve all books and report all orders, an outer-join is necessary.

Table name: STOCK

prodcode	category	title
600123	general	Risks in LIfe - % Gain or Loss
600780	general	Women Writers
600451	general	Greece and Beyond
600489	general	Mountaineering Skills
600125	general	The Maestro

Table name: ORDERS

prodcode	quantity	totsale
600125	350	2432.50
600125	12	83.40
600780	103	885.80
600125	100	1250.00
600489	25	137.50
600125	600	8580.00

The query has been rewritten to include a left outer join in the next example. The resulting report now shows all general category book titles that the Bluesky Publishing Company has in stock together with the sales details. The *stock* table may contain records that do not match a record in the *orders* table. The *stock* table is to the left of the join keyword; therefore a left join is required.

```
LIBNAME bluesky "C:\mydata\bluesky bookstore\";

TITLE1    'Sales of General Category Books';

SELECT    stock.title "Title" format= $40.,
          sum(orders.quantity) "# Sold" format= 8.0,
          sum(orders.totsale) "Total Sale" format= Dollar10.2

FROM      bluesky.stock LEFT JOIN bluesky.orders
          ON stock.prodcode = orders.prodcode

WHERE     stock.category='general'
GROUP BY stock.title;
```

```
Sales of General Category Books

Title                                           # Sold  Total Sale
------------------------------------------------------------------
Greece and Beyond                                    .           .
Mountaineering Skills                               25     $137.50
Risks in Life - % Gain or Loss?                      .           .
The Maestro                                       1062  $12,345.90
Women Writers                                      103     $885.80
```

Tip: All rows in the table that precede the LEFT JOIN keyword are reported even if they do not have a corresponding entry in the table to which they are joined. The query can be rewritten to use a right join if the position of the *stock* and *orders* tables are reversed in the FROM clause.

These forms of joins can be useful when checking the integrity of your tables. For example, if an accidental entry were made in the *orders* table for a book that is not listed in the *stock* table, an equijoin would not reveal the error. In the next example a right join between the *stock* and the *orders* tables allows us to check for orders that contain product codes that are not in the *stock* table. Notice that the results include a record with sale information but a missing title.

```
LIBNAME bluesky "C:\mydata\bluesky bookstore\";

TITLE1    'All general and missing book category orders and stock';

SELECT    stock.title "Title" format= $40.,
          sum(orders.quantity) "# Sold" format= 8.0,
          sum(orders.totsale) "Total Sale" format= Dollar10.2

FROM      bluesky.stock RIGHT JOIN bluesky.orders
          ON stock.prodcode = orders.prodcode

WHERE     stock.category IN ('', 'general')
GROUP BY stock.title;
```

```
All general and missing book category orders and stock

Title                                          # Sold  Total Sale
------------------------------------------------------------------

                                                  400  $13,600.00
Mountaineering Skills                              25     $137.50
The Maestro                                      1062  $12,345.90
Women Writers                                     103     $885.80
```

Caution: If you add a WHERE clause to a query used to check for data integrity errors, you have to build your condition so that a missing or incorrect entry will meet the criteria. Without the addition of a blank category to the IN values in the previous example, books without entries in the *stock* table, the very ones we're looking for, would not meet the criteria. It is often easier when checking the integrity of your tables to exclude a WHERE clause criterion.

Tip: To prevent an order for a nonexistent book from occurring, a foreign key relationship between the prodcode columns in the *stock* and the *orders* tables could be used. Refer to Chapter 6, "Creating and Managing Tables and Views," for more information on the use of foreign keys for data integrity.

Full outer join

SELECT
INTO
▸ FROM
▸ ON
WHERE
GROUP BY
HAVING
ORDER BY
USING;

General form:

FROM <libref.>table <alias> FULL JOIN <libref.>table <alias>

ON <table|alias.>column | expression
OPERATOR <table|alias.>column | expression
<, table|alias JOIN KEYWORD table|alias ON join condition…>
<LOGICAL OPERATOR condition…>

A full outer join includes rows from each of two tables that do not have matching rows. Essentially, it is a complete record of the rows in each table with column values where available. If we use our modified *orders* table as part of a full join, we can easily see what happens. Notice in the next example that both books without an entry in the *stock* table and books without an entry in the *orders* table are included in this report.

Tip: What is the difference between a full outer join and a Cartesian product? A Cartesian product matches each row in one table to every row in the other table. The number of rows returned by the query will always equal the number of rows in the first table multiplied by the number of rows in the second table.

A full outer join matches rows in the two tables based on the join criteria and includes extra entries for those rows without a match. The number of rows returned by the query cannot be predicted without detailed information on the values stored in the columns used to construct the join.

```
LIBNAME bluesky "C:\mydata\bluesky bookstore\";

TITLE1    'All general and missing book category orders and stock';

SELECT    stock.title "Title" format= $40.,
          sum(orders.quantity) "# Sold" format= 8.0,
          sum(orders.totsale) "Total Sale" format= Dollar10.2

FROM      bluesky.stock FULL JOIN bluesky.orders
          ON stock.prodcode = orders.prodcode

WHERE     stock.category IN ('', 'general')
GROUP BY stock.title;
```

```
All general and missing book category orders and stock

Title                                        # Sold  Total Sale
---------------------------------------------------------------

                                                400  $13,600.00
Greece and Beyond                                 .           .
Mountaineering Skills                            25     $137.50
Risks in Life - % Gain or Loss?                   .           .
The Maestro                                    1062  $12,345.90
Women Writers                                   103     $885.80
```

Tip: When a FULL join is specified, all rows in both tables that meet the criteria set out in the WHERE clause are reported, including those that do not have a corresponding entry in the table to which they are joined.

Set operators

SET operators provide another method of joining tables. They can also be helpful in combining results from more than one table when complex selection criteria are included in the query. Moreover, they can be much easier to understand than self-joins and many outer join operations.

Tip: SET operations do not change or remove rows in any of the tables. A new table can be created from the results of a SET operation using the CREATE TABLE AS statement discussed in Chapter 6, "Creating and Managing Tables and Views."

There are several SET operators available through PROC SQL including UNION, OUTER UNION, EXCEPT, and INTERSECT. The nature of the merge operation differs depending on the SET operator used. The SELECT expressions are often referred to as table expressions because each provides results or rowsets from a table based on one or more criteria.

Tip: Table joins may be included in one or more of the SELECT expressions used in conjunction with SET operators. The joins are processed first and the resulting rowsets passed to the SET operation. The SET operation next connects these rowsets to generate the result set.

Queries or SELECT statements incorporating set operators have two or more SELECT expressions as shown in the form below. Each of the SELECT expressions is evaluated separately, and the resulting rowsets are merged to produce the result set. Only the columns listed in each SELECT expression become part of the rowsets passed to the SET operation. The final result set can be sorted using an optional ORDER BY statement.

General form:

```
SELECT expression

    SET OPERATOR <ALL>

SELECT expression

    <<SET OPERATOR <ALL>
    SELECT expression >...>

<ORDER BY >
;
```

SET operations between tables with different numbers of columns in the SELECT clause of each SELECT expression are processed using virtual columns. The table with fewer columns is altered to include one or more virtual columns during processing. Each virtual column is populated with null values and assigned the same type as the column that matches it positionally on the SELECT clause with more columns.

Tip: Although PROC SQL allows SET operations between tables with different numbers of columns in the SELECT clause, the addition of virtual columns to a table adds to the memory requirement of the operation. If processing time or memory requirements are a problem, consider creating a view or table with the required structure for use in the SET operation.

Check your SAS log for a warning message reporting that one or more of the tables has been extended:

```
WARNING: A table has been extended with null columns to
         perform the UNION set operation.
```

In the next example the intersection set of the current and historical orders tables, *orders* and *order_2001_2002,* based on client number is first created. A union between the resulting rowsets, those client numbers occurring in both the current and historical orders tables and the *client* table is then processed to obtain the company name for each client number. The intersection operation is based on a single common column and client number. The union operation, however, operates with an additional column from the *client* table that is not present in the intersection result set. The SAS log reports that a table has been extended to include an extra column (company) that is populated with null values in order to complete the union operation.

```
LIBNAME bluesky "C:\mydata\bluesky bookstore\";

TITLE1  'Clients for which there are orders in both order tables';

        SELECT  clientno
        FROM    bluesky.orders

INTERSECT

        SELECT  clientno
        FROM    bluesky.order_2001_2002

UNION
        SELECT  distinct clientno, company
        FROM    bluesky.client;
```

```
WARNING: A table has been extended with null columns to perform the
UNION set operation.
```

SAS/ACCESS and SQL Pass-Through Facility users: The ANSI standard for set operations requires that the number and data type of columns included in the SELECT clause in each expression must be identical except when the OUTER UNION operator is used. To bypass this restriction, place the SET operation in an outer SELECT statement for the SQL Pass-Through Facility or use the SAS/ACCESS LIBNAME statement.

A SELECT statement may contain more than two SELECT expressions joined through a SET operator. Regardless of the number of pairs of SELECT expressions joined through a SET operator, SAS works with only two rowsets at a time, generating a new rowset from the operation. The rowset generated from the first set operation becomes the input for the next set operation.

Tip: If more than two set operators are included in a single SELECT statement, the INTERSECT operation is evaluated first. All other set operations have the same precedence; they are processed in order of occurrence.

In the next example several INTERSECT operations are used to generate a report of all product codes for general category books ordered in both the 2001-2002 and 2003-2004 periods. The intersect operation between the rows resulting from the SELECT expressions against the *stock* and *order_2001_2002* tables occurs first. The rowset from the first intersect operation is then compared to the rows of the *orders* table to generate the report. Only those rows and columns that are common to all three of the tables are included in the report.

```
LIBNAME bluesky "C:\mydata\bluesky bookstore\";

TITLE1    'General category books ordered
           in 2001-2002 and 2003-2004';

           SELECT *
           FROM bluesky.stock
           WHERE category = 'general'
INTERSECT corr

           SELECT *
           FROM bluesky.order_2001_2002

INTERSECT corr
           SELECT *
           FROM bluesky.orders;
```

```
General category books ordered in 2001-2002 and 2003-2004

prod
Code
______

600125
600489
600780
```

Tip: Although an asterisk appears in the SELECT clause of each of the SELECT expressions above, only one column appears in the report. The CORR keyword directs SAS to match the columns in each of the tables by name. As there is only a single column in each of the tables with the same name (prodcode), it is the only column reported.

By default, duplicate values are eliminated from the combined results of a SET operation for all SET operators except OUTER UNION. The keyword ALL must be specified to override this default. When SET operators are applied to a SELECT statement, a second pass is made through the result set to check for duplicate values. This additional processing may degrade performance slightly. As a result, the ALL keyword should be added whenever the elimination of duplicates is unnecessary.

Tip: Duplicate values are removed from the final result set for all SET operations except OUTER UNION. The ALL keyword should be added if duplicates are not problematic to prevent extra processing which can adversely affect performance.

UNION operator

General form:

UNION <ALL><CORRESPONDING|CORR>

The UNION operator reports the unique results formed by the concatenation of rows retrieved by one SELECT statement with those of a second SELECT statement. The columns to be included in the result set are determined from the first SELECT statement; rows retrieved from the execution of each of the SELECT statements are included in the result set. Common columns are merged, with values contributed by each of the tables. By default, all duplicate rows are eliminated from the result set.

The SELECT clause of each SELECT statement lists the columns from each table that are to be included in the rowset processed by the SET operator. By default, SAS will match each column in the first table with a column in the second table by their position in the SELECT clause. The columns and column names for the result set are derived from the table in the first SELECT statement, where available. If an unnamed expression is included in the first SELECT statement, SAS will attempt to name the column using the second table. However, if a name is not assigned to the expression in the second SELECT statement, a name will not be included in the result set.

Tip: In order to avoid confusion, especially when working with UNION operators between more than two tables include all of your formats, aliases, and labels on the first SELECT clause whenever possible.

In the next example the UNION set operator is used to combine the results from two SELECT statements, each of which contains a table join and CASE expression. A different label has been assigned to the clientno and country columns of each SELECT statement. However, the CASE expression, based on the results of a substring (SUBSTR or SUBSTRN) function applied to the client number (clientno), is named only in the second SELECT statement. Notice that the result set uses the column labels from the first SELECT statement, with the exception of the unnamed CASE expression, which takes the label *Client Category* from the second statement.

Tip: The LABEL= keyword has been added to the CASE expression to avoid confusion among the character values assigned based on each CASE condition and the label or heading applied to the result. It is good practice to include optional keywords or comments when writing complex queries where confusion might arise.

```
LIBNAME bluesky "C:\mydata\bluesky bookstore\";

TITLE1  'Client orders in US dollars or Clients located in the USA';
TITLE2  'Between January 1, 2004 and August 30, 2004';


        SELECT  orders.clientno "Client", country "Country",
                CASE(SUBSTR(put(orders.clientno,4.),4,1))
                     when '0' then 'Discount = 7%'
                     when '1' then 'No discount'
                     else 'Disc ount = 5%'
                     end
        FROM    bluesky.orders, bluesky.address
        WHERE   orders.clientno = address.clientno
                AND currency = 'USD'
                AND ord_date between '01JAN2004'd and '30AUG2004'd

UNION
        SELECT  client.clientno 'Client Number', country 'Cntry',
                CASE(SUBSTR(put(client.clientno,4.),4,1))
                     when '0' then 'Discount = 7%'
                     when '1' then 'No discount'
                     else 'Discount = 5%'
                     end LABEL='Client Category'
        FROM    bluesky.client, bluesky.address
        WHERE   client.clientno = address.clientno
                AND country ='USA' ;
```

```
Client orders in US dollars or Clients located in the USA
Between January 1, 2004 and August 30, 2004

                                           Client
  Client  Country                          Category
-----------------------------------------------------
    1001  USA                              No discount
    2010  USA                              Discount = 7%
    8003  Canada                           Discount = 5%
```

Tip: The SELECT expression that occurs immediately before the UNION operator controls the columns to be output from the UNION operation. Priority is given to aliases and labels in the first SELECT clause. Aliases and labels in the second SELECT clause are used only if none are associated with expressions appearing in the first SELECT clause.

For comparison, the same query is written as a single SELECT statement joining the *address*, *client,* and *orders* tables in the next example. The WHERE clause criteria are much more complex than that shown in the previous example; as a result, they are more prone to errors. Notice that the DISTINCT keyword was added to the SELECT statement to eliminate duplicate records.

```
LIBNAME bluesky "C:\mydata\bluesky bookstore\";

TITLE1    'Client orders in US dollars
           or Clients located in the USA';
TITLE2    'Between January 1, 2004 and August 30, 2004';

SELECT     DISTINCT orders.clientno, country,
           CASE(SUBSTR(put(orders.clientno,4.),4,1))
                when '0' then 'Discount = 7%'
                when '1' then 'No discount'
                else 'Discount = 5%'
                end LABEL='Client Category'
FROM       bluesky.address, bluesky.client, bluesky.orders
WHERE      address.clientno = client.clientno
           and orders.clientno = client.clientno
           AND ((currency = 'USD'
           AND (orders.ord_date
                between '01JAN2004'd and '30AUG2004'd))
           OR country = 'USA');
```

```
Client orders in US dollars or Clients located in the USA
Between January 1, 2004 and August 30, 2004

                                        Client
clientNo  country                       Category
------------------------------------------------------

    1001  USA                           No discount
    2010  USA                           Discount = 7%
    8003  Canada                        Discount = 5%
```

Set and join operations each have advantages and disadvantages. In the former example each SELECT statement includes a single join operation, and the criteria in the WHERE clause are therefore not as complex. But the repetition of the CASE expression makes it more cumbersome. In the latter example the query is more compact but the WHERE clause is complex. The combination of AND and OR operators can be tricky, and the need for the DISTINCT keyword is not immediately obvious.

> **Tip:** Generally I use SET operations when the columns involved do not require manipulation. I also use them when I have complex criteria that differ for each table.

ALL keyword

The ALL keyword alters the handling of duplicate rows. By default, a union operation eliminates duplicate rows in the result set. If the ALL keyword is added, all rows in the row sets used in the union operation are included in the result set. All other aspects of the union operation remain unchanged. The example below includes an earlier query, modified to include the ALL keyword and the result set produced by the query.

```
LIBNAME bluesky "C:\mydata\bluesky bookstore\";

TITLE1    'Client orders in US dollars or Clients located in the USA';
TITLE2    'Between January 1, 2004 and August 30, 2004';

          SELECT  orders.clientno "Client", country "Country",
                  CASE(SUBSTR(put(orders.clientno,4.),4,1))
                      when '0' then 'Discount = 7%'
                      when '1' then 'No discount'
                      else 'Discount = 5%'
                      end
          FROM    bluesky.orders, bluesky.address
          WHERE   orders.clientno = address.clientno
                  AND currency = 'USD'
                  AND ord_date between '01JAN2004'd and '30AUG2004'd

UNION ALL

          SELECT  client.clientno 'Client Number', country 'Cntry',
                  CASE(SUBSTR(put(client.clientno,4.),4,1))
                      when '0' then 'Discount = 7%'
                      when '1' then 'No discount'
                      else 'Discount = 5%'
                      end LABEL='Client Category'
          FROM    bluesky.client, bluesky.address
          WHERE   client.clientno = address.clientno
                  AND country ='USA' ;
```

```
Client orders in US dollars or Clients located in the USA
Between January 1, 2004 and August 30, 2004

                                         Client
  Client  Country                        Category
-------------------------------------------------------------

    2010  USA                            Discount = 7%
    2010  USA                            Discount = 7%
    2010  USA                            Discount = 7%
    2010  USA                            Discount = 7%
    8003  Canada                         Discount = 5%
    1001  USA                            No discount
    2010  USA                            Discount = 7%
```

Tip: Another way to eliminate the duplicate rows in the result set in the above example is to add a DISTINCT keyword to the first SELECT expression. In some cases, a DISTINCT keyword has to be added to more than one of the SELECT expressions. Using UNION instead of UNION ALL is a much simpler way to ensure unique rows in your result set.

OUTER UNION operator

General form:

OUTER UNION <CORRESPONDING|CORR>

An outer union combines information from two or more tables in much the same way as the UNION operator. However, with an outer union all rows meeting the criteria of the SELECT expressions are concatenated and included in the output. Columns selected from each table are reported separately unless the CORR keyword is added.

Tip: The ALL keyword does not apply to the OUTER UNION operation.

In order to show how these set operators differ, the next example includes the same SELECT statement shown in the previous section, but the CASE expression has been excluded. The OUTER UNION operator has replaced the UNION operator. The reported client numbers are the same as those obtained through the UNION operation; however, they are organized differently. The first two columns of the report show the data retrieved from the *orders* table while the next two columns contain the data retrieved from the *address* table. Notice that the labels for the columns are still drawn solely from the first SELECT expression.

```
LIBNAME bluesky "C:\mydata\bluesky bookstore\";

TITLE1    'Client orders in US dollars or Clients located in the USA';

          SELECT   orders.clientno "Client", country "Country"
          FROM     bluesky.orders, bluesky.address
          WHERE    orders.clientno=address.clientno
                   AND currency = 'USD'
                   AND ord_date between '01JAN2004'd and '30AUG2004'd

OUTER UNION

          SELECT   client.clientno "Client Number", country "Cntry"
          FROM     bluesky.client, bluesky.address
          WHERE    client.clientno = address.clientno
                   AND country ='USA' ;
```

```
  Client orders in US dollars or Clients located in the USA

                                               Client
    Client  Country                            Number  Cntry
  ------------------------------------------------------------
      2010  USA                                     .
      2010  USA                                     .
      2010  USA                                     .
      2010  USA                                     .
      8003  Canada                                  .
         .                                       1001  USA
         .                                       2010  USA
```

The OUTER UNION operator is used in much the same way as the SET option of a DATA step. The two sets of retrieved rows are concatenated to form a common result set that continues to treat the rows somewhat separately.

CORR keyword

If we add the CORR keyword to the OUTER UNION operator, corresponding columns are merged. The next example shows a modified version of the previous query with corresponding columns overlaid. The corresponding column has been assigned the same alias on each SELECT expression. For clarity, the selected columns have been labeled differently on each SELECT clause to show that column labels for the report are derived from the first SELECT expression.

```
LIBNAME bluesky "C:\mydata\bluesky bookstore\";

TITLE1    'Client orders in US dollars or Clients located in the
           USA';

          SELECT o.clientno as client "Client1", country as country
          "Country1"
          FROM   bluesky.orders o, bluesky.address a
          WHERE  o.clientno=a.clientno
                 AND currency = 'USD'
                 AND ord_date between '01JAN2004'd and '30AUG2004'd

OUTER UNION CORR

          SELECT c.clientno as client "Client2", a.country as country
          "Country2"
          FROM   bluesky.client c, bluesky.address a
          WHERE  c.clientno = a.clientno
                 AND country ='USA' ;
```

```
Client orders in US dollars or Clients located in the USA

Client1  Country1
__________________________________

   2010  USA
   2010  USA
   2010  USA
   2010  USA
   8003  Canada
   1001  USA
   2010  USA
```

There are several important points to note about the CORR keyword when table joins are also part of one or more of the SELECT expressions involved in a set operation.

If table qualifiers are prefixed to the common column in both SELECT clauses, SAS will consider these columns to be different. If column aliases are assigned differently in each SELECT clause, the columns will not be overlaid. Labels or headings for each of the columns however, can differ.

In the next example, different aliases have been added to the client column in each SELECT expression; however, the labels for corresponding columns are the same. The *orders* and *client* tables have all been assigned aliases, but the *address* table has not. The table qualifer added to the country columns causes these columns to be reported separately although the column names and aliases are the same. The client columns are reported separately because each column has been assigned a different alias.

```
LIBNAME bluesky "C:\mydata\bluesky bookstore\";

TITLE1 'Client orders in US dollars or Clients located in the
        USA';

        SELECT o.clientno as client1 "Client", address.country
        "Country"
        FROM   bluesky.orders o, bluesky.address
        WHERE  o.clientno=address.clientno
               AND currency = 'USD'
               AND ord_date between '01JAN2004'd and '30AUG2004'd

OUTER UNION CORR

        SELECT c.clientno as client2 "Client", address.country
        "Country"
        FROM   bluesky.client c, bluesky.address
        WHERE  c.clientno = address.clientno
               AND address.country ='USA' ;
```

```
    Client orders in US dollars or Clients located in the USA

     client1  Country                             client2  Country
    -------------------------------------------------------------------
        2010  USA                                       .
        2010  USA                                       .
        2010  USA                                       .
        2010  USA                                       .
        8003  Canada                                    .
           .                                         1001  USA
           .                                         2010  USA
```

Tip: If two columns in different tables have the same name, SAS will treat them as a common column as long as table qualifers have not been added. If different aliases are assigned to each column, they will no longer be treated as a common column.

The first-level name or table-qualifer is required if a column exists in two or more tables listed in the FROM clause of a SELECT statement. In such a case, you cannot avoid adding a table qualifer to the columns in your SELECT clause.

My advice is to always add matching aliases to the columns you wish to overlay to avoid problems.

EXCEPT operator

General form:

EXCEPT <ALL> <CORRESPONDING|CORR>

The UNION operator described above combines the results from two SELECT expressions. The EXCEPT operator, however, is used to compare the rows returned from two or more SELECT expressions and generate a result set containing only those rows that are not in common.

If the CORR keyword is added to the EXCEPT operator, the query is processed as described for the UNION CORR operator in the previous section. The CORR keyword directs SAS to use the name of each column rather than its position in the SELECT clause when determining which columns are to be compared.

The next example contains a slightly modified version of the SELECT expression shown in the "OUTER UNION operator" section above. In this case, however, the EXCEPT operator is used between the two SELECT expressions. The use of the EXCEPT operator limits the result set to those clients not located in the United States who placed an order in US currency between January 1, 2004, and August 30, 2004.

```
LIBNAME bluesky "C:\mydata\bluesky bookstore\";

TITLE1    'Client orders in US dollars';
TITLE2    'For clients located outside of the USA';

          SELECT   orders.clientno as client, country
          FROM     bluesky.orders, bluesky.address
          WHERE    orders.clientno=address.clientno
                   AND currency = 'USD'
                   AND ord_date between '01JAN2004'd and
                    '30AUG2004'd
EXCEPT
          SELECT   client.clientno as client, country
          FROM     bluesky.client, bluesky.address
          WHERE    client.clientno = address.clientno
                   AND country ='USA' ;
```

```
Client orders in US dollars
For clients located outside of the USA

  client  country
------------------------------------
Canada
```

The logic applied to the processing of this SELECT statement appears straightforward, but many errors occur in the use of the EXCEPT operator. The query has been broken into two independent SELECT statements to show precisely which rows are compared by the EXCEPT operator. In the next example the first SELECT expression run as an independent SELECT statement returns all clients who placed an order in US currency between two dates. Two clients are retrieved; each is reported more than once because multiple product orders were placed by the clients during the specified period. The order date (ord_date) and product code (prodcode) have been included for clarity.

```
LIBNAME bluesky "C:\mydata\bluesky bookstore\";

TITLE1    'Client orders in US dollars';

SELECT    orders.clientno as client, country, ord_date, prodcode
FROM      bluesky.orders, bluesky.address
WHERE     orders.clientno=address.clientno
          AND currency = 'USD'
          AND ord_date between '01JAN2004'd and '30AUG2004'd;
```

```
Client orders in US dollars

                                            prod
client  country                  ord_date   code
----------------------------------------------------
  2010  USA                       07JUN04   500127
  2010  USA                       05MAY04   600125
  2010  USA                       12APR04   200145
  2010  USA                       12APR04   400128
  8003  Canada                    10MAR04   500500
```

The second SELECT expression retrieves all clients located in the United States. If it is run separately, it generates the results shown in this example.

```
LIBNAME bluesky "C:\mydata\bluesky bookstore\";

TITLE1   'Clients located in the United States';

SELECT   client.clientno as client, country
FROM     bluesky.client, bluesky.address
WHERE    client.clientno = address.clientno
         and country ='USA' ;
```

```
Clients located in the United States

  client  country
--------------------------------------

    1001  USA
    2010  USA
```

Now consider what happens when the two SELECT expressions are joined by an EXCEPT operator. The retrieved rows for client 2010 are common to both row sets; therefore, this client is not included in the final result set. Client 8003 is located in Canada, and it is not included in the row set of the second SELECT expression; therefore, it meets the criteria. However, why is client 1001 included in the final result set? The rowset generated by the second SELECT expression is used only to set the criteria that rows retrieved from the first SELECT expression must pass. None of the rows retrieved by the second SELECT expression is passed to the result set.

The order in which the SELECT statements are presented must be carefully considered. The retrieved rows of all SELECT statements other than the first one are used only for comparison purposes. If the SELECT statements are reversed, a different result is achieved.

The next example presents the same query as shown on page 223. However, the SELECT expressions have been reversed. Clients 1001 and 2010 are both located in the United States, and, as such, they are retrieved by the first SELECT expression. These rows are then compared to the second rowset which contains clients 2010 and 8003. Only the clients retrieved from the first SELECT expression that are not also retrieved by the second SELECT expression meet the EXCEPT criteria. As a result, only client 1001 is reported.

```
LIBNAME bluesky "C:\mydata\bluesky bookstore\";

TITLE1  'Clients located in the United States';
TITLE2  'Who did not use USD or place order between
         Jan 1 - Aug 30, 2004';


         SELECT  client.clientno as client, country
         FROM    bluesky.client, bluesky.address
         WHERE   client.clientno = address.clientno
                 and country ='USA'

 EXCEPT

         SELECT  orders.clientno as client, country
         FROM    bluesky.orders, bluesky.address
         WHERE   orders.clientno=address.clientno
                 and currency = 'USD'
                 and ord_date between '01JAN2004'd and '30AUG2004'd ;
```

```
Clients located in the United States
Who did not use USD or place order between Jan 1 - Apr 30, 2004

  client  country
------------------------------------

   1001     USA
```

ALL keyword

If the ALL keyword is added to the EXCEPT operator, the processing of the query is altered. The resulting rowset of the first SELECT expression is still compared to the rowset generated by the second SELECT expression. However, not all rows in the first rowset with a matching value in the second rowset are eliminated; instead the number of matched rows between the first and second rowset becomes important. Each matched pair of rows from the two rowsets are eliminated and rows in the first rowset without a matched row in the second rowset is passed to the result set.

The next example presents the same query shown on page 223. But now the ALL keyword has been added to the EXCEPT operator. If you compare these results to those of the earlier query, you will notice that both clients 2010 and 8003 are now reported. Client 8003 is included in the output because it does not have a matching entry in the second rowset. On the other hand, client 2010 is found in both rowsets; four rows for this client appear in the first rowset and one row appears in the second. Only the single matched pair of rows for client 2010 in the first and second rowset is eliminated from the result set. The remaining three rows are unmatched and pass to the result set.

```
LIBNAME bluesky "C:\mydata\bluesky bookstore\";

TITLE1    'Client orders in US dollars';
TITLE2    'For clients located outside of the USA';


          SELECT  orders.clientno as client, country
          FROM    bluesky.orders, bluesky.address
          WHERE   orders.clientno=address.clientno
                  AND currency = 'USD'
                  AND ord_date between '01JAN2004'd and
                  '30AUG2004'd
EXCEPT all
          SELECT  client.clientno as client, country
          FROM    bluesky.client, bluesky.address
          WHERE   client.clientno = address.clientno
                  AND country ='USA' ;
```

```
Client orders in US dollars
For clients located outside of the USA

  client  country
___________________________________

    2010  USA
    2010  USA
    2010  USA
    8003  Canada
```

Tip: To include all rows in two or more row sets except for those in common, add the ALL keyword. Without the ALL keyword, only rows from the first row set that do not match a row in the second row set are reported.

Let's take a closer look at the processing. The following illustration shows the results from each of the SELECT expressions. Recall that only rows in the first rowset are reported; those in the second rowset are used for comparison purposes only. The highlighted rows in the first rowset have a matching entry in the second rowset. One of the rows in the first rowset for client 2010 matches the row in the second rowset. As a result, it is eliminated. The three remaining rows for this client do not have a matching record in the second rowset, so they are included in the report. Client 8003 does not have a matching entry in the second rowset; therefore, it is passed to the result set.

Rowset from first SELECT expression			
client	**country**	**ord_date**	**prodcode**
2010	USA	12APR04	200145
2010	USA	12APR04	400128
2010	USA	05MAY04	600125
2010	USA	10MAR04	500127
8003	Canada	107JUN04	500127

Rowset from second SELECT expression	
client	**country**
1001	USA
2010	USA

Tip: The number of times a row is included in the result set or report when EXCEPT ALL is used in a query is equal to the number of rows in the first row set minus the number of matching rows in the second rowset.

INTERSECT operator

General form:

INTERSECT <ALL> <CORRESPONDING|CORR>

The INTERSECT operator is used when only common rows retrieved by two or more SELECT expressions are desired. Unless the CORR keyword is included, column positions in the SELECT clause are used to determine which columns in the two tables are shared.

The use of the INTERSECT operator is less subject to errors than some of the other set operators because the rows retrieved by each SELECT expressions contribute to the result set. The order in which the SELECT expressions are placed does not affect the outcome, unless the ALL keyword is used.

Caution: If columns are included in one of the SELECT clauses and not the other, no rows will be included in the result set. The intersection operation requires that the rows selected from each table are exactly the same in terms of column names and column values.

In the next example the SELECT expressions used in previous examples are shown, but with an INTERSECT operator between them. As illustrated in the preceding example, only client 2010 is present in the row sets resulting from each of the SELECT expression. Therefore, it is the only row included in the report or result set.

```
LIBNAME bluesky "C:\mydata\bluesky bookstore\";

TITLE1   'Client orders in US dollars';
TITLE2   'From US-based clients';

          SELECT orders.clientno as client, country
          FROM   bluesky.orders, bluesky.address
          WHERE  orders.clientno=address.clientno
                 AND currency = 'USD' AND ord_date
                between '01JAN2004'd
                AND '30AUG2004'd

INTERSECT

          SELECT client.clientno as client, country
          FROM   bluesky.client, bluesky.address
          WHERE  client.clientno = address.clientno
                 AND country ='USA' ;
```

```
Client orders in US dollars
From US-based clients

  client  country
-----------------------------------
    2010  USA
```

ALL keyword

By default, the INTERSECT set operation generates a result set that contains only distinct rows that successfully meet the criteria. If the ALL keyword is used, the rows resulting from the first SELECT expression are matched one-to-one with the rowset generated by the second SELECT expression. The order of the SELECT expressions is important because the number of matching rows in the second rowset determines the number of rows passed to the result set.

The next example illustrates an INTERSECT operation without the ALL keyword and the resulting report. To effectively illustrate the processing differences that occur with the addition of the ALL keyword, a second address for client 2010 was added to the Bluesky *address* table. The INSERT statement used to add the new address is included in the example. More information on the INSERT statement is included in Chapter 6, "Creating and Managing Tables and Views."

```
LIBNAME bluesky "C:\mydata\bluesky bookstore\";

TITLE1   'Clients in the address and orders tables';

INSERT into bluesky.address
         values (2010, '121 East 61 Street',
         'New York','NY','10022','USA',' ');

         SELECT  *
         FROM    bluesky.address

INTERSECT CORR

         SELECT  *
         FROM    bluesky.orders;
```

```
Clients in the address and orders tables

clientNo
________

    1001
    2010
    3007
    4008
    5005
    6090
    7008
    8003
```

Although there are two rows in the *address* table for client 2010, only one occurrence of the client number is reported. Compare the above results with those of the same query but with the addition of the ALL keyword shown in the next example. Client 2010 is reported twice in this report, once for each occurrence in the *address* table.

```
LIBNAME bluesky "C:\mydata\bluesky bookstore\";

TITLE1   'Clients in both the address and orders tables';

         SELECT  *
         FROM    bluesky.address

INTERSECT CORR ALL

         SELECT  *
         FROM    bluesky.orders;
```

Tip: Wondering why the report includes the clientno even though an asterisk is used in the SELECT clause? The INTERSECT operation returns only columns common to each contributing rowset.

```
Clients in both the address and orders tables

clientNo
--------
    1001
    2010
    2010
    3007
    4008
    5005
    6090
    7008
    8003
```

Subqueries

SQL statements containing subqueries are similar in many ways to those incorporating joins. In both cases, the goal is to retrieve or otherwise use information from one or more tables to control the rows retrieved from another table. In addition, the performance of SQL queries using joins and subqueries is similar.

Many users, especially those starting out with SQL, find subqueries more difficult to understand and construct than joins. Why then bother with subqueries? Although join operations provide a powerful tool, subqueries offer several unique advantages over joins. Subqueries can be used to compare every row in a table to a single retrieved or calculated value from another table or the same table. It is also possible to easily compare each variable in a SELECT statement to a set of values retrieved from another table. In addition, complex nested subqueries with each statement relying on the outcome of a nested or other statement can also be constructed.

Guidelines

- Subqueries are usually included in SELECT, WHERE, or HAVING clauses of SELECT, UPDATE, or INSERT statements.
- The SELECT statement that includes the subquery is referred to as the outer query. Subqueries are often referred to as inner queries.
- Subqueries must return a single value or a single column of values. An asterisk can only be used when a subquery is part of an existence test.
- All valid SELECT statements can be used in a subquery, although neither ORDER BY nor INTO clauses are permitted.
- Subqueries can reference other subqueries. Nested subqueries are processed from the innermost subquery outward.
- Subqueries can be included on the right or left side of an operator in a WHERE or HAVING clause. All queries included in this chapter are written with the subquery on the right of the operator to provide appropriate examples for SQL Pass-Through Facility users.

SAS/ACCESS and SQL Pass-Through Facility users: In the ANSI-92 standard, a subquery is allowed on both the left and right side of the operator. Database systems that have adopted other standards permit a subquery only on the right side of the operator.

FROM clause subqueries

Although a subquery may be included in a FROM clause, it does not produce the expected results. This form of subquery does not generate one or more values for comparison with variables in the outer query. Instead, it generates a view from which the outer query draws its data.

Tip: A subquery in a FROM clause generates an IN-LINE VIEW, a topic that is covered in more detail in Chapter 6, "Creating and Managing Tables and Views." Only subqueries in WHERE and HAVING clauses are discussed in this chapter.

The next example shows a SELECT statement with a subquery in the FROM clause. The SELECT statement in the subquery retrieves the table names (memname) in the Bluesky library that meet the WHERE clause criteria from a dictionary table called *members*. Only the *orders* table is returned by the subquery with a prefix of *Bluesky* added. You might expect the outer query to now read as `SELECT * FROM BLUESKY.ORDERS` and return all of the rows of the *orders* table. However, the outer SELECT clause does not retrieve the contents of the tables, but rather retrieves all of the rows resulting from the inner query.

```
LIBNAME bluesky "C:\mydata\bluesky bookstore\";

SELECT    *
FROM      (SELECT 'bluesky'||'.'||memname
          FROM dictionary.members
          WHERE memname like "ORDERS " and memtype = "DATA"
          and libname = 'BLUESKY') ;
```

```
________________________________________

bluesky.ORDERS
```

Tip: The subquery selects the table name from the data dictionary *members* table. The data dictionary is covered in detail in Chapter 7, "Building Interactive Applications," with additional information contained in Appendix B, "Dictionary Table Descriptions."

Subqueries returning single values

SELECT
INTO
FROM
ON
▸ WHERE
GROUP BY
▸ HAVING
ORDER BY
USING;

General form:

WHERE <table|alias.>column|expression =
(SUBQUERY EXPRESSION)
<LOGICAL OPERATOR condition…>

HAVING <table|alias.>column|expression =
(SUBQUERY EXPRESSION)
<LOGICAL OPERATOR condition…>

Tip: Notice that ORDER BY and INTO clauses are not allowed in a subquery. The inclusion of an ORDER BY clause in the subquery will cause an error message, and processing of the query will stop. However, if you include an INTO clause in your subquery, it will generate the following WARNING message and processing will continue:

```
WARNING: INTO clause that is not in the outermost query
         block will be ignored.
```

The simplest form of subquery is that involving the comparison of the values in each row of one table against another table. A separate SELECT statement is used to retrieve a single, specific value from another table. This allows for maximum flexibility and program reusability. Instead of hardcoding a value into the SELECT statement, a specific value is retrieved as required.

The next example shows a query that generates a report of all invoices placed by a client in Paris. It assumes that the client number of the Paris customer must be retrieved before the report can be generated.

```
LIBNAME bluesky "C:\mydata\bluesky bookstore\";

SELECT   invoice,prodcode,ord_date
FROM     bluesky.orders

WHERE    clientno = (SELECT clientno
                     FROM   bluesky.address
                     WHERE  city= 'Paris');
```

invoice	prod code	ord_date
040310-01	100345	10MAR04
030411-01	400128	11APR03
041223-04	500116	23JUL04
040412-03	600489	12APR04

The subquery portion included in parentheses in the WHERE clause determines the client number for the Paris customer. The subquery is replaced by the retrieved client number (clientno) value when the outer SELECT statement is processed. At this stage, internally the outer SELECT statement would appear as shown in the next example.

```
LIBNAME bluesky "C:\mydata\bluesky bookstore\";

SELECT   invoice,prodcode,ord_date
FROM     bluesky.orders
WHERE    clientno = 7008;
```

invoice	prod code	ord_date
040310-01	100345	10MAR04
030411-01	400128	11APR03
041223-04	500116	23JUL04
040412-03	600489	12APR04

Tip: A subquery coupled with an EQUAL operator in a WHERE clause criterion must return a single value. In the above example, only a single Paris customer can be retrieved by the subquery. If the subquery returns more than one value, the following error message will be printed to the SAS log and the query will not be processed:

```
ERROR: Subquery evaluated to more than one row.
```

Although the value returned by the subquery SELECT statement may be a single, specific value, it is often the result of a summary function such as MAX or AVG. Consider how you would generate a report detailing all client orders, which are higher than the average size or dollar amount of all book orders received. A query could be written to first obtain the average book order size and sale amount for the company and those results used to generate the client order report. The set of queries needed to generate the report and the result of each are shown in the next example.

Step 1: Calculate the average quantity and total sale values from the existing orders.

```
LIBNAME bluesky "C:\mydata\bluesky bookstore\";

SELECT   round(avg(quantity)) "Average Order",
         round (avg(totsale)) "Average Total Sale"
FROM     bluesky.orders;
```

Average Order	Average Total Sale
538	18770

Step 2: Compare all orders against the average values.

```
SELECT   clientno "Client", invoice "Invoice",
         ord_date "Order Date" format=date10.,
         quantity "Quantity" format=comma5.,
         totsale "Total Sale" format=dollar12.2
FROM     bluesky.orders
WHERE    quantity GE 538 OR totsale GE 18770;
```

Client orders in US dollars
For clients located outside of the USA

Client	Invoice	Order Date	Quantity	Total Sale
1001	030506-01	06MAY2003	500	$32,875.00
1001	030506-01	06MAY2003	600	$20,700.00
4008	031110-01	10NOV2003	1,400	$76,972.00
2010	031020-01	20OCT2003	2,900	$3,390.00
8003	030109-01	09JAN2003	800	$14,400.00
1001	030906-01	06SEP2003	1,000	$34,500.00
6090	030927-01	27SEP2003	500	$27,490.00
2010	040412-01	12APR2004	700	$39,375.00
2010	040412-01	12APR2004	1,230	$41,820.00
2010	040505-01	05MAY2004	600	$8,580.00
3007	041212-02	12JUN2004	5,000	$225,000.00
3007	041223-01	23JUL2004	590	$15,487.50
5005	041223-02	23JUL2004	1,500	$82,500.00

However, book orders change over time so the average order size and average total sale also change. A query that encompasses both of the tasks above into a single statement would allow the report to be easily generated for any time period. The next example contains a SELECT statement that includes two subqueries that generate the same report as shown in the above example.

```
LIBNAME bluesky "C:\mydata\bluesky bookstore\";

TITLE1   'Order details for above-average sales and quantity';

SELECT   clientno "Client", invoice "Invoice",
         ord_date "Order Date" format=date10.,
         quantity "Quantity" format=comma5.,
         totsale "Total Sale" format=dollar12.2
FROM     bluesky.orders

WHERE    quantity GE   (SELECT   round(avg(quantity))
                        FROM bluesky.orders)

         OR totsale GE (SELECT   round(avg(totsale))
                        FROM bluesky.orders);
```

Order details for above-average sales and quantity

Client	Invoice	Order Date	Quantity	Total Sale
1001	030506-01	06MAY2003	500	$32,875.00
1001	030506-01	06MAY2003	600	$20,700.00
4008	031110-01	10NOV2003	1,400	$76,972.00
2010	031020-01	20OCT2003	2,900	$3,390.00
8003	030109-01	09JAN2003	800	$14,400.00
1001	030906-01	06SEP2003	1,000	$34,500.00
6090	030927-01	27SEP2003	500	$27,490.00
2010	040412-01	12APR2004	700	$39,375.00
2010	040412-01	12APR2004	1,230	$41,820.00
2010	040505-01	05MAY2004	600	$8,580.00
3007	041212-02	12JUN2004	5,000	$225,000.00
3007	041223-01	23JUL2004	590	$15,487.50
5005	041223-02	23JUL2004	1,500	$82,500.00

Subqueries bypass many of the restrictions imposed on the inclusion of summary functions in SELECT statements. If you recall, a summary function cannot be used as part of the criteria in a WHERE clause. However, as shown in the above example, both of the subqueries in the WHERE clause contain a summary function. The subqueries are processed first, resulting in a single value of 505 and 21560 respectively, with which the *orders* table quantity values are subsequently compared.

> **Tip:** Summary functions such as the ROUND function here may only be included in HAVING and SELECT clauses in a SELECT statement, whether it is part of an outer or inner subquery. In this example, the subquery is evaluated first, returning a single value for substitution into the WHERE clause criteria. When the WHERE clause is processed, the returned value rather than the summary function is seen.

Although it is possible to achieve this result using a join, a SELECT statement with a subquery provides a simpler solution. The next example gives one possible query that would produce the same result as the subquery above. Notice that the join is achieved through a linking of both the invoice and product code columns. This is necessary because it is only the combination of these two columns that uniquely identifies each row in the table. The query also includes a HAVING clause that allows for the inclusion of a summary function in the outer query.

```
LIBNAME bluesky "C:\mydata\bluesky bookstore\";

SELECT  order1.clientno, order1.invoice,
        order1.ord_date,
        order1.quantity,order1.totsale format=dollar10.2

FROM    bluesky.orders order1,
        bluesky.orders order2

WHERE   order1.invoice = order2.invoice
        and order1.prodcode = order2.prodcode

HAVING  order1.quantity >= round(avg(order2.quantity))
        OR order1.quantity >= round(avg(order2.totsale));
```

clientNo	invoice	ord_date	quantity	totsale
8003	030109-01	09JAN03	800	$14,400.00
3007	041223-01	23JUL04	590	$15,487.50
2010	040412-01	12APR04	700	$39,375.00
4008	031110-01	10NOV03	1400	$76,972.00
3007	041212-02	12JUN04	5000	$225000.00
2010	031020-01	20OCT03	2900	$3,390.00
5005	041223-02	23JUL04	1500	$82,500.00
2010	040412-01	12APR04	1230	$41,820.00
1001	030506-01	06MAY03	600	$20,700.00
1001	030906-01	06SEP03	1000	$34,500.00
2010	040505-01	05MAY04	600	$8,580.00

Tip: The remerging capability of SAS is used in this example. The average values are calculated on a first pass through the table and those results are remerged automatically with the *orders* table as an extra column value.

Subqueries returning multiple values

SELECT
INTO
FROM
ON
► WHERE
GROUP BY
► HAVING
ORDER BY
USING;

General form:

WHERE <table|alias.>column|expression IN
(SUBQUERY EXPRESSION)|
<LOGICAL OPERATOR condition…>

HAVING <table|alias.>expression IN (SUBQUERY EXPRESSION)
<LOGICAL OPERATOR condition…>

The subquery examples in the previous section all returned a single value, but subqueries may also return multiple values from a single column. The next example shows a subquery which returns several client numbers. The WHERE clause allows for the possibility of several values resulting from the subquery by using an IN operator instead of an EQUAL operator.

```
LIBNAME bluesky "C:\mydata\bluesky bookstore\";

TITLE1 'All orders for customers in the USA';

SELECT clientno, ord_date, invoice
FROM   bluesky.orders

WHERE  clientno IN (SELECT clientno
                    FROM bluesky.address
                    WHERE country = 'USA');
```

```
All orders for customers in the USA

clientno  ord_date  invoice
_____________________________
    2010   12APR04  040412-01
    1001   07FEB03  030207-01
    1001   06MAY03  030506-01
    2010   20OCT03  031020-01
    2010   12APR04  040412-01
    1001   06MAY03  030506-01
    1001   06MAY03  030506-01
    1001   06SEP03  030906-01
    2010   07JUN04  040607-01
    2010   05MAY04  040505-01
```

Tip: If you are unsure whether multiple values may be returned by a subquery, use an IN operator rather than an EQUAL operator.

The subquery in the previous example is executed first and the results substituted into the WHERE clause. Only those rows in the *orders* table that meet the WHERE clause condition generated by the subquery are selected as summarized in the next example.

ORDERS table: sample rows with results from outer query highlighted		
clientno	**ord_date**	**invoice**
1001	07FEB03	030207-01
1001	06MAY03	030506-01
1001	06MAY03	030506-01
1001	06MAY03	030506-01
4008	10NOV03	031110-01
2010	20OCT03	031020-01
4008	15MAR03	030315-01
7008	11APR03	030411-01
5005	11APR03	030411-01

Results of INNER QUERY
clientno
1001
2010

A more complex subquery is given in the next example. Here a join between the *orders* and *client* tables is included so that the company name rather than the client number appears in the report. There are several important aspects of the syntax of this SQL statement that should be reviewed. Notice that not all of the column names in the outer or main query are prefixed by the table name.

As discussed earlier in this chapter, the table name is required if the column occurs in more than one table and the table name is often added to other columns in the SELECT statement for clarity. However, in the next example neither the inner nor outer queries include a table qualifer in the SELECT clause nor is the table qualifier required although the *address* table is referenced in both queries. This example is given to show the independent nature of a subquery.

Recall that the subquery is processed first, and the values returned are substituted in the outer query before the outer query is processed. At the time of processing, SAS sees only the subquery and not the outer query. All columns listed in the SELECT clause of a subquery are assumed to belong to the table referenced in the nearest FROM clause. As a result, there is no need to include table qualifers in the inner query unless a join is included. When the outer query is executed, the values from the subquery, rather than the subquery itself, are seen.

When working with queries, you must qualify columns with the table name if the same column name is included in more than one table. Otherwise, an error message such as the following will be written to the SAS log:

```
ERROR: Ambiguous reference, column clientno is in more than one
table.
```

However, within a subquery, all columns are assumed to belong to the table in the nearest FROM clause, that is, the FROM clause within the inner query. As a result, it is not necessary to qualify columns included in the SELECT clause of an inner query that may also be found in a table in the outer query.

> **Tip:** It is never incorrect to qualify columns. Many SQL programmers routinely add table qualifers to all column names in their queries when they are working with more than one table, whether or not the query includes a subquery. If you use meaningful but short aliases for your tables, it takes very little extra effort to qualify each column.

```
LIBNAME bluesky "C:\mydata\bluesky bookstore\";

TITLE1   'All orders for customers in the USA';

SELECT   client.company, orders.ord_date, orders.invoice
FROM     bluesky.orders, bluesky.client

WHERE    orders.clientno IN (SELECT clientno
                             FROM   bluesky.address
                             WHERE  country = 'USA')

         AND orders.clientno = client.clientno;
```

```
All orders for customers in the USA

company                                      ord_date  invoice
_______________________________________________________________

University of Texas                           07FEB03  030207-01
University of Texas                           06MAY03  030506-01
University of Texas                           06MAY03  030506-01
University of Texas                           06MAY03  030506-01
University of Texas                           06SEP03  030906-01
Chicago State University                      20OCT03  031020-01
Chicago State University                      12APR04  040412-01
Chicago State University                      12APR04  040412-01
Chicago State University                      05MAY04  040505-01
Chicago State University                      07JUN04  040607-01
```

A single SELECT statement may include more than one subquery. In the next example the criteria for the both the quantity and client number are built from subqueries. The quantity in the *orders* table is compared to a single value, the average quantity of all orders placed, to find only the above-average orders. The clients are again limited to those in the USA using a check of each client number in the *orders* table against the *address* table.

```
LIBNAME bluesky "C:\mydata\bluesky bookstore\";

TITLE1    'Above-average orders for US Customers';
TITLE2    'Based on average for all customer orders';

SELECT    clientno "Client", invoice "Invoice#",
          ord_date "Date", quantity "Quantity", totsale "Sale Total"
FROM      bluesky.orders ord1

WHERE     quantity GE (SELECT round(avg(quantity))
                       FROM bluesky.orders ord2)

          AND clientno IN (SELECT clientno
                           FROM bluesky.address
                           WHEREcountry = 'USA');
```

```
Above-average orders for US Customers
Based on average for all customer orders
                                                  Sale
  Client  Invoice#          Date  Quantity       Total
----------------------------------------------------------
    1001  030506-01    06MAY03        600        20700
    2010  031020-01    20OCT03       2900         3390
    1001  030906-01    06SEP03       1000        34500
    2010  040412-01    12APR04        700        39375
    2010  040412-01    12APR04       1230        41820
   2010  040505-01    05MAY04        600        8580
```

Tip: Subqueries written with an IN operator are often easier to write and understand than join operations. Another advantage subqueries give you is the ability to compare to a column or expression in a WHERE clause to the result of a summary function. Summary functions are limited to SELECT and HAVING clauses unless subqueries are included in the SELECT statement.

Correlated subqueries

SELECT
INTO
▶ FROM
ON
▶ WHERE
GROUP BY
▶ HAVING
ORDER BY
USING;

General form:

FROM <libref.>table <alias>

WHERE <table|alias.>column|expression OPERATOR
(SUBQUERY EXPRESSION)
<LOGICAL OPERATOR condition…>

HAVING <table|alias.>expression OPERATOR
(SUBQUERY EXPRESSION)
<LOGICAL OPERATOR condition…>

SUBQUERY EXPRESSION:

(SELECT **clause**
FROM <libref.>table <alias>
<ON clause>

WHERE <table|alias.>column|expression = table|alias.column|expression
<LOGICAL OPERATOR condition…>

<GROUP BY clause>

<HAVING <table|alias.>expression = table|alias.expression
<LOGICAL OPERATOR condition…>>

NOTE: The highlighted alias name in the subquery references a table alias in the outer query as shown in the main syntax description above.

In the previous examples, the subquery has been used to return a value or values for comparison to a column in a WHERE clause criterion. In each case, the subquery was an independent part of the SQL statement. However, it is also possible for a subquery to reference a column value that is part of the outer or main query. Such subqueries are called correlated subqueries because each time the subquery is executed, the value returned by the subquery is compared to or correlated with a value returned by the outer query. These subqueries are not processed independently from the main query. Furthermore, they are not processed only once before the execution of the main or outer query. Instead they are processed each time the column value in the outer query changes.

Tip: A correlated subquery can return only a single column of values; only one column or a summary function can be included in the SELECT clause. The column used in the WHERE clause to establish a relationship between the rows returned by the outer query and the values of the subquery is also implicitly retrieved.

The next example shows a correlated subquery that is based on a query shown in the preceding example. In the previous query, a single average order quantity and value for all orders placed at Bluesky Publishing was calculated by the subquery. This average value was then compared to the order quantities for each row in turn from the *orders* table. The subquery was executed only once, and it was completely independent from the outer or main query.

In the next example, on the other hand, the inner query returns an average value and sale amount for each client. Each row in the *orders* table is still compared to the average order quantity, but now the average changes for each client. In order to process this SQL statement, the subquery must be executed several times. The average value and sale amount is recalculated in the subquery for each client number read from a row in the *orders* table.

Tip: Column correlation must be specified in a WHERE clause. An ON clause requires a FROM clause with a JOIN keyword between two tables. Adding the table to the FROM clause of the inner subquery generates a new join within the subquery. However, the function of a subquery is to join or correlate columns in a table referenced in the outer query with a table in the inner query.

```
LIBNAME bluesky "C:\mydata\bluesky bookstore\";

TITLE1    'Order details for above-average order size or sale amount' ;
TITLE2    'by Customer';

SELECT    clientno "Client", invoice "Invoice#",
          ord_date "Date" format=date9., quantity "Qty" format=comma8.,
          totsale "Sale Total" format= dollar12.2
FROM      bluesky.orders ord1

WHERE     quantity GE (SELECT  round(avg(quantity))
                       FROM   bluesky.orders
                       WHERE  orders.clientno = ord1.clientno )

          OR totsale GE  (SELECT  round(avg(totsale))
                          FROM   bluesky.orders
                          WHERE  orders.clientno = ord1.clientno )
ORDER BY clientno ;
```

```
Order details for above-average order size or sale amount
by Customer

   Client  Invoice#          Date         Qty     Sale Total
--------------------------------------------------------------

     1001  030506-01   06MAY2003          500    $32,875.00
     1001  030506-01   06MAY2003          600    $20,700.00
     1001  030906-01   06SEP2003        1,000    $34,500.00
     2010  040412-01   12APR2004        1,230    $41,820.00
     2010  040412-01   12APR2004          700    $39,375.00
     2010  031020-01   20OCT2003        2,900     $3,390.00
     3007  041212-02   12JUN2004        5,000   $225,000.00
     4008  031110-01   10NOV2003        1,400    $76,972.00
     5005  041223-02   23JUL2004        1,500    $82,500.00
     6090  030927-01   27SEP2003          500    $27,490.00
     7008  041223-04   23JUL2004          400    $13,600.00
     7008  040310-01   10MAR2004          180    $11,700.00
     8003  030109-01   09JAN2003          800    $14,400.00
     8003  030109-01   09JAN2003          275     $4,661.25
     8003  040310-02   10MAR2004          350    $15,312.50
```

An alias has been assigned to the *orders* table referenced in the outer query to distinguish it from the *orders* table in the inner query. Because aliases in the FROM clauses of each of the inner queries are optional, they have not been included in this example.

> **Tip:** When referencing the same table in both an inner and outer query, you must assign an alias to the common column of the queries.

You will notice that the columns in the SELECT clause in both the inner and outer queries in the preceding example are not qualified with the table name. When a subquery is processed all columns are assumed to belong to the tables in the nearest FROM clause. For example, when the inner query retrieving the average total sale (totsale) is processed, columns are assumed to be drawn from the *orders* table included in the FROM clause within the inner query.

As discussed in the previous section, qualified column names can be routinely used throughout your query. In most cases this makes the query easier to read. However, I find when using correlated subqueries that it is often easier to interpret the SQL statement if only the correlated columns are qualified.

A graphical version of the processing steps of the inner and outer queries is included in the next example. Each row of the outer query is compared to the corresponding value from the inner query. When the client number (clientno) of the outer query changes, the average values for the corresponding client number are calculated. For example, an average quantity of 510 and an average total sale value of $18,620 are compared to each row of the *orders* table with a client number value of 1001. The highlighted rows in the outer query results table would be included in the report. When the client number value in the *orders* table changes to 2010, the subquery will be reexecuted to calculate average values based on the orders for that client.

Tip: Each time the inner subquery is executed, a single value is returned for comparison with the column value of the current row in the outer table. As a result, operators such as =, <, and > can be used with a correlated subquery.

ORDERS table: sample rows with results from outer query highlighted			
clientno	**ord_date**	**totsale**	**quantity**
1001	07FEB03	2850.00	300
1001	06MAY03	2175.00	150
1001	06MAY03	32875.00	500
1001	06MAY03	20700.00	600
4008	10NOV03	76792.00	1400
2010	20OCT03	3390.00	2900
4008	15MAR03	5468.75	125
7008	11APR03	6800.00	200
5005	11APR03	8750.00	200

Results of first INNER QUERY	
clientno	**Average quantity**
1001	510

Results of second INNER QUERY	
clientno	**Average totsale**
1001	18620

As seen in the example above, the correlated subqueries are no longer independent from the outer query. Instead, each inner query references a column that exists in the outer query. In our example, the *orders* table is the source table for the outer query and also for each of the subqueries.

Tip: With correlated subqueries, the subquery or inner query is executed multiple times, once for each row in the outer query table. To optimize performance of correlated subqueries, the outer query should be carefully constructed to ensure that all unnecessary rows are eliminated from the table. In addition, an index of the inner query table may be beneficial. More information on indexes is provided in Chapter 6, "Creating and Managing Tables and Views."

Each time the subquery is executed, the value from the outer table and the result of the subquery are stored in an indexed cache. If the same value is encountered in another row of the outer table, the result is retrieved from the cache rather than reexecuting the subquery.

Nested subqueries

The above examples all included subqueries designed to generate one or more values that are incorporated into a WHERE or HAVING clause of an outer query. It is also possible for each subquery to call another subquery to establish criteria for the WHERE or HAVING clause of the inner query. The next example shows a modified version of the previous query. In this example, rather than calculating the average quantity ordered for all customers, the average is applied to the results returned by a subquery. The subquery that retrieves the client numbers for customers in the US is nested inside the subquery that calculates the average quantity for that group of customers.

```
LIBNAME bluesky "C:\mydata\bluesky bookstore\";

TITLE1   'Above-average orders for US Customers';
TITLE2   'Based on average for all US customers';

SELECT   clientno "Client", invoice "Invoice#",
         ord_date "Date", quantity "Quantity" format=comma6.,
         totsale "Sale Total" format=dollar10.2
FROM     bluesky.orders ord1

WHERE    quantity GE
         (SELECT round(avg(quantity))
         FROM    bluesky.orders ord2
         WHERE   ord2.clientno IN (SELECT clientno
                                  FROM    bluesky.address
                                  WHERE   country = 'USA'))

         AND clientno IN (SELECT clientno
                         FROM    bluesky.address
                         WHERE   country ='USA');
```

```
Above-average orders for US Customers
Based on average for all US customers

  Client  Invoice#         Date  Quantity  Sale Total
---------------------------------------------------
    2010  031020-01   20OCT03     2,900   $3,390.00
    1001  030906-01   06SEP03     1,000  $34,500.00
    2010  040412-01   12APR04     1,230  $41,820.00
```

Existence tests

SELECT
INTO
▶ FROM
ON
▶ WHERE
GROUP BY
▶ HAVING
ORDER BY
USING;

General form:

WHERE <table|alias.>column|expression EXISTS | NOT EXISTS (SUBQUERY EXPRESSION) <LOGICAL OPERATOR condition…>

HAVING <table|alias.>expression EXISTS |NOT EXISTS (SUBQUERY EXPRESSION) <LOGICAL OPERATOR condition…>

A special operator, EXISTS is available for use with subqueries. The EXISTS operator evaluates the subquery to its right as TRUE or FALSE based on whether any rows are retrieved by the subquery. The subquery itself does not return any values to the outer query. Instead, the retrieval of a single by the subquery causes the subquery to evaluate to TRUE and allows the outer query to be processed.

> **Tip:** An EXISTS or NOT EXISTS test can only evaluate to TRUE or FALSE. It is not possible for a result of NULL to occur.

The next example shows an example of a simple subquery using an EXISTS operator. Notice that the EXISTS operator is not preceded by a column or expression. The WHERE clause evaluates to TRUE if results are returned by the subquery. In this example, the title, ISBN, and prodcode for all rows in the *stock* table would be reported if a single order of more than 300 copies of a book priced at less than $50 was received.

```
LIBNAME bluesky "C:\mydata\bluesky bookstore\";

SELECT  title, isbn, prodcode
FROM    bluesky.stock
WHERE   exists    (SELECT *
                   FROM    bluesky.orders
                   WHERE   totsale le 15000 and quantity > 300);
```

Tip: If a subquery appears to the right of an EXISTS operator, a column of values is not returned by the subquery. Rather, the retrieval of at least one row by the subquery causes the existence test to evaluate to TRUE. As a result, the choice of column name(s) in the SELECT statement is arbitrary and an asterisk may be included instead.

A correlated subquery operates in a similar fashion when coupled with an EXISTS operator; however, there is one distinction. The product code (prodcode) from each row of the *stock* table is checked to determine whether a row with a corresponding product code exists or was retrieved from the inner query. Only those rows with product codes that exist in the subquery result set are reported.

The next example shows a correlated subquery and an EXISTS operator. The query is the same as the one presented in the previous example except that an additional WHERE clause criterion linking the outer and inner queries has been added. This correlation or link causes the existence test to be evaluated for each product code in the *stock* table. Only the four rows with corresponding product code values that meet the criteria set out in the subquery evaluate to TRUE and are included in the report.

```
LIBNAME bluesky "C:\mydata\bluesky bookstore\";

TITLE1   'Books less than $50 that sold more than 100 copies';

SELECT  title, isbn, prodcode
FROM    bluesky.stock
WHERE   exists (SELECT *
                FROM   bluesky.orders
                WHERE  totsale le 5000 and quantity > 100
                       and orders.prodcode = stock.prodcode);
```

```
Books less than $50 that sold more than 100 copies

                                                             prod
title                                         isbn           code
--------------------------------------------------------------------
Decorative Arts                               1-7890-1072-1  300678
The Ultimate Philosophy                       1-7890-2878-7  300456
The Underground Economy                       1-7890-5477-x  300680
Start a Business Using a Computer             1-7890-5634-9  500238
Women Writers                                 1-7890-3468-x  600780
The Maestro                                   1-7890-3007-2  600125
```

An alternative to the existence test is a nonexistence test which is achieved through the addition of a NOT keyword. The outer query can only retrieve rows if the subquery evaluates to FALSE.

The next example includes the same subquery as presented in the previous example, except that the NOT keyword has been added. This query does not retrieve any rows from the *stock* table because the subquery evaluates to TRUE. Put another way, there are rows in the *orders* table for which the WHERE clause criterion is TRUE. The existence of rows means that the test for nonexistence fails, and so none of the rows in the *stock* table can be retrieved by the outer query.

```
LIBNAME bluesky "C:\mydata\bluesky bookstore\";

SELECT   title, isbn, prodcode
FROM     bluesky.stock
WHERE    not exists  (SELECT *
                      FROM    bluesky.orders
                      WHERE   totsale le 15000 and quantity > 100);
```

SAS log:

```
NOTE: No rows were selected.
```

If a correlated subquery is used instead, the results are very different. In the next example a WHERE clause has been added to the subquery, linking or correlating the inner and outer queries. As a result, each row in the *stock* table is checked to determine if a row with corresponding product code exists in the subquery. Only the lack of a corresponding row in the subquery causes the test for nonexistence to pass. In this example, all rows from the *stock* table except the four shown in the example will pass the nonexistence test.

```
LIBNAME bluesky "C:\mydata\bluesky bookstore\";

SELECT  title, isbn, prodcode
FROM    bluesky.stock
WHERE   not exists  (SELECT *
                     FROM   bluesky.orders
                     WHERE  totsale le 15000 and quantity > 100
                     AND    stock.prodcode = orders.prodcode);
```

title	ISBN	prod Code
Democracy in America	1-7890-1256-2	300289
The Art of Computer Programming	1-7890-1209-0	500120
Introduction to Computer_Science	1-7890-3473-6	500890
Computer: Beginners Guide	1-7890-2829-9	500500
Engineering Infrastructure Modeling	1-7890-3245-8	200345
Space Sciences	1-7890-1290-2	200145
Managing Water Resources	1-7890-5698-5	200678
Materials Science	1-7890-1267-8	200507
Risks in Life - % Gain or Loss?	1-7890-4578-9	600123
Greece and Beyond	1-7890-2390-4	600451
Mountaineering Skills	1-7890-3278-4	600489
The 10% Solution	1-7890-4578-9	400457
Medications and Maintenance	1-7890-3467-1	400345
Unconventional treatments	1-7890-7893-8	400102
National Library of Medicine	1-7890-3479-5	400178
Book of Science and Nature	1-7890-4567-3	100890
Free Thinking in Mathematics	1-7890-3478-7	100601
Science and Technology	1-7890-1280-5	100406

Tip: An asterisk can also be used in the SELECT clause of a subquery that is combined with the NOT EXISTS operator.

The next example shows a SELECT statement that uses the NOT EXISTS operator to determine if there are any customers who have not placed an order between the dates shown. The inner and outer subqueries are related or correlated by the client number criteria in the WHERE clause of the subquery. The subquery still checks for the existence of orders in the *orders* table between the two dates. However, now the test for nonexistence is checked for each client number. As a result, each client who did not place an order between the indicated dates is assigned a FALSE result and passes the nonexistence test.

```
LIBNAME bluesky "C:\mydata\bluesky bookstore\";

TITLE1 'Clients who did not order books';
TITLE2 'Between January 1, 2004 and April 30, 2004';

SELECT   client.clientno, address.email
FROM     bluesky.address, bluesky.client
WHERE    not exists  (SELECT *
                      FROM    bluesky.orders
                      WHERE   ord_date between '01JAN2004'D and
                              '30APR2004'D
                      AND orders.clientno = client.clientno)
         AND address.clientno = client.clientno;
```

```
Clients who did not order books
Between January 1, 2004 and April 30, 2004

clientno  email
-----------------------------------------
1001      eagleton@usa.com
```

> **Tip:** Criteria built on either the EXISTS and NOT EXISTS operator can be part of a WHERE clause that includes other criteria.

The next figure gives a graphical representation of the processing of an EXISTS or NOT EXISTS test when a correlated subquery is used. The correlated subquery is processed first and retrieves a set of values. Next the outer query checks for the existence/nonexistence of a row in the subquery result set for each client number.

Step 1: Inner query is processed

ORDERS Table	
client no	**ord_date**
8003	01FEB04
4008	01FEB04
3007	07MAR04
7008	10MAR04
8003	10MAR04
8003	10MAR04
4008	10MAR04
4008	08APR04
6090	10APR04
2010	12APR04
2010	12APR04
5005	12APR04
7008	12APR04

Step 2: Each clientno value in *client* table is checked against inner query results for existence/nonexistence of a record **for that clientno**.

CLIENT Table	Comparison of each clientno with the subquery results	
clientno	**exists**	**not exists**
1001	FALSE	TRUE
2010	TRUE	FALSE
3007	TRUE	FALSE
4008	TRUE	FALSE
5005	TRUE	FALSE
6090	TRUE	FALSE
7008	TRUE	FALSE
8003	TRUE	FALSE

Tip: Only when a correlated subquery is used does the evaluation of TRUE or FALSE occur on a row-by-row basis.

An existence test may also be included in a HAVING clause. In this case, the WHERE clause of the subquery correlates a column of values from a table referenced in the subquery with the GROUP BY values.

The next example shows a correlated subquery and an existence test using a HAVING clause. A GROUP BY clause is used in the outer query to produce summary statistics for each currency in the *currency* table. The subquery builds a link between the currency values of the inner and outer query using the highlighted WHERE clause. The resulting query reports group statistics only for those currencies that have entries in the *orders* table.

```
LIBNAME bluesky "C:\mydata\bluesky bookstore\";

TITLE1    'Currency information';
TITLE2    'for orders of $250,000 or more';
TITLE3    'April 1, 2003 to March 31, 2004';

SELECT    currency "Currency", min(exchrate)  "Min" format=12.2,
          max(exchrate) "Max" format=12.2,avg(exchrate) "Avg"
          format=12.2
FROM      bluesky.currency c1
GROUP BY  currency
HAVING    exists   (SELECT  *
                    FROM     bluesky.orders
                    WHERE    orders.currency=c1.currency
                             and ord_date between '01APR2003'd and
                            '31MAR004'd
                    GROUP BY currency
                    HAVING   sum(totsale) ge 25000);
```

```
Currency information
for orders of $250,000 or more
April 1, 2003 to March 31, 2004

Currency              Min            Max            Avg
--------------------------------------------------------
EUR                  0.79           0.94           0.86
SGD                  1.68           1.78           1.73
USD                  1.00           1.00           1.00
```

If we take a close look in the next example at the totals for sales and quantity by currency in the *orders* table, the results of the previous example become clear. The existence test evaluates to TRUE only for the US and Singapore dollars and euro currencies because total sales for each of these currencies meets or exceeds $25,000.

```
LIBNAME bluesky "C:\mydata\bluesky bookstore\";

TITLE1    'Order totals for each currency';

SELECT    currency, sum(totsale) as total format=comma10.2
FROM      bluesky.orders
WHERE     ord_date between '01APR2003'd and '31MAR004'd
GROUP BY  currency;
```

```
Order totals for each currency

currency        total
_____________________
AUD          8,750.00
CAD         15,395.90
EUR         49,097.50
SGD         79,107.80
USD         95,285.00
```

Tip: Both GROUP BY and HAVING clauses can be included in a subquery. A correlated subquery is built between inner and outer queries through the WHERE clause of the subquery.

Quantified tests

SELECT
INTO
▶ FROM
ON
▶ WHERE
GROUP BY
▶ HAVING
ORDER BY
USING;

General form:

WHERE <table|alias.>column|expression OPERATOR ANY|ALL (SUBQUERY EXPRESSION)| <LOGICAL OPERATOR condition…>

HAVING <table|alias.>expression OPERATOR ANY|ALL (SUBQUERY EXPRESSION)| <LOGICAL OPERATOR condition…>

Another special form of test using ANY and ALL operators is available when subqueries are included in an SQL statement. These operators are used between a column or expression and a subquery in a WHERE clause or HAVING clause. They are similar in nature to the IN operator because they allow for a comparison of a column or expression value against a set of listed values.

If the EQUAL operator is used with the ANY operator, the comparison is analogous to a criterion that includes an IN operator and a list of values. However, both the ANY and ALL operators allow for comparisons such as greater than and less than against the values returned by the subquery. For example, a column or expression may be tested to ensure that its value is greater than all values returned by the subquery.

Tip: One important distinction between quantified and existence testing is that quantified tests retrieve a column of values in the subquery but existence tests simply evaluate to TRUE or FALSE. As a result, an asterisk can be included in the SELECT clause of an existence test subquery but a single column must be named in the SELECT clause of a quantified test subquery.

ANY operator

The ANY operator compares the value to the left of the operator with a list of values returned by the subquery and determines if the criterion is TRUE or FALSE. The criterion must evaluate to TRUE for at least one value in the outer query for the SELECT statement to be executed.

If a correlated subquery is used, a row-by-row comparison occurs. A row can only be included in the report or result set if the criterion evaluates to TRUE for the value in that row.

The next example shows the ANY operator used with an EQUAL operator. The WHERE clause compares each client number retrieved from the outer query against the list of values returned by the subquery. If the client number is in the list, the criterion evaluates to TRUE and the row is included in the report. In this example, the subquery returns all but client number 1001.

```
LIBNAME bluesky "C:\mydata\bluesky bookstore\";

SELECT   client.clientno, address.email
FROM     bluesky.address,bluesky.client

WHERE    client.clientno = ANY   (SELECT  clientno
                                  FROM    bluesky.orders
                                  WHERE   ord_date between
                                          '01JAN2004'D and
                                           30APR2004'D)

         AND address.clientno = client.clientno;
```

```
clientno  email
------------------------------------------
    2010  Hdavis@cat.org
    3007  allace@unimedya.net
    4008  clements@biz.comp
    5005  ebaird@eod.people
    6090  g_smith@home.com
    7008  cjennings@medien.print
    8003  acaston@usa.com
```

The next example shows the reverse operation. You may be surprised by the results because intuitively you may have expected only client number 1001 to be reported. However, every row in the *client* table is returned. The question posed by the NE ANY operator is whether there is any occurrence of a value for clientno in the subquery result set for which clientno in the *orders* table does not match.

```
LIBNAME bluesky "C:\mydata\bluesky bookstore\";

SELECT   client.clientno, address.email
FROM     bluesky.address,     bluesky.client

WHERE    client.clientno NE ANY(SELECT clientno
                                FROM   bluesky.orders
                                WHERE  ord_date between '01JAN2004'D
                                       and '30APR2004'D)

         AND address.clientno = client.clientno;
```

```
clientno  email
------------------------------------------
    1001  eagleton@usa.com
    2010  Hdavis@cat.org
    3007  allace@unimedya.net
    4008  clements@biz.comp
    5005  ebaird@eod.people
    6090  g_smith@home.com
    7008  cjennings@medien.print
    8003  acaston@usa.com
```

The following figure gives a graphical representation of what happens in the above query. Each row in the client table is compared to the set of client numbers retrieved by the subquery. If an unequal value is found, the criterion evaluates to TRUE and the row is passed to the result set. Processing continues with each client number in the *client* table being compared to the client numbers in the subquery result set. For example, the highlighted client number 1001 from the client table evaluates to TRUE because it does not match client number 8003 in the subquery result set.

Step 1: Inner query is processed

Subquery result set from ORDERS table	
clientno	**ord_date**
8003	01FEB03
4008	01FEB03
3007	07MAR03
7008	10MAR03
8003	10MAR03
8003	10MAR03
4008	10MAR03
4008	08APR03
6090	10APR03
2010	12APR03
2010	12APR03
5005	12APR03
7008	12APR03

Step 2: Each clientno value in the *client* table is checked against inner query results for at least one unequal value. If a single unequal value is found, the NE ANY test is TRUE and the value is returned.

CLIENT Table	Comparison of each clientno with the subquery results	
clientno	**NE ANY**	**Sample clientno value that does not match**
1001	TRUE	8003
2010	TRUE	8003
3007	TRUE	8003
4008	TRUE	8003
5005	TRUE	8003
6090	TRUE	8003
7008	TRUE	8003
8003	TRUE	4008

Tip: The NE ANY test can also be written as NOT *column-name* = ANY (SELECT…). However, using the more standard form of *column-name* NE ANY (SELECT…) is preferred because it makes for a more understandable query.

Caution: The NE or NOT quantified tests can degrade performance because they cannot generally be optimized by the SQL optimizer.

When other operators such as <, >, GE, and LE are combined with ANY, the same comparison of values occurs. For example, each value for the column in the outer query would be checked against the value of every row in the subquery result set to determine if there is at least one value greater than or less than the current outer query value.

ALL operator

If a criterion is built on an ALL operator, the test must evaluate to TRUE for all values in the subquery result set. The value to the left of the operator is compared to the list of values returned by the subquery evaluating to TRUE or FALSE. If every comparison evaluates to TRUE, the row passes to the result set; otherwise processing continues to the next value in the outer query.

The next example shows a query using the ALL quantitative test. In this query, we are seeking the highest total sale value in the *orders* table. Each totsale value in the *orders* table is checked against all of the totsale values in the same table retrieved by the subquery. Only the highest total sale value evaluates to TRUE when compared to every value in the *orders* table.

```
LIBNAME bluesky "C:\mydata\bluesky bookstore\";

SELECT   clientno, totsale,quantity
FROM     bluesky.orders
WHERE    orders.totsale >= ALL (SELECT  totsale
                                FROM    bluesky.orders);
```

clientNo	totsale	quantity
3007	225000	5000

Caution: If > ALL instead of >= ALL were used in the above example, no rows would be retrieved. To be greater than the entire list of column values retrieved by the subquery would require a value that is not in the *orders* table. With the >= operator, we select the value from the *orders* table that is greater than all of the other values.

The ALL operator can also be used with the NOT keyword. The next example presents a query that seeks to report only those clients who do not have a matching entry in the *orders* table. If you recall, during the processing of the ANY and ALL quantitative tests, each value from the outer query is compared to every value from the inner query and evaluates to TRUE or FALSE. Therefore, if the ALL operator is used, only client 1001 evaluates to TRUE because this client did not place an order during the specified period.

```
LIBNAME bluesky "C:\mydata\bluesky bookstore\";

SELECT   client.clientno, address.email
FROM     bluesky.address, bluesky.client

WHERE    client.clientno ne ALL(SELECT clientno
                           FROM      bluesky.orders
                           WHERE     ord_date between '01JAN2004'D
                                     AND '30APR2004'D)
         AND address.clientno = client.clientno;
```

```
clientno  email
------------------------------------------
    1001  eagleton@usa.com
```

Tip: I prefer to use a NOT IN operator rather than a NE ALL operator. I find it more intuitive to ask the question "Is it not in the list?" rather than "Is it not equal to any value in the list?"

Putting it all together

The next example combines many of the concepts covered in this chapter. The query generates a report outlining order details for above-average book quantities ordered by universities located in the United States. Both FROM-ON and WHERE clause joins are used here. The FROM-ON clause join is used in the outer query and a WHERE clause join is used in the third subquery.

The order quantity for each university order is compared against the average order quantity for that client using a correlated subquery. This subquery uses another subquery to generate a list of university clients located in the United States. Client numbers for clients in the United States are compared against those with company names that include "university" using an INTERSECT set operator. The client numbers in the *orders* table are then compared against the list of client numbers returned by the innermost subquery using the =ANY operator.

A second subquery is used to limit the rows reported in the outer query to the appropriate clients. The subquery includes an inner join between the *client* and *address* tables to determine the university clients in the United States.

> **Tip:** The INTERSECT and JOIN operations included in the subqueries can be used interchangeably. The same is true for the =ANY and IN operators.

```
LIBNAME bluesky "C:\mydata\bluesky bookstore\";

TITLE1   'Above-average orders by Universities in the United States';

SELECT   c.company as university "University" format=$25.,
         count(invoice) "Number of invoices",
         count(prodcode) "Book titles ordered",
         max(quantity) "Maximum Quantity" format=comma8.,
         min(quantity) "Minimum Quantity" format=comma8.,
         max(totsale) as maxsale "Maximum Sale Total" format=
         dollar10.2,
         min(totsale) "Minimum Sale Total" format=dollar10.2

FROM     bluesky.orders ord1 JOIN bluesky.client c
ON       ord1.clientno=c.clientno

WHERE    quantity GE
         (SELECT avg(round(quantity))
         FROM           bluesky.orders ord2
         WHERE          ord2.clientno =ANY (SELECT clientno
                                            FROM    bluesky.address
                                            WHERE   country = 'USA'
                                       INTERSECT
                                            SELECT  clientno
                                            FROM    bluesky.client
                                            WHERE   company like
                                                    '%University%'
                                           )
         AND ord2.clientno = ord1.clientno
         )

         AND ord1.clientno IN (SELECT    address.clientno
                     FROM      bluesky.address, bluesky.client
                     WHERE     country ='USA'
                                 AND address.clientno=client.clientno
                                 AND company like '%University%'
          )
GROUP BY university
ORDER BY maxsale;
```

Above-average orders by Universities in the United States

University	Number of invoices	Book titles ordered	Maximum Quantity	Minimum Quantity	Maximum Sale Total	Minimum Sale Total
University of Texas	2	2	1,000	600	$34,500.00	$20,700.00
Chicago State University	2	2	2,900	1,230	$41,820.00	$3,390.00

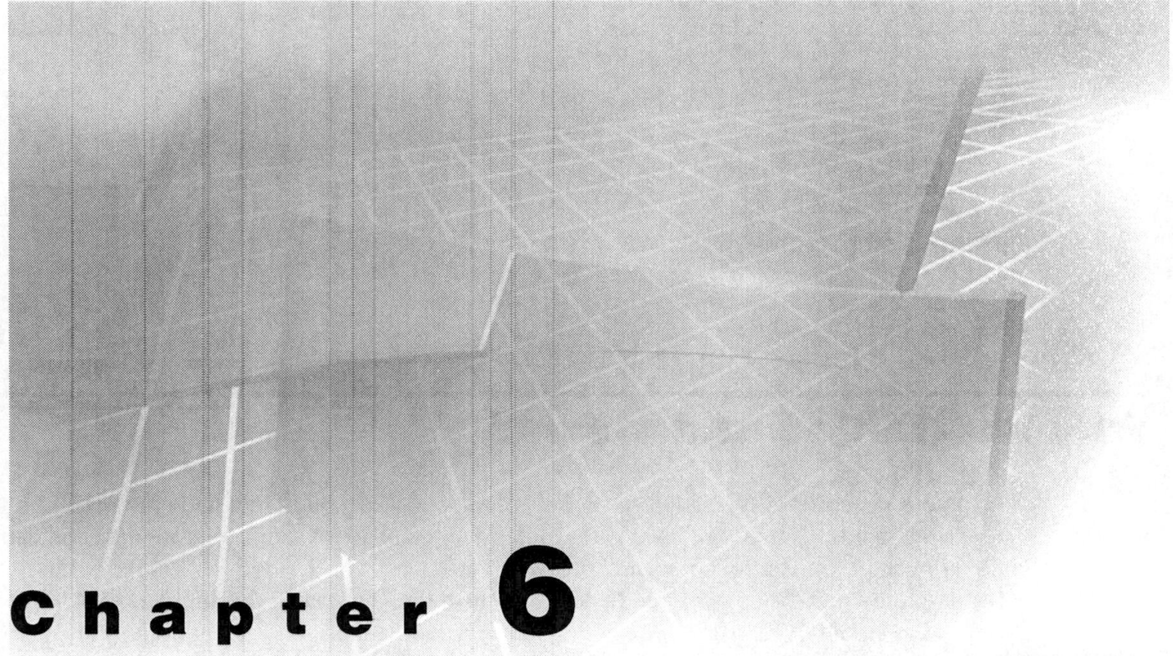

Chapter 6

Creating and Managing Tables and Views

Why use tables and views?

A table's structure of formatted rows and columns is well-suited to a wide range of reporting needs. Tables are used within relational database systems to store data and can be referenced in SAS/ACCESS and the SQL Pass-Through facility. Within the SAS System, they may be constructed to accommodate data generated through a DATA step or a query in the SQL procedure.

Constraints may be imposed on one or more columns in a table. These constraints can be used to establish relationships between tables within an RDBMS or to check incoming data null values or uniqueness.

As seen in the previous chapters of this book, the SQL procedure can be used to simplify the data merging process through joins and set operations. Summary information is easily generated from data in one or more tables using the various SELECT statement clauses. However, the need for summary information often results in complex queries with many calculations, GROUP by clauses, joins, and subqueries. Views store queries, eliminating the need to reconstruct the SELECT statement to retrieve up-to-date information.

The problem of merging summary statistics with records in one or more data sets is not uncommon. Often SAS users attempt to compare statistical measures against a value in a data set. In the next example, the check value is dependent on the total number of orders as well as a comparison of the order quantity against a percentage of the stock. The mean and sum values of the books are necessary because not all books have been ordered more than once.

```
LIBNAME bluesky "C:\mydata\bluesky bookstore\";

PROC SUMMARY data=bluesky.orders nway;
  class prodcode;
  var quantity;
  id quantity;;
  output out=bluesky.ord_stat n=qtycnt mean=qtymean sum=qtysum;

PROC SORT data=bluesky.stock;
  by prodcode;
```

```
DATA BLUESKY.STKORD;
  MERGE bluesky.ord_stat bluesky.stock (in=in1);
  by prodcode;

     * include only orders with matching records in the stock
       table;
       if in1;

    if qtycnt > 1 then
        ord_qty=qtysum;
    else
        ord_qty = quantity;

        qtymean = round(qtymean);

         if qtymean ge stock*.75 then
          do;
           if ord_qty ge (stock*.9) then check=90;
             else
           if ord_qty ge (stock*.75) then check = 75;
             else
           if ord_qty ge (stock*.5) then check=50;
             else
           check = 0;
           output;
          end;

PROC PRINT noobs label;
  TITLE 'Product Stock Check Report';
  var title prodcode stock qtycnt ord_qty qtymean check;
  LABEL title = 'Title'
        prodcode = 'Prodcode'
        stock = 'Stock'
        qtycnt = '# of Orders'
        ord_qty = 'Order size'
        qtymean = 'Avg. Order'
        check = '% of Stock';
RUN;
```

```
Product Stock Check Report

                                                 # of  Order  Avg.   % o
Title                            Prodcode Stock Orders  size  Order Stock

Geology: Volcanos                 100340    400      2    820   410    90
Managing Water Resources          200678   6000      1   5000  5000    75
The Ultimate Philosophy           300456    100      3    405   135    90
The Underground Economy           300680   1000      2   3050  1525    90
Medical Education in School       400100    300      3    675   225    90
Unconventional treatments         400102   1000      1   1500  1500    90
National Library of Medicine      400178     35      2    510   255    90
Medications and Maintenance       400345     30      1     25    25    75
New User's Guide to Computers     500127    350      1    324   324    90
The Maestro                       600125    100      4   1062   266    90
```

A table may be constructed to hold the summary information, which eliminates the need to rerun the entire query in order to report some of the summary information. Once created, simplified SELECT statements can then be issued against the new table. The summary table must only be recreated when new summary information is required. Such a solution would work well in an environment where summary information changes infrequently.

Alternatively, a virtual table or view may be constructed from such queries. Views are referenced in SELECT statements in the same fashion as tables. They are updated with the current information in the source tables each time they are accessed. Only the query used to construct the view is stored, and it is rerun when the view is referenced in a SELECT statement. They are often an ideal solution when information must be current but complex queries are required to generate routine reports.

> **Tip:** Views are generated when they are referenced in a SELECT statement, so they always contain the most current information.

In the next example, a view called *stats* is created from the *stock* and *orders* tables including the stock details as well as summary information. The SELECT statement enclosed in brackets completes the same tasks as the DATA step in the preceding example providing the columns and rows for the view. A nested CASE expression has been added to generate the values of the check variable. Each time the SELECT statement is issued against the view, the view is generated using the current *stock* and *orders* tables.

```
PROC SQL;
LIBNAME bluesky "C:\mydata\bluesky bookstore\";

CREATE VIEW bluesky.stats AS
   (SELECT  title 'Title' format=$30.,
            stock.prodcode 'Prodcode', stock 'Stock',
            round(mean(quantity)) as qtymean 'No. of Orders',
            sum(quantity) as ord_qty 'Order size',
            count(quantity) as qtycnt 'Avg. Order',
                 CASE when (CALCULATED qtymean ge stock*.75) then
                      CASE  when (CALCULATED ord_qty GE stock*.9)
                                 then 90
                            when (CALCULATED ord_qty GE stock*.75)
                                 then 75
                            when (CALCULATED ord_qty GE stock*.5)
                                 then 50
                      END
                   ELSE 0
                END as check '% of Stock'
    FROM        bluesky.stock, bluesky.orders
    WHERE       stock.prodcode = orders.prodcode
    GROUP BY    stock.prodcode, title, stock
    HAVING      qtymean >= (stock*.75)
    );

SELECT *
FROM   bluesky.stats;
```

Product Stock Check Report

Title	Prodcode	Stock	No. of Orders	Order size	Avg. Order	% of Stock
Geology: Volcanos	100340	400	2	820	410	90
Managing Water Resources	200678	6000	1	5000	5000	75
The Ultimate Philosophy	300456	100	3	405	135	90
The Underground Economy	300680	1000	2	3050	1525	90
Medical Education in School	400100	300	3	675	225	90
Unconventional treatments	400102	1000	1	1500	1500	90
National Library of Medicine	400178	35	2	510	255	90
Medications and Maintenance	400345	30	1	25	25	75
New User's Guide to Computers	500127	350	1	324	324	90
The Maestro	600125	100	4	1062	266	90

Tip: The CALCULATED keyword was added in the above example to allow the alias of each of the summary functions to be included in the CASE expression. The CALCULATED keyword eliminates the need to repeat an expression if you want to use it more than once in a SELECT statement. When the CALCULATED keyword and an alias are encountered, the expression in the SELECT clause associated with the alias is automatically substituted during processing.

Views are also useful when you need to create subsets of a table for different groups of users. With a view, it is possible to control both the columns and rows that a user can access but to still draw current information from the table.

UPDATE and DELETE statements issued against the view act on only the rows in the underlying table that are included in the view. The rows affected by UPDATE and DELETE statements are also limited to those represented in the view. INSERT statements add new data only to the columns that are part of the view.

Tip: When working with views, the user is still working with the underlying tables; data can be added to the tables and existing values can be modified through the view.

Caution: A DELETE statement issued against a view will delete rows in the underlying tables even if only selected columns of the table are included in the view.

In the next example a view is created for the individual at the Bluesky Bookstore responsible for printing books in the arts category. The view includes only the arts category books and does not include any of the sales information related to the orders. When a report is required, a simple SELECT statement is issued against the view and up-to-date information is displayed. Notice that the column labels in the report are those assigned in the CREATE VIEW statement.

Tip: Labels, aliases, and formatting associated with a column at the time a view is created are stored. If you require different formatting or labels for groups of users, consider creating views for each group that includes their preferences.

```
LIBNAME bluesky "C:\mydata\bluesky bookstore\";

CREATE VIEW bluesky.arts AS
   (SELECT     title 'Title' format=$25.,
               stock.prodcode 'Prodcode', stock 'Stock',
               quantity 'Order Qty', ord_date 'Order Date'
    FROM       bluesky.stock, bluesky.orders
    WHERE      stock.prodcode = orders.prodcode
               and category = 'arts');

SELECT *
FROM   bluesky.arts
ORDER  BY title;
```

Title	Prodcode	Stock	Order Qty	Order Date
Decorative Arts	300678	1500	275	09JAN03
Democracy in America	300289	55	30	12JUN04
The Ultimate Philosophy	300456	100	55	10APR04
The Ultimate Philosophy	300456	100	300	07FEB03
The Ultimate Philosophy	300456	100	50	07FEB03
The Underground Economy	300680	1000	2900	20OCT03
The Underground Economy	300680	1000	150	06MAY03

Tip: A view acts much like a mask on a table because it controls the columns and rows that can be accessed through a SELECT statement.

Views can be very useful when you want to hide rows and/or columns in a table from your users or to automate calculations. For example, you might want to create a view for users that limits the e-mail addresses and phone numbers to nonmanagement staff only (restricted rows) and protect salaries from view (hidden column). The view might also automate the calculation of staff ages from stored birthdate information.

Creating tables

When creating a table, three options are available. First, a table can be defined in its entirety with column names and data types indicated. Second, new tables can have a structure based on an existing table. Third, the structure of a new table can be based on an existing table and rows of data from that table can be used to populate the new table. If a libref is specified, the newly created table will be permanent.

> **SAS/ACCESS and SQL Pass-Through Facility users:** Having difficulty creating a table in a database using PROC SQL? Permission to create objects is required in order to successfully create a table in a database. Modify your CREATE statement so that the newly created table resides in a native SAS library instead of a database. If the modified statement is successful, lack of appropriate permission is the reason you cannot create your table in the database. Contact your database administrator to arrange for the necessary permission to be added to your user account.

Regardless of the form of the CREATE statement, the INSERT statement can be used after the table is created to add rows of data. The ALTER statement can also be applied to the tables to change the structure.

New table definition

General form:

```
CREATE TABLE    table-name
( column-name   data type <column modifier>
<,column-name   data type <column modifier>...>
);
```

Data types:

CHARACTER| CHAR| VARCHAR <(width)>
INTEGER| INT| SMALLINIT
DECIMAL| DEC| NUMERIC| FLOAT <(width <,ndec>)>
REAL| DOUBLE PRECISION
DATE

Column modifiers:

INFORMAT=informat w.d
FORMAT=format w.d
LABEL='label'
LENGTH='length'

The CREATE statement can be used to create a table with each column name and data type specified. An optional column modifier can be applied to specify the default label or format of the column. The newly created table does not contain any rows of data. The INSERT statement, covered in detail later in this chapter, is used to add rows to the table.

New rows can also be added through a DATA step or PROC APPEND. PROC APPEND may reference a SAS data set or an SQL table or view as the source or target of new rows. In the following example, the rows in table *orders* are added to a table called *neworders:*

```
PROC APPEND base=bluesky.neworders data=bluesky.order;
run;
```

SAS/ACCESS and SQL Pass-Through Facility users: PROC APPEND can also be used to add data to a table residing in a database.

The column name must be one allowed by the SAS system. Column names can be up to 32 characters in length, and they must adhere to SAS variable naming conventions.

Just because something is allowed does not mean it is a good idea. Avoid using ANSI reserved words as column names in your tables. They cause confusion and can make your queries difficult to debug. The reserved words according to the ANSI-92 standard are included in Chapter 2, "Working with PROC SQL."

SAS/ACCESS and SQL Pass-Through Facility users: Column and table names consisting of reserved words such as max or mean may not be allowed in tables residing in an RDBMS. It depends on how closely the RDBMS adheres to the ANSI-92 standard.

Data types

All data types supported by the SAS System can be used in the CREATE TABLE statement. However, there are a few important points to remember when specifying a data type.

If a character data type is specified, the width defaults to eight unless a width is included in the definition. Data values stored within a column defined as CHARACTER are padded with blanks to the defined width.

All numeric data types such as INTEGER, DECIMAL, REAL, DATE, and FLOAT are treated as the SAS data type NUMERIC. Numeric columns are always created with the maximum allowed precision, even if width and the number of decimal places is included in the column definition. However, a LENGTH statement can be submitted in a DATA step to reduce the amount of storage space allocated to it.

Tip: Dates are numeric data types in the SAS System with a DATE informat or format. A separate data type called DATE exists in most database systems. Additional DATE data types such as TIME and TIMESTAMP are found in some databases. Detailed information on SAS data types is provided in *SAS Language Reference: Concepts.*

SAS/ACCESS and SQL Pass-Through Facility users: Data type definitions vary between database systems. The width and number of decimal place (*ndec*) arguments that are common when you are defining columns using most commercial SQL products associated with databases are ignored in SAS. In addition, column attributes and the length of allowed names for columns may differ.

Appendix C, "Information for Database Users," contains ANSI standard SQL-92 naming guidelines and data types. Other data types are available within each DBMS and users should consult a reference appropriate to their specific database.

The next example shows the CREATE TABLE statement used to generate the *orders* table in the Bluesky Publishing Company.

```
LIBNAME bluesky "C:\mydata\bluesky bookstore\";

CREATE TABLE BLUESKY.ORDERS (BUFSIZE=8192) (
            prodCode   char(6),
            ord_date   date,
            quantity   num,
            totsale    num,
            currency   char(3),
            delCode    char(3),
            clientNo   num,
            invoice    char(10));
```

Tip: A BUFSIZE value that specifies a permanent buffer page size for a table can be set at the time the table is created. It is added in parentheses after the table name as shown in this example.

Column modifiers: Labels, informats, and formats

Column labels, informats, and formats can be applied to all columns, regardless of the data type. More information on labels is provided in Chapter 3, "Understanding the SELECT Statement." Informats and formats are described in detail in the *SAS Language Reference: Dictionary*.

Tip: Labels of more than 32 characters can be associated with columns at the time the table is created. If you want to associate an ANSI reserved word with your column, it is better to use it as a label than the column name.

In the chapters presented thus far, labels and formats for the columns have been assigned in the SELECT clause used to generate reports. The next example includes a simple SELECT statement that reports the order details for client 1001. The column labels and formats included in the SELECT clause are applied to the report as can be seen in the example.

```
LIBNAME bluesky "C:\mydata\bluesky bookstore\";

TITLE1  Order information for client 1001';

SELECT  PRODCODE 'Product Code',
        ord_date 'Order Date' format=DATE10.,
        quantity 'Quantity',
        totsale  'Total Sale' format=dollar10.2,
        currency 'Currency',
        delCode  'Delivery Code',
        clientNo 'Client Number',
        invoice  'Invoice'
FROM    bluesky.orders
WHERE   clientno = 1001;
```

```
Order information for client 1001

Product                                                  Delivery     Client
Code      Order Date  Quantity  Total Sale  Currency     Code         Number  Invoice
-------------------------------------------------------------------------------------
300456    07FEB2003        300   $2,850.00  USD          UPS            1001  030207-01
300680    06MAY2003        150   $2,175.00  USD          EXE            1001  030506-01
400178    06MAY2003        500  $32,875.00  USD          UPS            1001  030506-01
500120    06MAY2003        600  $20,700.00  USD          UPS            1001  030506-01
500120    06SEP2003       1000  $34,500.00  USD          UPS            1001  030906-01
```

However, it is possible to assign a set of labels and formats to all of the columns in the table at the time the table is created. This eliminates the need to specify formats and labels in the SELECT clause of a query.

SAS/ACCESS and SQL Pass-Through Facility users: Column modifiers cannot be specified for tables that are stored in a database. However, they can be added to CREATE VIEW statements built from tables stored in a database.

In the next example, the CREATE TABLE statement for the orders table shown in the example in the "Data types" section preceding has been modified to include format and label column assignments. A simple SELECT statement generates the report shown here.

```
LIBNAME bluesky "C:\mydata\bluesky bookstore\";

CREATE TABLE bluesky.new_order (
         prodCode char(6)  label = 'Product Code',
         ord_date date     label = 'Order Date' format=DATE10.,
         quantity num      label = 'Quantity',
         totsale num       label = 'Total Sale' format=dollar10.2,
         currency char(3)  label = 'Currency',
         delCode char(3)   label = 'Delivery Code',
         clientNo num      label = 'Client Number',
         invoice  char(10) label = 'Invoice'
         );

INSERT into bluesky.new_order
  SELECT * from bluesky.orders;


TITLE    'Order Information for Client 8003';
SELECT   *
FROM     bluesky.new_order
WHERE    clientno=8003;
```

Order Information for Client 8003

Product Code	Order Date	Quantity	Total Sale	Currency	Delivery Code	Client Number	Invoice
300678	09JAN2003	275	$4,661.25	CAD	GRN	8003	030109-01
100340	09JAN2003	800	$14,400.00	CAD	UPS	8003	030109-01
600125	01FEB2004	12	$83.40	CAD	GRN	8003	040101-01
400100	10MAR2004	350	$15,312.50	CAD	EXA	8003	040310-02
500500	10MAR2004	70	$1,645.00	USD	EXA	8003	040310-02
100340	12JUN2004	20	$360.00	CAD	GRN	8003	041212-01

Tip: This example includes an INSERT statement that was used to populate the new table to generate a report illustrating the new labels and formats. More information is provided on the INSERT statement later in this chapter.

The use of column modifiers offers several advantages as seen in the previous example. The SELECT statement needed to generate the report has been greatly simplified because the burden of labeling and formatting has been removed from the user. Moreover, consistent labels and formats will be applied to every report generated from the table.

Tip: Column modifiers can be assigned to columns after a table has been created through the ALTER TABLE statement covered later in this chapter.

Column modifiers can be overridden through the assignment of a new attribute in a SELECT clause.

Constraints

The CREATE TABLE statement allows for two forms of constraint specification, in-line and out-of-line. In-line constraints are those that are specified on the same line as the column name and column modifiers. Out-of-line constraints are specified after all columns have been set out.

In-line constraint specification

General form:

```
CREATE TABLE        table-name
( column-name       data type  <column modifier> <column-constraint >
<, ...>
);
```

Column constraints:

```
PRIMARY KEY <message-options>

FOREIGN KEY references <table-name>
                  <ON UPDATE referential-action
                  ON DELETE referential-action
                  message-options>

CHECK (WHERE clause criteria) <message-options>

NOT NULL <message-options>

UNIQUE <message-options>
```

Message:

MESSAGE= message string
MSGTYPE= NEWLINE | USER

Referential action:

CASCADE | RESTRICT | SET NULL

Column modifiers include the data type, informat and default labels associated with a column in a table discussed in detail earlier in this chapter. Both column modifiers and constraints can be added to each column specified in a CREATE TABLE statement.

In the next example two new tables called *newreprint* and *newstock* are created using the same structure as the *reprint* and *stock* tables for the Bluesky Publishing Company, respectively. Several constraints are added to each table at the time of creation. The *newreprint* table has a primary key in the reprint column, preventing duplicate values from being entered into that column. The *newstock* table includes a primary key in the ISBN column and a check constraint in each of the stock and publication year (yrpubl) columns. In addition, it has a foreign key constraint relating the values in the reprint column to the reprint column of the *newreprint* table.

Tip: Constraints are also discussed in Chapter 2, "Working with PROC SQL."

```
CREATE table newreprint
         (reprint char(1) primary key,
          cutoff        num
         );

CREATE table newstock
        (isbn            char(13) primary key,
         title           char(50),
         auth_fst        char(10),
         auth_lst        char(15),
         category        char(20),
         reprint         char(1) references work.newreprint
                         on update cascade on delete set null
                         message="Violates Foreign Key - check
                                  reprint value. " msgtype=user,
         stock           num check ((yrpubl > 1990 and stock >=25)
                                    or (yrpubl <= 1990 and  stock
                                    >=10)),
         yrpubl          num check(yrpubl > 1900),
         prodcode        char(6) unique,
         price           num not null
             );
```

An optional message of up to 250 characters can be associated with a constraint by using the MESSAGE= option. The default setting of MSGTYPE=NEWLINE results in both the specified message together with the default error message relating to the constraint reported in the SAS log if the constraint is violated. If MSGTYPE=USER is specified, the SAS portion of the error message is suppressed and only the specified message is printed in the SAS log when the constraint is violated.

> **Tip:** Messages can be set for every constraint. These messages are reported to the SAS log when the constraint is violated. If you create your constraints in-line, it is a good idea to add a message because default constraint names that are not meaningful are automatically assigned to each constraint.

In the "Messages" section later in this chapter you will find the output of a DESCRIBE statement issued against each of the newly created tables. Notice that the CREATE statement in the SAS log does not reference the constraints; rather a separate section detailing the constraints for the table is now included. The details of the constraint report are discussed below.

Several indexes are automatically created for the tables. A unique index is created for the primary key columns as well as those with a UNIQUE constraint. A non-unique index is also automatically created for the foreign key column. Foreign key columns may contain duplicate values; however, the table column referenced by the foreign key constraint must contain unique values. In this example, a primary key constraint has been applied to the reprint column of the *reprint* table (reference or parent table) to enforce uniqueness.

Constraint name and type

Each constraint has been assigned a name preceded by an underscore and a set of letters indicating the type of constraint. For example, the primary key constraint in the *reprint* table has been assigned a name of –PK0001–. The number portion of the constraint name is incremented by one for each integrity constraint of the same type. For example, the check constraints in the *stock* table are assigned names of –CK0001– and –CK0002–.

Out-of-line constraint specifications allow for the assignment of a descriptive name to a constraint at the time of creation. It is a good idea to use out-of-line constraints if you have two or more of the same constraint in a single table. At minimum, a unique message should be associated with each to distinguish between them when a violation occurs. Out-of-line constraints are discussed in the next section.

> **SAS/ACCESS and SQL Pass-Through Facility users:** When creating a unique constraint in DB2, the DISTINCT keyword is substituted for UNIQUE.

Variables and WHERE clause

The column or variable upon which the constraint has been placed is indicated. Notice, however, that the check constraint does not reference a column; instead a WHERE clause that indicates the criterion against which impending changes or incoming data are checked is included. The check constraint used in this example shows the complexity possible in the criteria of this form of constraint.

Tip: All valid WHERE clause criteria can be added to a CHECK constraint.

Reference and referential action

For foreign key constraints, the reference or parent table is indicated using a two-level name. Both an action ON UPDATE and an action ON DELETE are included. The *reprint* table is the reference or parent table and the *stock* table is the child table. The reprint column in each table is linked through a foreign key constraint.

Table: STOCK (child table)	
isbn	**reprint**
1-7890-2878-7	C
	↑
	FOREIGN KEY

Table: REPRINT (parent)	
reprint	**cutoff**
C	50
↑	
PRIMARY KEY	

There are several options relating to the action in the linked column when a value in the reference table column is either updated or deleted. These referential actions maintain the integrity of the data in linked columns.

RESTRICT: Values in the reference or parent table column cannot be deleted or changed if the value occurs in the linked column in one or more rows in the child table.

SET NULL: in the reference or parent table is deleted or modified, matching values in the linked column in the child table are changed to NULL.

CASCADE: Changes to values in the reference or parent table are applied to each of the matching values in the linked column of the child table. This option is available only for the UPDATE statement in SAS Version 8 and later.

The CASCADE option for the foreign key constraint discussed above is used to make adjustments to the child table when key values in the reference or parent table are modified using an UPDATE statement. If key values in the reference table are deleted, all matching entries in the child table are set to null if the SET NULL option is in effect. In this way, the two tables are always synchronized.

In this example, if a reprint value in the *reprint* table is deleted, the corresponding reprint value in the *stock* table will be set to NULL. Changes to the reprint value in the *reprint* table will result in the same change to all corresponding reprint values in the *stock* table.

Messages
A message has been indicated for the foreign key constraint. This message will be output to the SAS log if the user tries to modify existing data or insert new data that violates the foreign key constraint. The MSGTYPE=USER option causes the default SAS error message to be suppressed; only the specified message will be reported to the SAS log.

SAS log:

```
1065  describe table newreprint;
NOTE: SQL table WORK.NEWREPRINT was created like:

create table WORK.NEWREPRINT( bufsize=4096 )
  (
   reprint char(1),
   cutoff num
  );
create unique index reprint on WORK.NEWREPRINT(reprint);
```

```
          -----Alphabetic List of Integrity Constraints-----

     Integrity                                                    On        On
#   Constraint   Type          Variables  Reference        Delete    Update
---------------------------------------------------------------------------
1   _PK0001_     Primary Key   reprint
2    _FK0001_    Referential   reprint    WORK.NEWSTOCK    Set Null  Cascade
```

```
1066  describe table newstock;
NOTE: SQL table WORK.NEWSTOCK was created like:

create table WORK.NEWSTOCK( bufsize=12288 )
  (
   isbn char(13),
   title char(50),
   auth_fst char(10),
   auth_lst char(15),
   category char(20),
   reprint char(1),
   stock num,
   yrpubl num,

   prodcode char(6),
   price num
  );
create unique index prodcode on WORK.NEWSTOCK(prodcode);
create index reprint on WORK.NEWSTOCK(reprint);
create unique index isbn on WORK.NEWSTOCK(isbn);
```

-----Alphabetic List of Integrity Constraints-----

#	Integrity Constraint	Type	Variables	Where Clause	Reference	On Delete	On Update	User Message	Message Type
1	_CK0001_	Check		((yrpubl>1990) and (stock>=25)) or ((yrpubl<=1990) and (stock>=10))					
2	_CK0002_	Check		yrpubl>1900					
3	_FK0001_	Foreign Key	reprint		WORK.NEWREPRINT	Set Null	Cascade	Violates Foreign Key -check reprint value.	user
4	_NM0001_	Not Null	price						
5	_PK0001_	Primary Key	isbn						
6	_UN0001_	Unique	prodcode						

Out-of-line constraint specification
General form:

```
CREATE TABLE        table-name
( column-name       data type  <column modifier>
<,…>

CONSTRAINT          constraint-name constraint
);
```

Constraint:

PRIMARY KEY <message-options>

FOREIGN KEY references <*table-name*>
<ON UPDATE referential-action
ON DELETE referential-action
message-options>
CHECK (*WHERE clause criteria*) <message-options>

NOT NULL <message-options>

UNIQUE <message-options>

Message:
MESSAGE= message string
MSGTYPE= NEWLINE | USER

Referential action:
CASCADE | RESTRICT | SET NULL

There are several advantages to specifying constraints out-of-line, that is, at the end of the CREATE TABLE statement rather than on the same line as the column definition. First, a name of up to 32 characters can be specified for the constraint. This allows for easier recognition of offending data values when the SAS log reports a constraint violation error, especially when the same constraint type is applied to several columns in a single table. It is not uncommon to have several NOT NULL or CHECK constraints, for example, in a single table.

Out-of-line constraints also allow for the creation of a constraint on more than one column such as required for composite primary keys.

> **Tip:** Meaningful constraint names make constraint reports and errors easier to interpret. A portion of the column name associated with the constraint together with an identifier such as PK or CK is a good idea. For composite keys, a name that includes some portion of each of the columns in the order they occur in the key is often used. The order of the columns affects query optimization. Information on indexes and the SQL optimizer is included later in this chapter.

The next example shows the creation of an *orders* table with several constraints created out-of-line. The SAS log report generated from the DESCRIBE statement is included in the example.

```
CREATE table ORDERS
  (
   PRODCODE char(6),
   ORD_DATE num format=DATE. informat=DATE.,
   QUANTITY num,
   TOTSALE  num,
   CURRENCY char(3),
   DELCODE  char(3),
   CLIENTNO num,
   INVOICE  char(10),

   CONSTRAINT pk_prod_invoice PRIMARY KEY(prodcode,invoice),
   CONSTRAINT date_chk CHECK(ord_date> '01JAN2004'D),
   CONSTRAINT qty_null NOT NULL(quantity),
   CONSTRAINT totsale_null NOT NULL(totsale),
   CONSTRAINT clientno_null NOT NULL(clientno)
  );
DESCRIBE table orders;
```

SAS log:

```
NOTE: SQL table WORK.ORDERS was created like:

CREATE table WORK.ORDERS( bufsize=8192 )
   (
    PRODCODE char(6),
    ORD_DATE num format=DATE. informat=DATE.,
    QUANTITY num,
    TOTSALE  num,
    CURRENCY char(3),
    DELCODE  char(3),
    CLIENTNO num,
    INVOICE  char(10)
   );
create unique index pk_prod_invoice on WORK.ORDERS(PRODCODE,INVOICE);
```

```
          -----Alphabetic List of Integrity Constraints-----

  Integrity                                       Where
# Constraint        Type          Variables        Clause
---------------------------------------------------------------------

1 clientno_null     Not Null      CLIENTNO
2 date_chk          Check                          ORD_DATE>'01JAN2004'D
3 pk_prod_invoice   Primary Key   PRODCODE INVOICE
4 qty_null          Not Null      QUANTITY
5 totsale_null      Not Null      TOTSALE
```

The next example includes an INSERT statement for the *orders* table with an invalid date. Although an optimal message has not been specified for the check constraint in the *orders* table, the error message is more easily interpreted because of the name of the constraint.

When views are created from tables having integrity constraints in one or more columns, you must give careful thought to how the view will be used. For example, if a column with a primary key constraint is excluded from a view, all INSERT statements issued against that view will fail. All columns in which a PRIMARY KEY and NOT NULL constraints are built must be included in the view.

```
INSERT into orders
values ('500890','21JAN1990'D, 10, 100.00, 'USD', 'UPS', 1001,
        '000121-01');
```

SAS log:

```
ERROR: Add/Update failed for data set WORK.ORDERS because data
       value(s) do not comply with integrity constraint date_chk.
NOTE:  This insert failed while attempting to add data from VALUES
       clause 1 to the data set.
NOTE:  Deleting the successful inserts before error noted above to
       restore table to a consistent state.
```

Tip: The INSERT statement is discussed in detail later in this chapter.

Using an existing table structure

General form:

CREATE TABLE LIKE table-name <(DROP= column <column ...>)>

It is possible to use an existing table or data set as a template for the new table. The new table has the same column names and data types as the existing table but does not contain any rows of data. The SAS data set option DROP= can be added to the statement if one or more of the columns in the existing table are not required in the new table.

In the next example a new table called *newcomp* is generated using the structure of the *client* table. Several of the columns in the *client* table have been excluded from the new table. The SAS log confirms that the new, empty table has been created.

```
LIBNAME bluesky "C:\mydata\bluesky bookstore\";

CREATE TABLE BLUESKY.NEWCOMP
  LIKE bluesky.client(DROP=dept phone fax);
```

SAS log:

```
708   CREATE table bluesky.newcomp
709   LIKE bluesky.client (DROP=dept phone fax);
NOTE: Table BLUESKY.NEWCOMP created, with 0 rows and 5 columns.
```

Guidelines

- The new table contains all of the columns in the original table, except for those listed after the DROP option.
- The data types of the original columns are used for the columns in the new table.

- Column modifiers assigned to the original columns are assigned to the columns in the new table.

Using an existing table structure and data

General form:

> **CREATE TABLE** table-name
> AS (**SELECT** statement)
> <**ORDER BY** clause>;

The CREATE TABLE statement can be combined with an SQL query. This form of the CREATE statement both creates a new table and populates the table with data. The structure of the new table will be limited to the columns included in the SELECT statement. The rows of data added to the table will be limited by the criteria that you set in the WHERE or HAVING clause.

> **Tip:** The use of parentheses around the query or SELECT statement in a CREATE TABLE statement is optional. However, I recommend including them because they make the statement easier to read.

> **SAS/ACCESS and SQL Pass-Through Facility users:** The syntax used by some databases when creating a table from an existing structure differs from that shown here. In some cases, parentheses are required; in others, the query precedes an INTO keyword followed by the new table name. Check the SQL reference specific to your RDBMS for more information.

In the next example a new table called *company* is created from the *client* and *address* tables of the Bluesky Publishing Company. Only the rows in the table at the time the CREATE TABLE statement is issued will be inserted into the new table.

```
LIBNAME bluesky "C:\mydata\bluesky bookstore\";

CREATE TABLE BLUESKY.COMPANY
AS  (SELECT    c.company, a.address, a.city,
               a.state, a.zip_post, a.country
     FROM      bluesky.client c, bluesky.address a
     WHERE     c.clientno = a.clientno);

SELECT   *
FROM     bluesky.company;
```

Tip: A table that is created using columns and data from one or more tables is not linked to those underlying tables. Modifications and new data added to the underlying table(s) after the CREATE statement is issued are not reflected in the new table. Views, on the other hand, are dependent on the underlying table(s) used to create them. As a result, they will always reflect the current data in the table(s) from which the view was constructed. More information on views is provided later in this chapter.

Guidelines

- The new table contains only the columns listed in the SELECT clause of the query.
- The data type of the original columns or expressions are used for the column in the new table.
- Column modifiers assigned to the original columns are assigned to the columns in the new table, unless replaced in the SELECT clause of the query.
- An ORDER BY clause can be added to the CREATE TABLE statement, setting the order in which the rows retrieved from the query are loaded into the new table.
- All valid SELECT statements or queries may be used, although the following restrictions apply:
  - A GROUP BY clause is allowed in the query; however, variables in a GROUP BY clause are not included as columns in the table unless they are also in the SELECT clause.
  - An ORDER BY clause is not allowed in the query. It can be included outside of the parenthesis in the CREATE TABLE statement.

The next example shows a new table called *prodchk* built from a more complex SELECT statement. The SELECT statement or query draws columns and rows from several tables and generates summary statistics. Notice the position of the ORDER BY and GROUP BY clauses. There are two GROUP BY clauses in the query—one in the outer or main query and the other in the inner or subquery. However, the ORDER BY clause is part of the CREATE TABLE statement; it is positioned outside of the query parentheses. The ORDER BY clause operates on the newly created table after the SELECT statement or query is processed. An ORDER BY clause is not allowed in the query portion of a CREATE TABLE statement.

```
LIBNAME bluesky "C:\mydata\bluesky bookstore\";

CREATE TABLE bluesky.prodchk
AS (SELECT   s.title, s.prodcode,
```

```
                max(s.stock) as stock,
                mean(o.quantity) as qtymean,
                count(o.invoice) as salecnt
       FROM     bluesky.orders o,
                bluesky.stock s
       WHERE    o.prodcode = s.prodcode
                and o.quantity >(SELECT   mean(o1.quantity)
                                FROM     bluesky.orders o1
                                WHERE    o1.prodcode=o.prodcode
                                GROUP BY o1.prodcode )
   GROUP BY s.title, s.prodcode)
ORDER BY  prodcode;
```

If you do not include the parentheses around the SELECT statement of the CREATE TABLE statement, it may appear that the ORDER BY clause is allowed in the query. If the ORDER BY clause is moved into the query of a CREATE TABLE statement where parentheses are included, an error is reported in the SAS log as shown in the next example.

SAS log:

```
601  CREATE TABLE bluesky.prodchk
602  AS (SELECT   s.title, s.prodcode,
603               max(s.stock) as stock,
604               mean(o.quantity) as qtymean,
605               count(o.invoice) as salecnt
606      FROM     bluesky.orders o,
607               bluesky.stock s
608      WHERE    o.prodcode = s.prodcode
609               and o.quantity >(SELECT   mean(o1.quantity)
610                                FROM     bluesky.orders o1
611                                WHERE    o1.prodcode=o.prodcode
612                                GROUP BY o1.prodcode )
613
614  GROUP BY s.title, s.prodcode
615  ORDER BY prodcode);
     -----
     79
ERROR 79-322: Expecting a ).

615! ORDER BY prodcode);
                      -
                      79
ERROR 79-322: Expecting a (.
```

The next example provides a description of the new table. The variable data types are based on the data types of the table or data set from which the column is drawn. If an expression based on one or more columns is included in the SELECT clause, the data type of the result is used in the new table.

SAS log:

```
NOTE: SQL table BLUESKY.PRODCHK was created like:

create table BLUESKY.PRODCHK( bufsize=8192 )
  (
   title char(50),
   prodCode char(6),
   stock num,
   qtymean num,
   salecnt num
  );
```

If you are using expressions in your SELECT clause, an alias should be assigned using the AS keyword. If an alias is not provided, SAS will assign a nondescriptive name to the column as shown in a report generated by a DESCRIBE statement.

SAS log:

```
create table BLUESKY.STAT( bufsize=8192 )
  (
   TITLE char(30),
   PRODCODE num,
   STOCK num,
   _TEMA004 num,
   _TEMG002 num,
   _TEMG003 num
  );
```

If you find yourself in this situation, there are several options available other than dropping and recreating the table. The problem column(s) can be dropped and re-added using the ALTER statement discussed later in this chapter. Alternatively, the columns can be renamed using a SAS DATA step. A RENAME= option is available for the SELECT statement; however, it behaves like an alias or label in that it does not permanently rename the column:

```
SELECT * FROM bluesky.stat (rename=_TEMA004=meanqty);
```

The newly created table, which is based on the *stock* table, resembles the output of the Base SAS SUMMARY procedure. A report generated from the *prodchk* table is included in the following table.

title	prod Code	stock	qtymean	salecn
Geology: Volcanos	100340	400	800	1
Engineering Infrastructure Modeling	200345	2400	1400	1
The Ultimate Philosophy	300456	100	300	1
The Underground Economy	300680	1000	2900	1
Medical Education in School	400100	300	350	
Tibetan Medicine	400128	2000	1230	1
National Library of Medicine	400178	35	500	1
The Art of Computer Programming	500120	1600	1000	1
The Maestro	600125	100	475	2

This form of the CREATE TABLE statement can also be used to accomplish data type conversions. An INPUT or PUT function can be applied to a column in the SELECT clause. The data type conversion will be assigned to the column in the new table only.

In the next example a new table called *prodsmry* is created from columns in the *orders* and *stock* tables. The SELECT clause contains an INPUT function that converts the product code (prodcode) column to a numeric data type with a width of four. Notice that the alias of the newly created numeric product code (prodcode) column is included in the GROUP BY clause. The data type definition of the product code column in the new table is confirmed as numeric in the results from the DESCRIBE statement. However, the original *orders* and *stock* tables remain unchanged.

```
LIBNAME bluesky "C:\mydata\bluesky bookstore\";

CREATE TABLE bluesky.prodsmry
AS (SELECT   s.title, input(s.prodcode,4.) as code, s.stock,
             mean(o.quantity) as qtymean, count(o.quantity) as
                  qtycnt
    FROM     bluesky.orders o,
             bluesky.stock s
    WHERE    o.prodcode = s.prodcode
    GROUP BY s.title, code, s.stock);
```

SAS log:

```
NOTE: SQL table BLUESKY.PRODSMRY was created like:

create table BLUESKY.PRODSMRY( bufsize=8192 )
  (
   TITLE char(50),
   CODE num,
   STOCK num,
   QTYMEAN num,
   QTYCNT num
  );
```

Tip: Data type conversions specified in the SELECT statement used in a CREATE TABLE statement apply to both the column definition and the values added to the column from the source table.

Creating views

General form:

CREATE VIEW <libref.>name
AS (query)
<**ORDER BY** clause>
<**USING LIBNAME** libref 'path' | **RDBMS** connection parameters>
;

NOTE: The use of parentheses around the SELECT statement or query is optional.

Views are generated through a single form of the CREATE statement that takes both structure and data from an existing table. However, only the CREATE statement is stored either in the WORK or USER library or the storage location associated with the libref on the LIBNAME statement, not the view itself. Views are dynamic in nature, and, as a result, they are created each time they are referenced.

Views will always reflect the current data in the table or tables from which they are constructed. Moreover, because only the query is stored, views do not require the storage space of a table. However, these advantages come at a cost; processing is involved each time the view is accessed. If your view is built from very large tables or complex queries, you might consider using tables instead of views, especially if the view will be frequently accessed.

Guidelines

- Although views may be assigned to a library, only the CREATE statement and not the data itself is permanently stored.
- The view contains only the columns listed in the SELECT clause of the query.
- If a column in the underlying table upon which the view is built is deleted, an error message will be reported when the view is accessed.
- Column modifiers assigned to the columns in the view source tables are passed on to the view. All reports generated from the view will use the column modifiers unless a new attribute is assigned to a column in the SELECT clause.
- An ORDER BY clause is allowed in the CREATE VIEW statement.
- A USING clause can be added to the CREATE VIEW statement, embedding a LIBNAME statement into the view.
- All valid SELECT statements or queries can be used, although the following exceptions apply:
  - A GROUP BY clause is allowed; however, variables in a GROUP BY clause are not included as columns in the view unless they are also in the SELECT clause.
  - An ORDER BY clause is not allowed in the query. It can, however, be included in the CREATE VIEW statement.

Tip: Views created in Version 6 are automatically converted for use in Version 7, 8, or 9 when the view is referenced in a SAS program or SQL Pass-Through Facility.

The next example shows a view used to generate orders in the last 30 days for the Bluesky Publishing Company. The query associated with the view is stored permanently in the bluesky library; therefore, it can be accessed in future sessions. The view joins the *orders* and *stock* table and limits the rows in the view to those between the current date and 30 days prior.

```
LIBNAME bluesky "C:\mydata\bluesky bookstore\";

CREATE VIEW bluesky.ordrpt AS
       (SELECT stock.prodcode 'Product Code', stock.title 'Title',
               orders.invoice 'Invoice', orders.ord_date 'Order Date'
        FROM   bluesky.stock, bluesky.orders
        WHERE  ord_date between DATE() and DATE()-30
               AND stock.prodcode=orders.prodcode
        )
ORDER BY orders.ord_date;
```

Tip: Remember that parentheses around the query used to build the view are optional. In the above example, they are used to make clear that the ORDER BY clause is part of the CREATE VIEW statement rather than the query.

Give careful consideration to the inclusion of an ORDER BY clause in the CREATE VIEW statement. Each time the view is created, the sort must be processed increasing the required resources and processing time.

A DESCRIBE statement issued against the *ordrpt* view is included in the next example. Notice that the query used to generate the view, rather than the structure of the view, is reported. The column names in the view are evident only if the SELECT clause in the CREATE statement includes specific columns rather than an asterisk. Although the column names are shown, the data types are not; the data types are associated with the underlying table and can only be viewed when a DESCRIBE statement is issued against the underlying *stock* and *orders* tables.

Tip: The DESCRIBE statement includes the keyword VIEW rather than TABLE when issued against a view. The dictionary tables can be used to provide the correct keyword based on the name of the table or view, constructing the correct form of the DESCRIBE statement for interactive applications. Information on SAS dictionary tables is included in Chapter 7, "Building Interactive Applications."

```
LIBNAME bluesky "C:\mydata\bluesky bookstore\";

DESCRIBE VIEW BLUESKY.ORDRPT;
```

SAS log:

```
NOTE: SQL view BLUESKY.ORDRPT is defined as:

select stock.prodcode label='Product Code', stock.title label='Title',
      orders.invoice label='Invoice', orders.ord_date label='Order
      Date'
from BLUESKY.STOCK, BLUESKY.ORDERS
where ord_date between DATE() and DATE()-30 and
      (stock.prodcode=orders.prodcode)
order by orders.ord_date asc;
```

Tip: If you compare the SELECT statement from the SAS log above with the CREATE VIEW statement for *ordrpt* in the previous example, you will notice slight differences in the syntax. SAS automatically adds table qualifiers to all column names as well as parentheses in WHERE or HAVING clauses that contain multiple criteria.

When a report is required from the view, the user enters a simple SELECT statement. The view is generated at the time of the query; therefore, only those orders within 30 days of the current date are included in the report. The next example shows the SELECT statement and the resulting report.

```
LIBNAME bluesky "C:\mydata\bluesky bookstore\";

TITLE1  'Orders placed in the last 30 days';
TITLE2  'Report Date: ' &SYSDATE;

SELECT  *
FROM    bluesky.ordrpt;
```

```
Orders placed in the last 30 days
Report Date:  11JUL04

Product                                                         Order
Code      Title                                   Invoice         Date
----------------------------------------------------------------------

------

100340    Geology: Volcanos                       041212-01     12JUN04
300289    Democracy in America                    041212-03     12JUN04
200678    Managing Water Resources                041212-02     12JUN04
```

Tip: Unlike the DESCRIBE statement, a SELECT statement makes no distinction between a view and a table.

The use of views can be very helpful when complex or dynamic queries are necessary to generate the required reports. The next example includes a much more complex query upon which a view is built. This view includes details of orders placed by U.S. universities for above-average book quantities.

```
LIBNAME bluesky "C:\mydata\bluesky bookstore\";

CREATE VIEW univrpt as
         (SELECT clientno "Client", invoice "Invoice#",
                          ord_date "Date", quantity "Quantity",
                          totsale "Sale Total" format dollar10.2
          FROM   bluesky.orders ord1
          WHERE quantity GE
                             (SELECT round(avg(quantity))
                              FROM    bluesky.orders ord2
                              WHERE   ord2.clientno =ANY

                                      (SELECT clientno
                                      FROM    bluesky.address
                                      WHERE   country = 'USA'
                       INTERSECT
                              SELECT  clientno
                              FROM    bluesky.client
                              WHERE   company like '%University%'
                 )

           AND ord2.clientno = ord1.client
           )

AND clientno IN  (SELECT  address.clientno
                  FROM    bluesky.address JOIN bluesky.client
                  ON          address.clientno = client.clientno
                  WHERE   country ='USA'
                          AND company like '%University%'
                     )
      );
```

Tip: When a view is created, SAS does not generate any output. Rather, a simple message indicating that the view has been defined is reported in the log. This message confirms that the syntax was correct, the underlying tables exist, and the variables were correctly used.

```
NOTE: SQL view WORK.UNIVRPT has been defined.
```

Remember, if the underlying tables are later deleted or columns used in the view are dropped, a SELECT statement referencing the view will generate an error message. The following error messages are reported when the clientno column of the *orders* table is dropped and a SELECT statement is issued against the *univrpt* view created in the preceding example.

SAS log:

```
1405   SELECT * FROM univrpt;
ERROR: Column clientno could not be found in the table/view identified
       with the correlation name ORD2.
ERROR: Unresolved reference to table/correlation name ord2.
ERROR: Column clientno could not be found in the table/view identified
       with the correlation name ORD2.
ERROR: Unresolved reference to table/correlation name ord2.
ERROR: Column clientno could not be found in the table/view identified
       with the correlation name ORD1.
ERROR: The following columns were not found in the contributing
       tables: clientno.
```

USING clause

The USING clause can be added to a SELECT statement included in a CREATE VIEW statement. The LIBNAME statement is permanently stored with the view, allowing for automatic update of the view data without the reassignment of the library.

> **Tip:** The LIBNAME libref embedded in the CREATE VIEW statement is local to the statement. The same libref can be used in your SAS session without conflict.

The LIBNAME statement may reference a database or disk location. In the next example a view called *newaddress* is created from the Bluesky Publishing *address* table. The Bluesky libref is associated with a disk location in the USING clause of the CREATE VIEW statement. Each time the view is referenced in a SELECT statatement, the Bluesky libref is assigned to the location and then cleared.

```
CREATE   view newaddress as
SELECT   *
FROM     bluesky.address
USING    LIBNAME bluesky "C:\mydata\bluesky bookstore\";
```

When a USING clause that references a database is encountered within a CREATE VIEW statement, a connection with the database is made using the database connection parameters specified in the clause. The library reference is de-assigned and the connection terminated after the view is processed.

> **SAS/ACCESS users:** Appendix C, "Information for Database Users," contains details on the connection parameters used in a LIBNAME statement or USING clause.

In the next example a view is created from the order-related tables stored in both an Oracle database and a SAS native library. The USING clause assigns a libref to both the database and disk locations using forms of the LIBNAME statement suitable to each. The SAS/ACCESS form of the LIBNAME statement assigning a libref of ORALIB to the Oracle database includes the parameters needed to establish a connection to the database. By contrast, the LIBNAME statement for the BLUESKY library includes only the libref and pathname.

```
LIBNAME bluesky "C:\mydata\bluesky bookstore\";

CREATE  view bluesky.allorders AS
        (SELECT  *
         FROM    oralib.orders, bluesky.orders
         USING   libname oralib oracle
           user = scott password = tiger path= master,
           libname bluesky "C:\mydata\bluesky bookstore\");
```

SAS log:

```
NOTE: SQL view BLUESKY.allorders has been defined.
NOTE: PROCEDURE SQL used (Total process time):
      real time           12.32 seconds
      cpu time            0.77 seconds
```

In the next example, the user treats the view created in the previous example as any other with no additional keywords, clauses, or statements required to access the database. However, the CREATE VIEW statement included an embedded LIBNAME statement that connects to an Oracle database. If problems are encountered when establishing a connection to the database, it can generate error messages confusing to the user. Notice that the error message indicates that an Oracle connection could not be made; however, it does not indicate that the connection parameters are part of an embedded LIBNAME statement in a CREATE VIEW statement. In fact, the error message does not include anything that would suggest the user is accessing a view rather than a table.

The problem is not limited to database connections. If an embedded LIBNAME statement in a CREATE VIEW statement references a disk location that is not available when the user accesses the view, an error message stating that the library does not exist is generated.

```
LIBNAME bluesky "C:\mydata\bluesky bookstore\";

PROC SQL;
SELECT  *
FROM    bluesky.emp;
```

SAS log:

```
ERROR: ORACLE connection error: ORA-01034: ORACLE not availableORA-27101:
shared memory realm does not exist.
```

SAS/ACCESS users: Keep in mind that every time a user accesses the view containing an embedded LIBNAME statement referencing a database, a connection is made to that database. If a connection is not possible because the database is unavailable or the maximum number of connections has been reached, the SELECT statement issued against the view will fail. This can be confusing for the user because the error message appears to be unrelated to the SQL statement submitted.

In-line views

General form:

FROM (query)

NOTE: The query in the FROM clause must adhere to the guidelines for queries used to generate views.

In the examples above, the view was first created and then a SELECT statement was issued against the view to generate a report. However, both of these steps can be combined when in-line views are used.

The query needed to generate the view is included in the FROM clause instead of the name of a view or table. The FROM clause is executed first, generating the view from which the SELECT clause draws its columns. When a view is used in this fashion, it is not permanently stored. Rather, it is dynamically created during the processing of the query.

The next example includes two in-line views, each of which is highlighted in the example. The first in-line view given an alias of "a" generates the total sales and quantities for the past 30 days for each client. The second in-line view given an alias of "c" generates company total sales and quantities from all orders in the current *orders* table. An equijoin is made between the client numbers in view "a" and the Bluesky *orders* table to provide comparison by client of total sales and quantity to the 30-day totals. A Cartesian join is then made between these results and the totals for the company.

```
LIBNAME bluesky "C:\mydata\bluesky bookstore\";

TITLE1    'Comparison of:';
TITLE2    '1.  Total Client to Company sales and quantity ';
TITLE3    "2.  Comparison of Total Client sales and quantity to
               Client's last 30 days";

SELECT    a.clientno 'Client',
          sum(b.totsale) as csales 'Client Total Sales'
              format=comma10.,
          sum(b.totsale)/sum(c.sales) as cosales
          'Percent Company Total sales' format=percent.,
          sum(a.sales30) as csales30 'Client Sales in last 30
          days' format=comma10.,
          sum(b.quantity) as cqnty 'Client Total quantity'
          format=comma10.,
          sum(b.quantity)/sum(c.quantity) as coqnty 'Percent
              Company Total quantity'
          format=percent.,
          sum(a.quantity30) as cqnty 'Client Quantity in last 30
          days' format=comma10.

FROM      (SELECT    orders.clientno,
                     sum(orders.totsale) as sales30,
                     sum(orders.quantity)as quantity30
          FROM       bluesky.stock, bluesky.orders
          WHERE      ord_date between DATE() and DATE()-30
                     AND stock.prodcode=orders.prodcode
          group by orders.clientno
          ) a,

     bluesky.orders b,

     (select        sum(totsale)as sales, sum(quantity) as quantity
     from           bluesky.orders
     ) c

WHERE a.clientno = b.clientno
GROUP BY a.clientno;
```

The report generated by the above query is shown in the next example. Without the in-line views, a report of this nature would necessitate the creation of temporary tables because the grouping or summary variables are each calculated differently.

> **Tip:** A view can be created from the query included in the previous example allowing for simpler access or the inclusion of the variables in other SAS procedures. In order to reference expressions created in a view by name, an alias must be assigned to that expression at the time the view is created as shown in the previous example
>
> Remember, an alias is assigned with an AS keyword. Quoted strings associated with an expression are treated only as a column heading for the report.

```
Comparison of:
1.   Total Client to Company sales and quantity
2.   Comparison of Total Client sales and quantity to Client's last 30
     days

                        Percent    Client                 Percent    Client
               Client   Company   Sales in      Client    Company   Quantity
                Total     Total    last 30       Total      Total    in last
    Client      Sales     sales       days    quantity   quantity    30 days
--------------------------------------------------------------------------------
      3007    262,010        6%  1,350,000       6,295         5%     30,000
      6090     30,025        1%      4,320         595         1%        120
      8003     36,462        1%      2,160       1,527         1%        120
```

> **Tip:** In-line views do not have the same benefit as views created with a CREATE VIEW statement. They are not permanently stored, nor do they provide for simple SELECT statements. Rather they are more like subqueries described in the previous chapter. They create a new temporary table that includes all necessary calculations and combines columns from one or more tables that would ordinarily require more than one query.

Effective use of indexes

Indexes are physical structures that contain data values and row pointers or identifiers. When a column is indexed, every data value from the column is placed in the index along with a pointer to the row or rows in which the data occurs in the table. If several rows have the same data value, the index stores a list of the row locations in which the data value is found.

> **Tip:** Data that is already sorted in proper order does not have to be re-sorted at the time the index is created.

Significant performance improvements may be accomplished with carefully designed indexes. When the WHERE clause of a query includes criteria that reference an indexed column, the index rather than the table is accessed first. The index identifies which row or rows contains the values that meet the criteria. As a result, only a portion of the table must be accessed to obtain the rows to be included in the report.

> **Tip:** Indexes cannot be applied to views because views are stored as queries rather than physical structures. However, indexing the underlying tables from which the views draw data will improve performance.

Indexes may reduce performance. Indexes are automatically built for integrity constraints, and these indexes are checked against values in incoming rows to ensure that the rules established by the constraint are not violated. In addition, indexes associated with integrity constraints such as primary and foreign keys are updated at the time new rows are inserted.

> **Tip:** It is a good idea to build indexes on columns that change infrequently. Indexes must be checked and/or updated as new rows are added or values are changed. Keep in mind that indexes are created automatically for integrity constraints.

Creating indexes

Indexes can be created either in the SQL procedure or within the SAS DATA step. If an index is built in a permanent table, then the index is stored permanently. Alternatively, an index can be created for a temporary table. It will be available only during the current SAS session.

SAS/ACCESS and SQL Pass-Through Facility users: You cannot create a unique constraint (index) on a table unless you have the appropriate access to that table. The GRANT command can be issued within the SQL Pass-Through Facility.

Simple indexes

General form:

```
CREATE      <UNIQUE> INDEX <index_name>
ON          <LIBREF.>table (column) ;
```

A simple index is an index built on a single column of either a permanent or a temporary table. The unique option can be applied to the index to ensure that each value within the column is distinct. The unique option is discussed in detail in a later section.

A simple index must be assigned with the same name as the column upon which it is built. When created, indexes are associated with a specific table. It is therefore possible for indexes with the same name to be associated with different tables. However, two indexes with the same name cannot be associated with the same table.

The next example shows a simple index created for the clientno column in the Bluesky *client* table. A DESCRIBE statement issued after the index creation statement provides information in the SAS log concerning both the table and the new index.

```
LIBNAME bluesky "C:\mydata\bluesky bookstore\";

CREATE    INDEX CLIENTNO ON BLUESKY.CLIENT(CLIENTNO);
DESCRIBE  table bluesky.client;
```

SAS log:

```
NOTE: SQL table BLUESKY.CLIENT was created like:

create table BLUESKY.CLIENT( bufsize=12288 )
  (
   clientNo num,
   company  char(40),
   cont_fst char(10),
   cont_lst char(15),
   dept     char(25),
   phone    char(25),
   fax      char(25)
  );
create index clientNo on BLUESKY.CLIENT(clientNo);
```

Simple indexes can increase the performance of queries that include criteria based on the indexed column. However, indexes also use resources because they are updated each time the contents of the column changes. More performance-related information is included in a later section.

Composite indexes

General form:

```
CREATE        <UNIQUE> INDEX <index_name>
ON            <LIBREF.>table (column, column,<column...>) ;
```

The SAS System will not allow a composite index to have the same name as one of the columns included in the index. As simple indexes are named after a column, this rule prevents any confusion between the two types of indexes. Any name that SAS allows can be applied to a composite index.

Composite indexes can be any valid SAS name except the name of any columns that are part of another index. It is best to assign a name that is meaningful to your composite indexes. Names that combine part of each of the contributing column names or indicate the purpose of the index are often used.

The columns included in a composite index do not have to be the same data type. For example, columns containing dates, numbers, and characters can be combined into a single composite index.

Only one composite index can be generated for a specific set and order of columns. SAS will report an error message in the SAS log if you attempt to create a composite index for a set of columns for which a composite index exists. However, the same set of columns can be included in more than one composite index if the order in which they are specified is different.

The next example shows two composite indexes using the same set of columns but specified in a different order. Notice that the columns have various data types.

```
LIBNAME     bluesky "C:\mydata\bluesky bookstore\";

CREATE       INDEX orderx
             ON bluesky.orders(ord_date, invoice, clientno);
CREATE       INDEX clientx ON bluesky.orders(clientno,
             ord_date,invoice);
DESCRIBE     table bluesky.orders;
```

SAS log:

```
NOTE: SQL table BLUESKY.ORDERS was created like:

create table BLUESKY.ORDERS( bufsize=8192 )
  (
   PRODCODE char(6),
   ORD_DATE num format=DATE. informat=DATE.,
   QUANTITY num,
   TOTSALE  num,
   CURRENCY char(3),
   DELCODE  char(3),
   CLIENTNO num,
   INVOICE  char(10)
  );
create index CLIENTX on BLUESKY.ORDERS(CLIENTNO,ORD_DATE,INVOICE);
create index ORDERX on BLUESKY.ORDERS(ORD_DATE,INVOICE,CLIENTNO);
```

Tip: A column may be part of one or more composite indexes, and it may also have its own simple index.

Unique indexes

Although indexes are commonly created to enhance performance, they may also be used to prevent duplicate values in a column. When created in this way the index is used to apply an integrity constraint to the table column. A common form of integrity constraint is the PRIMARY KEY constraint, which ensures that each row of a table is uniquely identified. A unique index is automatically generated for a primary key.

Caution: A single missing or null value is allowed when a unique index is applied to a column. However, PRIMARY KEY constraints do not permit even a single null value in the column. There is a second constraint, NOT NULL, that is also associated with a PRIMARY KEY constraint.

The unique option can be applied to either simple or composite indexes. If a unique simple index is built, the values within that column must be unique. However, when a unique composite index is created, the combination of all of the columns making up a composite index must be unique. With such indexes, there may be duplicate values within any of the columns included in the composite index.

Tip: A UNIQUE constraint and a unique index operate the same way. An index is often created to enforce uniqueness for a set of operations and then dropped. Although the UNIQUE constraint can be dropped from a table using the ALTER statement, it is often safer in interactive applications to create and later drop an index rather than manipulating a table structure.

If you attempt to build a unique index on a column or combination of columns that contain duplicate values, an error message will be written to the SAS log. An error message is also generated if the column contains multiple null or missing entries.

Consider the next example. The creation of three indexes in the *address* table for the Bluesky Publishing Company has been attempted. In each case, the index specified as unique requires unique values within the column or columns.

SAS log:

```
136   CREATE UNIQUE INDEX state ON bluesky.address(state);
ERROR: Duplicate values not allowed on index STATE for file ADDRESS.

141   CREATE UNIQUE INDEX country ON bluesky.address(country);
ERROR: Duplicate values not allowed on index COUNTRY for file ADDRESS.

139   CREATE UNIQUE INDEX stcntry ON bluesky.address(state,country);
NOTE: Composite index CSC has been defined.
```

The failure of the index in the country column is caused by the occurrence of USA in two of the rows in the table. The failure of the index in the state column is caused by the occurrence of five null values in that column. However, notice that the composite index built in the state and country is successful. If you closely examine the table entries below, you will find that when the state and country values are taken together unique combinations are produced.

Table name: ADDRESS		
city	**state**	**country**
Austin	TX	USA
Chicago	IL	USA
Cambridge		UK
Singapore		Singapore
Adelaide		Australia
Berlin		Germany
Paris		France
Vancouver	BC	Canada

SQL optimizer

The SQL optimizer, automatically invoked with PROC SQL, determines the most cost-efficient method of processing a query. The SQL optimizer evaluates whether a sequential search of a file or the use of an index is more efficient in terms of cost. Several join options including hash, index, and merge joins are also evaluated. Statistical information relating to the distribution of values within a table is stored by the system allowing for better assessment of the most cost-efficient method of data access.

SAS/ACCESS and SQL Pass-Through Facility users: To optimize performance, the SQL optimizer may transfer join processing to the database(s) involved in the query. Appendix C, "Information for Database Users," contains additional information on working with databases and PROC SQL.

MSGLEVEL=

The MSGLEVEL= option controls the level of information written to the SAS log. When you set MSGLEVEL= I, more information concerning index usage is written to the SAS log including whether an index was used and which index was selected. This information is invaluable when trying to optimize performance.

In the next example, the SAS log is included for a query used to retrieve the arts and science books with a specific reprint cutoff code. The index selected by the SQL optimizer is indicated in the log because the MSGLEVEL has been set.

```
LIBNAME bluesky "C:\mydata\bluesky bookstore\";

PROC SQL;

CREATE   INDEX reprint on bluesky.stock(reprint);
CREATE   INDEX category on bluesky.stock(category);

OPTIONS  msglevel=I;

SELECT   *
FROM     bluesky.stock
WHERE    category in ('arts', 'science') and reprint='A';
```

SAS log:

```
INFO: Index reprint selected for WHERE clause optimization.
NOTE: No rows were selected.
```

_METHOD

The SQL optimizer develops an execution plan that outlines each step in the processing of the query and includes the indexes and join methods used. To check the execution plan of a query, _METHOD is specified in the PROC SQL statement. The execution plan uses the codes shown in the next table to indicate the action associated with each step.

Module code	Meaning
sqxcrta	Create table as Select
sqxfil	Filter Rows
sqxjsl	Step Loop Join (Cartesian)
sqxjm	Merge Join
sqxjndx	Index Join
sqxjhsh	Hash Join
sqxnsct	Nested Select
sqxslct	Select
sqxsort	Sort
sqxsrc	Source Rows from table
sqxsubq	Subquery
sqxsumg	Summary Statistics (with Group BY)
sqxsumn	Summary Statistics (not grouped)
sqxuniq	Distinct rows only

There is another option, _TREE, that can be used instead of, or in addition to, _METHOD. The _TREE option generates the execution plan in a graphical format. Both the _METHOD and _TREE options are undocumented PROC SQL options.

In the next example a complex query is included together with its execution plan. Notice that a separate execution plan is provided for each of the subqueries. Although this is a complex query, the plan includes only the major processing steps.

```
LIBNAME bluesky "C:\mydata\bluesky bookstore\";
PROC SQL _method;
SELECT    clientno "Client", invoice "Invoice#",
                         ord_date "Date", quantity "Quantity",
                         totsale "Sale Total" format dollar10.2
          FROM   bluesky.orders ord1
          WHERE  quantity GE
                         (SELECT (avg(quantity))
                         FROM    bluesky.orders ord2
                         WHERE   ord2.clientno =ANY
                         (SELECT clientno
```

```
                        FROM    bluesky.address
                        WHERE   country = 'USA'
                  INTERSECT
                        SELECT  clientno
                        FROM    bluesky.client
                        WHERE   company like '%University%'
               )
             AND ord2.clientno = ord1.clientno
             )
AND clientno IN  (SELECT address.clientno
                  FROM   bluesky.address JOIN bluesky.client
                  ON     address.clientno = client.clientno
                  WHERE  country ='USA'
                         AND company like '%University%'
                  )
;
```

SAS log:

```
NOTE: SQL execution methods chosen are:

      sqxslct
          sqxfil
              sqxsrc( BLUESKY.ORDERS(alias = ORD1) )

NOTE: SQL subquery execution methods chosen are:

          sqxsubq
              sqxsumn
                  sqxfil
                      sqxsrc( BLUESKY.ORDERS(alias = ORD2) )
NOTE: SQL subquery execution methods chosen are:

          sqxsubq
              sqxnsct
                  sqxuniq
                      sqxsrc( BLUESKY.ADDRESS )
                  sqxuniq
                      sqxsrc( BLUESKY.CLIENT )
```

At first glance the output generated by the _METHOD option appears difficult to interpret because of the coding. However, even with a complex query only a few codes are included in the plan. In addition, the plan is divided into logical groupings when subqueries are included.

WHERE clause processing

An index will be used in the processing of a WHERE clause if the SQL optimizer determines that approximately 15 percent or fewer rows from a table will be selected using the index. If more than one index is available, the SAS System will use the index that will select the fewest observations. The algorithm used by the optimizer in its evaluation of index usage is most accurate in its prediction if values within the indexed column are uniformly distributed. The SQL optimizer is invoked automatically at the time the SQL statement is parsed; it does not require any user intervention.

An index cannot be used if it will not provide all of the rows in a table that satisfy a set of conditions in the WHERE clause. If the use of an index might eliminate rows that meet the criteria specified in the WHERE clause, index use will be rejected by the SAS System.

In the next example, two indexes for the *orders* table have been built—one on the order date column and the other on the client number column. The ord_date index could be used to quickly identify the rows that meet the date condition. However, by limiting the rows accessed in the table to those within the specified date range, rows that meet the client number condition could be eliminated. The same problem exists if the clientno index is used to identify the rows with the specified client numbers. As a result, this query would not use either index.

```
LIBNAME bluesky "C:\mydata\bluesky bookstore\";
PROC SQL _METHOD;
OPTIONS msglevel=I;

CREATE  INDEX ORD_DATE ON BLUESKY.ORDERS(ORD_DATE);
CREATE  INDEX clientno ON bluesky.orders(clientno);

SELECT  *
FROM    bluesky.orders
WHERE   (ord_date between '01MAY04'D and '30DEC04'D)
        OR clientno in (1001, 2010);
```

SAS log :

```
NOTE: SQL execution methods chosen are:

      sqxslct
          sqxsrc( BLUESKY.ORDERS )
```

> **Tip:** If you often select all rows from a table using an asterisk, consider adding a format and label to each column when the table is created. It avoids the problem of having to specify each of the columns in the SELECT statement in order to generate a more polished report.

The next example shows multiple WHERE clause criteria in which indexes would be used. In this case, all of the conditions must be true so the identification of specific rows through each of the indexes does not eliminate rows.

```
LIBNAME bluesky "C:\mydata\bluesky bookstore\";
PROC SQL _METHOD;
OPTIONS msglevel=I;

CREATE INDEX ORD_DATE ON BLUESKY.ORDERS(ORD_DATE);
CREATE INDEX currency ON bluesky.orders(currency);
CREATE INDEX totsale ON bluesky.orders(totsale);

SELECT   ord_date "Order Date", clientno "Client",
         totsale "Total Sale" Format=comma8.2
FROM     bluesky.orders
WHERE    (ord_date between '01MAY04'D and '30DEC04'D)
         AND totsale > 300 and currency = 'USD';
```

SAS log:

```
NOTE: SQL execution methods chosen are:

      sqxslct
          sqxsrc( BLUESKY.ORDERS )
INFO: Index currency selected for WHERE clause optimization.
```

When multiple criteria are included in a WHERE clause, composite indexes may be advantageous. In the above example, three indexes were created for the columns used in the criteria in the WHERE clause. The SQL optimizer selects only one of the indexes when the query is run. However, a composite index created from the three columns would allow for indexed searching within all of the columns. A composite index includes all possible combinations of the included columns so it can be used to quickly identify the rows in the table that meet the WHERE clause condition.

> **Tip:** A composite index can only be used if the AND operator joins multiple criteria based on the columns in the index in the WHERE clause.

The first column of the composite index must be included in the criteria of an SQL query in order for the index to be utilized. For example, if a composite index is built on the invoice number and date, then the invoice number must be included in the criteria. If only the date is included in the WHERE clause, then the index will not be used.

> **Tip:** Although the first column in a composite index must be included in the WHERE criteria, it is not necessary for all columns in the composite index to be included in the criteria.

IDXWHERE=YES

Setting the option IDXWHERE =YES directs the SQL optimizer to use indexes in the processing of a WHERE clause without evaluating whether they are cost-efficient. In the next example a simple query directs the SQL optimizer to use the newly created category index when processing the WHERE clause of the query. Notice that the index is not named, but rather the direction to use an index is given. The choice of index is based on the standard guidelines discussed later in this section.

> **Tip:** If you are using SAS 8.2 and the IDXWHERE option does not appear to be working, check the SAS Web site for the appropriate hotfix.

```
LIBNAME bluesky "C:\mydata\bluesky bookstore\";

PROC SQL;
OPTIONS msglevel=I;

CREATE index category on bluesky.stock(category);

SELECT *
FROM   bluesky.stock (idxwhere=yes)
WHERE  category = 'arts';
```

SAS log:

```
INFO: Data set option (IDXWHERE=YES)forced an index to be used rather
      than a sequential pass for where-clause processing.
INFO: Index category selected for WHERE clause optimization.
```

> **Tip:** If you specify IDXWHERE=YES and an index that can be used to optimize the WHERE clause does not exist, the SAS log will report the following message:
>
> ```
> ERROR: IDXWHERE=YES but no index exists for optimizing a
>        where clause.
> ```

IDXNAME=

The IDXNAME= option directs the SQL optimizer to use the named index in the optimization of the WHERE clause of a query. A specific single or composite index can be indicated for use with a PROC SQL statement with the IDXNAME= option. This is helpful if you have more than one index defined for a table column and you would like to direct the optimizer to use a specific index.

> **Tip:** A simple or composite index may be specified with the IDXNAME option for optimizing the WHERE clause condition of a query. Choose carefully if you have a WHERE clause with a number of criteria as only a single index may be named with this option.

In the next example two indexes are associated with the category column of the *stock* table; a simple index named *category* and a composite index named *catprod*. The optimizer selects the simple index to optimize the WHERE clause of the SELECT statement. However, the IDXNAME=catprod option in the second SELECT statement forces the optimizer to instead use the composite index.

```
LIBNAME bluesky "C:\mydata\bluesky bookstore\";

PROC SQL;
OPTIONS msglevel=I;

CREATE  INDEX category on bluesky.stock(category);
CREATE  INDEX catprod on bluesky.stock(category,prodcode);

SELECT  *
FROM    bluesky.stock
WHERE   category = 'arts';

SELECT  *
FROM    bluesky.stock (idxname=catprod)
WHERE   category='arts';
```

SAS log:

```
3162   SELECT   *
3163   FROM     bluesky.stock
3164   WHERE    category = 'arts';
INFO: Index category selected for WHERE clause optimization.

3165   SELECT   *
3166   FROM     bluesky.stock (idxname=catprod)
3167   WHERE    category='arts';
INFO: Index catprod selected for WHERE clause optimization.
```

The SQL optimizer will check the WHERE clause condition to ensure that it can be optimized through the named index. If the WHERE clause condition includes an expression or function, the index cannot be used. In addition, the condition must reference the first column upon which the index was built if a composite index is named.

In the next example the IDXNAME= option directs the optimizer to use a composite index called prodcat built on the product code and category columns of the *stock* table. However, the WHERE clause criteria include the category column, which is the second column in the composite index. An error message is generated because the named index cannot be used to optimize the query.

```
LIBNAME bluesky "C:\mydata\bluesky bookstore\";

CREATE  index prodcat on bluesky.stock(prodcode,category);
SELECT  *
FROM    bluesky.stock (idxname=prodcat)
WHERE   category = 'arts';
```

SAS log:

```
ERROR: IDXNAME=prodcode, but first or only index variable does not
       match any optimizable WHERE clause condition
```

Tip: You cannot use IDXNAME= to override the rules associated with index usage. The named index will only be used if it is appropriate for the WHERE clause.

If the WHERE clause of a SELECT statement includes comparative criteria, an index can improve performance. If for example we wanted to find all entries in the *orders* table on May 6, 2003, we would use a query similar to that shown in the following example.

```
LIBNAME bluesky "C:\mydata\bluesky bookstore\";

SELECT  *
FROM    bluesky.orders
WHERE   ord_date = '06MAY03'D;
```

If the order dates are not indexed, every row in the table must be checked because a date of May 6, 2003, may occur anywhere within the table. This full-table scan processing can take a long time if the table is very large.

Warning: Full-table scans that involve checking every row in a table are conducted even if the values in the column are stored in sorted order.

However, if the order date column is indexed, the index rather than the table is searched for the required date. When the value is found in the index, the row pointer indicates exactly which row or range of rows within the table must be retrieved. There is no need to check every row in the table because SAS knows exactly where the value is located. The next example shows the same query as above; however, an index is created for the ord_date column of the *orders* table prior to the execution of the query.

```
LIBNAME bluesky "C:\mydata\bluesky bookstore\";
OPTIONS msglevel=I;
PROC SQL;

CREATE  INDEX ord_date ON bluesky.orders(ord_date);

SELECT  *
FROM    bluesky.orders
WHERE   ord_date = '06MAY03'D;
```

SAS log:

```
113  CREATE INDEX ord_date ON bluesky.orders(ord_date);
NOTE: Simple index ORD_DATE has been defined.

114
115  SELECT *
116  FROM bluesky.orders
117  WHERE  ord_date = '06MAY03'D;
INFO: Index ORD_DATE selected for WHERE clause optimization.
```

> **Tip:** Set the system option MSGLEVEL= I to have index usage information reported in the SAS log.

Indexes may also be used to optimize the performance of WHERE clauses comparing column values to patterns using LIKE and NOT LIKE operators. They can also be used when the IN or BETWEEN operator is used to construct WHERE clause criteria. The next example shows the query that limits the returned rows from the *orders* table to those with specific product codes. The prodcode index is used to optimize this query.

```
LIBNAME bluesky "C:\mydata\bluesky bookstore\";

CREATE INDEX PRODCODE ON BLUESKY.ORDERS(PRODCODE);

TITLE1 'Orders of product 300456 and 400345';

SELECT  prodcode, ord_date, quantity
FROM    bluesky.orders
WHERE   prodcode in ('300456','400345');
```

SAS log:

```
CREATE INDEX prodcode ON bluesky.orders(prodcode);
NOTE: Simple index PRODCODE has been defined.

TITLE1 'Orders of product 300456 and 400345';

SELECT prodcode, ord_date, quantity
FROM   bluesky.orders
WHERE  prodcode in ('300456','400345');
INFO: Index PRODCODE selected for WHERE clause optimization.
```

Tip: Notice that the index is not referenced in the query. The SAS System will use available indexes automatically if it determines that an index would provide more efficient processing of the query. There are two options, IDXNAME and IDXWHERE, that allow you to direct the SQL optimizer index usage. These options were discussed earlier in this section.

Table joins

The SQL optimizer has four join processing methods available: index look-up joins, hash joins, sort-and-merge joins, and step-loop joins. The optimizer first considers whether a hash or index look-up join is possible. Hash joins do not require sorting or indexes; instead the rows from the smaller of two tables are loaded into memory and a hash algorithm is used to process the join. The existence of one or more indexes allows the optimizer to evaluate index look-up joins. If neither of these options is possible, a sort-and-merge join that generates a cross-product between the join tables is evaluated. Finally the least efficient option, the step-loop join that generates a Cartesian product is considered.

The optimizer evaluates the use of indexes in the join process when at least one of the columns involved in the join expression is indexed. If several columns in one table are used to construct the join, indexes for all of the columns should exist. The SQL query optimizer will access the nonindexed table sequentially and find the matching row values in the second table using an index.

Tip: Consider creating an index for a table that is often involved in joins if that table is not frequently updated. It allows the SQL optimizer to consider an index look-up to optimize processing of the join.

It is not necessary to create indexes for the joined column(s) in all of the tables. If at least one index is available, the SQL optimizer can assess the advantage of index usage. It is best to create indexes for a table that will not frequently change to avoid the performance cost of checking and/or updating the index with data changes.

In the next example a SELECT statement that joins two tables together and limits the report to rows that meet a criterion built on a correlated subquery is shown. The client number (clientno) column of the *orders* table and the product code (prodcode) column of the *stock* table have been indexed. However, the optimizer uses both indexes in the execution of the query.

```
LIBNAME bluesky "C:\mydata\bluesky bookstore\";

PROC SQL;
OPTIONS msglevel=I;
CREATE INDEX prodcode ON bluesky.stock(prodcode);
CREATE INDEX clientno ON bluesky.orders(clientno);

TITLE1 'Above-average Orders by Client';

SELECT  o.prodcode, o.invoice, s.title, s.yrpubl
FROM    bluesky.stock s, bluesky.orders o
WHERE   s.prodcode = o.prodcode
        and o.totsale > (SELECT     mean(o1.totsale)
                         FROM       bluesky.orders o1
                         WHERE      o1.clientno=o.clientno
                         GROUP BY   o1.clientno);
```

SAS log:

```
TITLE1 'Above-average Orders by Client';

SELECT  o.prodcode, o.invoice, s.title, s.yrpubl
FROM    bluesky.stock s, bluesky.orders o
WHERE   s.prodcode = o.prodcode
        and o.totsale > (SELECT   mean(o1.totsale)
                         FROM     bluesky.orders o1
                         WHERE    o1.clientno=o.clientno
                         GROUP BY o1.clientno);
INFO: Index clientNo selected for WHERE clause optimization.
INFO: Use of index clientNo for WHERE clause optimization cancelled.
INFO: Index clientNo selected for WHERE clause optimization.
INFO: Use of index clientNo for WHERE clause optimization cancelled.
INFO: Index clientNo selected for WHERE clause optimization.
INFO: Use of index clientNo for WHERE clause optimization cancelled.
INFO: Index clientNo selected for WHERE clause optimization.
INFO: Use of index clientNo for WHERE clause optimization cancelled.
INFO: Index clientNo selected for WHERE clause optimization.
INFO: Use of index clientNo for WHERE clause optimization cancelled.
INFO: Index clientNo selected for WHERE clause optimization.
INFO: Use of index clientNo for WHERE clause optimization cancelled.
INFO: Index clientNo selected for WHERE clause optimization.
INFO: Use of index clientNo for WHERE clause optimization cancelled.
INFO: Index clientNo selected for WHERE clause optimization.
INFO: Index prodCode selected for WHERE clause optimization.
```

Compare the index use of the above example with that shown in the next example. Here an index is generated for the product code column of the *orders* table instead of the *stock* table. The client number index (clientno) for the *orders* table is still available, but all other indexes have been dropped. Notice that the SQL optimizer has chosen only the client number index in the execution of this query.

```
LIBNAME bluesky "C:\mydata\bluesky bookstore\";
PROC SQL;
OPTIONS msglevel=I;

CREATE INDEX PRODCODE ON BLUESKY.ORDERS(PRODCODE);
CREATE INDEX clientno ON bluesky.orders(clientno);

TITLE1  'Above-average Orders by Client';

SELECT   c.company, o.prodcode, o.invoice, s.title, s.yrpubl
FROM     bluesky.stock s, bluesky.orders o, bluesky.client c
```

```
WHERE     o.clientno =    c.clientno and s.prodcode = o.prodcode
          AND o.totsale>( SELECT  mean(o1.totsale)
                          FROM    bluesky.orders o1
                          WHERE   o1.clientno=o.clientno
                          GROUP BY o1.clientno);
```

SAS log:

```
968  TITLE1 'Above-average Orders by Client';
969
970  SELECT  c.company, o.prodcode, o.invoice, s.title, s.yrpubl
971  FROM    bluesky.stock s, bluesky.orders o, bluesky.client c
972  WHERE   o.clientno = c.clientno and s.prodcode = o.prodcode
973          and o.totsale > (SELECT   mean(o1.totsale)
974                           FROM     bluesky.orders o1
975                           WHERE    o1.clientno=o.clientno
976                           GROUP BY o1.clientno);
INFO: Index clientNo selected for WHERE clause optimization.
INFO: Use of index clientNo for WHERE clause optimization cancelled.
INFO: Index clientNo selected for WHERE clause optimization.
INFO: Use of index clientNo for WHERE clause optimization cancelled.
INFO: Index clientNo selected for WHERE clause optimization.
INFO: Use of index clientNo for WHERE clause optimization cancelled.
INFO: Index clientNo selected for WHERE clause optimization.
INFO: Use of index clientNo for WHERE clause optimization cancelled.
INFO: Index clientNo selected for WHERE clause optimization.
INFO: Use of index clientNo for WHERE clause optimization cancelled.
INFO: Index clientNo selected for WHERE clause optimization.
INFO: Use of index clientNo for WHERE clause optimization cancelled.
INFO: Index clientNo selected for WHERE clause optimization.
INFO: Use of index clientNo for WHERE clause optimization cancelled.
INFO: Index clientNo selected for WHERE clause optimization.
```

Tip: If your queries are carefully constructed, the SQL optimizer will use indexes whenever they improve performance. In situations where you want to direct the optimizer to use a specific index, you can use the IDXWHERE= and IDXNAME= options discussed in this chapter.

A hash join rather than an indexed join may be selected by the SQL optimizer to optimize performance. With a hash join, records from the smaller of the two tables are loaded into an indexed cache and a hash key is generated. Each row in the other table is then processed, comparing the value of the join variable to the hash keys to determine the position in the cache of the matching record.

The next example shows a query that draws data from the *orders*, *stock*, and *client* tables. An index is generated for the product code (prodcode) and client number (clientno) columns of the *client* and *stock* tables. Additions and changes to these tables occur infrequently, which makes them better choices for indexing than the *orders* table. In this example, the optimizer chose to use the product code index for the *stock* table; hash-join processing was utilized as indicated by the sqxjhsh code in the execution plan.

> **Tip:** When a hash join is processed, one of the tables is used to build a set of distinct values or hash keys and the other table is matched to those keys. A hash join does not use indexes associated with a table.

```
LIBNAME bluesky "C:\mydata\bluesky bookstore\";
PROC SQL _method;
OPTIONS msglevel = I;

CREATE INDEX prodcode ON bluesky.stock(prodcode);
CREATE INDEX clientno ON bluesky.client(clientno);

TITLE1 'Orders by Client';

SELECT c.company, o.prodcode, o.invoice, s.title, s.yrpubl
FROM   bluesky.stock s, bluesky.orders o, bluesky.client c
WHERE  o.clientno = c.clientno
       AND s.prodcode = o.prodcode;
```

SAS log:

```
NOTE: SQL execution methods chosen are:

      sqxslct
          sqxjhsh
              sqxjhsh
                  sqxsrc( BLUESKY.ORDERS(alias = O) )
                  sqxsrc( BLUESKY.CLIENT(alias = C) )
              sqxsrc( BLUESKY.STOCK(alias = S) )
```

> **Tip:** When joining tables, the SQL optimizer also evaluates the use of merge joins. With merge joins, each of the join variables is sorted and a cross-product of the rows in the tables generated.

Subqueries

Indexes can also improve performance when subqueries are included in a WHERE statement. When this form of criteria is processed, each value from a table row in the outer query is compared to a single value or set of values generated by an inner query. When a subquery is included in a SELECT statement, it is executed first. The column value for each row in the outer table is then compared against the value or values returned by the subquery. As a result, an index for the outer query table column does not affect performance.

> **Tip:** Indexes on columns used in the inner query, rather than the outer query, improve overall performance.

The next example shows the use of a subquery that checks the product code (prodcode) in the *orders* table against a list of selected product codes from the *stock* table. Notice that the index for the prodcode column of the *orders* table is not used to optimize this query. Rather, the index on the stock column is used to improve performance in the inner query.

```
OPTIONS msglevel=I;
PROC SQL;

CREATE INDEX prodcode ON bluesky.orders(prodcode);
CREATE INDEX category ON bluesky.stock(category);
CREATE INDEX stock ON bluesky.stock(stock);

TITLE1 'Medicine and Science book orders';
TITLE2 'Stock on-hand between 1000 and 2000';

SELECT  prodcode, ord_date, quantity
FROM    bluesky.orders
WHERE   prodcode in (SELECT prodcode
                  FROM   bluesky.stock
                  WHERE  category in ('medicine','science')
                         AND stock between 1000 and 2000);
```

SAS log:

```
INFO: Index STOCK selected for WHERE clause optimization.
```

The tables shown in the next example summarize the rows retrieved by the inner and outer queries of the previous example in graphical form. The inner query is executed first retrieving three product codes from the *stock* table for books in the medicine and science categories that meet the stock criteria. These values are substituted into the WHERE clause and each row of the *orders* table is checked against the WHERE clause criteria. Only the highlighted row would be selected from the sample rows shown.

ORDERS Table: sample rows used in the OUTER QUERY		
prodcode	**ord_date**	**quantity**
300456	07FEB03	300
300680	06MAY03	150
400178	06MAY03	500
500120	06MAY03	600
200345	10NOV03	1400
300680	20OCT03	2900
400100	15MAR03	125
400128	11APR03	200
400100	11APR03	200

STOCK Table: results of INNER QUERY	
prodcode	**quantity**
400128	2000
400102	1000
100890	1000

If a correlated subquery is included in a WHERE clause, it can be beneficial to index the column being compared with the correlated reference. With correlated subqueries, the subquery is evaluated against the value of each row of the outer query. The comparison variable is the column within the subquery while the constant value is the value of the outer query column. As a result, columns that are part of the inner query should be indexed. The SQL optimizer will not use an index built on the correlated column of the table in the outer query.

> **Tip:** When using correlated subqueries it is important that columns that are part of the inner query are indexed to ensure that performance is optimized.

The next example shows a query that contains a correlated subquery. An index has been built for the stock column of the *stock* table used in the outer query. A second index has been built for the product code of the *orders* table, which is part of the inner query. Notice that the SQL optimizer has rejected the use of the stock index in favor of the prodcode index of the inner query.

```
OPTIONS msglevel=I;
PROC SQL;
LIBNAME bluesky "C:\mydata\bluesky bookstore\";

CREATE INDEX prodcode ON bluesky.orders(prodcode);
CREATE INDEX stock ON bluesky.stock(stock);

TITLE1 'Book stocks below average order quantities';
```

```
SELECT   prodcode, title, stock, yrpubl
FROM     bluesky.stock s
WHERE    s.stock < (SELECT mean(o.quantity)
                    FROM   bluesky.orders o
                    WHERE  s.prodcode = o.prodcode );
```

SAS log excerpt:

```
INFO: Index PRODCODE selected for WHERE clause optimization.
INFO: Use of index PRODCODE for WHERE clause optimization cancelled.
INFO: Index PRODCODE selected for WHERE clause optimization.
INFO: Use of index PRODCODE for WHERE clause optimization cancelled.
INFO: Index PRODCODE selected for WHERE clause optimization.
INFO: Use of index PRODCODE for WHERE clause optimization cancelled.
INFO: Index PRODCODE selected for WHERE clause optimization.
INFO: Use of index PRODCODE for WHERE clause optimization cancelled.
INFO: Index PRODCODE selected for WHERE clause optimization.
INFO: Use of index PRODCODE for WHERE clause optimization cancelled.
INFO: Index PRODCODE selected for WHERE clause optimization.
```

Tip: The selection and cancellation of index use shown in the above log is repeated numerous times, because the SQL statement is parsed for each pass of the inner query. The final entry in the log shows the selection of the product code index for optimization. With correlated subqueries, the subquery is executed each time the correlated value in the outer query changes. Correlated subqueries are covered in Chapter 5, "Working with Two or More Tables."

The next example shows the same query as the previous example, but here the product code column of the *stock* table rather than the *orders* table has been indexed. Notice that the new index is not selected for use by the SQL optimizer. The DROP statement used to eliminate the index in the *orders* table is discussed in detail later in this chapter.

```
LIBNAME bluesky "C:\mydata\bluesky bookstore\";
PROC SQL;
OPTIONS msglevel=I;

DROP INDEX prodcode ON bluesky.orders;
CREATE INDEX prodcode ON bluesky.stock(prodcode);

TITLE1 'Book stocks below average order quantities';

SELECT   prodcode, title, stock, yrpubl
FROM     bluesky.stock s
WHERE    s.stock < (SELECT mean(o.quantity)
                    FROM   bluesky.orders o
                    WHERE  s.prodcode = o.prodcode );
QUIT;
```

SAS log:

```
DROP INDEX prodcode ON bluesky.orders;
NOTE: Index PRODCODE has been dropped.

CREATE INDEX prodcode ON bluesky.stock(prodcode);
NOTE: Simple index PRODCODE has been defined.


TITLE1 'Book stocks below average order quantities';

SELECT  prodcode, title, stock, yrpubl
FROM    bluesky.stock s
WHERE   s.stock < (SELECT mean(o.quantity)
                   FROM   bluesky.orders o
                   WHERE  s.prodcode = o.prodcode );
```

The following tables summarize the rows retrieved by the inner and outer queries of the previous example in graphical form. The inner query is executed once for each row in the outer query. When the second row of the *stock* table is read, a prodcode value of 300456 is passed to the inner query for execution. Three rows are retrieved from the *orders* table and the quantities for each used in the calculation of the mean quantity for that product code. When the next row of the *stock* table is read, the prodcode value changes and the inner query is re-executed.

STOCK Table: sample rows used in the OUTER QUERY

prodcode	title	stock	yrpubl
300678	Decorative Arts	1500	1999
300456	The Ultimate Philosophy	100	1999
300289	Democracy in America	55	2003
300680	The Underground Economy	1000	2000
500120	The Art of Computer Programming	1600	1999
500127	New user's Guide to Computers	350	2003
500168	Visual Basic for Beginners	1000	2002
500238	Start a Business Using a Computer	1000	2002
500890	Introduction to Computer_Science	100	2000

ORDERS Table: rows selected by INNER QUERY used to calculate MEAN(QUANTITY)

prodcode	quantity
300456	300
300456	50
300456	55

Tip: With correlated subqueries the correlated column is always implicitly returned so that it can be compared with the current value of the correlated column in the outer query.

Maintaining indexes

Indexes are synchronized with column values and as such, they must be modified if the data within the column changes. Changes include modification of one or more data values, the deletion of a row or the addition of a new row. In each case, the index must be updated to accurately reflect the current data in the table column. Index maintenance occurs automatically, and it uses computer resources. As a result, careful selection of columns for indexing is required to ensure optimal overall performance. Tables that are frequently changed should not be indexed unless the performance gains for common queries against such tables outweigh the resources required for maintenance.

Index updates may be delayed until after all new records have been added to a table for which an index exists. This can result in significant performance gains when several indexed columns occur in a table.

Tip: Use either PROC APPEND or the INSERT INTO <table-name> AS SELECT form of the INSERT statement to delay index updates until after all new rows are added to the table or data set. The new incoming data is sorted and then inserted into the index in sequential order, reducing the processing load. This processing option applies only if an index is not associated with a referential integrity constraint.

Unique indexes use even more additional resources because of their constraining nature. Once a unique index has been created, all incoming data must adhere to the restrictions imposed by the constraint. Each time a new row of data is added to a table, the index must first be checked to determine if the new value is already in the table. If the incoming value is unique, the table and the index are both updated.

Tip: Unique indexes are automatically built for primary and foreign keys.

If you create a unique index, FOREIGN KEY, or PRIMARY KEY constraint after adding rows to your table, SAS will check all existing rows to ensure that the constraint you are adding has not been violated. If duplicate values are found in the table, SAS returns an error message, and it will not create the index.

Tip: Indexes are maintained by the SAS System for all modifications to a table, whether the changes originate from the SQL procedure or some other source.

Indexes also must be modified if indexed columns are renamed. The name of a simple index must match the name of the column on which it is built. Therefore, if an indexed column is renamed, the associated simple index is also renamed. However, composite indexes can be assigned any valid SAS name. If a column included in a composite index is renamed, the column name is updated within the index but the index name remains unchanged.

If either the table or column associated with an index is deleted, the index is also dropped automatically. It is also possible to drop an index without deleting the column or table. Further information on the DROP INDEX statement is included later in this chapter.

Indexes are not stored as separate members of a SAS library, but rather are stored together in a single index file that has the same name as the data set. If the data set name is changed, the index file name is also changed. Index files are deleted automatically if the associated data set is deleted.

The index name and columns are displayed if you issue a DESCRIBE statement against the table associated with the index. The next example shows the results of a DESCRIBE statement for the *orders* table taken from the SAS log. Notice that the CREATE statements for both the table and indexes are included in the report.

SAS log:

```
 create table WORK.ORDERS( bufsize=8192 )
  (
   prodCode char(6),
   ord_date num format=DATE. informat=DATE.,
   quantity num,
   totsale num,
   currency char(3),
   delCode char(3),
   clientNo num,
   invoice char(10)
  );
create index CLIENTNO on WORK.ORDERS(clientNo);
create index ORDERX on WORK.ORDERS(ord_date,invoice,clientNo);
create index CLIENTX on WORK.ORDERS(clientNo,ord_date,invoice);
```

Tip: The *work.orders* table was created using a CREATE *orders* AS (SELECT * from *bluesky.orders*) statement, a form of the CREATE statement covered earlier in this chapter. Only the table structure and data are taken from *bluesky.orders*; indexes on the *bluesky.orders* table are not automatically added to the new table. If you review the output in the next example, you will find that the indexes shown above do not match those associated with the *bluesky.orders* table. The indexes on *work.orders* were generated for the table using CREATE index statements issued after the new table was created.

Information about indexes can be obtained from other sources. The SAS dictionary tables, covered in detail in Chapter 7, "Building Interactive Applications," can be queried to generate summary reports. The dictionary tables are accessed in the same way as other views and tables in PROC SQL. One of the advantages of using the dictionary tables is the ability to generate customized reports interactively. The names of columns and tables accessed by a SELECT statement can be retrieved from the dictionary tables at the time the SELECT statement is executed.

In the next example the *indexes* dictionary table is queried to obtain information on all indexes in the Bluesky library. A portion of the output of a DESCRIBE statement issued against the indexes view is included in the example for reference. Instead of viewing indexes only for the *orders* table, selected information for all of the indexes in the Bluesky library is reported. Notice that each column has pre-defined column headings and formats. In the query, the format for the memname column has been overridden to generate a more compact report.

```
LIBNAME    bluesky "C:\mydata\bluesky bookstore\";

DESCRIBE    table dictionary.indexes;
SELECT      memname format=$10., memtype, name, idxusage,
            indxname
FROM        dictionary.indexes
WHERE       libname='BLUESKY'    ;
```

SAS log:

```
NOTE: SQL table DICTIONARY.INDEXES was created like:
create table DICTIONARY.INDEXES
  (
   libname char(8) label='Library Name',
   memname char(32) label='Member Name',
   memtype char(8) label='Member Type',
   name char(32) label='Column Name',
   idxusage char(9) label='Column Index Type',
   indxname char(32) label='Index Name',
   indxpos num label='Position of Column in Concatenated Key',
   nomiss char(3) label='Nomiss Option',
   unique char(3) label='Unique Option'
  );

                                                        Column
Member       Member                                     Index
Name         Type       Column Name                     Type         Index Name
-------------------------------------------------------------------------------

------
CLIENT       DATA       clientNo                        SIMPLE       clientNo
ORDERPEND    DATA       ord_date                        SIMPLE       ord_date
ORDERPEND    DATA       prodCode                        COMPOSITE    prodinv_pk
ORDERPEND    DATA       invoice                         COMPOSITE    prodinv_pk
```

Tip: SAS dictionary tables can be queried to generate custom reports containing detailed or summary information about libraries, tables, indexes, and views. More information on the SAS dictionary tables and views is included in Chapter 7, "Building Interactive Applications," and Appendix B, "Dictionary Table Descriptions."

PROC CONTENTS can also be used to obtain detailed table or library information, including information about indexes. The next example displays the results of the CONTENTS procedures run against the Bluesky publishing *orders* table. Notice that the columns in each of the composite indexes are listed in the order of their occurrence within the index. However, the column associated with a simple index is not indicated because the simple index name must match the column name.

```
LIBNAME bluesky "C:\mydata\bluesky bookstore\";

PROC CONTENTS data=bluesky.orders;
RUN;
```

SAS log:

```
The CONTENTS Procedure

Data Set Name BLUESKY.ORDERS                          Observations          0
Member Type   DATA                                    Variables             8
Engine        V9                                      Indexes               6
Created       Friday, July 9, 2004 10:38:52 AM Observation Length    56
Last Modified Friday, July 9, 2004 10:38:56 AM Deleted Observations  0
Protection                                            Compressed            NO
Data Set Type                                         Sorted                NO
Label
Data Representation  WINDOWS_32
Encoding             wlatin1  Western (Windows)


                   Engine/Host Dependent Information

Data Set Page Size          8192
Number of Data Set Pages    2
First Data Page             1
Max Obs per Page            145
Obs in First Data Page      0
Index File Page Size        4096
Number of Index File Pages  8
Number of Data Set Repairs  0
File Name                   C:\mydata\bluesky bookstore\orders.sas7bdat
Release Created             9.0101M0
Host Created                XP_PRO


    Alphabetic List of Variables and Attributes

#    Variable     Type    Len    Format     Informat

7    clientNo     Num       8
5    currency     Char      3
6    delCode      Char      3
8    invoice      Char     10
2    ord_date     Num       8    DATE.      DATE.
1    prodCode     Char      6
3    quantity     Num       8
4    totsale      Num       8
```

(continued on the next page)

(continued)

```
      Alphabetic List of Indexes and Attributes

                       # of
                      Unique
#     Index           Values    Variables

1     clientNo          0
2     clientx           0       clientNo ord_date invoice
3     currency          0
4     ord_date          0
```

Tip: PROC CONTENTS provides a wealth of information on tables and views. It can be run on an entire library in a single step, making it very useful in generating project or program summary documentation.

Caution: PROC CONTENTS reports can generate hundreds of pages for a large library. Consider the dictionary tables for summary reports. Information on dictionary tables and their associated SASHELP views can be found in Chapter 7, “Building Interactive Applications,” and Appendix B, “Dictionary Table Descriptions.”

Finally, a PROC DATASETS statement can also be used to view all members of a SAS library and the associated indexes. In the next example the PROC DATASETS statement and a portion of the report generated to the SAS log for the bluesky library are shown. Notice that in this report, details such as the column on which the index was constructed are not included.

```
LIBNAME bluesky "C:\mydata\bluesky bookstore\";

PROC DATASETS library=bluesky;
RUN;
```

SAS log:

```
  Directory

Libref          BLUESKY
Engine          V9
Physical Name   C:\mydata\bluesky bookstore
File Name       C:\mydata\bluesky bookstore


                        Member    File
 #  Name                Type      Size  Last Modified

 1  ADDRESS             DATA     17408  11May04:11:15:52
 2  ALLORDERS           VIEW      5120  09Jul04:13:08:14
 3  ARTS                VIEW      5120  11May04:11:15:52
 4  CLIENT              DATA     25600  09Jul04:13:08:19
    CLIENT              INDEX     9216  09Jul04:13:08:19
 5  COMPANY             DATA     17408  11May04:11:15:54
 6  CONTACTS            DATA      9216  09Jul04:13:05:50
 7  CURRENCY            DATA      5120  02Jul04:16:25:03
```

Tip: There are many options available for reporting index and table information. I most often use the DESCRIBE statement because it provides a concise summary. I keep a SAS file with several queries against the dictionary tables such as the one shown earlier as the second example in the "Maintaining indexes" section. I select from the file when I need other details.

Modifying tables and views

Several options are available for modifying tables after creation. Views built on a modified table reflect many of the changes made to the tables. Indexes also change when a table is modified.

ALTER statement

The ALTER statement can be used to modify the structure of an existing table. The nature of the modification is determined by the clause added to the statement. The ADD clause allows new columns or constraints to be defined. The MODIFY clause is used to change attributes such as the format or label of an existing column. Columns and constraints may also be deleted from a table using the DROP clause.

Tip: The ALTER statement cannot be applied to a PROC SQL view because a view does not have a stored structure. If you recall, a view stores the query used to create it. If the USING clause included in the view, the LIBNAME statement for the view is also stored.

To alter the structure or the embedded LIBNAME statement of a view, the view must be deleted and recreated using the CREATE statement.

SAS/ACCESS and SQL Pass-Through Facility users: The ALTER statement is only allowed in some databases and is often available only in specific versions. For example, an ALTER statement can be used in Oracle 8i and Oracle 9i, but it is not available in earlier versions. Many of the clauses in an ALTER statement are also limited to specific databases. See the documentation for your database to confirm whether specific clauses can be used.

Caution: You must have appropriate permission in an RDBMS to alter a table.

General form:

```
ALTER TABLE            table-name
<ADD CONSTRAINT        constraint- name constraint>
<DROP CONSTRAINT       constraint-name>
);
```

Constraints are dropped or added to existing tables using the same syntax discussed earlier in this chapter for the specification of out-of-line integrity constraints using the CREATE TABLE statement.

SAS/ACCESS and SQL Pass-Through Facility users: The syntax of the DROP clause changes slightly for DB2 users when either a FOREIGN KEY or PRIMARY KEY constraint is dropped from a table:

```
ALTER TABLE table-name
DROP FOREIGN KEY constraint-name;
ALTER TABLE table-name
DROP PRIMARY KEY;
```

If an integrity constraint is added to a column in an existing table, all of the current data values are checked to ensure that none violate the constraint. The ALTER statement in the next example attempts to add a UNIQUE constraint to the product code column of the *orders* table. Because there are several orders for each book, identified by product code in the table, the UNIQUE constraint cannot be applied to the column. The error message reported in the SAS log is included in the example.

```
LIBNAME bluesky "C:\mydata\bluesky bookstore\";

ALTER TABLE BLUESKY.ORDERS
  ADD constraint prod_unique UNIQUE(prodcode);
```

SAS log:

```
ERROR: Duplicate values not allowed on index prodCode for file ORDERS.
```

If an existing constraint is dropped, all of the indexes associated with the constraint are also eliminated. In the second example following the UNIQUE constraint is removed from the product code (prodcode) column of the *newstock* table. The indexes associated with the *newstock* table before the ALTER statement are shown in the next example. The same report run after the constraint is dropped is included in the second example. The reports, drawn from the *indexes* dictionary table confirm that the unique constraint index associated with the product code column was dropped when the constraint was dropped.

> **Tip:** DESCRIBE, PROC CONTENTS, and PROC DATASETS will all provide information on indexes, constraints, and constraint names. The dictionary table *indexes* used in the previous example provides the ability to selectively report index information for one or more tables. There are also two dictionary tables new to SAS Version 9 that provide constraint information: constraint_column_usage and constraint_table usage. More information on dictionary tables can be found in Chapter 7, "Building Interactive Applications," and in Appendix B, "Dictionary Table Descriptions."

```
CREATE table newstock
        (isbn         char(13) primary key,
        title         char(50),
        auth_fst      char(10),
        auth_lst      char(15),
        category      char(20),
        reprint       char(1) references work.newreprint
                      on update cascade on delete set null
                      message="Violates Foreign Key - check reprint
                      value. "
                      msgtype=user,
        stock         num  check ((yrpubl > 1990 and stock >=25)
                      or (yrpubl <= 1990 and  stock >=10)),
```

```
                yrpubl   num check(yrpubl > 1900),
        prodcode    char(6) unique,
        price       num not null
        );

SELECT   memname format=$10., memtype, name, idxusage, indxname
FROM     dictionary.indexes
WHERE    memname='NEWSTOCK' and libname='WORK';
```

Member Name	Member Type	Column Name	Column Index Type	Index Name
NEWSTOCK	DATA	prodcode	SIMPLE	PRODCODE
NEWSTOCK	DATA	reprint	SIMPLE	REPRINT
NEWSTOCK	DATA	isbn	SIMPLE	ISBN

```
ALTER table newstock
 drop constraint _UN0001_;

SELECT memname format=$10., memtype, name, idxusage, indxname
FROM dictionary.indexes
WHERE memname='NEWSTOCK' and libname='WORK' ;
```

Member Name	Member Type	Column Name	Column Index Type	Index Name
NEWSTOCK	DATA	reprint	SIMPLE	REPRINT
NEWSTOCK	DATA	isbn	SIMPLE	ISBN

Tip: The constraint *_UN0001_* was added to the *newstock* table using an inline constraint specification on a CREATE TABLE statement. Only constraints added using out-of-line constraint specifications on a CREATE TABLE statement or constraints added using an ALTER statement can be assigned a descriptive name.

Deletion of columns associated with constraints

A column for which an integrity constraint has been defined cannot be deleted from a table without first dropping the constraint. If a column is part of a composite PRIMARY KEY constraint, the PRIMARY KEY constraint must be eliminated or modified so that the column marked for deletion is no longer referenced.

In the next example a series of ALTER statements are issued to illustrate the steps necessary to delete a column associated with a constraint. A DESCRIBE statement for the table and the output generated by the statement is included for reference. The first ALTER statement is unsuccessful because of the check constraint associated with the exchrate column. Only after the constraint is first dropped with an ALTER statement is it possible to delete the column.

```
CREATE table currency
         (CURRENCY char(3),
         CUR_DATE num format=DATE. informat=DATE.,
         EXCHRATE num,
         CONSTRAINT pk_currency PRIMARY KEY(currency, cur_date),
         CONSTRAINT exch_ck CHECK(exchrate > 0)
         );

ALTER TABLE currency
  DROP exchrate;

ALTER TABLE currency
  DROP constraint exch_ck;

ALTER TABLE currency
  DROP exchrate;
```

SAS log:

```
90    ALTER TABLE currency
91      DROP exchrate;
ERROR: The column named EXCHRATE cannot be dropped because it
       participates in an integrity constraint named exch_ck.
NOTE:  Only a column that doesn't participate in any integrity
       constraint can be dropped.

92    ALTER TABLE currency
93      DROP constraint exch_ck;
NOTE: Integrity constraint exch_ck deleted.
NOTE: Table WORK.CURRENCY has been modified, with 3 columns.
94
95    ALTER TABLE currency
96      DROP exchrate;
NOTE: Table WORK.CURRENCY has been modified, with 2 columns.
```

> **Tip:** Notice that the error message does not indicate the type of integrity constraint exch_ck defines. The assignment of a meaningful constraint name, possible when defining out-of-line constraints, makes it easier to understand error messages. In this case, a CK added to the constraint name helps identify it as a check constraint in the error message.

When foreign keys have been defined for a table, the order in which the constraints are dropped becomes important. Foreign keys forge a relationship or dependency among columns in different tables. The FOREIGN KEY constraint in the child table must be dropped prior to deleting the PRIMARY KEY constraint in the parent or reference table that is referenced in the FOREIGN KEY constraint.

In the next example the reprint column of the *newstock* table is dependent on the values in the reprint column of the *newreprint* table. A foreign key constraint has been defined for the reprint column of the *newstock* table, relating it to the primary key of the *newreprint* table.

> **Tip:** For ideas on how to create and populate linked tables such as these, refer to the example at the end of this chapter.

Table: NEWSTOCK (child)	
isbn	**reprint**
1-7890-2878-7	C
	↑
	FOREIGN KEY

Table: NEWREPRINT (parent)	
reprint	**cutoff**
C	50
↑	
PRIMARY KEY	

> **Tip:** A primary key constraint can only be removed from a table if it is not referenced in a foreign key constraint in another table. Drop all foreign key constraints referencing the primary key prior to issuing the ALTER statement dropping the primary key.

In the table below, the ALTER statement is issued to drop the primary key in the newreprint table. However, the SAS log reports an error because the primary key is referenced by a FOREIGN KEY constraint in the newstock table.

```
ALTER table newreprint
  DROP constraint _PK0001_;
```

SAS log:

```
NOTE: SQL table WORK.NEWREPRINT was created like:

create table WORK.NEWREPRINT( bufsize=4096 )
  (
   reprint char(1),
   cutoff num
  );
create unique index reprint on WORK.NEWREPRINT(reprint);

                -----Alphabetic List of Integrity Constraints-----

     Integrity                                               On
On
#    Constraint    Type          Variables   Reference       Delete
Update
--------------------------------------------------------------------

1   _PK0001_  Primary Key  reprint
   _FK0001_  Referential  reprint   WORK.NEWSTOCK  Set Null   Cascade
8381  ALTER table newreprint
8382    DROP constraint _PK0001_;
ERROR: Unable to delete primary key _PK0001_.  It is referenced by one
       or more foreign keys.  The foreign key(s) must be deleted
       first.
```

An ALTER statement dropping the FOREIGN KEY constraint must be issued before the PRIMARY KEY constraint in the reprint table can be deleted. The required SQL statements in the correct order are included in the next example.

```
ALTER table newstock
  DROP constraint _FK0001_;

ALTER table newreprint
  DROP constraint _PK0001_;
```

SAS log:

```
1293  PROC SQL;
1294  ALTER table newstock
1295    DROP constraint _FK0001_;
NOTE: Integrity constraint _FK0001_ deleted.
NOTE: Table WORK.NEWSTOCK has been modified, with 10 columns.
1296
1297  ALTER table newreprint
1298    DROP constraint _PK0001_;
NOTE: Integrity constraint _PK0001_ deleted.
NOTE: Table WORK.NEWREPRINT has been modified, with 2 columns.
```

Tip: A DESCRIBE statement provides valuable information concerning constraints and it can save much frustration when trying to delete constraints. Remember, FOREIGN KEY constraints link two tables together; the values in the column of one table affect the other table. It is best to avoid creating foreign keys unless data integrity is critical as they complicate table maintenance.

ADD clause

General Form:

```
ALTER    TABLE <libref.>table-name
ADD      column-name          data type <column modifier>
         <, column-name data type <column modifier> ...;
```

Additional columns can be added to a table after it is created using the ADD clause of the ALTER statement. For each row currently in the table, a missing or null value is inserted into the new column. The column name, data type, and column modifier function in the ADD clause follow the same specifications and rules as described for the CREATE TABLE statement.

The next example illustrates the addition of a new column in the *reprint* table of the Bluesky Publishing Company using the ALTER statement. The SAS log reports the successful modification of the table. The DESCRIBE statement provides more information on the new structure of the *reprint* table.

```
LIBNAME bluesky "C:\mydata\bluesky bookstore\";

ALTER table bluesky.reprint
  ADD maximum numeric LABEL = 'MAX';

DESCRIBE table bluesky.reprint;
```

SAS log:

```
NOTE: SQL table BLUESKY.REPRINT was created like:

create table BLUESKY.REPRINT( bufsize=8192 )
  (
   REPRINT char(1),
   CUTOFF num,
   MAXIMUM num label='MAX'
  );
```

If we review the data stored in the *reprint* table shown in the next example, we find that the new maximum column is empty. An UPDATE statement can be used to change the missing value in one or more of the rows. The UPDATE statement is discussed later in this chapter.

```
LIBNAME bluesky "C:\mydata\bluesky bookstore\";

SELECT    *
FROM  bluesky.reprint;
```

REPRINT	CUTOFF	MAX
A	0	.
B	10	.
C	50	.
D	100	.
E	500	.
F	1000	.

It is important to remember that the addition of a column may affect views built for the table. If the view references each column by name, then the new column will not automatically be added to the view. However, if the view is created using an asterisk in the SELECT clause, then the new column will be included the next time the view is accessed.

Tip: If you anticipate frequent changes to the structure of a table, use the asterisk option in the SELECT clause used to create views based on the table if possible.

Modify clause

General Form:

```
ALTER      TABLE <libref.>table-name
MODIFY     column-name  data type column-modifier
           <,column-name, data type column-modifier...> ;
```

Several characteristics of a column can be modified through the MODIFY clause of the ALTER TABLE statement. These characteristics include the length, informat, format, and label of an existing column. In addition, the width of character can be adjusted. The MODIFY clause can also be applied to constraints.

Caution: The data type of a column cannot be changed except through the deletion and recreation of the column. If your queries frequently include INPUT and PUT statements altering the data type of a column, you might want to consider changing the column data type because the conversion process (INPUT/PUT) may slow down processing.

Refer to the section on the UPDATE clause for a suggested approach for modifying the data type of an existing column.

Tip: A column's name cannot be changed through the ALTER TABLE statement. The RENAME= data set option is used to effect this change within a DATA step. PROC DATASETS can also be used. Although the RENAME= option can be added to the SELECT clause, it behaves like an alias in that it temporarily renames the column for the duration of the SELECT statement only.

If the width of a column containing character data is changed to a smaller value, then the values stored in that column in the table are truncated. If the width of the column is increased, blanks are added to character values stored in that column to expand the current values to the new length.

Columns of numeric data type, however, behave differently. Although an ALTER statement can be issued changing the width or number of decimal places, the storage space is changed. Numeric values are always stored with the maximum available precision and a length of 8 bytes unless a LENGTH modifier is specified at the time of table creation. Precision can be lost if inadequate storage space is allocated to the column.

In the second example following the Bluesky Publishing *client* table is altered to reduce the length of the phone column from 25 to 10. The clientno column, specified as a numeric data type, is also altered to reduce its width to 3. For reference, see the first example following. Here the table description and the table contents are provided before the table is altered.

```
LIBNAME  bluesky "C:\mydata\bluesky bookstore\";

DESCRIBE TABLE BLUESKY.CLIENT;
SELECT   clientno, phone
FROM     bluesky.client;
```

SAS log:

```
NOTE: SQL table BLUESKY.CLIENT was created like:

create table BLUESKY.CLIENT( bufsize=8192 )
  (
   CLIENTNO  num,
   COMPANY   char(25),
   CONT_FST  char(10),
   CONT_LST  char(15),
   DEPT      char(25),
   PHONE     char(25),
   FAX       char(25)
  );
```

SAS output:

```
clientNo  phone
______________________________

1001   512-495-4370
2010   312-756-7890
3007   01223-568568
4008   874-2339
5005   61-8-8303-4402
6090   49-30-8252573
7008   33-14-362-1899
8003   604-261-3612
```

Notice in the next example that the contents of the phone column are truncated to adjust to the new length. However, the client numbers remain unchanged. Although the new table description includes a modified length for the phone column, the clientno column values have not been truncated to a length of 3.

```
LIBNAME bluesky "C:\mydata\bluesky bookstore\";

ALTER  TABLE BLUESKY.CLIENT
  MODIFY phone char(10);

ALTER  table bluesky.client
  MODIFY clientno num(3);

DESCRIBE table bluesky.client;

SELECT clientno, phone
FROM   bluesky.client;
```

SAS log:

```
NOTE: SQL table BLUESKY.CLIENT was created like:

create table BLUESKY.CLIENT( bufsize=8192 )
  (
   CLIENTNO num,
   COMPANY  char(25),
   CONT_FST char(10),
   CONT_LST char(15),
   DEPT     char(25),
   PHONE    char(10),
   FAX      char(25)
  );
```

SAS output:

```
clientNo  phone
____________________

    1001  512-495-43
    2010  312-756-78
    3007  01223-5685
    4008  874-2339
    5005  61-8-8303-
    6090  49-30-8252
    7008  33-14-362-
    8003  604-261-36
```

Tip: By default, numeric variables are assigned a length of 8 bytes allowing for maximum precision with 16-decimal digits. Reducing the length of a numeric column reduces its storage space, which in turn may adversely affect the precision of the data values within the column.

In the next example an attempt is made to return the phone column width to its original size. Although the DESCRIBE statement output confirms that the phone column is now 25 characters in length, the phone numbers in the column remain at the truncated length of 10 characters.

```
LIBNAME bluesky "C:\mydata\bluesky bookstore\";

ALTER table bluesky.client
  MODIFY phone char(25);

DESCRIBE     bluesky.client;
SELECT       clientno, phone
FROM         bluesky.client;
```

SAS log:

```
           create table BLUESKY.CLIENT( bufsize=12288 )
             (
              clientNo num,
              company  char(25),
              cont_fst char(10),
              cont_lst char(15),
              dept       char(25),
              phone      char(25),
              fax        char(25)
             );
```

SAS output:

```
                  clientNo  phone
              ___________________________________

                  1001   512-495-43
                  2010   312-756-78
                  3007   01223-5685
                  4008   874-2339
                  5005   61-8-8303-
                  6090   49-30-8252
                  7008   33-14-362-
                  8003   604-261-36
```

> **Tip:** Use caution when altering the length of character data columns. If you set a column length that is smaller than the length of the data contained in the column, the data is truncated and it cannot be recovered.

If a column is modified, the index will be updated automatically. For example, if all values in a column are truncated due to the shortening of the length of a column, then the index will be updated to include the new truncated values.

DROP clause

General Form:

```
ALTER     TABLE <libref.>table-name
DROP      column-name <, column-name ...> ;
```

The DROP statement can be used to both delete the contents of a column and eliminate it from the structure of a table simultaneously.

> **SAS/ACCESS and SQL Pass-Through Facility users:** In some databases, you cannot drop a column that has values. Values within the column must be deleted prior to the removal of the column itself.

In the next example a new table is created from the existing Bluesky *orders* table for orders taken during 2004. In this example, we want the new table to have the same table structure and data as the original *orders* table but without the delivery information. One way to accomplish this task is to generate a new table using all columns and data from the original and then drop the unwanted column.

```
LIBNAME bluesky "C:\mydata\bluesky bookstore\";

CREATE  table bluesky.ord2004 AS
       (SELECT *
       FROM    bluesky.orders
       WHERE   year(ord_date) = 2004);

ALTER   table bluesky.ord2004
  DROP  delcode;
```

Alternatively, the SELECT clause of the CREATE TABLE statement could have listed all of the desired columns as shown in the creation of *ord2004* in the next example.

```
LIBNAME bluesky "C:\mydata\bluesky bookstore\";

CREATE   table bluesky.ord2004 AS
         SELECT  prodcode, ord_date, quantity, totsale,
                 currency, clientno, invoice
         FROM    bluesky.orders
         WHERE   year(ord_date) = 2004;
```

Give careful consideration to the effect of the deletion of a column in a table. When a column is dropped, all indexes built on the column are also dropped. This includes composite indexes.

In the next example a composite index is built on the invoice and prodcode columns of the new *ord2004* table. Next, the table is altered to remove the invoice column and its data. A DESCRIBE statement issued against the table confirms that the invoice column is no longer part of the table. Notice that the newly created index is also absent although no message appears in the SAS log about its deletion.

```
LIBNAME bluesky "C:\mydata\bluesky bookstore\";

CREATE INDEX invprod on bluesky.ord2004(invoice,prodcode);

ALTER   table bluesky.ord2004
  DROP  invoice;

DESCRIBE table bluesky.ord2004;
```

SAS log:

```
1031  CREATE INDEX invprod ON bluesky.ord2004(invoice,prodcode);
NOTE: Composite index invprod has been defined.
1032
1033  ALTER   table bluesky.ord2004
1034  DROP    invoice;
NOTE: Table BLUESKY.ORD2004 has been modified, with 6 columns.
1035
1036  DESCRIBE table bluesky.ord2004;
NOTE: SQL table BLUESKY.ORD2004 was created like:

create table BLUESKY.ORD2004( bufsize=8192 )
  (
   prodCode char(6),
   ord_date num format=DATE. informat=DATE.,
   quantity num,
   totsale      num,
   currency char(3),
   clientNo num
  );
```

Tip: Simple and composite indexes based on a dropped column are deleted automatically without a message reported in the SAS log even if OPTIONS MSGLEVEL=I is set.

The deletion of a column can also affect views. Views that reference a dropped column in either their WHERE or HAVING clause criteria or their SELECT clause will become invalid. If a SELECT clause uses the asterisk to reference all columns in the table, the view will not be affected.

Consider the next example. Here a view is built from the *orders* table columns prior to the elimination of the currency column from that table. When the view is queried, an error message is reported to the SAS log and the SELECT statement is not processed.

```
LIBNAME bluesky "C:\mydata\bluesky bookstore\";
CREATE view view2004 AS
       (SELECT prodcode, ord_date, clientno, totsale, currency
        FROM   bluesky.orders
        WHERE  year(ord_date)=2004);

ALTER table bluesky.orders
  DROP currency;

DESCRIBE view view2004;

SELECT *
FROM view2004;
```

SAS log:

```
1054  CREATE view view2004 AS
1055      (SELECT prodcode, ord_date, clientno, totsale, currency
1056      FROM   bluesky.orders
1057      WHERE  year(ord_date)=2004);
NOTE: SQL view WORK.VIEW2004 has been defined.
1058
1059  ALTER table bluesky.orders
1060    DROP currency;
NOTE: Table BLUESKY.ORDERS has been modified, with 7 columns.
1061
1062  describe view view2004;
NOTE: SQL view WORK.VIEW2004 is defined as:

        select prodcode, ord_date, clientno, totsale, currency
          from BLUESKY.ORDERS
         where YEAR(ord_date)=2004;

1063
1064  SELECT *
1065  FROM view2004;
ERROR: The following columns were not found in the contributing tables:
currency.
```

Tip: A view cannot be rebuilt or queried if one of the columns included when the view was created is subsequently dropped. Create views using SELECT * instead of listing each column to avoid invalid views when the structure of the underlying table is altered.

INSERT statement

The INSERT statement is used to insert one or more new rows into a table. A new row can be added with or without data for one or more of the columns unless a PRIMARY KEY, FOREIGN KEY, or NOT NULL constraint exists in the table. An UPDATE statement can be used later to change the null or missing value.

Incoming data must meet the conditions set out in constraints defined for the table columns. If a unique constraint or index exists for a column, then the incoming data value must not already be stored within that column. A single null or missing value is allowed in a column for which a unique index or constraint has been created unless the column is a primary key. PRIMARY KEY constraints both enforce uniqueness and prevent null values from being added to the column or columns that are part of the key.

Tip: The unique constraint or index allows a single null or missing value in a column. However, a NOT NULL constraint prevents a column from storing even a single null or missing value. The two constraints can be combined in a single column; alternatively a NOT NULL constraint and a unique index may be placed on a single column.

A PRIMARY KEY constraint imposed on one or more table columns prevents the insertion of a null or missing value into those columns because it combines NOT NULL and UNIQUE constraints.

Two forms of the INSERT statement are available. The first form allows specific values to be inserted into a single new row in the table. The second form adds one or more new rows with data selected from an existing table.

Tip: A common mistake is to use the INSERT statement to add a value to a column for one or more rows that already exist in a table. SAS will not report an error message, but will simply create a new row in the table with the values specified in the INSERT statement. The UPDATE statement covered in the next section is used to add new data to an existing row.

Insertion of a single new row

General form:

```
INSERT INTO table-name [column1,column2 ...]
VALUES      (value1, value2...)
<VALUES...>;
```

This form of the INSERT statement adds one or more new rows of data values to an existing table. The data values included after the VALUES keyword within parentheses are added to the columns of the corresponding new row.

Guidelines

- Each VALUES clause supplies the data for a single new row in the table.
- Unless columns are listed in parentheses after the table name, the VALUES clause must include a value for each column in the table, presented in the same order as the columns in the table. A DESCRIBE statement can be issued to determine the column order within the table.
- If one or more columns are included in parentheses after the table name, values are inserted into only the specified columns. The values in parentheses after the VALUES keyword are inserted into each of the listed columns in order, and null values are entered into all other columns.
- Character values must be enclosed in quotes.
- Date values must adhere to the SAS date format guidelines.
- Null values for character-defined columns are indicated by a pair of quotes or a blank enclosed by quotes. An alternative character can be specified through the MISSING statement.
- Missing values for numeric-defined columns are indicated with a period. An alternative character can be specified through the SAS MISSING statement.

The INSERT statement is not well suited to the population of a table using in-stream record images. The next example shows a PROC SQL table creation statement followed by the insertion of 2 rows. Compare the PROC SQL statements with the SAS DATA step example given in the second example following.

Notice that the PROC SQL INSERT statement requires a VALUES keyword and that the complete record must be enclosed in a set of parentheses. Also, all character variables must be enclosed in quotes. As most files that are imported contain, at best, a delimiter between fields, the added syntax required by the INSERT statement can significantly add to the workload of data imports. The SAS DATA step does not require any additional syntax or keywords in the data. It offers a wide range of delimiters and other formatting options commonly encountered in data files.

> **Tip:** In the following examples, PROC SQL and the DATA step are used to create identical tables or data sets called *customer* in the SAS WORK library.

```
PROC SQL;
CREATE table customer
         (name char(25),
         address char(20),
         city char(10),
         phone num);

INSERT into customer
         VALUES ('John Smith', '123 West Link
                  Road','Seattle',2068701453)
         VALUES('Jane Doe','999 Garden
                 Boulevard','Miami',8134209143);
QUIT;

DATA customer;
  Infile cards DLM = ',' DSD;
               Input name : $25.
               Address : $20.
               City : $10.
               phone
               ;
cards;
John Smith, 123 West Link Road, Seattle, 2068701453
Jane Doe, 999 Garden Boulevard, Miami, 8134209143
;
RUN;
```

Missing values can create some difficulties when using the PROC SQL INSERT statement. Notice in the next example that a set of quotes is required for the missing address in the first record and a period represents a missing phone number in the second record.

```
CREATE table customer
         (name char(25),
         address char(20),
         city char(10),
         phone num);
```

```
INSERT into customer
        VALUES ('John Smith','','Seattle',2068701453)
        VALUES('Jane Doe','999 Garden Boulevard','Miami',.);
```

The next example shows an alternate form that allows you to indicate which variable or column you are inserting.

```
CREATE table customer
         (name char(25),
         address char(20),
         city char(10),
         phone num);

INSERT into customer
         SET name='John Smith', city='Seattle', phone=2068701453
         SET name='Jane Doe', address='999 Garden Boulevard',
                   city='Miami';
```

The SAS DATA step more easily handles missing values; a space and a comma delimiter is all that is needed to represent a missing value, as shown in the next example. Because this is a typical output from other sources such as spreadsheets, the DATA step offers much more flexibility. The SAS INPUT statement also allows for named input as shown in the second example below.

```
LIBNAME bluesky "C:\mydata\bluesky bookstore\";

DATA customer;
     Infile cards DSD DLM =',' MISSOVER;
     Input name : $25.
     Address : $20.
     City : $10.
     phone
     ;
cards;
John Smith, , Seattle, 2068701453
Jane Doe, 999 Garden Boulevard, Miami,
;
RUN;


LIBNAME bluesky "C:\mydata\bluesky bookstore\";
```

```
DATA customer;
     Input name= $25.
     Address= $20.
     City= $10.
     phone =
     ;
cards;
name=John Smith, city=Seattle phone=2068701453
name=Jane Doe address=999 Garden Boulevard city=Miami
;
RUN;
```

Whether the DATA step or INSERT statement are used, all indexes on the table are updated when a new row is entered into a table, If a unique index or primary key are present, the incoming data will be checked against all other values in the column before the row is added.

The next example includes several INSERT statements used to add three new entries to the *orders* table of the Bluesky Publishing Company for client 7008. A DESCRIBE statement and its output are included in the example for reference. The quantity and delivery code in the first INSERT statement are missing, while all columns are assigned values in the second and third statements.

> **Tip:** INSERT statements issued against a view add rows to the underlying tables and must meet all constraints imposed in those tables.

Messages related to the INSERT statement are written to the SAS log. Although the first two INSERT statements were executed successfully, the third failed. A unique composite index on the order date, product code, and invoice number exists for the table. The third INSERT statement attempts to enter values for these columns that are the same as the previous INSERT statement. Both of these statements have an order date of November 23, 2004, a product code of 300678, and an invoice number of 041123-02.

```
LIBNAME bluesky "C:\mydata\bluesky bookstore\";

CREATE   UNIQUE INDEX ordprod on
bluesky.orders(ord_date,prodcode,invoice);
CREATE   INDEX clientno on bluesky.orders(clientno);
CREATE   INDEX ord_date on bluesky.orders(ord_date);

DESCRIBE table bluesky.orders;

INSERT into bluesky.orders

VALUES('500890','23Nov2004'D,.,13000,'EUR','',7008,'041123-01');
```

```
INSERT into bluesky.orders

VALUES('300678','23Nov2004'D,300,7000,'EUR','UPS',7008,'041123-02');

INSERT into bluesky.orders (prodcode, ord_date, invoice)
         VALUES('300678','23Nov2004'D,'041123-02');
```

SAS log:

```
1984
1985   INSERT into bluesky.orders
1986   VALUES('500890','23Nov2004'D,.,13000,'FRF','',7008,'041123-01');
NOTE: 1 row was inserted into BLUESKY.ORDERS.

1987
1988   INSERT into bluesky.orders
1989     VALUES('300678','23Nov2004'D,300,7000,'FRF','UPS',7008,'041123-
02');
NOTE:   1 row was inserted into BLUESKY.ORDERS.

1990
1991   INSERT into bluesky.orders (prodcode, ord_date, invoice)
1992       VALUES('300678','23Nov2004'D,'041123-02');
ERROR: Duplicate values not allowed on index ORDPROD for file ORDERS.
NOTE: This insert failed while attempting to add data from VALUES
      clause 1 to the data set.
NOTE: Deleting the successful inserts before error noted above to
      restore table to a consistent state.
```

Tip: If a problem is encountered with any of the incoming data, all data for that row is deleted and the new row is eliminated from the table. A message is written to the SAS log concerning the action. The successful inserts referenced in the SAS log above refer to data inserted into the columns of the current row prior to the check against the index.

To confirm that the new entries have been made to the *orders* table, a SELECT statement must be issued. The next example includes the query and the resulting report of all orders for client 7008.

```
LIBNAME   bluesky "c:\mydata\blueskybookstore\";
SELECT    *
FROM      bluesky.orders
WHERE     clientno = 7008;
```

prod Code	ord_date	quantity	totsale	currency	del Code	clientNo	invoice
400128	11APR03	200	6800	EUR	UPS	7008	030411-01
100345	10MAR04	180	11700	EUR	EXP	7008	040310-01
600489	12APR04	25	137.5	EUR	EX	7008	040412-03
500116	23JUL04	400	13600	EUR	EXP	7008	041223-04
500890	23NOV04	.	13000	EUR		7008	041123-01
300678	23NOV04	300	7000	EUR	UPS	7008	041123-02

The UNDO_POLICY=REQUIRED option is in effect for INSERT statements to ensure that partially successful INSERT statements cannot insert a partial row in a table. All successful data is rolled back or deleted from the table when an error in the INSERT statement is encountered.

If we attempt to insert all of the rows in a single INSERT statement, the UNDO_POLICY option causes a different outcome. In the previous example, two of the three INSERT statements were successful. However in the next example none of the rows is inserted because all of the rows are part of the same INSERT statement. All of the data successfully inserted by the first two VALUES clauses is rolled back when an error is encountered in the third VALUES clause.

> **Tip:** In the previous example, the third INSERT statement specified that the VALUES clause defined values for only three of the columns in the ORDERS table. In this example, missing values would have to be included in the VALUES clause for the row to correct the error.

```
LIBNAME bluesky "c:\mydata\bluesky bookstore\";
INSERT into bluesky.orders
VALUES('500890','23Nov2004'D,.,13000,'EUR','',7008,'041123-01')
VALUES('300678','23Nov2004'D,300,7000,'EUR','UPS',7008,
       '041123-02')
VALUES('300678','23Nov2004'D,'041123-02');

SELECT   *
FROM     bluesky.orders
WHERE    clientno=7008;
```

SAS log:

```
13788 PROC SQL;
13789 INSERT into bluesky.orders
13790   VALUES('500890','23Nov2004'D,.,13000,'EUR','',7008,'041123-01')
13791   VALUES('300678','23Nov2004'D,300,7000,'EUR','UPS',7008,'041123-02')
13792   VALUES('300678','23Nov2004'D,'041123-02');
ERROR: VALUES clause 3 attempts to insert fewer columns than specified
       after the INSERT table name.
ERROR: Value 3 of VALUES clause 3 does not match the data type of the
       corresponding column in the object-item list (in the SELECT
       clause).
13793
```

prod Code	ord_date	quantity	totsale	currency	del Code	clientNo	invoice
400128	11APR03	200	6800	EUR	UPS	7008	030411-01
100345	10MAR04	180	11700	EUR	EXP	7008	040310-01
600489	12APR04	25	137.5	EUR	EX	7008	040412-03
500116	23JUL04	400	13600	EUR	EXP	7008	041223-04

Tip: If an INSERT statement is attempting to insert more than one row into a table and an error is encountered, all of the successful inserts are deleted or rolled back. In this example, all of the rows in the existing *stock* table are being inserted into the *newstock* table as part of a single INSERT statement. As a result, if even one problem data value is encountered none of the rows is inserted.

Care must be taken when inserting new rows into tables if integrity constraints have been defined for the table or the table is related to another table through a referential constraint.

In the next example an INSERT statement for a new book title in the *stock* table is shown together with the SAS log error message. The new entry violates several constraints. First, the stock amount does not meet the minimum set out in the check constraint associated with this column. Second, the PRIMARY KEY constraint is violated because the new ISBN value exists in the *newstock* table. Third, the reprint code of H does not exist in the *newreprint* table, resulting in a violation of the FOREIGN KEY constraint. Notice that the SAS log reports only the first violation encountered, not all three. In addition, it reports that any inserts that were successfully entered are backed out because the UNDO_POLICY=REQUIRED option is set by default.

Tip: Only one constraint violation is reported in the SAS log even if several constraints are violated by the INSERT or UPDATE statement.

```
insert into newstock
  values ('1-7890-1267-8','Alternative therapies','Brown',
          'Thomas','medicine','H',
          5,1980,'123444',10.0);
```

SAS log:

```
ERROR: Add/Update failed for data set WORK.NEWSTOCK because data
       value(s) do not comply with integrity constraint _CK0001_.
NOTE:  This insert failed while attempting to add data from VALUES
       clause 1 to the data set.
NOTE:  Deleting the successful inserts before error noted above to
       restore table to a consistent state.
```

Tip: By default, if an integrity constraint is violated, the entire statement fails and none of the rows specified in the INSERT statement is saved to the table.

In the next example, the same entry is made but with a different ISBN and stock value; the reprint value remains the same. Notice that the SAS log reports the message specified with the MESSAGE= option when the FOREIGN KEY constraint was created rather than the usual error message. Because the message type was set to user, the specified message overrides the entire SAS error message.

```
insert into newstock
  values ('1-7890-7888-1','Alternative
therapies','Brown','Thomas',
          'medicine','H',
          10,1980,'123444',10.0);
```

SAS log:

```
ERROR: Violates Foreign Key - check reprint value.
NOTE: This insert failed while attempting to add data from VALUES
      clause 1 to the data set.
NOTE: Deleting the successful inserts before error noted above to
      restore table to a consistent state.
```

Tip: Adding an optional message to an integrity constraint enables a user to understand why an INSERT or UPDATE statement in a table failed. Set MSGTYPE=USER to replace the entire SAS error message with your message. Otherwise, the message associated with the constraint is written to the SAS log together with the usual SAS error message :

```
ERROR: Violates Foreign Key - check reprint value.
       Observation was not added/updated because a
       matching primary key value was not found for
       foreign key _FK0001_.
```

Insertion of one or more rows from an existing table

General form:

> **INSERT INTO** <libref.>table-name <(column list)>
> |query ;

This form of the INSERT statement adds one or more rows from an existing table to another table. An SQL query is used to select data from an existing table for the columns in the new rows.

> **Tip:** If the query does not return any rows, then the INSERT statement will not add any rows to the table; a row of null values cannot be added to a table.

Guidelines

- The order of the columns listed in the SELECT clause of the query must match the column order of the table into which the data is inserted.
- All valid queries can be used; however, the ORDER BY clause cannot be added to the query.
- Indexes associated with the table are not updated until all new rows have been added.

> **Tip:** If you are entering many new rows of data into a table with one or more indexes using the INSERT INTO and VALUES statements you might consider inserting your rows into a temporary table. The new rows can then be added from the temporary table into the final table using an INSERT INTO SELECT statement, delaying index updates until all rows have been entered.

The next example shows the query form of the INSERT statement used to populate a new table called *ordsmry*. The table is first created, and then the INSERT statement adds rows of selected data from the *orders*, *client* and *currency* table. The contents of the new table are included in the example.

```
LIBNAME bluesky "C:\mydata\bluesky bookstore\";

CREATE    table bluesky.ordsmry
          (company  char(25) label='Company',
          ord_date  date format=DATE9. label='Order Date',
          contact   varchar(20) label = 'Contact',
          totsale   num format=dollar10.2 label='Total Sale',
          currency  char(3) label = 'Currency',
          exchrate  num format=10.4 label='Exchange Rate');

INSERT into bluesky.ordsmry
          SELECT    c.company, o.ord_date,
                    compress(c.cont_fst)||'
                    '||compress(c.cont_lst),
                    o.totsale, o.currency, cn.exchrate
          FROM      bluesky.client c, bluesky.orders o,
                    bluesky.currency cn
          WHERE     c.clientno = o.clientno
                    and o.currency = cn.currency
                    and month(cn.cur_date) = month(o.ord_date);

SELECT    *
FROM      bluesky.ordsmry;
```

Company	Order Date	Contact	Total Sale	Currency	Exchange Rate
Chicago State University	12APR2004	Holee Davis	$39,375.00	USD	1.0000
Chicago State University	12APR2004	Holee Davis	$41,820.00	USD	1.0000
Cosmos 2000	11APR2003	Curtis Jennings	$6,800.00	EUR	0.9208
Heymann's	10APR2004	Gary Smith	$797.50	EUR	0.9208
Cosmos 2000	12APR2004	Curtis Jennings	$137.50	EUR	0.9208
National University of Si	08APR2004	John Clements	$1,490.00	SGD	1.7771
University of Adelaide	11APR2003	Emily Baird	$8,750.00	AUD	1.6398
University of Adelaide	12APR2004	Emily Baird	$4,450.00	AUD	1.6398
University of Texas	06MAY2003	Alice Eagleton	$2,175.00	USD	1.0000
University of Texas	06MAY2003	Alice Eagleton	$32,875.00	USD	1.0000
University of Texas	06MAY2003	Alice Eagleton	$20,700.00	USD	1.0000
Chicago State University	05MAY2004	Holee Davis	$8,580.00	USD	1.0000
Heffers Booksellers	12MAY2004	Marge Wallace	$17,940.00	EUR	0.8656
National University of Si	11MAY2004	John Clements	$2,150.00	SGD	1.7357
Chicago State University	07JUN2004	Holee Davis	$8,505.00	USD	1.0000

(*continued on the next page*)

(continued)

```
Heffers Booksellers       24JUN2003  Marge Wallace     $2,432.50  EUR      0.8534
Heffers Booksellers       12JUN2004  Marge Wallace    $225000.00  EUR      0.8534
Heymann's                 12JUN2004  Gary Smith        $1,080.00  EUR      0.8534
Lawrence Books            12JUN2004  Alan Caston         $360.00  CAD      1.3530
Heffers Booksellers       23JUL2004  Marge Wallace    $15,487.50  EUR      0.8756
Heymann's                 23JUL2004  Gary Smith          $657.50  EUR      0.8756
Cosmos 2000               23JUL2004  Curtis Jennings  $13,600.00  EUR      0.8756
University of Adelaide    20JUL2004  Emily Baird      $11,390.00  AUD      1.5306
University of Adelaide    23JUL2004  Emily Baird      $82,500.00  AUD      1.5306
```

If integrity constraints are defined for a table, each incoming row is checked against the constraints to ensure that the data values do not violate the constraints.

In the next example an INSERT statement is used to populate the *newreprint* table from the existing Bluesky *reprint* table, and the SAS log messages are shown. The reprint values in each of the incoming six rows were checked against the PRIMARY KEY constraint of the *newreprint* table to ensure that the value was not a duplicate of one already in the table. The SAS log reports that six rows were added to the table without incident.

Tip: I often use a DATA step to import my data and then use PROC SQL to manipulate, subset, and report from the data. Complex selection criteria can be used to selectively retrieve records for insertion from one data set into another data set or table. In addition, two or more data sets or tables may contribute information to the new records.

```
PROC SQL;
LIBNAME bluesky "C:\mydata\bluesky bookstore\";

/* Newreprint and newstock tables were created in earlier in this
chapter.  The CREATE statements are repeated here for easy
reference*/

CREATE table newreprint
         (reprint char(1) primary key,
          cutoff        num
         );
```

```
CREATE table newstock
        (isbn           char(13) primary key,
        title           char(50),
        auth_fst        char(10),
        auth_lst        char(15),
        category    char(20),
        reprint     char(1) references work.newreprint
                    on update cascade on delete set null
                    message="Violates Foreign Key - check reprint
value. "
                    msgtype=user,
        stock       num check ((yrpubl > 1990 and stock >=25)
                                or (yrpubl <= 1990 and  stock
>=10)),
        yrpubl      num check(yrpubl > 1900),
        prodcode    char(6) unique,
        price       num not null
        );

/* Insert new rows into the newreprint table*/

INSERT into work.newreprint
        SELECT *
        FROM bluesky.reprint;
```

SAS log:

```
WARNING: The SQL option UNDO_POLICY=REQUIRED is not in effect. If an error
         is detected when processing this INSERT statement, that error
         will not cause the entire statement to fail.
WARNING: PROC SQL was unable to honor the REQUIRED UNDO policy because the
         data set contains a primary key having one or more foreign keys
         referencing it that have the SET NULL or CASCADE referential
         action set. UNDO_POLICY=NONE will be used instead and will
         override the specified policy in this situation.

NOTE: 6 rows were inserted into WORK.REPRINT.
```

Tip: The foreign key relationship between the *newstock* and *newreprint* tables requires that each value added to the reprint column of the *newstock* table exists in the corresponding column of the *newreprint* table. As a result, values are first added to the *newreprint* table to avoid violating the FOREIGN KEY constraints when adding data to the *newstock* table.

For a complete example of the creation and population of linked tables, refer to the first example in the "Putting it all together" section at the end of this chapter.

The warnings in the SAS log in the preceding example concerning the UNDO_POLICY are due to the referential actions associated with the foreign key in the *newstock* table defined for the reprint column of the *newreprint* table. As set, the referential actions cause the *newstock* table to be automatically updated if one of the reprint codes in the *newreprint* table changes or is deleted. If you recall from in Chapter 2, "Working with PROC SQL," the UNDO_POLICY=REQUIRED option setting means that all inserts or updates that have been completed to the point of error are reversed. Because this can conflict with referential integrity actions, the UNDO_POLICY is automatically reset to NONE for this table.

> **Tip:** The UNDO_POLICY is automatically set to NONE for every INSERT and UPDATE statement issued against a table whose primary key is linked to a FOREIGN KEY constraint defined in another table if the foreign key is associated with referential integrity actions.

The primary key, which enforces uniqueness on the ISBN column is violated in an attempt to insert the rows of the Bluesky *stock* table into the *newstock* table. The entire INSERT statement is rolled back when the error is encountered, leaving the *newstock* table empty. A check of the Bluesky *stock* table reveals a duplicate ISBN number; the SELECT statement is modified to eliminate records with the duplicate ISBN, and 28 rows are successfully entered into the table.

```
/* The first insert statement violates the primary key
constraint*/

INSERT into work.newstock
        SELECT *
        FROM bluesky.newstock;

/* All of the successful inserts are deleted or rolled-back when
the error is encountered*/

SELECT   *
FROM     work.newstock;

/* If the offending record is eliminated from the incoming rows,
the insert is successful*/

INSERT into work.newstock
        SELECT *
        FROM bluesky.stock
        WHERE isbn ne '1-7890-4578-9';
```

SAS log:

```
13328  INSERT into work.newstock
13329  SELECT *
13330  FROM bluesky.stock;
ERROR: Add/Update failed for data set WORK.NEWSTOCK because data
       value(s) do not comply with integrity constraint _PK0001_.
NOTE:  Deleting the successful inserts before error noted above to
       restore table to a consistent state.

13331  SELECT *
13332  FROM work.newstock;
NOTE: No rows were selected.

13333  INSERT into work.newstock
13334  SELECT *
13335  FROM bluesky.stock
13336  WHERE isbn ne '1-7890-4578-9';
NOTE: 28 rows were inserted into WORK.NEWSTOCK.
```

SAS/ACCESS and SQL Pass-Through Facility users: You must have the appropriate authorization to INSERT rows into a table. Changes made to a table must be committed before they become permanent. Other users see only the new rows in the table after the action has been committed. Refer to Appendix C, "Information for Database Users," for more information.

UPDATE statement

The UPDATE statement is used to enter or modify the value of one or more columns in existing rows of a table. The UPDATE statement differs from the INSERT statement in that it does not add new rows to a table.

Tip: When a table is updated, views built on that table are also updated. Views are created when requested. Therefore, the data values reported by a view are always current. Indexes are also automatically updated when values within an indexed column change.

General form:

UPDATE	<libref.>table-name
SET	column = value| column| expression|query | CASE expression <,column=...>
<WHERE	condition <LOGICAL OPERATOR condition ...>>;

Tip: Details on the CASE expression can be found in Chapter 3, "Understanding the SELECT Statement."

This version of the UPDATE statement resets a column value in one or more rows of a table to a new value based on a column, value, or expression. New values can be conditionally assigned to columns based on the outcome of criteria set out within a CASE expression. An optional WHERE clause is added to limit the rows on which the data change operates.

SAS/ACCESS and SQL Pass-Through Facility users: You must have the appropriate authorization to update a table. Changes made to a table must be committed before they become permanent. Other users see only the new rows in the table after the action has been committed. Refer to Appendix C, "Information for Database Users," for more information.

In the next example the *reprint* table for the Bluesky Publishing Company is altered to include a new column called maximum. An UPDATE statement is then issued to generate values for the new column based on an expression using the existing cutoff column in the table. Every row in the table has been updated as shown in the report included in the example.

```
LIBNAME bluesky "C:\mydata\bluesky bookstore\";

UPDATE   BLUESKY.REPRINT
         SET maximum = cutoff*1.50;

SELECT   *
FROM     bluesky.reprint;
```

```
 REPRINT     CUTOFF   MAXIMUM
 ____________________________

 A                0         0
 B               10        15
 C               50        75
 D              100       150
 E              500       750
 F             1000      1500
```

In the example above, the maximum column was updated for every row in the table. The addition of a WHERE clause limits the modifications to specific rows within the table. In the next example, the UPDATE statement is used to update the fax number for Chicago State University.

```
LIBNAME bluesky "C:\mydata\bluesky bookstore\";
```

```
UPDATE   BLUESKY.CLIENT
         SET fax='312-861-9871'
         WHERE  clientno = 2010;

SELECT   clientno, company, phone, fax
FROM     bluesky.client;
```

```
clientNo   company                             phone            fax
--------------------------------------------------------------------------------
1001  University of Texas                  512-495-4370     512-495-4374
2010  Chicago State University             312-756-7890     312-861-9871
3007  Heffers Booksellers                  01223-568568     01223-354936
4008  National University of Singapore     874-2339
5005  University of Adelaide               61-8-8303-4402   61-8-8830-4405
6090  Heymann's                            49-30-8252573    49-30-8242690
7008  Cosmos 2000                          33-14-362-1899   33-14-352-1929
8003  Lawrence Books                       604-261-3612     604-261-3756
```

Caution: A common mistake is to forget to include the WHERE clause and update the column value for all rows in the table rather than the desired few.

The new value for a column can also be set to the outcome of a subquery. The subquery must return a single value that is then used to update the column in the table. If a correlated subquery is used, the updated column value will differ for each value within the correlated column.

Tip: Using correlated subqueries to update table columns may be resource intensive. Consider creating a temporary table from the query and then use a join to update the table.

In the next example a new column (reorder) is added to the *stock* table to hold the quantity of books to be reordered to top up inventory. An UPDATE statement is used to add values to the new column based on information stored in the *orders*, *stock,* and *reprint* tables.

Two subqueries are used. The first calculates the total quantity of each book ordered from the *orders* table. Notice that the subquery correlates the product code in the *stock* and *orders* tables to ensure that the appropriate order quantities are used for each book. The second correlated subquery determines the reprint cutoff value for each book by joining the reprint code in the *stock* table to the *reprint* table. A report is generated from the updated table to show the original stock values and the required reorder quantity of each book in the medicine category.

```
LIBNAME bluesky "C:\mydata\bluesky bookstore\";

ALTER table bluesky.stock
  add reorder num;

UPDATE  bluesky.stock
        SET reorder = abs(stock-
                         (SELECT   sum(quantity)
                         FROM      bluesky.orders
                         WHERE     orders.prodcode =
                                   stock.prodcode
                         ))
                       + (SELECT cutoff
                         FROM bluesky.reprint
                         WHERE reprint.reprint =
                         stock.reprint);

SELECT    title 'Title', prodcode 'Prod Code', stock 'Original Stock',
          reorder 'To be reordered'
FROM      bluesky.stock
WHERE     category = 'medicine'
ORDER BY title;
```

```
                                               Prod     Original      To be
Title                                          Code        Stock  reordered
----------------------------------------------------------------------------
Medical Education in School                    400100        300        385
Medications and Maintenance                    400345         30         15
National Library of Medicine                   400178         35        475
The 10% Solution                               400457        400          .
Tibetan Medicine                               400128       2000       1570
Unconventional treatments                      400102       1000        550
```

If you examine the report above, you will find a missing reorder value for the book with a product code of 400457. The next example includes a query that generates a report that shows the original stock values and the orders for each book in the medicine category. A left outer join is used to ensure that all medical books listed in the *stock* table are reported, regardless of whether an order for the book has been placed.

> **Tip:** Missing values in a column used to update another column's values can produce unsatisfactory results. Outer joins can be used to obtain the desired report or result set.

The report shows that the original stock value associated with product code 400457 is 400. However, the book has not been ordered. When the expression in the UPDATE statement was processed for this book, the missing value caused the expression to evaluate to missing.

```
LIBNAME bluesky "C:\mydata\bluesky bookstore\";

SELECT   s.title, s.prodcode, s.stock, sum(o.quantity) 'Orders'
FROM     bluesky.stock s LEFT JOIN bluesky.orders o
         ON stock.prodcode = orders.prodcode
WHERE    s.category = 'medicine'
GROUP BY s.title,s.prodcode, s.stock
ORDER BY s.title;
```

```
                                           prod
title                                      Code        stock    Orders
------------------------------------------------------------------------
Medical Education in School                400100        300       675
Medications and Maintenance                400345         30        25
National Library of Medicine               400178         35       510
The 10% Solution                           400457        400         .
Tibetan Medicine                           400128       2000      1430
Unconventional treatments                  400102       1000      1500
```

Tip: An ORDER BY clause was added to the above SELECT statement to ensure that the report in this example was sorted in the same order as the one shown in the previous example. Although a GROUP BY clause is included in the query, it does not always generate a sorted report. Information on GROUP BY clause processing is provided in Chapter 3, "Understanding the SELECT Statement."

The goal of the previous UPDATE statement was to retain the current stock value if no orders for the book had been placed. The conditional application of changes to a column can be achieved using a CASE expression. CASE expressions allow you to update a column with one value depending on the outcome of a criterion.

In the next example a new table called *reorder* is created to facilitate the reordering of books. The table structure and data is taken from the existing *stock* table for the Bluesky Publishing Company and altered to include a new column called orders. The UPDATE statement with a CASE expression is then used to conditionally add values to the orders column. If orders for the book have been placed, the column is updated with the total quantity of all placed orders. However, if the book has not been sold, the column is updated with a zero.

```
LIBNAME bluesky "C:\mydata\bluesky bookstore\";

CREATE table bluesky.reorder AS
         SELECT *
         FROM   bluesky.stock;

ALTER table bluesky.reorder
         ADD  orders num;

UPDATE bluesky.reorder
 SET orders =
 CASE
      WHEN  (SELECT  sum(quantity)
                     FROM  bluesky.orders
                     WHERE orders.prodcode = reorder.prodcode )ne.
      THEN   (SELECT sum(quantity)
                     FROM  bluesky.orders
                     WHERE orders.prodcode = reorder.prodcode )
          ELSE 0
     END;
```

Tip: Without the ELSE clause in the CASE expression the orders column would contain a missing value for books that are not in the *orders* table.

In the next example, a SELECT statement is issued against the new table to generate a report of the books that must be reprinted. The number of books in stock, less the orders, is compared with the cutoff in the *reprint* table to determine the number of books to be reprinted. The report is included in the example.

```
LIBNAME bluesky "C:\mydata\bluesky bookstore\";
TITLE1 'Books to be reprinted';

SELECT  title 'Title' format=$40.,
        prodcode 'Product Code', stock 'Original Stock',
        orders 'Orders', reprint.cutoff 'Cutoff',
        abs(stock-reprint.cutoff-orders) as rpt_amt 'Reprint Amt'
FROM    bluesky.reorder, bluesky.reprint
WHERE   reorder.reprint = reprint.reprint
        AND category='medicine'
ORDER BY title;
```

Books to be reprinted

Reprint	Product	Original			
Title	Code	Stock	Orders	Cutoff	Amt
Medical Education in School	400100	300	675	10	385
Medications and Maintenance	400345	30	25	10	5
National Library of Medicine	400178	35	510	0	475
The 10% Solution	400457	400	0	50	350
Tibetan Medicine	400128	2000	1430	1000	430
Unconventional treatments	400102	1000	1500	50	550

DELETE statement

General form:

DELETE **FROM** <libref.>table
<**WHERE** criteria>;

The DELETE statement is used to remove one or more rows from a table or view. However, the structure of the table remains intact. All indexes related to the table are automatically updated to exclude the removed values. All of the rows may be removed or only those that meet the conditions set out in the WHERE clause.

SAS/ACCESS and SQL Pass-Through Facility users: You must have the appropriate authorization to delete rows from a table. Changes made to a table must be committed before they become permanent. Other users see only the new rows in the table after the action has been committed. Refer to Appendix C, "Information for Database Users," for more information.

In the next example all of the rows in the ord2004 table are deleted. A DESCRIBE statement issued for the table confirms that the structure of the table is intact. However, the SELECT statement issued against the table does not generate a report.

```
LIBNAME bluesky "C:\mydata\bluesky bookstore\";

DELETE FROM BLUESKY.ORD2004;
DESCRIBE table bluesky.ord2004;

SELECT *
FROM   bluesky.ord2004;
```

SAS log:

```
create table BLUESKY.ORD2004( bufsize=8192 )
  (
   prodCode char(6),
   ord_date num format=DATE. informat=DATE.,
   quantity num,
   totsale num,
   clientNo num
  );
1656
1657  SELECT  *
1658  FROM    bluesky.ord2004;
NOTE: No rows were selected.
```

If a view has been built on a table and the rows are subsequently deleted from the table, the view will continue to be valid. However, the execution of the view will not retrieve any rows. If you issue a DELETE statement against a view, the rows in the underlying table are deleted. In the next example a view called *myview* is created from the rows in the *stock* table with one column and 30 rows. When a DELETE statement is issued against the view, the SAS log confirms that 30 rows were deleted from the *myview* view. Notice that there is no mention of action against the *stock* table. However, when a SELECT statement is run against the *stock* table, no rows are found.

```
PROC SQL;

CREATE VIEW myview AS
         (SELECT category
         FROM bluesky.stock);

DELETE
FROM    myview;

SELECT  *
FROM    bluesky.stock;

SELECT  *
FROM    myview;
```

SAS log:

```
13897  DELETE FROM myview;
NOTE: 30 rows were deleted from WORK.MYVIEW.

13898
13899  SELECT *
13900  FROM bluesky.stock;
NOTE: No rows were selected.

13901  SELECT *
13902  FROM myview;
   NOTE: No rows were selected.
```

Caution: If a view is created with an embedded LIBNAME statement on a USING clause, the location of the underlying table(s) is not always obvious. Consider restricting access to the underlying table(s) to eliminate accidental deletion of rows in the table(s).

Compress and reuse options

It is important to note that when one or more rows are deleted from a table, the space occupied by those rows may still be allocated to the table. For large tables with frequent deletions, this unused space may be especially problematic.

Tip: Although COMPRESS and REUSE control wasted space, tables that are subjected to frequent DELETE statements will have wasted space. Rebuilding such tables from time to time is the best way to avoid wasted space.

By default, the REUSE and COMPRESS options are set to NO; space allocated to rows that are subsequently deleted is not reused and space is added to the table to accommodate incoming rows. In the following table, which is a portion of the Bluesky Publishing Company *shipping* table, five observations are shown. The highlighted rows in the table represent observations that were deleted previously. The space occupied by these observations is still in use by the table, although they no longer have any values associated with them.

SAS/ACCESS and SQL Pass-Through Facility users: Each RDBMS has a method for compressing tables to recover unused space and to de-fragment storage space associated with tables. These commands or steps are more often found in DBA handbooks than in SQL references.

Table name: SHIPPING		
delcode	**deltype**	**charge**
EXE	2 day Express shipping	15
UPS	US postal service	10
EXP	express mail	10
EXA	express air delivery	15
GRN	ground delivery	10

If the REUSE option is set to YES and the COMPRESS option is set to YES at the time the table is created, incoming observations may be inserted into the space freed up by deleted rows.

Tip: Compression will only occur if the table size decreases with compression. There are cases where compression results in a larger table size. In my experience, this happens most often with corrupted tables or fragmented storage. If you find compression has not occurred, it is best to create a new table from the old using a statement of a form such as CREATE TABLE <*newtable*> AS SELECT * from <*oldtable*>.

DROP statement

General form:

```
DROP      TABLE | VIEW
          <libref.>table-name | view-name  ;

DROP      INDEX index-name ON|FROM <libref.>table-name;
```

The DROP statement is used to eliminate permanent or temporary tables, views, or indexes. All references to the member are eliminated from the data dictionary. The data dictionary is covered in more detail in Chapter 7, "Building Interactive Applications," with additional information contained in Appendix B, "Dictionary Table Descriptions."

Indexes associated with columns in a table are automatically eliminated when the table is dropped. However, it is possible for a view that references a dropped table to continue to exist. SAS does not report the interdependencies between tables and views at the time the table is dropped. When a SELECT statement is executed against the view an error message will occur indicating that the table does not exist.

> **Tip:** An error message indicating that a table does not exist may be the result of a DROP statement. However, such messages also occur when the table name is misspelled or an incorrect libref is specified. Check your table name and LIBNAME statements carefully before assuming the worst.

The next example illustrates the results of a DROP statement issued against a table that is used as a source for a view. The query used to create the *ordrpt* view is reported using the DESCRIBE statement. The view is built in part on the *stock* table for the Bluesky Publishing Company. The *stock* table is dropped and the DESCRIBE statement is reissued. The view still exists and continues to reference the dropped table. An error message is only reported when a SELECT statement is issued against the view.

```
LIBNAME bluesky "C:\mydata\bluesky bookstore\";

CREATE VIEW bluesky.ordrpt as
         SELECT s.prodcode, s.title, o.invoice, o.ord_date
         FROM   bluesky.orders o JOIN bluesky.stock s
         ON     s.procode=o.prodcode
         WHERE  ord_date between DATE() and DATE()-356);

DROP TABLE bluesky.stock;

SELECT *
FROM   bluesky.ordrpt;
```

SAS log:

```
513  DROP TABLE bluesky.stock;
NOTE: Table BLUESKY.STOCK has been dropped.

514   select  *
515 FROM     bluesky.ordrpt;
ERROR: File BLUESKY.STOCK.DATA does not exist.
```

> **Tip:** It is best to drop all views associated with a table immediately after dropping the table to prevent problems.

It is often necessary to drop and recreate indexes and views due to changes to reporting requirements. The DROP statement for views is identical to the one used to drop a table. However, the DROP statement for an index must include the name of the associated table as well as the name of the index. Each index associated with a specific table must be assigned a unique name, but there is no requirement that an index name be unique in a library or SAS session.

In the next example a DESCRIBE statement issued for the *orders* table indicates that a composite index based on the order date, product code, and invoice is associated with the table. If we decide that we require a new composite index based on the same columns but with a different column order, the existing index may be dropped. The column order is important because a composite index is used only if the first column in the index is included in a WHERE clause criterion.

```
LIBNAME bluesky "C:\mydata\bluesky bookstore\";

DESCRIBE table bluesky.orders;
```

SAS log:

```
create table BLUESKY.ORDERS( bufsize=8192 )
  (
   PRODCODE char(6),
   ORD_DATE num format=DATE. informat=DATE.,
   QUANTITY num,
   TOTSALE num,
   CURRENCY char(3),
   DELCODE char(3),
   CLIENTNO num,
   INVOICE char(10)
  );

create unique index ORDPROD on
       BLUESKY.ORDERS(ORD_DATE,PRODCODE,INVOICE);
create index CLIENTNO on BLUESKY.ORDERS(CLIENTNO);
create index ORD_DATE on BLUESKY.ORDERS(ORD_DATE);
```

In the next example the original *ordprod* index is dropped and a new index using the same columns in a different order is created. The DESCRIBE statement confirms that the original composite index was dropped and the new index created.

> **Tip:** Either the ON or FROM keyword can be used in the DROP INDEX statement. My preference is the ON keyword because it is consistent with the CREATE INDEX statement.

```
LIBNAME bluesky "C:\mydata\bluesky bookstore\";

DROP INDEX       ordprod ON bluesky.orders;
CREATE INDEX     prodord ON
bluesky.orders(prodcode,ord_date,invoice);

DESCRIBE table bluesky.orders;
```

SAS log:

```
create table BLUESKY.ORDERS( bufsize=8192 )
  (
   prodCode char(6),
   ord_date num format=DATE. informat=DATE.,
   quantity num,
   totsale num,
   currency char(3),
   delCode char(3),
   clientNo num,
   invoice char(10)
  );
create unique index prodord on BLUESKY.ORDERS(prodCode,ord_date,invoice);
create index ord_date on BLUESKY.ORDERS(ord_date);
create index clientNo on BLUESKY.ORDERS(clientNo);
```

Tip: A view or index built on a table can be dropped without also dropping the associated table.

Dropping tables associated with constraints

A table cannot be dropped if it has integrity constraints associated with it. Each of the constraints must first be removed using a series of ALTER TABLE statements before a DROP TABLE statement can be issued. Moreover, if a foreign key in another table references the table to be dropped, the FOREIGN KEY constraint must be deleted before the reference table can be dropped.

The next example includes the CREATE statements used earlier in this chapter to create the *newreprint* and *newstock* tables. A description of each of the tables generated using the DESCRIBE statement is included in the "Constraints" section early in this chapter. If a DROP statement is issued against either of the tables, an error message is written to the SAS log as shown in the second example following. The tables are linked through a FOREIGN KEY constraint on the reprint column. As a result, neither table can be dropped without first dropping the constraint.

```
CREATE  table newreprint
        (reprint char(1) primary key,
        cutoff    num
        );

CREATE table newstock
        (isbn           char(13) primary key,
        title           char(50),
        auth_fst        char(10),
        auth_lst        char(15),
        category        char(20),
        reprint         char(1) references work.newreprint
                        on update cascade on delete set null
                        message="Violates Foreign Key - check
                        reprint value. "
                                msgtype=user,
        stock           num check ((yrpubl > 1990 and stock >=25)
                        or (yrpubl <= 1990 and  stock >=10)),
        yrpubl          num check(yrpubl > 1900),
         prodcode       char(6) unique,
        price           num not null
        );
```

SAS log:

```
1665  DROP table newreprint;
ERROR: A rename/delete/replace attempt is not allowed for a data set
       involved in a referential integrity constraint.
WORK.NEWREPRINT.DATA
WARNING: Table WORK.NEWREPRINT has not been dropped.
1666  DROP table newstock;
ERROR: A rename/delete/replace attempt is not allowed for a data set
       involved in a referential integrity constraint. WORK.NEWSTOCK.DATA
WARNING: Table WORK.NEWSTOCK has not been dropped.
```

The next example includes the statements needed to drop the *newreprint* and *newstock* tables created earlier in this chapter. The FOREIGN KEY constraint is first dropped from the *newstock* table allowing both the *newstock* or the *newreprint* tables to be dropped.

```
PROC SQL;
ALTER table newstock
  DROP constraint _FK0001_;

DROP table newreprint;
DROP table newstock;
```

Putting it all together

The next example includes many of the statements and concepts discussed in this chapter. Several tables are created using the various forms of the CREATE TABLE statement. A new table called *stock_new* takes its structure and rows from the existing *stock* table. It is altered to add column modifiers to the title column and a PRIMARY KEY constraint. The *currency_new* table, on the other hand, takes only the structure from the existing *currency* table. The ALTER statement is used to create a primary key on the table and to specify column modifiers. Rows are then added to the *currency_new* table using the INSERT statement.

Each column of the *orders_new* tables is defined in a CREATE TABLE statement. Several constraints using out-of-line syntax are also specified in the CREATE TABLE statement.

The *shipping_new* table is constructed using a series of steps designed to create a table that provides labels and rates for each delivery code and validates incoming delivery codes for entries in the *orders_new* table. A *shipping_new* table with a single column delcode is created and populated with unique values from the delcode column of the *orders_new* table. Next the *shipping_new* table is altered, adding two columns for a delivery type description (deltype) and delivery rates (charge). An UPDATE statement is used to populate the delivery type column with descriptions assigned to each delivery code using a CASE expression. Delivery rates are then associated with each delivery code using a WHERE expression to assign different rates to selected codes.

A primary key is next added to the *shipping_new* table to prepare it for the foreign key relationship. An ALTER statement is then issued against the *orders_new* table to add a FOREIGN KEY constraint, linking its delivery code to the delivery code column of the *shipping_new* table. Each of the constraints associated with the *orders_new* table has a user message associated with it, overriding the SAS error message normally generated when the constraint is violated. The primary keys in the *shipping_new* and *stock_new* tables must be created before the FOREIGN KEY constraints in the *orders_new* table can be generated.

From this point on, the delivery code for every order entered into the *orders* table is checked against the *shipping_new* table. Only those rows that contain a delivery code that is in the *shipping_new* table will be added to the *orders_new* table. The foreign key relationship between the *orders* and *currency_new* tables serves to validate the currency code of an order. Only currency codes currently in the *currency_new* table can be specified on incoming rows to the *order_news* table.

Tip: The steps used to create the *shipping_new* table can be applied to tables used to simulate the PROC FORMAT procedure. The *shipping_new* table associates a label with each delivery code in the *orders_new* table in the same fashion as PROC FORMAT.

This strategy can also be applied to data warehouse ETL processes. For example, tables can be created to remap codes, store formulae for modifying values, or calculating segments. Table joins are then used to transform source data to a common form for loading into data warehouse tables.

Next an index is created for the *orders_new* table and a view called *neworders* is built to join all of the tables. The view takes the descriptive information relating to the delivery code from the *shipping_new* table, rather than reporting the code itself. The view contents are included in the second example in this section. Notice that the labels and formatting specified when the tables were created or in an ALTER statement are used in the view report.

The *shipping_new* table is modified to remove one of the entries in the *shipping_new* table, and the entries in the *stock_new* table are updated. The delCode column of the *shipping_new* table is part of a foreign key relationship. As a result, the *orders* table is updated automatically when the changes are made to the *shipping_new* table.

The foreign key relationship between *shipping_new* and *orders_new* in the delivery code column prevents a new order with a delivery code that does not exist in the *shipping_new* table to be entered. When the foreign key was created, a user message was attached to it. The user message is displayed in the SAS log when the INSERT statement fails. The portion of the SAS log with the INSERT statement and the message is shown in the third example in this section.

The *orders_new* table is shown in the fourth example after the changes to the *shipping_new* table were applied. The delCode value in the *orders_new* table for the book entitled Unconventional Treatments, with a product code (prodcode) 400102, has been set to null. The null value replaces GRN because the GRN value was deleted from the *shipping_new* table. In addition, the delCode value for product code 200145, Space Sciences, reflects the change from EXE to EX2 made to the *shipping* table.

The view after all updates have been applied is shown in the fifth example. Notice that the entry for product code 400102, Unconventional Treatments, is missing from the view. An outer join is required to retrieve rows in the *orders* table whose delCode column values do not match the *shipping_new* table. The view must be dropped and recreated using a different join expression in order to retrieve the row associated with product code 400102. However, each of the changes made to the tables, including the new title in the *stock_new* table, are included in the view. Views are regenerated when they are queried, taking the current data from each of the tables involved in the view.

Finally, each of the tables is dropped. The order of the statements is important here. The FOREIGN KEY constraints must be dropped before the DROP TABLE statements are issued for tables that are linked through such a constraint. In this example, the *stock_new* and *shipping_new* tables are parent or reference tables to the *orders_new* table. The foreign key relationship between these tables is eliminated by removing the FOREIGN KEY constraint from the child table, *orders_new* with an ALTER statement. DROP TABLE statements issued against the three tables can then be executed.

```
PROC SQL;
LIBNAME bluesky "C:\mydata\bluesky bookstore\";

* Create a new stock table using the structure and data of an
existing table;

CREATE table bluesky.stock_new
  as (SELECT * from bluesky.stock);

* Add a label and formatting to the title column;

ALTER table  bluesky.stock_new
  modify title 'Title' format=$30.;

* Add a primary key to the new table;

ALTER table bluesky.stock_new
  add constraint prodcode_pk primary key (prodcode);

* Create a new currency table using only the structure of an
existing table;

CREATE table bluesky.currency_new
  like bluesky.currency;

* Add a primary key to the new table;

ALTER table bluesky.currency_new
  add constraint curr_pk primary key(currency);

* Add a labels and formats to columns in the currency table;

ALTER table bluesky.currency_new
  modify exchrate 'Exchange Rate' format=6.4;

ALTER table bluesky.currency_new
  modify cur_date 'Date';

ALTER table bluesky.currency_new
```

```
  modify currency 'Currency';

* Add rows to the new table;

INSERT into bluesky.currency_new
  values('USD','01JUL04'D,1)
  values('EUR','01JUL04'D,0.87561)
  values('SGD','01JUL04'D,1.76712)
  values('AUD','01JUL04'D,1.53064)
  values('CAD','01JUL04'D,1.38795);

* Create the orders table, adding several constraints;

CREATE table bluesky.orders_new (
         prodCode       char(6) 'Product Code',
         ord_date       date 'Order Date',
         quantity       num 'Order Qty' format=comma8.,
         totsale        num 'Total Sale' format=dollar12.2,
         currency       char(3) 'Currency',
         delCode        char(3) 'Delivery Code',
         clientNo       num 'Client No.',
         invoice        char(10) 'Invoice No.',
         constraint orders_pk primary key(invoice)
           message='Violated primary key' msgtype=user,
         constraint sale_nn not null (totsale)
           message='Total sale cannot be null' msgtype=user,
         constraint qty_nn not null (quantity)
           message='Quantity cannot be null' msgtype=user,
         constraint date_ck check (ord_date > '01JAN2004'd)
           message='Date must be after January 1, 2004'
msgtype=user,
         constraint prodcode_fk foreign key (prodcode) references
                    bluesky.stock_new
           on update cascade on delete set null
           message='Book product code not in stock table'
msgtype=user);

* Add orders to the table;

INSERT into bluesky.orders_new
  values('100601','23Jul2004'D,590,15487.5,'EUR','EXP',3007,
        '041223-01')
  values('400102','23Jul2004'D,1500,82500,'AUD','GRN',5005,
        '041223-02')
  values('400178','23Jul2004'D,10,657.5,'CAD','EXA',6090,
        '041223-03')
```

```
  values('600125','23Jul2004'D,400,13600,'SGD','UPS',7008,
         '041223-04')
  values('200145','23Jul2004'D,700,39375,'USD','EXE',2010,
         '041223-05');

* Create a new shipping table with a single column populated with
  unique values from the
  orders delivery code column;

CREATE table bluesky.shipping_new
as select distinct delCode from bluesky.orders_new;

* Alter the shipping table, adding the remaining columns;

ALTER table bluesky.shipping_new
  add delType    char(25) 'Delivery';

ALTER table bluesky.shipping_new
  add charge     num  'Cost' format=dollar8.2;

* Add a column modifier to the delCode column;
  ALTER table bluesky.shipping_new
  MODIFY delCode 'Delivery Code';

* Add additional details to the shipping table;
  UPDATE bluesky.shipping_new
  set delType =
         CASE delcode
               WHEN 'EXE' then '2 day Express shipping'
               WHEN 'UPS' then 'US postal service'
               WHEN 'EXP' then 'express mail'
               WHEN 'EXA' then 'express air delivery'
               WHEN 'GRN' then 'ground delivery'
         END;

UPDATE bluesky.shipping_new
  set charge = 10
  where delcode in ('UPS','GRN','EXP');

UPDATE bluesky.shipping_new
  set charge = 15
  where delcode in ('EXE','EXA');

* Add a primary key to the shipping table;

ALTER table bluesky.shipping_new
  add constraint delcode_pk primary key (delcode);
```

```
* Alter the orders table to add another foreign key constraint,
linking the orders and shipping tables;

ALTER table bluesky.orders_new
  add constraint del_fk foreign key (delcode) references
  bluesky.shipping_new on update cascade on delete set null
  message='Delivery code not in shipping table' msgtype=user;

* Add indexes to the order date column, often used in WHERE
  clauses;

CREATE index ord_date on bluesky.orders_new(ord_date);

* Create a view joining the tables
- description of delivery code is reported rather than code
- exchange rate is obtained from the currency table;

CREATE view NewOrders as
(SELECT  n.title, o.ord_date, o.quantity,
         o.totsale, o.currency, c.exchRate,
         s.delType
FROM     bluesky.orders_new o, bluesky.stock_new n,
         bluesky.shipping_new s, bluesky.currency_new c
WHERE    o.prodcode = n.prodcode
         and o.delcode = s.delcode
         and month(o.ord_date) = month(c.cur_date)
         and o.currency = c.currency
);

TITLE 'Current Orders';

SELECT   *
FROM     neworders
ORDER BY title;

* Modify the shipping table, deleting the ground shipping option;

DELETE from bluesky.shipping_new
  where delCode= 'GRN';

* Modify the shipping table, updating one of the codes;

UPDATE bluesky.shipping_new
  set delCode='EX2'
  where delCode='EXE';
```

```
* Modify the currency table, updating an exchange rate;

UPDATE bluesky.currency_new
  set exchrate= 1.35178
  where currency = 'CAD' and cur_date='01JUL04'D;

* Change the title of the Space Science book';

 UPDATE bluesky.stock_new
  set title= 'The Science of Outer Space'
  where title ='Space Sciences';

* Foreign key relationship between the shipping_new and orders_new
tables causes the INSERT statement to fail because delivery code
is not in shipping table;

INSERT into bluesky.orders_new

values('500890','25Jul2004'D,250,8125.00,'EUR','GRN',3007,'040725-
01');

* INSERT statement shipping value of GRN changed to EXE.  Order is
successfully entered into the orders_new table;

INSERT into bluesky.orders_new

values('500890','25Jul2004'D,250,8125.00,'EUR','EX2',3007,'040725-
01');

TITLE 'New Orders Table';

SELECT  *
FROM    bluesky.orders_new;

* View reflects all changes.  It does not need to be recreated;

TITLE 'Current Orders - updated';

SELECT  *
FROM neworders
ORDER BY title;

* Drop the foreign key constraints so the tables can be dropped;

ALTER table bluesky.orders_new
  drop constraint del_fk;
```

```
ALTER table bluesky.orders_new
  drop constraint prodcode_fk;

* Drop the tables;

DROP table bluesky.stock_new;
DROP table bluesky.shipping_new;
DROP table bluesky.orders_new;
DROP table bluesky.currency_new;
```

Current Orders

Title Delivery	Order Date	Order Qty	Total Sale	Currency	Exchange Rate
Free Thinking in Mathematics express mail	23JUL04	590	$15,487.50	EUR	0.8756
National Library of Medicine express air delivery	23JUL04	10	$657.50	CAD	1.3880
Space Sciences 2 day Express shipping	23JUL04	700	$39,375.00	USD	1.0000
The Maestro US postal service	23JUL04	400	$13,600.00	SGD	1.7671
Unconventional treatments ground delivery	23JUL04	1,500	$82,500.00	AUD	1.5306

SAS log excerpt:

```
* Foreign key relationship between the shipping_new and
  orders_new tables causes the INSERT statement to fail
 because delivery code is not in shipping table;

INSERT into bluesky.orders_new
  values('500890','25Jul2004'D,250,8125.00,'EUR','GRN',3007,'
  040725-01');
ERROR: Delivery code not in shipping table
NOTE: This insert failed while attempting to add data from VALUES
      clause 1 to the data set.
NOTE: Deleting the successful inserts before error noted above to
      restore table to a consistent state.
```

New Orders Table

Product Code	Order Date	Order Qty	Total Sale	Currency	Delivery Code	Client No.	Invoice No.
100601	23JUL04	590	$15,487.50	EUR	EXP	3007	041223-01
400102	23JUL04	1,500	$82,500.00	AUD		5005	041223-02
400178	23JUL04	10	$657.50	CAD	EXA	6090	041223-03
600125	23JUL04	400	$13,600.00	SGD	UPS	7008	041223-04
200145	23JUL04	700	$39,375.00	USD	EX2	2010	041223-05
500890	25JUL04	250	$8,125.00	EUR	EX2	3007	040725-01

Current Orders - updated

Title Delivery	Order Date	Order Qty	Total Sale	Currency	Exchange Rate
Free Thinking in Mathematics express mail	23JUL04	590	$15,487.50	EUR	0.8756
Introduction to Computer_Scien 2 day Express shipping	25JUL04	250	$8,125.00	EUR	0.8756
National Library of Medicine express air delivery	23JUL04	10	$657.50	CAD	1.3518
The Maestro US postal service	23JUL04	400	$13,600.00	SGD	1.7671
The Science of Outer Space 2 day Express shipping	23JUL04	700	$39,375.00	USD	1.0000

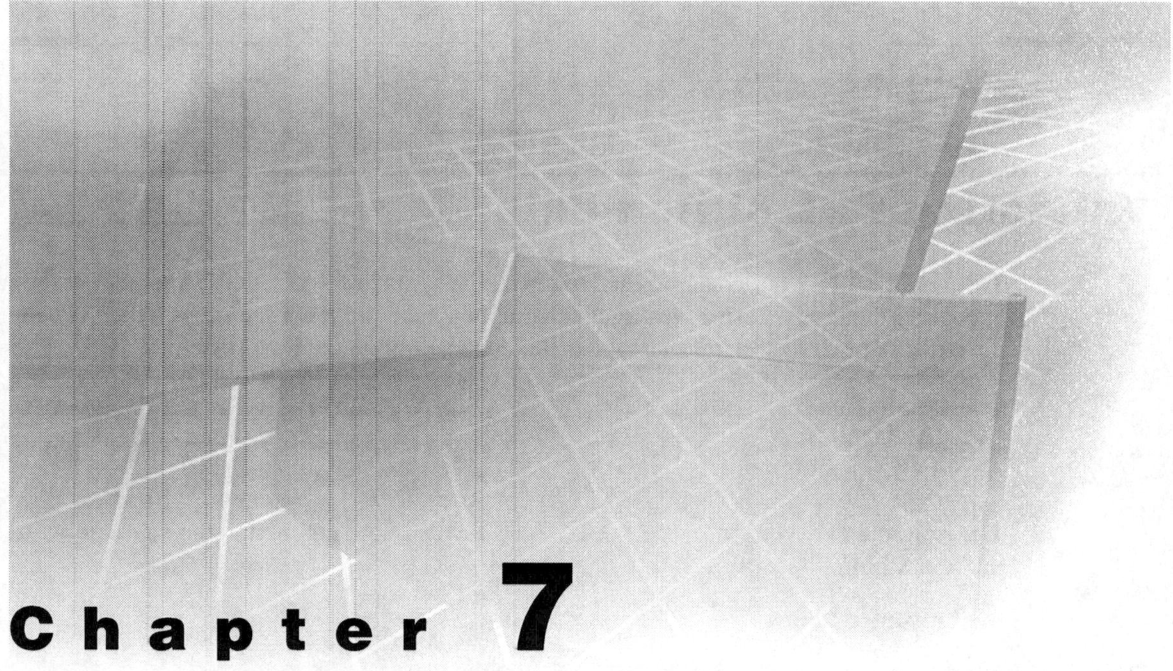

Chapter 7

Building Interactive Applications

Validating SQL statements

The VALIDATE option can be used to check the syntax of a SELECT statement without executing the query. Error messages relating to syntax are recorded only in the SAS log; the exact nature of the error message differs depending on the host system.

General form:

VALIDATE
SELECT statement;

The example following shows a VALIDATE SELECT statement and the message written to the SAS log.

```
LIBNAME bluesky "C:\mydata\bluesky bookstore\";
PROC SQL;

VALIDATE
SELECT   *
FROM     bluesky.orders
WHERE    totsale between 50 and 1000;
```

SAS log:

```
NOTE: PROC SQL statement has valid syntax.
```

SQL SELECT statements which include macro variables can also be debugged with the VALIDATE statement. The automatic macro variable SQLRC is set to a status value that indicates whether the statement is successful. A value of 4 (warning) or less for the SQLRC return code indicates that the program will correctly run. A return code of 8 indicates severe errors and the program cannot be executed. More information on the SQLRC variable is provided in the next section.

Use of macro variables

The INTO clause of the SELECT statement assigns values retrieved through the execution of the query to one or more macro variables. Either a single value or the contents of an entire column can be stored in a macro variable.

Tip: The CALL SYMPUT routine in the DATA step provides the same functionality as the INTO clause within PROC SQL.

Specify a single value for each macro variable listed

General form:

SELECT *column1* <, *column2* ...>
INTO **:macro-variable1 <, macro-variable2 ... >**
FROM <libref.>table <alias> ;

Guidelines

- Each macro variable specified in the INTO clause is assigned a single value. If more than one value is returned by the SELECT statement, the macro variable is assigned the first returned value.
- Any number of macro variables can be specified using this format.
- Single value macro variables may be combined with other forms of macro variables.
- The number of columns or expressions in the SELECT clause must match the number of macro variables or a warning will be generated.
- By default, leading and trailing blanks are not trimmed before they are stored in the macro variables.

The next example shows a SELECT statement that calculates several summary statistics based on column values in the *orders* table. These statistical values are stored in a set of macro variables that can then be passed to a macro for further processing. This query produces a report that provides for easy checking of the macro variable values, although it does not report the macro variable values unless additional options are added. Notice that formatting and labeling can be added to the SELECT statement; it does not affect the macro variable assignment.

```
LIBNAME bluesky "C:\mydata\bluesky bookstore\";
PROC SQL;

SELECT   sum(totsale), sum(quantity) ,
         mean(totsale/quantity) format= 6.2
INTO     :bksum, :bkamt, :bkprice
FROM     bluesky.orders
WHERE    ord_date between '01MAR2004'd and '30APR2004'd;

%put Total sales =  &bksum;
%put Total quantity = &bkamt;
%put Price per book =  &bkprice;
```

SAS log:

```
1180  %put Total sales =  &bksum;
Total sales =  118652.5
1181  %put Total quantity =  &bkamt;
Total quantity =       2975
1182  %put Price per book =  &bkprice;
Price per book =   33.34
```

Tip: %PUT is a commonly used SAS statement that writes comments and variable values to the Log. It is especially useful for debugging your programs or checking values without generating reports. Notice that the message string on the %PUT statement is not enclosed in quotes.

A %TRIM option can be specified on the %PUT statement to trim trailing blanks from macro variables before printing.

Macro variables assigned using this format can only be assigned a single value. Only summary functions are used on the SELECT clause in the preceding example; therefore, a single value is calculated for each of the macro variables. If the SELECT statement retrieves more than one row of information, each macro variable would be assigned the values of the first row retrieved from the table.

The next example contains a SELECT statement similar to the one in the previous example. However, the summary functions have been removed. The SAS log reports the values of the macro variables bksum, bkamt, and bkprice to be 675, 45, and 15.00 respectively. These values are taken from the first row of the *orders* table, shown in the second example below.

```
LIBNAME bluesky "C:\mydata\bluesky bookstore\";
PROC SQL;

SELECT   totsale, quantity ,
         totsale/quantity as priceper format= 6.2
INTO     :bksum, :bkamt, :bkprice
FROM     bluesky.orders
WHERE    ord_date between '01MAR2004'd and '30APR2004'd;

%put Total sales =  %trim(&bksum) ;
%put Total quantity =  %trim(&bkamt);
%put Price per book =  %trim(&bkprice);
```

SAS log:

```
556  %put Total sales =  %trim(&bksum) ;
Total sales =  675
557  %put Total quantity =  %trim(&bkamt);
Total quantity =  45
558  %put Price per book =  %trim(&bkprice);
Price per book =  15.00

                     totsale  quantity  priceper
                     ----------------------------
                         675        45     15.00
                       11700       180     65.00
                     15312.5       350     43.75
                        1645        70     23.50
                        1250       100     12.50
                        1490        20     74.50
                       797.5        55     14.50
                       39375       700     56.25
                       41820      1230     34.00
                        4450       200     22.25
                       137.5        25      5.50
```

Tip: When testing a query that includes macro variables, it is best not to use the NOPRINT option for the SQL procedure. When PRINT is in effect, the results of the SELECT statement are written to the output window. This allows you to easily confirm that the macro variables have been assigned the correct values.

Numbered list of macro variables

An entire column of values in a table can also be assigned to a set of macro variables in a single pass with numbered lists. Three forms of the numbered list are allowed in an INTO clause:

1. Range of macro variables indicated on either side of a hyphen (-)

   INTO *:macro-variable1 - :macro-variablen <NOTRIM>*

2. Range of macro variables indicated with THROUGH keyword

   INTO *:macro-variable1 THROUGH :macro-variablen<NOTRIM>*

3. Range of macro variables indicated with THRU keyword

   INTO *:macro-variable1 THRU :macro-variablen<NOTRIM>*

Guidelines

- A single SELECT statement may include several numbered lists of macro variables using any of the above keywords or symbols.
- Numbered lists of macro variables may be combined with other forms of macro variables.
- The DISTINCT option can be applied to the SELECT clause resulting in only unique column values stored in each macro variable.
- The first *n* rows of the column in the SELECT clause are retrieved from the table and stored in the macro variables.
- By default, leading and trailing blanks are trimmed before they are stored in the macro variables.
- The NOTRIM option can be added to the INTO clause to override the default. This option can be applied to one set of macro variables and not to another as in the following examples.

The next example shows an INTO clause utilizing all three forms of numbered list to create twenty-four macro variables. The set of six macro variables storing client numbers drawn from the *orders* table is written to the SAS log with the %PUT statement.

```
LIBNAME bluesky "C:\mydata\bluesky bookstore\";
PROC SQL;

SELECT   clientno, totsale "Total sales" , quantity "Total
                           quantity",
         totsale/quantity "Price per book" format= 6.2
INTO     :client1- :client6, :bksum1 - :bksum6,
         :bkamt1 through :bkamt6, :bkpr1 thru :bkpr6
FROM     bluesky.orders
WHERE    ord_date between '01MAR2004'd and '30APR2004'd;

%put Clients = &client1, &client2, &client3, &client4, &client5,
               &client6;
```

SAS log:

```
1934  %put Clients = &client1, &client2, &client3, &client4, &client5,
   &client6;
Clients = 3007, 7008, 8003, 8003, 4008, 4008
```

Tip: When referencing a numbered list of macro variables in a %PUT statement, it is necessary to list each macro variable explicitly.

Single macro variable storing all values in a column

General form:

SELECT <DISTINCT> column|expression <column|expression…>
INTO **: macro-variable separated by 'character(s)' <NOTRIM>**
<, …>
FROM <libref.>table <alias>;

Guidelines

- All of the rows in the column are stored in a single macro variable. The values in the macro variable are stored as a list with the indicated character(s) used to separate one from another.
- A SELECT statement may include several multivalue single macro variables.
- Multivalue single macro variables may be combined with other forms of macro variables.
- The DISTINCT option can be applied to the SELECT clause resulting in only unique column or expression values stored in the macrovariable list.
- By default, leading and trailing blanks are trimmed before they are stored in the macro variable.
- The NOTRIM option can be applied to the values of one column prior to storage in the macro variable and not to other columns listed in the SELECT clause.

Any character can be used as a separator between the values. The next example shows two single macro values. Each of the macro variables store the column value for each row in the table selected by the query. The %PUT statement causes the results to be written to the SAS log, as shown.

```
LIBNAME bluesky "C:\mydata\bluesky bookstore\";
PROC SQL;
TITLE1   "Sales information for March 1 to April 30, 2004";

SELECT    clientno, totsale "Total sales"
INTO      :client separated by ',',
          :bksum separated by ','
FROM      bluesky.orders
WHERE     ord_date between '01MAR2004'd and '30APR2004'd;

 %put Client =  &client;
 %put Sales = &bksum;
```

```
        Sales information for March 1 to April 30, 2004

                                    Total
                        clientNo    sales
                        ------------------
                            3007      675
                            7008    11700
                            8003  15312.5
                            8003     1645
                            4008     1250
                            4008     1490
                            6090    797.5
                            2010    39375
                            2010    41820
                            5005     4450
                            7008    137.5
```

SAS log:

```
611   %put Client =  &client;
Client =  3007,7008,8003,8003,4008,4008,6090,2010,2010,5005,7008
612   %put Sales = &bksum;
Sales = 675,11700,15312.5,1645,1250,1490,797.5,39375,41820,4450,137.5
```

> **Tip:** Various data dictionary tables can be accessed in this manner to provide a list of column names for input into another query. A full discussion of data dictionary tables is included later in this chapter, with additional information contained in Appendix B, "Dictionary Table Descriptions."

Global macro variables are created outside of a macro, while local macro variables are generated within a macro. Global macro variables are stored in a global symbol table created when the SAS session starts; they can be referenced anywhere in the SAS session or job. Local macro variable values, on the other hand, are stored in a local symbol table created when the macro is invoked. These variables can only be used and modified within the macro in which they were created; they cease to exist once the macro has ended.

If both a global and local macro variable of the same name exist within a single macro, the local macro variable is used. It is also important to note that macro variables reside in symbol tables stored in memory and are not cleared between runs.

> **Tip:** Check the scope of your macro variables if your macro results are not as expected. Add %PUT _GLOBAL_ and %PUT _LOCAL_ to your SAS statements to generate a report of user-defined macro variables of local and global scope in the SAS log. Although %PUT _ALL_ can be used to give both local and global variables, it also reports all automatic variables resulting in more information than is needed to resolve most problems.
>
> New to SAS Version 9 are two new macro functions, %SYMLOCAL and %SYMGLOBAL, that can be used to check the scope of a specific macro variable. Refer to Chapter 8, "PROC SQL Enhancements in Version 9," for more information on these new functions.

There are several options available with %PUT that are helpful when dealing with macros. Each is described briefly in the following table. In each case, the defined macro variables and their current values are written to the SAS log together with the scope of the variable. An example of the information generated by each of these statements is included below

Statement	Macro symbol table written to the SAS log
%PUT _ALL_	user-defined and automatic macro variables
%PUT _AUTOMATIC_	all automatic macro variables
%PUT _GLOBAL_	user-defined global macro variables
%PUT _LOCAL_	user-defined local macro variables
%PUT _USER_	user-defined global and local macro variables

Tip: The %GLOBAL and %LOCAL statements override the default scope of a macro variable. Refer to the *SAS Macro Language: Reference* for more information.

To reference a macro variable, add a single ampersand as a prefix to the macro variable name. This allows SAS to substitute the value of the macro variable during the processing of the statement.

Macro variables initialized in the INTO clause of the SELECT statement follow the scoping rules of the %LET macro statement. When the INTO clause is processed, an appropriate symbol table is opened for the macro variables.

All values assigned to macro variables through an INTO clause are treated as text strings using a BEST12. format and case is preserved. Leading and trailing blanks are removed from values as they are assigned to the macro variables unless the NOTRIM option is specified.

Tip: The PROC SQL NOPRINT option prevents the generation of a result set from a query. It is useful when you are running a query only to obtain a set of macro variable values for input into a macro program.

In the next example, the macro variables created in the SQL query are passed to a macro program, that generates one or more reports. The total sales for the selected period are greater than $3000, and the average book price is greater than $25, causing two reports to be printed as shown in the second example following.

```
LIBNAME bluesky "C:\mydata\bluesky bookstore\";
PROC SQL noprint;

SELECT   sum(totsale), sum(quantity) ,
         mean(totsale/quantity)
INTO     :bksum, :bkamt, :bkprice
FROM     bluesky.orders
WHERE    ord_date between '01MAR2004'd and '30MAY2004'd;

%macro orderck;
       %if &bkprice > 25.00 %then %do;
              PROC SQL;
              TITLE1 "Average price per book > $25 for the
                       period";
              SELECT ord_date, clientno, prodcode,
                     totsale format=comma10.,
                     quantity format=comma6.
               FROM  bluesky.orders
               WHERE ord_date between '01MAR2004'd and
                                      '30MAY2004'd;
              %end;
```

```
        %if &bksum < 10000 %then %do;
               PROC SQL;
               TITLE1  "Total sales < $10,000 for the period";
               SELECT  clientno, prodcode,
               totsale format=comma10.
               FROM    bluesky.orders
               WHERE   ord_date between '01MAR2004'd and
                                        '30MAY2004'd;
               %end;
        %if &bkamt > 3000 %then %do;
               PROC SQL;
               TITLE1  "Total quantity sold > 3000 for the
                        period";
               SELECT   clientno, prodcode,
                        quantity format=comma6.
               FROM     bluesky.orders
               WHERE ord_date between '01MAR2004'd and
                                      '30MAY2004'd;
               %end;
%mend orderck;
%orderck;
%put _LOCAL_;
%put _GLOBAL_;
```

Report 1:

Average price per book > $25 for the period

ord_date	clientNo	prod Code	totsale	quantity
08APR04	4008	200507	1,490	20
10APR04	6090	300456	798	55
12APR04	2010	200145	39,375	700
12APR04	2010	400128	41,820	1,230
12APR04	5005	500238	4,450	200
12APR04	7008	600489	138	25
05MAY04	2010	600125	8,580	600
11MAY04	4008	400345	2,150	25
12MAY04	3007	100890	17,940	260

Report 2:

```
        Total quantity sold > 3000 for the period

                          prod
                clientNo  Code     quantity
                ------------------------------
                    4008  200507         20
                    6090  300456         55
                    2010  200145        700
                    2010  400128      1,230
                    5005  500238        200
                    7008  600489         25
                    2010  600125        600
                    4008  400345         25
                    3007  100890        260
```

Tip: Why the extra PROC SQL invocation statements in the above query? The first PROC SQL statement includes the NOPRINT option so that the SELECT statement assigns the macro variables and does not generate output. Since there is no way to know in advance which of the remaining SELECT statements will be executed, a PROC SQL statement appears before each.

The %PUT statements included in the previous query generate a list of the currently defined local and global macro variables as shown in the following example. Notice that in addition to the macro variables created by the INTO clause, four additional variables, SQLXOBS, SQLRC, SQLOBS, and SQLOOPS are reported. These automatic variables are created when PROC SQL is invoked and they are reported as user-defined variables.

Tip: The PROC SQL automatic macro variables SQLXOBS, SQLRC, SQLOBS, and SQLOOPS are discussed in more detail later in this chapter.

SAS log:

```
GLOBAL SQLOBS 9
GLOBAL SQLOOPS 20
GLOBAL BKPRICE 41.81111
GLOBAL SQLXOBS 0
GLOBAL SQLRC 0
GLOBAL BKAMT     3115
GLOBAL BKSUM   116740
```

Macro variables can be referenced indirectly though the use of multiple ampersands. Two ampersands added to a variable name cause SAS to substitute a single ampersand when the statement is processed. This enables the use of a macro variable defined in a previous step within a macro.

Notice that in the next example we now have the ability to compare numerous macro variable values to a constant using a loop. Each of the macro variables is referenced by an increasing value of an index variable *i*. With each increase of the index variable, the value of the macro variable retrieved from another row of the table is referenced.

The SAS log output from the macro program showing a list of client number and sales figures is included in the example. The %PUT statement is included in a loop inside a macro program causing a separate entry for each row meeting the criteria to be printed.

```
LIBNAME bluesky "C:\mydata\bluesky bookstore\";
PROC SQL;

SELECT   clientno, totsale "Total sales" , quantity "Total
                             quantity",
         totsale/quantity "Price per book" format= 6.2
INTO     :client1- :client10, :bksum1 - :bksum10,
         :bkamt1 through :bkamt10, :bkpr1 thru :bkpr10
FROM     bluesky.orders
WHERE    ord_date between '01MAR2004'd and '30MAY2004'd;

%macro printck;
   %do i=1 %to 10;
         %if &&bksum&i > 10000 %then %do;
                TITLE "Client report: Sales < $10,000 for the
                       period";
                %put Client =   &&client&i  Sales = &&bksum&i;
           %end;

   %end;
%mend printck;
%printck;
```

SAS log:

```
Client =   6090  Sales = 797.5
Client =   2010  Sales = 39375
Client =   2010  Sales = 41820
Client =   7008  Sales = 137.5
Client =   3007  Sales = 17940
```

In the previous query, 10 macro variables were created to hold the values from the rows retrieved by the SELECT statement. However, as seen in the next example, there are actually 14 rows returned by the query.

```
Client report: Sales < $10,000 for the period

                                          Price
              Total       Total            per
clientNo      sales    quantity           book
________________________________________________

    4008       1490          20          74.50
    6090      797.5          55          14.50
    2010      39375         700          56.25
    2010      41820        1230          34.00
    5005       4450         200          22.25
    7008      137.5          25           5.50
    2010       8580         600          14.30
    4008       2150          25          86.00
    3007      17940         260          69.00
```

If the SELECT statement were modified to assign values to more macro variables than the query is expected to generate, all of the retrieved rows would be accommodated. However, many of the macro variables would not be created or initialized. A warning message is generated if an uninitialized macro variable is referenced.

The next example contains the same query as the previous example. However, in this INTO clause 20 macro variables are created although the SELECT statement retrieves only 14 rows. Notice that creation of unassigned macro variables in the query does not generate a warning message. A warning is generated, however, when the %PUT statement references the first nonassigned macro variable, the 15th.

```
LIBNAME bluesky "C:\mydata\bluesky bookstore\";
PROC SQL;

SELECT  clientno, totsale "Total sales" , quantity "Total
                         quantity",
         totsale/quantity "Price per book"
 INTO    :client1- :client20, :bksum1 - :bksum20,
         :bkamt1 through :bkamt20, :bkpr1 thru :bkpr20
  FROM    bluesky.orders
 WHERE   ord_date between '01MAR2004'd and '30MAY2004'd;
%macro printck;
    %do i=1 %to 20;
       %put Client =    &&client&i;
    %end;
 %mend printck;
 %printck;
```

SAS log:

```
Client =   3007
Client =   7008
Client =   8003
Client =   8003
Client =   4008
Client =   4008
Client =   6090
Client =   2010
Client =   2010
Client =   5005
Client =   7008
Client =   2010
Client =   4008
Client =   3007
WARNING: Apparent symbolic reference CLIENT15 not resolved.
Client =   &client15
WARNING: Apparent symbolic reference CLIENT16 not resolved.
Client =   &client16
WARNING: Apparent symbolic reference CLIENT17 not resolved.
Client =   &client17
WARNING: Apparent symbolic reference CLIENT18 not resolved.
Client =   &client18
WARNING: Apparent symbolic reference CLIENT19 not resolved.
Client =   &client19
WARNING: Apparent symbolic reference CLIENT20 not resolved.
Client =   &client20
```

> **Tip:** With SAS Version 9, it is now possible to create macro variables with leading zeros such as client01. More information on SAS Version 9 enhancements is included in Chapter 8, "PROC SQL Enhancements in Version 9."

In the previous example, the unassigned macro variables generated a warning in the SAS log each time the %PUT statement was encountered and processing continued. However, unassigned macro variables can also generate error messages and stop processing. In the next example, 50 macro variables are assigned in the SELECT statement to ensure that all row values are captured. The problem arises in the macro printck with the comparison of a blank string to a numeric value.

```
LIBNAME bluesky "C:\mydata\bluesky bookstore\";
PROC SQL;

SELECT   clientno, totsale "Total sales" , quantity "Total
                              quantity",
         totsale/quantity "Price per book"
INTO     :client1- :client50, :bksum1 - :bksum50,
         :bkamt1 through :bkamt50, :bkpr1 thru :bkpr50
FROM     bluesky.orders
WHERE    ord_date between '01MAR2004'd and '30MAY2004'd;

  %macro printck;
     %do i=1 %to 50;
         %if &&bksum&i > 10000 %then %do;
            title "Client report -  < $10,000 for the period";
            %put Client =   &&client&i  Sales = &&bksum&i;
          %end;
     %end;
  %mend printck;
  %printck;
```

SAS log:

```
Client =   7008  Sales = 11700
Client =   8003  Sales = 15312.5
Client =   6090  Sales = 797.5
Client =   2010  Sales = 39375
Client =   2010  Sales = 41820
Client =   7008  Sales = 137.5
Client =   3007  Sales = 17940
```

```
WARNING: Apparent symbolic reference BKSUM15 not resolved.
ERROR: A character operand was found in the %EVAL function or %IF
       condition where a numeric operand is required. The
       condition was: &&bksum&i > 10000
ERROR: The macro PRINTCK will stop executing.
```

Several options are available to overcome this problem. First, the number of rows retrieved by a SELECT statement can be assigned to a single value macro and referenced in later macro processing. Another option is to use the automatic macro variable SQLOBS that stores the number of rows retrieved. Finally, the total number of rows in a table may be taken from the dictionary table *tables*.

In the next example, a SELECT statement that counts the number of retrieved rows in the *orders* table between the relevant dates is included as the first step in the processing. The macro variable numrow is assigned the row count value, which is then referenced in the macro printck to control the number of loop iterations. The numbered list of macro variables has been increased to accommodate up to 50 values. Although this results in unassigned macro variables, it does not affect the processing of the macro. Unlike the previous example, none of the unassigned macro variables is referenced because the numrow variable is set to the exact number of assigned macro variables.

```
LIBNAME bluesky "C:\mydata\bluesky bookstore\";
PROC SQL;

SELECT   count(clientno)
INTO     :numrow
FROM     bluesky.orders
WHERE    ord_date between '01MAR2004'd and '30MAY2004'd;

SELECT   clientno, totsale "Total sales" , quantity "Total
quantity",
         totsale/quantity "Price per book"
INTO     :client1- :client50, :bksum1 - :bksum50,
         :bkamt1 through :bkamt50, :bkpr1 thru :bkpr50
FROM     bluesky.orders
WHERE    ord_date between '01MAR2004'd and '30MAY2004'd;

 %macro printck;
   %do i=1 %to &&numrow;
         %if &&bksum&i > 10000 %then %do;
                title "Client report -  < $10,000 for the period";
                %put Client =   &&client&i  Sales = &&bksum&i;
           %end;

   %end;
%mend printck;
%printck;
```

Such multistep processing can be useful when values are passed to a macro for processing. However, there are problems associated with using macro variables in this fashion within SELECT statements outside of macros.

The next example shows the SAS log output resulting from a simple SELECT statement. The statement assigns the result of a count of the number of rows in the *stock* table to a macro variable called numrow. Notice that the output of the %PUT statement shows blank values preceding the value of 30. If you recall, all leading and trailing blanks are eliminated when a value is assigned to a macro variable. What happened? The count is converted to a text value with a default length of eight characters when it is assigned to the macro variable. As a result, blanks are included with this value.

```
LIBNAME bluesky "C:\mydata\bluesky bookstore\";
PROC SQL;

SELECT  count(prodcode)
INTO    :numrow
FROM    bluesky.stock;

%put The number of rows in the Stock table =&numrow;
```

SAS log:

```
The number of rows in the Stock table =       30
```

If this macro variable is used to control the number of macro variables created in an INTO clause, an error message is generated. The next example includes the query above, but now the numrow macro variable is used as part of another SELECT statement. The expected result is for a range of macro variables **title1–title30** to be assigned in the INTO clause. The conversion, however, generates an error message and stops processing. This is because the numrow value was converted to a character string with blanks padding the variable to a length of 8.

```
LIBNAME bluesky "C:\mydata\bluesky bookstore\";
PROC SQL;

SELECT  count(prodcode)
INTO    :numrow
FROM    bluesky.stock;
%put The number of rows in the Stock table =&numrow;

SELECT  title
INTO    :title1 - :title&numrow;
```

SAS log:

```
The number of rows in the Stock table =       30

486   PROC SQL;
487
488   SELECT   title
489   INTO    :title1 - :title&numrow;
NOTE: Line generated by the macro variable "NUMROW".
1     title      30
                 --
                 22
                 76
ERROR 22-322: Syntax error, expecting one of the following: ',', FROM, NOTRIM.

ERROR 76-322: Syntax error, statement will be ignored.
```

There are several alternatives available to overcome this situation. Functions such as %SYSEVALF and %EVAL can be used to convert a macro variable to an integer or perform integer arithmetic. The %LEFT function can also be used to eliminate leading blanks.

> **Tip:** The automatic SQLOBS macro variable can be used to determine the number of observations instead of the count used here. Another alternative is to query the dictionary table called *tables.* Details on both are provided later in this chapter.

In the next example, the %SYSEVALF function is used to eliminate the problem of leading blanks in the macro variables numrow included in the previous example. The conversion of the value to an integer results in the successful generation of the end point for the numbered list of macro variables.

```
LIBNAME bluesky "C:\mydata\bluesky bookstore\";
PROC SQL;

SELECT   count(prodcode)
INTO     :numrow
FROM     bluesky.stock;

%put The number of rows in the Stock table =&numrow;

SELECT   title
INTO     :title1 - :title%SYSEVALF(&numrow,integer)
FROM     bluesky.stock;
```

Alternatively, the %LEFT option can be applied to the numrow macro variable creating a suitable substitution variable for the macro list in the INTO clause.

```
%LET numrow=%left(&&numrow);
SELECT  title
INTO    :title1 - :title&numrow
FROM    bluesky.stock;
```

> **Tip:** Alternatives such as using a format option to set the length of the value assigned to the macro variables are available. However, the %LEFT and %SYSEVALF options provide more flexible solutions.

Automatic macro variables

The SQL procedure sets up automatic macro variables with certain values after it executes each statement. There are three automatic macro variables, SQLOBS, SQLRC, and SQLOOPS, associated with PROC SQL that are helpful in controlling the execution of SQL statements. Each of these macro variables is stored in the global macro symbol table. Additional automatic macro variables are assigned values when working with SAS/ACCESS and SQL Pass-Through.

> **Tip:** The values of SQLOBS, SQLRC, and SQLOOPS can also be obtained in a Screen Control Language (SCL) program. The section on SCL included later in this chapter provides more details.

SQLOBS

The SQLOBS variable is updated to reflect the number of rows processed by an SQL procedure statement. It is updated with SELECT, UPDATE, INSERT, and DELETE statements. It is very useful in the assignment of a sequence of macro variables, each storing a column of values.

The next example shows a query that generates summary statistics for each book category. A macro sequence is used to store the count and sum function values for each book category. The SQLOBS macro variable is used to indicate the range of the macro sequence. The final value of the SQLOBS variable is used to set the DO-loop endpoint within the bookcat macro.

> **Tip:** The %SYSEVAL function is not required when using SQLOBS because this macro variable is automatically trimmed to eliminate leading blanks when displayed.

```
LIBNAME bluesky "C:\mydata\bluesky bookstore\";
PROC SQL;

SELECT   category, count(s.category), sum(s.stock),
         sum(o.totsale), sum(o.quantity)
INTO     :cat1 - :cat&sqlobs, :cnt1 - :cnt&sqlobs, :stk1 -
         :stk&sqlobs,
         :sale1 - :sale&sqlobs, :qnty1 - :qnty&sqlobs
FROM     bluesky.stock s, bluesky.orders o
WHERE    s.prodcode = o.prodcode
GROUP BY category;

%macro bookcat;
%let space= *****;
%do i=1 %to &sqlobs;
 %put Category &i=  &&cat&i,
 Number of books = &&cnt&i ,
 Total stock = &&stk&i;
 %put  &space Total sales = $ &&sale&i
  &space Total quantity sold = &&qnty&i;
 %put;
%end;
%mend;

%bookcat
```

The SQLOBS variable is assigned a value of 0 when the SQL procedure is invoked. As a result, if a sequence of macro variables is created immediately after a PROC SQL statement is issued, the range will run from 1-0. A macro variable range end point must be greater than the start point; a range of 1-0 generates warning messages in the SAS log. The next example shows the messages that occurred the first time the previous query was executed.

SAS log:

```
WARNING: INTO Clause :cat1 thru :cat0 does not specify a valid sequence of
         macro variables.
WARNING: INTO Clause :cnt1 thru :cnt0 does not specify a valid sequence of
         macro variables.
WARNING: INTO Clause :stk1 thru :stk0 does not specify a valid sequence of
         macro variables.
WARNING: INTO Clause :sale1 thru :sale0 does not specify a valid sequence of
         macro variables.
WARNING: INTO Clause :qnty1 thru :qnty0 does not specify a valid sequence of
         macro variables.
```

When the query is re-executed, SQLOBS has a value of 6, which is the number of rows returned from the first execution of the statement in the same SQL block. In order to avoid this situation, a SELECT statement against the table should be executed before the assignment of the numbered list of macro variables. In the next example another SELECT statement is added to the query, setting the SQLOBS value correctly for the rest of the program.

Tip: To ensure that the correct row count for a table is stored in SQLOBS, issue a SELECT statement against the table immediately prior to the execution of the macro. The NOPRINT option can be added to this SELECT statement to eliminate output.

Caution: A QUIT statement terminating the SQL Procedure will reset the SQLOBS value.

```
LIBNAME bluesky "C:\mydata\bluesky bookstore\";
PROC SQL;

SELECT   count(category)
FROM     bluesky.stock s, bluesky.orders o
WHERE    s.prodcode = o.prodcode
GROUP BY category;

SELECT   category, count(s.category), sum(s.stock),
         sum(o.totsale), sum(o.quantity)
INTO     :cat1 - :cat&sqlobs, :cnt1 - :cnt&sqlobs, :stk1 -
         :stk&sqlobs,
         :sale1 - :sale&sqlobs, :qnty1 - :qnty&sqlobs
FROM     bluesky.stock s, bluesky.orders o
WHERE    s.prodcode = o.prodcode
GROUP BY category;

%macro bookcat;
%let space= *****;
%do i=1 %to &sqlobs;
 %put Category &i=  &&cat&i,
 Number of books = &&cnt&i ,
 Total stock = &&stk&i;
 %put  &space Total sales = $ &&sale&i
  &space Total quantity sold = &&qnty&i;
 %put;
%end;
%mend;

%bookcat
```

SAS log:

```
Category 1=  arts,  Number of books = 7 ,  Total stock = 3855
***** Total sales = $ 15428.75   ***** Total quantity sold = 3760

Category 2=  computer,  Number of books = 6 ,  Total stock = 5250
***** Total sales = $ 81190   ***** Total quantity sold = 2529

Category 3=  engineering,  Number of books = 5 ,  Total stock = 12350
***** Total sales = $ 370327   ***** Total quantity sold = 7620

Category 4=  general,  Number of books = 6 ,  Total stock = 1600
***** Total sales = $ 13369.2   ***** Total quantity sold = 1190

Category 5=  medicine,  Number of books = 9 ,  Total stock = 6000
***** Total sales = $ 196333.8   ***** Total quantity sold = 4140

Category 6=  science,  Number of books = 6 ,  Total stock = 3400
***** Total sales = $ 60562.5   ***** Total quantity sold = 1895
```

Tip: SQLOBS is set to zero under the following circumstances:

- At the start of a PROC SQL session.
- An INSERT, DELETE, SELECT, or UPDATE statement fails to access rows in a table.
- INSERT, DELETE, SELECT, or UPDATE statement failure due to syntax errors.

SQLRC

The SQLRC variable contains a code returned from the execution of an SQL procedure statement indicating its success or failure. The table below summarizes the values and meanings of each.

SQLRC value	Meaning	SQL statement executed?
0	Successful completion of SQL statement without errors or warnings.	Yes
4	Warning issued	Yes
8	Error encountered	No
12	Internal error encountered. Report to SAS Institute.	No
16	User error encountered at runtime.	No
24	System error encountered at runtime.	No
28	Internal error encountered at runtime. Report to SAS Institute	No

SQLRC values of 16 are difficult to debug through the use of a VALIDATE statement because they are encountered at runtime. The next example contains a query that reports valid syntax when the VALIDATE statement is added to the SELECT statement. However, when this query is run the subquery returns more than one value and an error message is reported in the SAS log.

SAS log:

```
LIBNAME bluesky "C:\mydata\bluesky bookstore\";
PROC SQL;

VALIDATE
SELECT *
FROM bluesky.orders
WHERE prodcode = (SELECT prodcode
                    FROM bluesky.stock
                    WHERE yrpubl = 2002);
NOTE: PROC SQL statement has valid syntax.


SELECT *
FROM bluesky.orders
WHERE prodcode = (SELECT prodcode
                    FROM bluesky.stock
                    WHERE yrpubl = 2002);
ERROR: Subquery evaluated to more than one row.
```

System errors are also exposed only at runtime because they involve system resources such as disk space that are accessed only when the statement is executed.

SQLOOPS

The SQLOOPS variable is updated with each pass through the PROC SQL process. It is related to the LOOPS option in the PROC SQL statement. Although the SQLOOPS variable can be used in much the same way as the SQLOBS to assign macro variable sequences, its use requires care. Each loop through the process increments the SQLOOPS variable. As a result, the values far exceed the number of rows produced by the report.

Consider the next example. There are 30 rows in the *orders* table, yet the SQLOOPS variable is assigned a value of 80. The execution of the SELECT statement would involve 80 passes through the process.

Tip: Checking the value of SQLOOPS can sometimes assist in determining whether one SQL query is more efficient than another. If you also add the _METHOD option specified in the PROC SQL invocation statement, the execution plan for the each query can be viewed in the SAS log.

```
LIBNAME bluesky "C:\mydata\bluesky bookstore\";
PROC sql;

SELECT  count(invoice)
FROM    bluesky.orders;
%put Number of loops = &sqloops;
```

SAS log:

```
Number of loops = 57
```

The SQLOOPS variable can be used to limit a query from consuming excessive computer resources. This can be very helpful with interactive SQL queries that may be incorrectly built. For example, a user may forget to include a criterion in a WHERE clause joining two or more tables. If the tables were very large, the Cartesian join process would take excessive time.

In the next example the number of rows in the *stock* table is retrieved from the *tables* dictionary table and is assigned to a macro variable rownum. Alternatively, a count function could have been issued against the *stock* table. The rownum variable is used to set the maximum number of loops or passes for the subsequent SELECT statement.

```
LIBNAME bluesky "C:\mydata\bluesky bookstore\";
PROC SQL;

SELECT  nobs
INTO    :rownum
FROM    dictionary.tables
WHERE   memname = 'STOCK' and libname = 'BLUESKY';
QUIT;

PROC SQL loops = &rownum;
SELECT  *
FROM    bluesky.stock,
        bluesky.orders;
```

SAS log:

```
NOTE: The execution of this query involves performing one or more Cartesian
      product joins that can not be optimized.
NOTE: PROC SQL statement interrupted by LOOPS=30 option.
```

Tip: The above query obtains the number of observations in the *stock* table from the *tables* dictionary table. Dictionary tables are discussed in detail later in this chapter.

Although this option may be useful to prevent endless processing, the LOOPS value must be such that legitimate processing is not stopped. The %EVAL function can be used with the rownum macro variable value to generate a LOOPS value that is a multiple of the number of rows in one of the source tables.

In the next example, the rownum variable value is multiplied by 10 to provide the loop limit rather than relying on a count from the *stock* table.

```
LIBNAME bluesky "C:\mydata\bluesky bookstore\";
PROC SQL loops = %EVAL(&rownum*10);

SELECT  *
FROM    bluesky.stock,
        bluesky.orders;
```

SAS log:

```
NOTE: The execution of this query involves performing one or more Cartesian
      product joins that can not be optimized.
NOTE: PROC SQL statement interrupted by LOOPS=300 option.
```

Macro programs can also benefit from a check for excessive loops. In the next example a limit of 500 is placed on the loops for the SQL procedure. Within the macro bookcat, a check has been added to ensure that the SQLOBS value is less than the loop limit.

Tip: The LOOPS= *n* option added to the PROC SQL statement in the previous example restricts all subsequent SQL statements to *n* iterations. It is very helpful when developing complex programs, especially those that use large tables or data sets. The automatic variable _N_ available in a DATA step works the same way, limiting the number of iterations or loops through a DATA step.

```
LIBNAME bluesky "C:\mydata\bluesky bookstore\";
PROC SQL loops = 500;

SELECT   category, count(s.category)
FROM     bluesky.stock s, bluesky.orders o
WHERE    s.prodcode = o.prodcode
GROUP BY category;
```

```
SELECT    category, count(s.category), sum(s.stock),
          sum(o.totsale), sum(o.quantity)
INTO      :cat1 - :cat&sqlobs, :cnt1 - :cnt&sqlobs, :stk1 -
          :stk&sqlobs,
          :sale1 - :sale&sqlobs, :qnty1 - :qnty&sqlobs
FROM      bluesky.stock s, bluesky.orders o
WHERE     s.prodcode = o.prodcode
GROUP BY category;

%macro bookcat;
%let space= *****;
%do i = 1 %to &sqlobs;
  %if &sqlobs < loops %then
    %do;
       %put Category &i=  &&cat&i,
       Number of books = &&cnt&i ,
       Total stock = &&stk&i;
       %put  &space Total sales = $ &&sale&i
        &space Total quantity sold = &&qnty&i;
       %put;
    %end;
 %end;
%mend;
```

SAS Component Language (SCL) for user input

The SAS Component Language (SCL) (formerly known as the SAS Screen Control Language) is used to develop program modules that allow for user interaction and input. It is used within SAS/AF, webAF, and SAS/FSP to associate programs with FRAME entries or icons. Both SQL and Base SAS statements can be included within an SCL program module.

SCL modules are ideally suited to object-oriented applications. Each module can support a single task or function, but it may be reused or accessed by a variety of applications or FRAME entries. Moreover, the SCL program module associated with a FRAME entry can be easily changed.

Window variables, variables associated with FRAME components such as text entry boxes, allow user-specified values to be passed to SCL modules. These variables also display messages and values generated by the SCL program.

SAS macro variables can be referenced in SCL programs allowing for even greater flexibility. Both macro variables defined within the current session or stored in autocall libraries are available within an SCL program.

SCL program form

SCL programs generally comprise three sections or phases accomplishing program initialization, main processing, and termination. Within each section, one or more SCL statements are included. Additional labeled sections may be added in any of the SCL program sections. If the label matches the name of a FRAME component, the component and the section are linked. Otherwise, a link statement specifying a section label can be used to direct the program to execute the statements contained in a section.

The figure following shows a simple FRAME built in SAS/AF that creates a new table. There are two text entry control objects, one for the entry of a new table name (dsn) and the other for messages returned by the program (message). In this example, a new table called *orders_august* is created in the bluesky library with a confirming message sent to the message text box. The SCL program associated with this SAS/AF example is shown in the example following the figure. Each section of the program is discussed in detail below.


```
DECLARE Char(20) newname;

INIT:
  norec = 10;
  model="BLUESKY.ORDERS";
RETURN;
```

```
MAIN:
  newname=dsn.text ;
  if (exist('bluesky.'||newname)) then
     message.text = 'Table  ' ||newname||'  already exists.';
  else
  do;
    call new('bluesky.'||newname,model,norec,'N');
    message.text='Table  '||newname||'  has been created.';
  end;
RETURN;

TERM:
RETURN;
```

Tip: The following LIBNAME statement was issued before working in SAS/AF:

```
LIBNAME bluesky "c:\mydata\Bluesky bookstore\";
```

This libref applies to all of the SCL programs in this section.

Variable declaration

Variables created for use within the SCL program may be declared as a character, numeric, list, or object outside of the labelled sections. In this example, the variable *newname* designed to hold the window variable entered into the text entry box (dsn) by the user is declared as a character data type.

INIT section

The INIT section of an SCL program serves to initialize the application. It executes only once when the FRAME is first opened. During this phase, variables are initialized, macro variable values are imported, and values that are passed to the FRAME entry by the user are processed.

In the INIT section for our FRAME SCL example the values of *norec* and *model* are set. Both *norec* and *model* are used in the NEW function within the MAIN section.

MAIN section

The MAIN section of an SCL program performs the tasks or functions of the module. Field values are validated, calculations are performed, and SAS statements are executed. In this phase, values from SAS data sets or external files are retrieved.

Each time the CREATE button icon in our FRAME SCL example is pressed, the MAIN section of the SCL program executes. The program assigns the value of the string entered into the *dsn* text entry box to the variable *newname* using dot notation. When the string is entered, it forms the value for the *text* attribute of the *dsn* text entry object.

> **Tip:** Dot notation is used to access the attribute of an SCL object using the general form:
>
> `object_name.attribute_name`

The EXIST function is used to check for the existence of a table in the bluesky library with the same name. If the table does not exist, the table is created in the bluesky library by the NEW function. The Bluesky *orders* table serves as the model for the structure of the new table and the variable *norec* controls the number of empty rows that are created in the table. Details on the NEW and EXIST functions are available in the *SAS Component Language: Reference*.

A message indicating whether the table exists or a new table has been created is displayed in the message text entry box. Dot notation is used to assign the text attribute of the message object to an appropriate message.

> **Tip:** The MAIN section of an SCL program executes each time the CREATE button in the associated FRAME is selected. The *newname* variable is initialized here instead of in the INIT section so that the newname variable is updated with the current table name in the *dsn* text box each time the MAIN section executes.

TERM section

The final stage of an SCL program is the TERM section. In this phase of processing, SAS data sets and external files are updated and closed and created SCL lists and objects are deleted. In addition, SCL variable values can be exported to macro variables for use in other programs.

In our FRAME SCL example, the TERM section does not contain any statements. In this situation, the TERM section is optional.

SQL statements in an SCL program

SQL statements can be used within a SUBMIT block in an SCL program. The statements contained in the block can be passed directly to the SQL procedure, eliminating the need for a PROC SQL or a QUIT statement.

Several options are available in the opening SUBMIT statement including CONTINUE and STATUS. The CONTINUE option causes processing to pass back to the SCL program after the statements within the block have been executed. Processing restarts at the first SCL statement after the endsubmit statement. The STATUS option gives a message showing the status of the submit block.

> **Tip**: Although a PROC SQL and QUIT statement can be included within a SUBMIT block, processing efficiency is improved through the SQL option on the SCL SUBMIT statement.

An example of an SCL program that uses SQL statements to generate a list containing an entry for each title in the Bluesky *stock* table is shown in the next example. A table called *tablist* is created and populated with the titles from the Bluesky *stock* table. Each of the observations in the *tablist* table is then added to a tables object (*tables*) as shown in the second example below.

> **Tip:** The OPEN statement cannot access a view, therefore a table must be created.

```
INIT:

  submit continue sql;

    DROP table bluesky.tablist;

    CREATE table bluesky.tablist as
      SELECT title
       FROM  bluesky.stock;

  endsubmit;


MAIN:
  titles = open('bluesky.tablist','I');
   if titles >0 then
  do;

   nv = attrn(titles,'nobs');
   namenum=varnum(titles,'title');

   tablist=makelist();

   do i = 1 to nv;

     var = fetchobs(titles,i);
     tabname = getvarc(titles,namenum);
     rc = insertc(tablist,tabname,i);

    end;

    tables.items=tablist;
    rc = close(titles);
  end;
```

```
  else
    _msg_ = sysmsg();
RETURN;

TERM:
RETURN;
```

The list is maintained entirely in memory and is dynamic in nature. The length of a list is dependent on the number of entries, although the number of entries displayed at one time without scrolling is dependent on the size attributes of the list box. In this example, the ATTRN function is used to obtain the number of observations in the *tablist* table, which controls the number of entries displayed. The *tables* object attribute *items* is assigned the values of the entries to be displayed using dot notation. The resulting list of stocked books is shown in the next figure.

Tip: The INIT section executes only once when the FRAME is invoked. As a result, the list generated by the above SQL procedure cannot be dynamically changed after initialization.

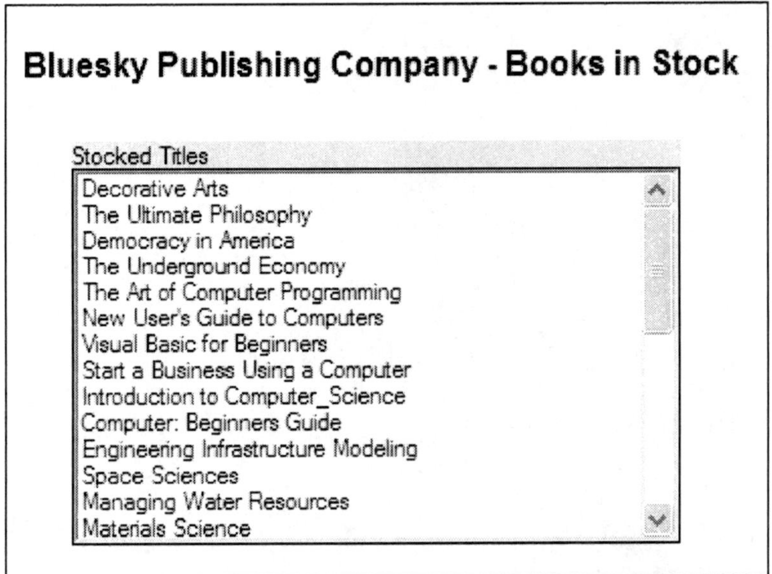

Use of substitution variables in an SQL statement

Variables entered into an object such as a text entry box in a FRAME may be referenced in SQL statements within a SUBMIT block. The variable is prefixed with a single ampersand when it is included in a clause in the SELECT statement. If the variable is part of a comparison that requires a character string, the variable name and ampersand are enclosed in double quotes.

The next figure expands on the previous example, allowing the user to enter the column name to be selected from the *stock* table. In this example, the user has entered the author last name column (auth_lst); when the enter key is pressed, the list box displays the contents of that column in the *stock* table.

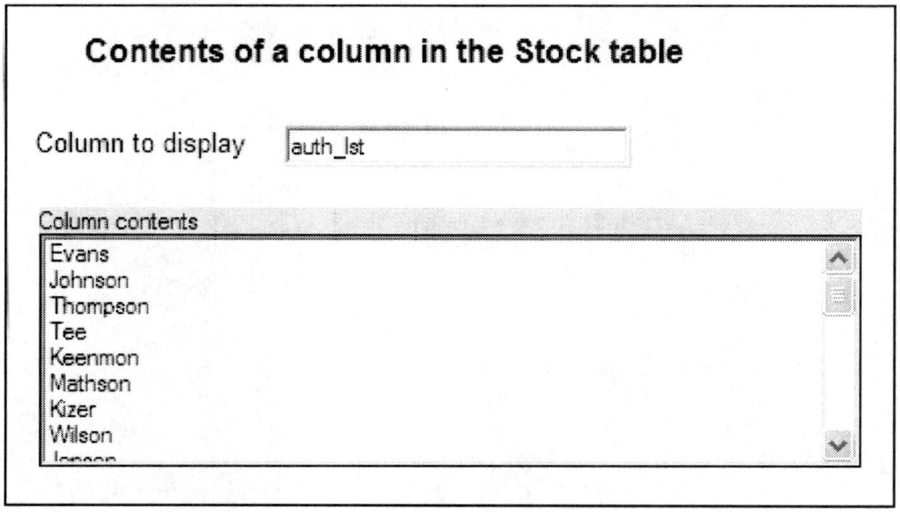

The column name is entered into a text entry box with a name attribute *col* that matches the labeled COL section of the SCL program associated with the FRAME shown in the next example. The SUBMIT block is included in a labeled section so that each time the value changes in the text entry box, the SELECT statement is reissued. The text attribute of the text entry object is assigned to the *colname* variable used in the SELECT statement using dot notation.

```
DCL Char(20) colname;

COL:
  colname = col.text;
  submit continue sql;

    DROP table bluesky.colvalue;

    CREATE table bluesky.colvalue as
    SELECT &colname
    FROM   bluesky.stock;

  endsubmit;
RETURN;

MAIN:
```

```
    datasets = open('bluesky.COLVALUE','I');
     if datasets >0 then
    do;

     nv = attrn(datasets,'NOBS');

     colvalue=makelist();

     do i = 1 to nv;

       var = fetchobs(datasets,i);
       tabname = getvarc(datasets,1);
       rc = insertc(colvalue,tabname,i);

     end;

     tables.items=colvalue;
     rc = close(datasets);
   end;

   else
   _msg_ = sysmsg();
  RETURN;

  TERM:
  return;
```

Macro variables

Resolution of macro variables occurs when the SCL program is compiled. When the program is executed, SYMGET or SYMGETN functions can be used to retrieve the value of the macro variable.

The automatic macro variables SQLOOPS, SQLOBS, and SQLRC values can be obtained through the SYMGET function. However, the number of observations and other data set attributes can also be obtained through the ATTRN function.

Tip: If a macro variable name is set to the same name as a window variable, you must use && (Boolean Symbol for "and") to pass resolution of the value to the macro processor. Both the SYMGET and SYMPUT functions can be used to retrieve the value of a macro variable at the time of execution.

CONTROL statement

The CONTROL statement directs aspects of the execution of labeled program sections in an SCL program. Several options, related to values entered for window variables, are important when using SQL in SUBMIT blocks within labeled program sections.

1. LABEL | NOLABEL

   Statements in a window variable section execute each time the variable value changes. The SCL section must be labeled with the same name as the window variable object for this option to operate. The MAIN section of the SCL program does not execute until all window variable sections have executed successfully. By default, FRAME SCL programs operate with the CONTROL LABEL option.

2. ERROR | NOERROR

   If the ERROR option is also included in the CONTROL statement, statements can be executed when window variable values are invalid. By default, CONTROL NOERROR is set to prevent the statements in the MAIN section from executing if an invalid value is encountered.

3. ALWAYS | NOALWAYS

   When this option is set to ALWAYS, the MAIN section executes regardless of whether the value entered for the window variable is valid or invalid. When the NOALWAYS option is set, the window variable value must be valid and the user must press either the ENTER key or a function key to start execution of the MAIN section. By default, the NOALWAYS option is set for SAS/AF or FSEDIT applications.

For a complete listing of CONTROL statement options, refer to the SAS Screen Control Language Reference.

> **Tip:** The MAIN section executes each time the ENTER or RETURN key or a function key is pressed after a field value is entered.

htmSQL

An HTML page, viewable through any standard browser, can incorporate SQL queries in the form of htmSQL. This enables the user to dynamically interact with tables and views using SQL statements such as SELECT, INSERT, and UPDATE directly from a Web page. The HTML page may also include other languages such as JavaScript adding rich functionality to the Web page.

All htmSQL statements issued from the Web page are submitted to the SAS/SHARE server for processing. Only the web browser software is required by the user. This allows for easy distribution of Web-based interactive reporting and data entry systems.

> **Tip:** htmSQL files have a .hsql extension; they can be invoked either from the Web through an HTML form or URL or from the command line prompt.

htmSQL program form

An htmSQL input file comprises one or more sections, each of which begins with a directive enclosed by braces and ends with the same directive preceded by a slash. A directive provides instructions on how the SQL statements should be processed and the results displayed.

SQL statements are contained within QUERY and UPDATE sections in the htmSQL input file. When an SQL statement is encountered it is sent directly to the SAS/SHARE server for processing.

> **Tip:** An htmSQL input file can include many SQL statements, but each SQL statement must be enclosed between {sql} and {/sql} and positioned within a QUERY or UPDATE section.

The following table summarizes the directives used in htmSQL to process SQL statements and the sections in which they may be found.

Directive	Section
{* }	Query, Update
{eachrow}	Query
{error}	Update
{include}	Cannot appear within a section
{label}	Query, Update
{library}	Query, Update
{norows}	Query
{query}	Query
{sql}	Query, Update
{success}	Update
{update}	Update

QUERY section

A QUERY section is delimited by the {query} and {/query} directives. The SAS/SHARE server and available libraries are indicated with the {query} directive together with a user id and password if required. Within each QUERY section, one or more pairs of SQL and EACHROW sections are included. An optional NOROWS section may also be contained within the QUERY section.

In the next example an htmSQL input file with a QUERY section that includes an SQL, NOROWS, and EACHROW section is shown. An SQL section with a single SELECT statement retrieves the rows of the *stock* table, applying a format to the price column in the process. The NOROWS section is executed only if the query does not retrieve any rows.

```
{*--------------------------------------------------------------*}
{* File name:    LIST.HSQL                                      *}
{* Description : This htmSQL input file lists the book titles   *}
{*--------------------------------------------------------------*}

<html>

<head>
  <title>Bluesky Publishing Titles</title>
</head>

<body bgcolor="white">
<center>

<h1>Bluesky Book Titles
</h1>

{*--------------------------------------------------------------*}
{* start the query section                                      *}
{* connect to the server and use a query to select the entries in *}
{* the stock table                                              *}
{*--------------------------------------------------------------*}

{query server="susieq.shr1"}

  {sql}
    SELECT isbn, title, auth_fst, auth_lst,
           category, stock, yrpubl, prodcode, price format=6.2
    FROM   bluesky.stock
  {/sql}
```

```
{*------------------------------------------------------------*}
{* Set up a norows section which executes if the query does not   *}
{* retrieve any                                                *}
{* rows                                                        *}
{*------------------------------------------------------------*}

  {norows}
    There are no entries in the Bluesky Publishing Stock table.
      <p>Click the <b>New Entry</b> button to enter a book.
    <p>
    <table>
      <tr>
        <td><form action="enter.html" method="post">
            <input type="submit" value="New Entry"></form></td>
      </tr>
    </table>
  {/norows}

{*------------------------------------------------------------*}
{* Create a table and add column headings                     *}
{*------------------------------------------------------------*}
  <table border="5">
    <tr>
      <th> ISBN</th>
      <th> Title</th>
      <th> Author </th>
      <th> Category </th>
      <th> Stocked </th>
      <th> Publ. </th>
      <th> Product Code </th>
      <th> Price </th>
    </tr>

{*------------------------------------------------------------*}
{* Set up an eachrow section.                                  *}
{* Get the query results one row at a time and place into table *}
{*------------------------------------------------------------*}

    {eachrow}
      <tr>
        <td>{&isbn} </td>
        <td>{&title}</td>
        <td>{&auth_fst} {&auth_lst}</td>
        <td>{&category}</td>
        <td align=right>{&stock}</td>
        <td>{&yrpubl}</td>
```

```
        <td>{&prodcode}</td>
        <td align=right>{&price}</td>

      </tr>
    {/eachrow}
  </table>
  <p>

{*----------------------------------------------------------------*}
{* End the query section                                          *}
{*----------------------------------------------------------------*}

{/query}

</center>
</body>
</html>
```

SQL section

The SQL section includes a single query or SELECT statement. The SELECT statement may include either specific references to column and table names or variable references that are resolved when the htmSQL is processed. All valid SELECT statements discussed in this book can be added to the SQL section.

> **Tip:** The format of the price column is set with a format option in the SELECT statement in the SQL section. All of the standard SAS formats are available for use in a SELECT statement.

EACHROW section

The EACHROW section is processed if the query in the SQL section returns one or more rows. The retrieved results are passed a row at a time to the EACHROW section and the reference variables are replaced with the appropriate values from the current row of the retrieved query results. The results are then formatted according to the details included in this section. The formatting options can include any valid HTML tags, text strings, and variable references for column names.

The following table is the result of the EACHROW section of the htmSQL input file above. The table shown is constructed one row at a time using the formatting information in the EACHROW section.

Bluesky Book Titles

ISBN	Title	Author	Category	Stocked	Publ.	Product Code	Price
1-7890-1072-1	Decorative Arts	Greg Evans	arts	1500	1999	300678	16.95
1-7890-2878-7	The Ultimate Philosophy	Cory Johnson	arts	100	1999	300456	9.50
1-7890-1256-2	Democracy in America	Jeff Thompson	arts	55	2003	300289	36.00
1-7890-5477-x	The Underground Economy	Arlene Tee	arts	1000	2000	300680	14.50
1-7890-1209-0	The Art of Computer Programming	Corinna Keenmon	computer	1600	1999	500120	34.50
1-7890-1378-x	New User's Guide to Computers	Jennifer Mathson	computer	350	2003	500127	26.25
1-7890-7648-x	Visual Basic for Beginners	Denise Kizer	computer	600	2003	500168	34.00
1-7890-5634-9	Start a Business Using a Computer	Roy Wilson	computer	1000	2002	500238	22.25
1-7890-3473-6	Introduction to Computer_Science	April Jensen	computer	1000	2002	500890	32.50
1-7890-2829-9	Computer: Beginners Guide	Rosanna Marossy	computer	100	2000	500500	23.50
1-7890-3245-8	Engineering Infrastructure Modeling	Merrill Frank	engineering	2400	1999	200345	54.98
1-7890-1290-2	Space Sciences	Ian Bishop	engineering	1500	2001	200145	56.25
1-7890-5698-5	Managing Water Resources	Brian Kerwin	engineering	6000	2001	200678	45.00
1-7890-1267-8	Materials Science	Andrew Bole	engineering	50	2000	200507	74.50
1-7890-4578-9	Risks in Life - % Gain or Loss?	Paul Smith	general	1000	2000	600123	14.30
1-7890-3468-x	Women Writers	Alex Paul	general	1000	2000	600780	8.60
1-7890-2390-4	Greece and Beyond	Clark Foutz	general	398	2000	600451	12.50
1-7890-3278-4	Mountaineering Skills	Chris Lillard	general	200	2000	600489	5.50
1-7890-3007-2	The Maestro	Alexander Dixon	general	100	2000	600125	6.95
1-7890-4578-9	The 10% Solution	Gabe Haney	medicine	400	1999	400457	74.65
1-7890-5475-3	Tibetan Medicine	Wendy Perry	medicine	2000	2000	400128	34.00
1-7890-3467-1	Medications and Maintenance	David Barry	medicine	30	2000	400345	86.00
1-7890-7893-8	Unconventional Treatments	Debbie Hedge	medicine	1000	2003	400102	55.00
1-7890-3479-5	National Library of Medicine	Robert Saravit	medicine	35	2001	400178	65.75
1-7890-3891-x	Medical Education in School	Beth Miler	medicine	300	2000	400100	43.75
1-7890-4567-3	Book of Science and Nature	Allison Clark	science	1000	2003	100890	69.00
1-7890-3478-7	Free Thinking in Mathematics	Ken McMurry	science	900	2001	100601	26.25
1-7890-1280-5	Science and Technology	Kay Davis	science	200	2002	100406	15.00
1-7890-5678-0	Science of Biology	Lisa Sharr	science	500	2000	100345	65.00
1-7890-2876-0	Geology: Volcanos	Jena Richardson	science	400	2001	100340	18.00

By default, all of the rows retrieved by the query in the SQL section are passed to the EACHROW section and formatted for output. If the option last=*n* is set in the eachrow directive, only *n* rows are retrieved. Alternatively, the first=*n* option can be set directing the EACHROW section to start with the *nth* row retrieved.

> **Tip:** The last and first options are mutually exclusive; if both are specified, the second option set on the EACHROW directive takes precedence.

NOROWS section

The NOROWS section includes one or more steps to be processed when a query does not return any results. Messages or actions can be part of the NOROWS section.

The next figure shows the HTML page displayed when the NOROWS section of the above htmSQL input file is executed. If the "New Entry" button is pressed, the enter.hsql input file is executed, displaying an HTML page where a new book can be entered.

Bluesky Book Titles

There are no entries in the Bluesky Publishing Stock table.

Click the **New Entry** button to enter a book.

[New Entry]

> **Tip:** The enter.htsql program and associated HTML Web page are included later in this section.

UPDATE section

An UPDATE section is delimited by the {update} and {/update} directives. The SAS/SHARE server and available libraries are indicated with the {update} directive together with a user id and password if required. Each UPDATE section requires at least one SQL section; ERROR and SUCCESS sections may also be included.

In the next example an htmSQL input file with an UPDATE section that includes SQL, SUCCESS, and ERROR sections is shown. An UPDATE section with a single INSERT statement adds the book particulars entered interactively into an html form. The values entered by the user are passed to this htmSQL file when it is invoked. The SUCCESS section is executed if the INSERT statement is successful; otherwise the error section is executed.

```
{*--------------------------------------------------------------*}
{* File name:     ADD.HSQL                                      *}
{* Description:   This htmSQL input file adds a new book in the *}
{*                stock table from information entered into     *}
{*                the webpage generated from enter.hsql         *}
{*--------------------------------------------------------------*}

<html>

<head>
  <title>Bluesky Publishing Company</title>
</head>

<body bgcolor="white">

<h1>Add Stock</h1>

<p>
{*--------------------------------------------------------------*}
{* start the update section                                     *}
{* connect to the server and use an INSERT statement to add a   *}
{* new book to the stock table                                  *}
{*--------------------------------------------------------------*}

{update server="susieq:5010"}

    {sql} insert into bluesky.stock
              set isbn="{&isbn}",
                  title="{&title}",
                  auth_fst="{&auth_fst}",
                 auth_lst="{&auth_lst}",
                  category="{&category}",
                 reprint="{&reprint}",
                  stock={&stock},
                  yrpubl={&yrPubl},
```

```
                prodcode="{&prodcode}",
                price={&price}

    {/sql}

{*----------------------------------------------------------------*}
{* set up an error section which executes if the INSERT          *}
{* statement fails                                               *}
{*----------------------------------------------------------------*}

    {error}
        <b>Add failed.
        </b>
    {/error}

{*----------------------------------------------------------------*}
{* set up a success section which executes if the INSERT statement*}
{* succeeds                                                       *}
{*----------------------------------------------------------------*}

    {success}
        <b>Entry added for "{&title}"
        </b>.
    {/success}

{/update}
{*----------------------------------------------------------------*}
{* end the update section                                         *}
{*----------------------------------------------------------------*}

</body>
</html>
```

SQL section

SQL data manipulation statements including ALTER, CREATE, DELETE, DROP, INSERT, and UPDATE statements can be issued in the UPDATE section. INSERT and UPDATE statements may include either specific values or they may include variable references. In addition, all statements may include variable references substituting for column and table names.

> **Tip:** It is possible to disable update actions by specifying a READONLY option in the htmSQL configuration file.

ERROR section

An ERROR section includes one or more steps to be processed when an UPDATE section SQL statement fails. Failure is indicated by a nonzero return code.

Tip: The section processed when a non-zero return code is encountered is controlled by the EMPTY option set on the sql directive. The default setting for this option is "error," which causes processing to transfer to the ERROR section if failure is encountered. If the empty option is set to "success," processing is transferred to the SUCCESS section if failure is encountered.

SUCCESS section

A SUCCESS section includes one or more steps to be processed when an UPDATE section SQL statement succeeds. Success is indicated by a return code of 0.

Variable references

SQL statements included in the query and update sections may include variable references instead of column names. All variable references are resolved before the SQL statement is passed to the SAS/SHARE server for processing.

In the next figure the user enters the specifics for the new book to be added to the Bluesky Publishing *stock* table. When the ADD button is pressed, the values are passed to the add.hsql file shown in the preceding example, resolving each of the variable references included in the UPDATE section.

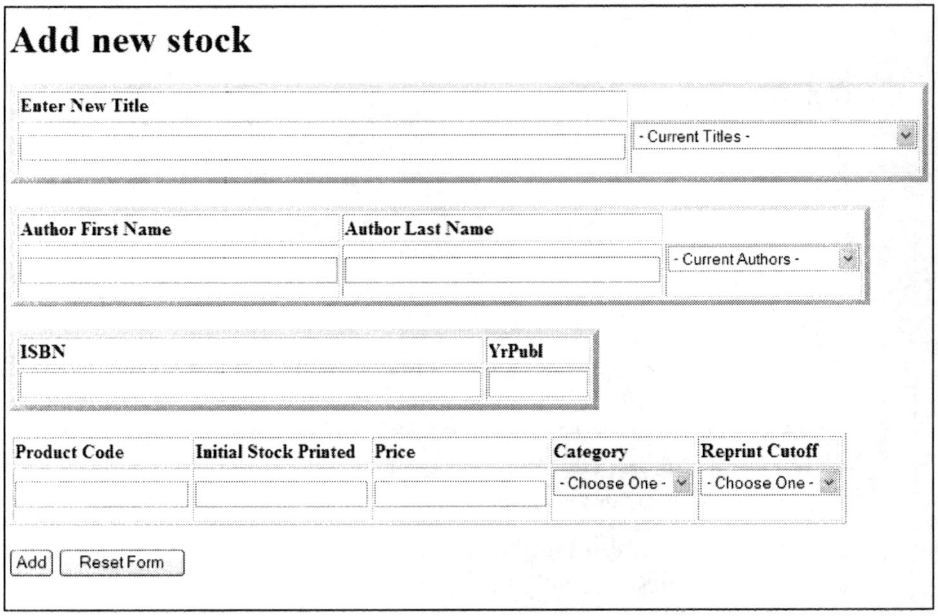

Add new stock

Enter New Title
- Current Titles -

Author First Name
Author Last Name
- Current Authors -

ISBN
YrPubl

Product Code
Initial Stock Printed
Price
Category
- Choose One -
Reprint Cutoff
- Choose One -

Add
Reset Form

The htmSQL input file used to generate the form shown above is included in the next example. Notice that this file contains a single QUERY section that includes several SQL sections. The SQL statements provide the list of values for the drop-down boxes relating to titles, authors, categories, and reprint values. The author and title drop-down boxes are provided for information only and supply the user with a list of current titles and authors in the *stock* table. The category and reprint drop-down boxes allow the user to select the value assigned to each from the list.

```
{*--------------------------------------------------------------*}
{* File name:   ENTER.HSQL                                      *}
{* Description: this htmSQL input file collects the information *}
{* required to add a new book to the stock table.  The          *}
{* information here is passed to the add.hsql                   *}
{* file for processing.                                         *}
{*--------------------------------------------------------------*}

   <html>

<head>
  <title>Bluesky Publishing Company</title>
  <script language="JavaScript" type="text/javascript"
  src="/lib/global.js"></script>
</head>

<body bgcolor="white">

{*--------------------------------------------------------------*}
{* If the ADD button is pressed, the add.hsql file will be      *}
{* processed using the values entered in the form.              *}
{*--------------------------------------------------------------*}

<h1>Add new stock</h1>
<p>
<p>

<form action="add.hsql" method="post">

{*--------------------------------------------------------------*}
{* Start a query section                                        *}
{*--------------------------------------------------------------*}

{query server="susieq:5010"}

<p>
<left>
```

```
<table border="5">

<tr align="left">
      <th> Enter New Title</th>
</tr>

<td align "left">

      <input name="title" size="80" value="">
</td>

{*-------------------------------------------------------------*}
{* use a query to select all current titles in the stock table *}
{* and add them to the drop down list for viewing              *}
{*-------------------------------------------------------------*}

<td align "left">

{sql}

   SELECT distinct title  as sel
   FROM bluesky.stock
{/sql}

<select name="titles" size="1">
      <option value="" size="100" selected>-    Current Titles   -
      {eachrow}
       <option>{&sel}
      {/eachrow}
</select> <br><p>
</td>
</table>

<p>
<p>
<p>

{*-------------------------------------------------------------*}
{* Create a table for the author names and apply headings      *}
{*-------------------------------------------------------------*}
<table border="5">

<!-- column headings -->
```

```
<tr align="left">
    <th>Author First Name</th>
    <th>Author Last Name</th>
</tr>


<td align "left">
      <input name="auth_fst" size="40" value="">
</td>

<td align "left">
      <input name="auth_lst" size="40" value="">
</td>

{*-------------------------------------------------------------*}
{* use a query to select all current authors in the stock table   *}
{* and add them to the drop down list for viewing                 *}
{*-------------------------------------------------------------*}

<td align "left">

{sql}
  SELECT distinct (auth_lst||', '||auth_fst) as sel
  FROM bluesky.stock
  ORDER BY auth_lst, auth_fst
{/sql}

    <select name="authors" size="1">
        <option value="" size="40" selected>- Current Authors -
        {eachrow}
        <option >{&sel}
        {/eachrow}
    </select> <br><p>

</td>
</table>

{*-------------------------------------------------------------*}
{* Create a table for the ISBN & Publication year.  Apply a       *}
{* heading to each.                                               *}
{*-------------------------------------------------------------*}
<p>
<p>
<p>
<p>
```

```
<table border="5">

<!-- column headings -->

<tr align="left">
      <th>ISBN</th>
      <th> YrPubl</th>
</tr>

<tr>
      <td align "left">
           <input name="isbn" size="60" value=""><br>
      </td>

      <td align "right">
           <input name="yrpubl" size="10" value="">
</td>
</table>
<p>
<p>
<p>

{*---------------------------------------------------------------*}
{* Create a table for the Product Code, Stock Printed, Price,    *}
{* Category and reprint cutoff.  Apply headings to each text     *}
{* box and drop down box                                         *}
{*---------------------------------------------------------------*}
<table border "5">

<tr align="left">
   <th>Product Code</th>
   <th>Initial Stock Printed</th>
   <th>Price </th>
   <th>Category</th>
   <th>Reprint Cutoff</th>
</tr>

<td align="left">
      <input name="prodcode" size="20" ><br>
</td>

<td align "left">
      <input name="stock" size="20" ><br>
</td>
```

```
<td align "right">
     <input name="price" size="20" ><br>
</td>

{*---------------------------------------------------------------*}
{* use a query to populate the drop down category list          *}
{*---------------------------------------------------------------*}

 <td align "left">
   {sql}
     SELECT distinct category as sel
     FROM bluesky.stock
     ORDER BY category
   {/sql}
   <select name="category" size="1">
   <option value="" selected>- Choose One -

   {eachrow}
     <option >{&sel}
   {/eachrow}

   </select> <br><p>
 </td>

{*---------------------------------------------------------------*}
{* use a query to populate the drop down reprint list           *}
{*---------------------------------------------------------------*}
 <td align "left">
   {sql}
      SELECT reprint as sel
      FROM bluesky.reprint
      ORDER BY reprint
   {/sql}

    <select name="reprint"  size="1">
    <option value="" selected>- Choose One -

     {eachrow}
       <option >{&sel}
     {/eachrow}

    </select> <br><p>

</td>
</tr>
</table>
```

```
</center>
<p>

{*-----------------------------------------------------------*}
{* create an ADD button which will invoke add.hsql and pass the *}
{* values                                                    *}
{* entered and selected on this form                         *}
{*-----------------------------------------------------------*}

<input type="submit" value="Add"></td>
<input type="reset"   value="Reset Form">

{/query}

</center>
</body>
</html>
```

Tip: I find it handy to invoke htmSQL from the command line when testing htmSQL input files with update sections. It is often faster and easier than entering all of the data into a form such as the one in the "Add a new stock" table preceding. The htmSQL input file in the code example last shown can be processed with a command that provides the values for each of the variable references:

```
htmsql add.hsql "title=The Age of
Reason&auth_fst=Bill&auth_lst=Newman&isbn=1-7890-1162-
2&yrpubl=2003&prodcode=300982&stock=100&price=10.50&
category=arts&reprint=A" >add.html
```

If the update is successful, the html page will display the success message; otherwise, the error message will be displayed.

The SAS/SHARE server must be running before the command is issued. The command must be issued from the directory in which the htmsql executable is located, or you must have your PATH environment variable set to that directory.

Dictionary tables

Dictionary tables provide information on SAS data libraries, data sets, system options, macros, and external files associated with the current SAS session. Although they are referred to as tables, they are actually a set of dynamic read-only views that are updated automatically each time they are accessed. The dictionary tables can be referenced in a PROC SQL query or view in the same way as other tables and views. They are also the basis for the SASHELP views.

Before you compile the information from the current SAS session for a dictionary table, one or more SAS processes may be executed, including the creation of additional views. As a result, care must be taken in the construction of queries referencing dictionary tables. A carefully constructed SELECT statement that restricts the variables returned and focuses the WHERE clause on just the required information can reduce processing.

> **Tip:** Many SQL queries that select data from dictionary tables are also available through SCL functions. Whenever possible, the SCL functions should be used instead of SQL statements within submit blocks because the SCL functions are more efficient. Refer to the SAS Screen Control Language Reference for more information.

The DESCRIBE TABLE statement can be applied to any of the dictionary tables to determine the columns in the table. Each column in a dictionary table has been associated with a descriptive label for ease of use.

The SELECT statement included in the example following queries the *members* dictionary table to generate a list of the SAS files in a SAS data library. The column headings are the default labels for the selected columns.

> **Tip:** To query a dictionary table, add DICTIONARY as a table qualifer; a LIBNAME statement is not required.

```
PROC SQL outobs=10;

TITLE1    'Dictionary.Members Sample Listing ';
SELECT    memname, memtype
FROM      dictionary.members;
```

```
Dictionary.Members Sample Listing

                                     Member
Member Name                          Type
_____________________________________________

ADDRESS                              DATA
ALLORDERS                            VIEW
ARTS                                 VIEW
CLIENT                               DATA
COMPANY                              DATA
CONTACTS                             DATA
COPYORDERS                           DATA
CURRENCY                             DATA
NEWCOMP                              DATA
NEWORDER                             DATA
```

Tip: Many of the dictionary tables return a large number of rows. If you want to print a sample listing from a table, add the OUTOBS option to your PROC SQL statement to limit the number of rows reported. Also use WHERE clauses wherever possible to select only the necessary variables or to restrict the search to specific libraries.

SAS/ACCESS and SQL Pass-Through Facility users: The preceding tip is especially important when DBMS librefs are active in your SAS session. Otherwise, your query could return information on the entire database!

These dictionary tables are useful in interactive programs because they provide valuable information. They are updated with information from the current SAS session. The table below summarizes the available dictionary tables. All tables new to SAS Version 9 are highlighted.

Dictionary table name	Description of contents
catalogs	Catalog information including SASUSER and SASHELP catalog details.
check_constraints	Information on check constraints
columns	Details on columns defined in tables, views, and SAS data sets.
constraint_column_usage	Information on columns associated with integrity constraints
constraint_table_usage	Information on tables associated with integrity constraints
dictionaries	Information on all DICTIONARY tables
engines	Available engines
extfiles	Directory path locations for libraries and catalogs.
formats	Formats and informats currently accessible
goptions	Information about currently defined graphics options
indexes	Details on indexes defined for tables and SAS data sets.
libnames	Currently defined SAS data libraries
macros	Current setting and scope of defined macro variables.
members	Information about all objects stored in currently defined SAS data librairies
options	Current settings of all SAS session and system options.
referential_constraints	Information about referential constraints
styles	Information about known ODS styles
tables	Number of rows/observations, columns and other details concerning tables and data sets.
table_constraints	Information about integrity constraints defined in known tables
titles	Titles and footnotes currently set.
views	Names of all defined views.

Tip: Only those libraries identified by a LIBNAME statement within the current SAS session are included in the dictionary tables. It is not necessary to identify standard SAS libraries such as SASUSER or WORK.

Detailed descriptions of each dictionary table are included in Appendix B, "Dictionary Table Descriptions." A brief description and examples of the use of the most commonly accessed tables are included in the following section.

Members

The *members* dictionary table contains information about each member of every library defined in the current SAS session. The next example includes a report on the columns of the *members* table generated with the DESCRIBE command.

```
PROC SQL;
DESCRIBE TABLE dictionary.members;
```

SAS log:

```
NOTE: SQL table DICTIONARY.MEMBERS was created like:

create table DICTIONARY.MEMBERS
  (
   libname char(8) label='Library Name',
   memname char(32) label='Member Name',
   memtype char(8) label='Member Type',
   dbms_memtype char(32) label='DBMS Member Type',
   engine char(8) label='Engine Name',
   index char(32) label='Indexes',
   path char(1024) label='Path Name'
  );
```

Tip: The dbms_memtype column in the *members* dictionary table is new to SAS Version 9.

The next example includes a SELECT statement that generates basic information about the members of the Bluesky library that have *order* as part of their name. The member name and type are reported along with the path and a yes/no indicator concerning indexes. Formats were added to the index and path columns to limit the size of each.

```
PROC SQL;

TITLE1   'Bluesky library member information - ORDER tables';
SELECT   memname, memtype,
         index format=$10.,path format=$30.
FROM     dictionary.members
WHERE    libname = 'BLUESKY'
         and memname like '%ORDER%';
```

```
Bluesky library member information - ORDER tables

Member Name          Type      Indexes     Path Name
--------------------------------------------------------------------
ALLORDERS            VIEW      no          C:\mydata\bluesky bookstore
COPYORDERS           DATA      yes         C:\mydata\bluesky bookstore
NEWORDER             DATA      no          C:\mydata\bluesky bookstore
NEW_ORDER            DATA      no          C:\mydata\bluesky bookstore
ORDER                DATA      no          C:\mydata\bluesky bookstore
ORDERPEND            DATA      yes         C:\mydata\bluesky bookstore
ORDERS               DATA      no          C:\mydata\bluesky bookstore
ORDER_2001_2002      DATA      no          C:\mydata\bluesky bookstore
REORDER              DATA      no          C:\mydata\bluesky bookstore
```

Tip: When trying to match to a libname, memname, or memtype, you must have the enclosed character string on the WHERE clause in uppercase.

Columns

The *columns* dictionary table provides detailed information on the columns defined for each table known to the SAS session. The next example includes a report on the columns of the *columns* table generated with the DESCRIBE command.

```
PROC SQL;
DESCRIBE table dictionary.columns;
```

SAS log:

```
NOTE: SQL table DICTIONARY.COLUMNS was created like:

create table DICTIONARY.COLUMNS
  (
   libname char(8) label='Library Name',
   memname char(32) label='Member Name',
   memtype char(8) label='Member Type',
   name char(32) label='Column Name',
   type char(4) label='Column Type',
   length num label='Column Length',
   npos num label='Column Position',
   varnum num label='Column Number in Table',
(   label char(256) label='Column Label',
```

```
 format char(49) label='Column Format',
 informat char(49) label='Column Informat',
 idxusage char(9) label='Column Index Type',
 sortedby num label='Order in Key Sequence',
 xtype char(12) label='Extended Type',
 notnull char(3) label='Not NULL?',
 precision num label='Precision',
 scale num label='Scale',
 transcode char(3) label='Transcoded?'
);
```

Tip: The highlighted columns were added to the columns dictionary table in SAS Version 9.

The next example includes a SELECT statement that gives information on the columns in a pending orders table of the Bluesky Publishing company. The type of index associated with each column is stored in the column index type (idxusage) column of the *columns* table. If a table column has both a simple and a composite index, the index type is set to BOTH.

```
PROC SQL;

TITLE1  'Report on Pending Order table columns';
SELECT  name, type, length, idxusage
FROM    dictionary.columns
WHERE   libname = 'BLUESKY' and memname = 'ORDERPEND';
```

```
Report on Pending Order table columns

                                                        Column
                                  Column     Column     Index
Column Name                       Type       Length     Type
------------------------------------------------------------------
prodCode                          char            6     COMPOSITE
ord_date                          num             8     SIMPLE
quantity                          num             8
totsale                           num             8
currency                          char            3
delCode                           char            3
clientNo                          num             8
invoice                           char           10     COMPOSITE
```

The next example shows another report generated from the *columns* dictionary table. In this case the format and label information for the table is reported. A column label was permanently assigned to the product code (prodcode) column when the *ordpend* table was created.

> **Tip:** Refer to Chapter 6, "Creating and Managing Tables and Views" for details on how to apply column labels, formats and informats to a column on the CREATE TABLE statement.

```
PROC SQL;

TITLE     'Report on Pending Order table columns';
TITLE2    'Formats and Labels';
SELECT    name format=$10., type, format format=$10., informat
          format=$10.,
          label format=$20.
FROM      dictionary.columns
WHERE     libname = 'BLUESKY' and memname = 'ORDERPEND';
```

```
Report on Pending Order table columns
Formats and Labels

Column       Column  Column       Column
Name         Type    Format       Informat     Column Label
------------------------------------------------------------------
prodCode     char
ord_date     num     DATE.        DATE.
quantity     num
totsale      num     COMMA10.2
currency     char
delCode      char                              Delivery Code
clientNo     num
invoice      char
```

The dictionary table values can also be assigned to macro variables for later use. In the next example the columns dictionary table is used to assign a list of numeric columns in the *orders* table to a macro variable. The macro variable is then used in a second SELECT statement to generate a report as shown in the second example following.

```
PROC SQL;

SELECT  name
INTO    :collist separated by ','
FROM    dictionary.columns
WHERE   libname = 'BLUESKY' and memname = 'ORDERS'
        and type = 'num';

%put List of numberic columns in orders table - &collist;
```

SAS log:

```
List of numeric columns in orders table -  ord_date,quantity,totsale,clientNo
```

```
LIBNAME bluesky "C:\mydata\bluesky bookstore\";
PROC SQL;

SELECT  &collist
FROM    bluesky.orders;
WHERE   ord_date > '01JUL2004'D;
```

ord_date	quantity	totsale	clientNo
20JUL04	335	11390	5005
23JUL04	590	15487.5	3007
23JUL04	1500	82500	5005
23JUL04	10	657.5	6090
23JUL04	400	13600	7008

Tables

The *tables* dictionary table provides detailed information on the tables known to the SAS session. This table is very useful in setting the number of observations and variables in a macro program. The next example includes a report on the columns of the *tables* dictionary table generated with the DESCRIBE command.

```
PROC SQL;
DESCRIBE table dictionary.tables;
```

SAS log:

```
NOTE: SQL table DICTIONARY.TABLES was created like:

create table DICTIONARY.TABLES
 (
  libname char(8) label='Library Name',
  memname char(32) label='Member Name',
  memtype char(8) label='Member Type',
  dbms_memtype char(32) label='DBMS Member Type',
  memlabel char(256) label='Dataset Label',
  typemem char(8) label='Dataset Type',
  crdate num format=DATETIME informat=DATETIME label='Date Created',
  modate num format=DATETIME informat=DATETIME label='Date Modified',
  nobs num label='Number of Physical Observations',
  obslen num label='Observation Length',
  nvar num label='Number of Variables',
  protect char(3) label='Type of Password Protection',
  compress char(8) label='Compression Routine',
  encrypt char(8) label='Encryption',
  npage num label='Number of Pages',
  filesize num label='Size of File',
  pcompress num label='Percent Compression',
  reuse char(3) label='Reuse Space',
  bufsize num label='Bufsize',
  delobs num label='Number of Deleted Observations',
  nlobs num label='Number of Logical Observations',
  maxvar num label='Longest variable name',
  maxlabel num label='Longest label',
  maxgen num label='Maximum number of generations',
  gen num label='Generation number',
  attr char(3) label='Dataset Attributes',
  indxtype char(9) label='Type of Indexes',
  datarep char(32) label='Data Representation',
  sortname char(8) label='Name of Collating Sequence',
  sorttype char(4) label='Sorting Type',
  sortchar char(8) label='Charset Sorted By',
  reqvector char(24) format=$HEX48 informat=$HEX48 label='Requirements
                     Vector',
  datarepname char(170) label='Data Representation Name',
  encoding char(256) label='Data Encoding',
  audit char(3) label='Audit Trail Active?',
```

```
  audit_before char(3) label='Audit Before Image?',
  audit_admin char(3) label='Audit Admin Image?',
  audit_error char(3) label='Audit Error Image?',
  audit_data char(3) label='Audit Data Image?'
);
```

Tip: A number of new columns, highlighted in the above example were added to the *tables* dictionary table in SAS Version 9.

The next example includes a report of selected columns from the dictionary table *tables* for the members of the bluesky library. In addition to information about the number of variables, it includes columns for both the number of observations and the number of deleted observations.

```
PROC SQL;

SELECT  memname, nobs, obslen, nvar, delobs,
FROM    dictionary.tables where libname = 'BLUESKY';
```

Member Name	Number of Observations	Observation Length	Number of Variables	Number of Deleted Observations
ADDRESS	23	160	7	14
CLIENT	16	133	7	8
CURRENCY	56	19	3	28
ORDERS	62	54	8	32
ORDRPT	.	80	4	0
ORD_DATA	30	64	8	0
REPRINT	12	9	2	6
SHIPPING	10	36	3	5
STOCK	120	139	10	90

On careful review of the table, you will notice that the *ordrpt* member does not have any observations, although there are four variables with a combined observation or row length of eighty. *Ordrpt* is a view and as such it does not hold observations.

Tip: The dictionary table *tables* will not provide the number of observations in a view because a view is populated with observations when it is referenced in a query. A SELECT statement with a count function issued against the view will report the number of observations in the view.

It is important to note that the *number of observations* column may include rows that have been deleted from the table. It is a count of the number of observations occupying space in the table, which is not necessarily equal to the number of observations with values. The space occupied by deleted rows cannot be used to store incoming rows in the table unless the COMPRESS and REUSE options were specified when the table was first created.

> **Caution:** To correctly assign the number of logical observations from *dictionary.tables* to a variable in a program the following calculation should be done:
>
> Number of observations - Number of deleted observations
>
> where the number of observations and the number of deleted observations are the column values taken from *dictionary.tables*

> **New to SAS Version 9 -** A new column called nlobs that contains the number of logical observations was introduced to the *tables* dictionary table. It stores the number of logical observations generated by the above calculation.

In the table following a portion of the Bluesky Publishing Company *shipping* table, with its five observations, is shown. The highlighted rows in the table represent observations that were deleted from the table previously. The space occupied by these observations is still in use by the table, although they no longer have any values associated with them. In the report generated from the *tables* dictionary table in the preceding example above, the *number of observations* for the *shipping* table is reported as ten and the *number of deleted observations* is five.

> **Tip:** Count functions and the macro variable SQLOBS report only the undeleted rows in a table because the deleted rows are not accessed during SQL queries. SQLOBS increments by one each time a new row is read from a table.

Table name: SHIPPING

delcode	deltype	charge
EXE	2 day Express shipping	15
UPS	US postal service	10
EXP	express mail	10
EXA	express air delivery	15
GRN	ground delivery	10

If the REUSE and COMPRESS options were specified when the table was first created, the space allocated to a row or observation in a table is freed up when the observation is deleted. In this case, the *number of deleted observations* column would always report zero. More information on these options is contained in the section on DELETE in Chapter 6, "Creating and Managing Tables and Views."

> **Tip:** Compression will only occur if the table size decreases with compression. There are cases where compression results in a larger table size. In my experience, this happens most often with corrupted tables or fragmented storage. If you find compression has not occurred, it is best to create a new table from the old using a statement such as CREATE TABLE <newtable> AS SELECT * from <oldtable>.

Indexes

The dictionary *indexes* table provides detailed information about indexes including their associated tables and columns. The next example includes a report on the columns of the dictionary *indexes* table generated with the DESCRIBE command.

```
PROC SQL;
DESCRIBE table dictionary.indexes;
```

SAS log:

```
NOTE: SQL table DICTIONARY.INDEXES was created like:
create table DICTIONARY.INDEXES
  (
   libname char(8) label='Library Name',
   memname char(32) label='Member Name',
   memtype char(8) label='Member Type',
   name char(32) label='Column Name',
   idxusage char(9) label='Column Index Type',
   indxname char(32) label='Index Name',
   indxpos num label='Position of Column in Concatenated Key',
   nomiss char(3) label='Nomiss Option',
   unique char(3) label='Unique Option'
  );
```

The next example shows a report generated on three new indexes created on the Bluesky Publishing *orders* table. The information on the composite index includes the position of the column within the index. As the first column in a composite index must be referenced in a WHERE clause in order for the index to be used, this positional value is important. A position value of zero indicates the leading column of the composite index. This position is incremented by the length of the variable providing the position of the next column in the composite index. For example, the product code (prodcode) column is reported in position 8 because the leading column, order date (ord_date), occupies positions 0-7 in the index.

```
LIBNAME bluesky "C:\mydata\bluesky bookstore\";
PROC SQL;

CREATE index ord_date on bluesky.orders(ord_date);
CREATE index clientno on bluesky.orders(clientno);
CREATE unique index ordprod on
       bluesky.orders(ord_date,prodcode,invoice);

TITLE    'Report on Orders Table Indexes';
SELECT    name format=$15., idxusage,
          indxname format=$15., indxpos, unique
FROM      dictionary.indexes
WHERE     libname = 'BLUESKY' and memname = 'ORDERS';
```

```
                Report on Orders Table Indexes

                                                  Position of
                 Column                            Column in
                 Index                          Concatenated  Unique
  Column Name    Type         Index Name                 Key  Option
  ------------------------------------------------------------------

  ord_date       COMPOSITE    ORDPROD                      0  yes
  prodCode       COMPOSITE    ORDPROD                      8  yes
  invoice        COMPOSITE    ORDPROD                     14  yes
  clientNo       SIMPLE       CLIENTNO                     .
  ord_date       SIMPLE       ORD_DATE                     .
```

Constraint_column_usage

The *constraint_column_usage* dictionary table, new to SAS Version 9, provides detailed information about constraints including their associated tables and columns. The next example includes a report on the constraints associated with the *newstock* table in the work library created in Chapter 6, "Creating and Managing Columns and Views."

```
LIBNAME bluesky "C:\mydata\bluesky bookstore\";
PROC SQL;

SELECT   table_name, column_name, constraint_name
FROM     dictionary.constraint_column_usage
WHERE    table_catalog = 'WORK' and table_name = 'NEWSTOCK';
```

Table	Column	Constraint Name
NEWSTOCK	isbn	_PK0001_
NEWSTOCK	reprint	_FK0001_
NEWSTOCK	stock	_CK0001_
NEWSTOCK	yrpubl	_CK0001_
NEWSTOCK	yrpubl	_CK0002_
NEWSTOCK	price	_NM0001_

Tip: The constraints associated with the *newstock* table were created in-line so each takes on a default name which includes two characters representing the constraint type and a number. Meaningful names can be assigned to constraints created out-of-line or added to a table with the ALTER statement.

Constraints are covered in detail in Chapter 6, "Creating and Managing Tables and Views." The statement used to create the *newstock* table is included in that chapter.

Putting it all together

The SCL program associated with the FRAME shown in the figure below includes many of the concepts discussed in this chapter. Each time a library name is entered in the text box a list of the data members in the library is generated. In addition, a message confirming a count of the number of data members in the library is displayed.

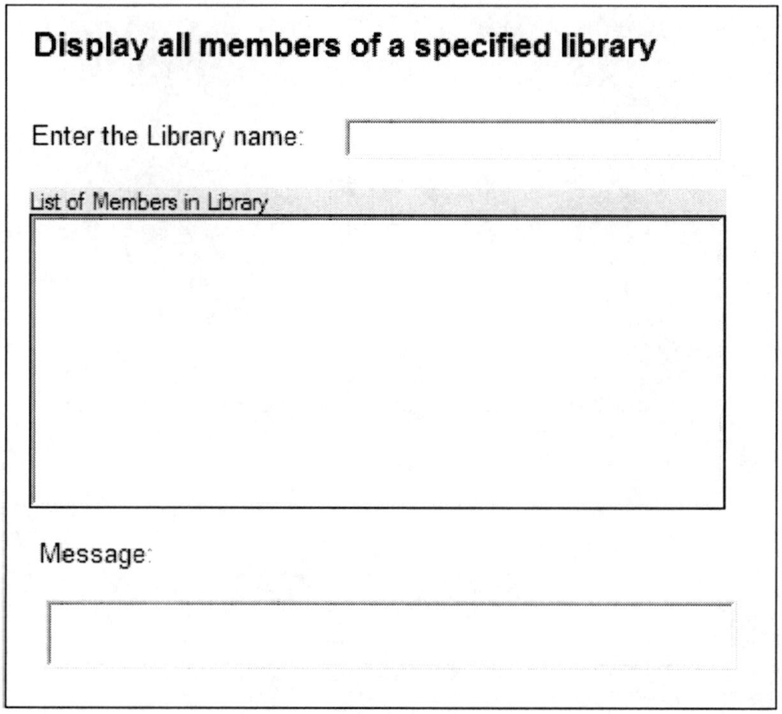

Display all members of a specified library

Enter the Library name:

List of Members in Library

Message:

The SCL program in the next example includes a labeled section that matches the name of the text entry object (libnew) in the associated FRAME. Each time the user enters a library name, the labeled section libnew is executed and the value entered object is passed to the program. The text attribute of the libnew object is substituted within the SELECT statement to retrieve the list of members in the library from the dictionary table *members*. The number of library members is determined from the automatic macro variable SQLOBS. An appropriate message is displayed in the FRAME; dot notation is used to assign a string to the text attribute of the message object.

```
/* Declare the library name variable assigned from the FRAME
   object*/

DCL Char(20) lib_name;


/* Initialize the program by creating a table with the necessary
data for the list*/


/* Execute labelled section each time the value in the text entry
box changes*/
```

```
LIBNEW:

/* Assign the current value of the LIBNEW text box to the
lib_name variable*/

  lib_name = libnew.text;


  /* Submit block with SQL statements sent directly
   to SQL processor*/

  submit continue SQL STATUS;

    /* Drop the table if it exists and recreate it with the
       library
    name from the text entry box.  Use the UPPER function to allow
    for user entry of upper, lower or mixed case*/

  DROP table bluesky.datlist;

  CREATE table bluesky.datlist as
    SELECT  memname
    FROM    dictionary.members
    WHERE   memtype = 'DATA'
            and libname = upper("&LIB_NAME");

  endsubmit;

  /* Check for a return code which would indicate that the
  statement is in error*/

  if symget ('SQLRC')>4 then
  message.text = 'The SQL statement is not valid';

  /* Check the number of observations read in the SELECT
  statement*/

  if symget ('SQLOBS') = 0 then
  message.text = 'There are no DATA members in the library';
  ELSE
  message.text = 'There are '||symget('SQLOBS')||' DATA members in
  the library';

RETURN;
```

```
/* Execute the MAIN section of the program*/

MAIN:

  /* Open the table in read-only mode and check that it opens
  (return code > 0) */

  datasets = open('bluesky.DATLIST','I');
  if datasets >0 then

  do;

  /* Obtain attribute information from the table including the
  number of observations and the variable number for the Member
  Name column*/

     nv = attrn(datasets,'NOBS');
     namenum=varnum(datasets,'MEMNAME');

  /* Create an empty list*/

     tablist=makelist();

  /* Loop through the observations in the table.  Fetch the
     current
  observation, obtain the value of the Member Name column and
      insert
  it into the list*/

   do i = 1 to nv;

     var = fetchobs(datasets,i);
     tabname = getvarc(datasets,namenum);
     rc = insertc(tablist,tabname,i);

   end;

   /* Associate the displayed list with the items from the table*/

   tables.items=tablist;

   /* Close the table and delete the created list*/

   rc = close(datasets);
   rc = dellist(tablist);
 end;
```

```
 else
   message.text = sysmsg();
RETURN;

/* Terminate the program*/

TERM:
RETURN;
```

Tip: The following LIBNAME statement was issued before working in SAS/AF:

```
LIBNAME bluesky "c:\mydata\Bluesky bookstore\";
```

Chapter 8

PROC SQL Enhancements in Version 9

Several enhancements have been made in SAS Version 9 that improve the functionality of PROC SQL. If you are migrating from SAS Version 6 or SAS Version 7, a review of the features introduced in SAS Version 8 is recommended. Major changes to PROC SQL designed to more closely tie PROC SQL to the ANSI SQL-92 standard were introduced in SAS Version 8.

Working with PROC SQL

PROC SQL options

THREADS option

PROC SQL now supports parallel processing for sort operations. The THREADS option is specified when PROC SQL is invoked enables multithreaded sorting. The default setting for this option is THREADS.

BUFNO and BUFSIZE options

The BUFNO option allows for the specification of the number of buffers to be allocated for processing a SAS data set or table. A permanent buffer page size can be set with the BUFSIZE option. Each of these options uses the same syntax as the system option of the same name.

In the next example the BUFSIZE option is added to a CREATE statement in PROC SQL to permanently assign a buffer page size to the *client* table. The output of a DESCRIBE statement issued against the newly created table is included in the example.

```
LIBNAME bluesky "C:\mydata\bluesky bookstore\";

CREATE table bluesky.client (bufsize=8704)
         (clientNo   num,
         company     char(40),
         cont_fst    char(10),
         cont_lst    char(15),
         dept        char(25),
         phone       char(25),
         fax         char(25)
         );

DESCRIBE table bluesky.client;
```

SAS log:

```
NOTE: SQL table BLUESKY.CLIENT was created like:

create table BLUESKY.CLIENT( bufsize=8704 )
  (
   clientNo num,
   company char(40),
   cont_fst char(10),
   cont_lst char(15),
   dept char(25),
   phone char(25),
   fax char(25)
  );
```

Output Delivery System

The Output Delivery System (ODS) has been enhanced to provide even more flexibility in generating custom reports. It is covered in detail in Chapter 2, "Working with PROC SQL."

ODS Destinations—DOCUMENT statement

SAS Version 9 introduced the ability to create a SAS document customized by the user in terms of content and order. Results generated from one or more procedures may be output to an ODS document in addition to other destinations such as traditional SAS listings and HTML formatted reports.

An ODS document stores the reports generated by each SQL or other SAS procedure in your program. It allows you to interactively direct these results to one or more destinations without rerunning the procedure. In addition to ODS destinations, an ODS document may be directed to a printed, comma-delimited output or rich-text-format documents in the order you prefer. ODS documents may also be replayed or rerun to generate new results from modified procedures.

In the next example two SELECT statements retrieve the contents of the *orders* and *order_2001_2002* tables. Two formatted destinations are included in the example. The output from the first SELECT statement is directed to an HTML formatted report while the output from the second SELECT statement is directed to a PDF document. The ODS DOCUMENT statement directs the result of each of the queries to a DOCUMENT destination. In each case, the traditional SAS listing is also generated.

```
PROC SQL;
LIBNAME bluesky "C:\mydata\bluesky bookstore\";

ODS document;

ODS html;
     TITLE1'Orders table ';

     SELECT     *
     FROM       bluesky.orders
     ORDER BY   BY     ord_date;
ODS html close;

ODS pdf;
     TITLE1 'Historical Orders';

     SELECT     *
     FROM       bluesky.order_2001_2002
     ORDER BY   ord_date;
ODS pdf close;

ODS document close;
QUIT;
```

> **Tip:** Each ODS destination is initiated before the report or reports to be output to that destination, and closed when the destination no longer applies. The PROC SQL invocation statement may occur either before or after the ODS DOCUMENT or ODS HTML statement in the above example.

The Results window after the execution of the above statements is shown in the following figure. For each SELECT statement, a set of query results has been generated including a SAS listing, an ODS document, and an HTML or PDF document depending on the query. The ODS document contains the raw output generated by the SELECT statement. It can be directed to one or more forms of formatted output from the Results window, eliminating the need to rerun the query.

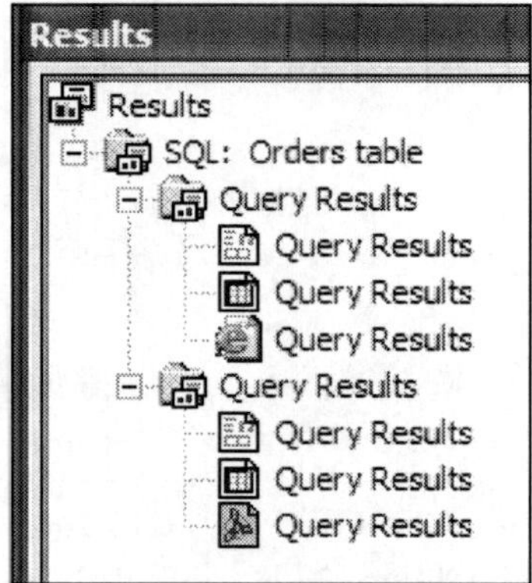

In the next figure the ODS document for the second query is highlighted and the right mouse button clicked to display a menu. The Open As option on the menu allows for the selection of a new destination for the output. The Replay option on the menu reexecutes the query, generating a new SAS listing.

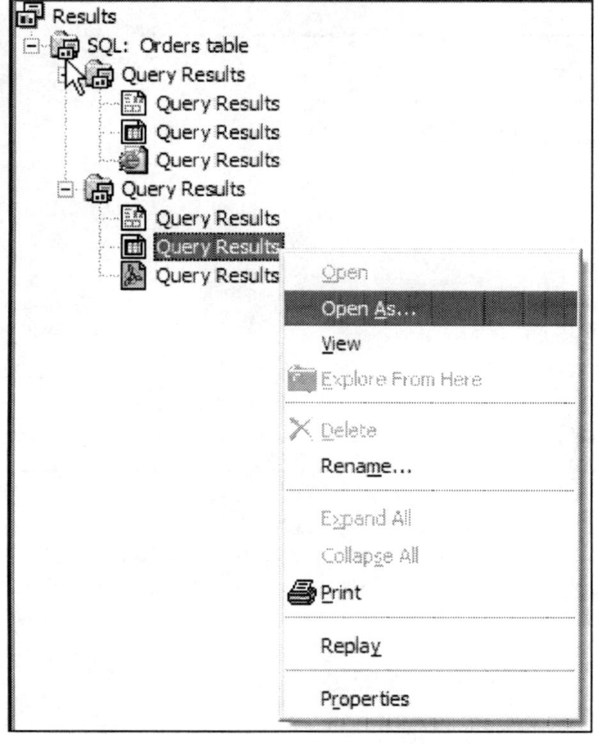

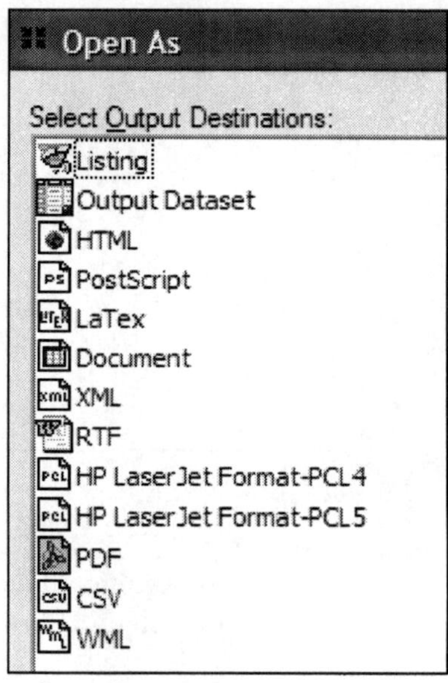

ODS third-party, formatted destinations and TEMPLATE procedures

Procedure output can be generated using markup languages such as HTML4 and XML. For added flexibility, SAS Version 9 has introduced the TEMPLATE procedure that allows you to create your own markup language tagsets or modify existing markup languages.

Three options are available for viewing available style templates: the SQL and TEMPLATE procedures and the SAS graphical user interface.

In the next example a SELECT statement is run against the *styles* dictionary table, retrieving the style names. A partial listing is provided in the example using the OUTOBS option to limit the number of rows reported.

```
PROC SQL outobs=10;

SELECT  style
FROM    dictionary.styles;
```

```
Style Name
________________________________

Styles.Analysis
Styles.Astronomy
Styles.Banker
Styles.BarrettsBlue
Styles.Beige
Styles.Brick
Styles.Brown
Styles.Curve
Styles.D3d
Styles.Default
```

Alternatively, PROC TEMPLATE shown in the next example can be used to generate the same list. Additional information such as the creation date may be requested through the addition of a STATS option as shown.

```
LIBNAME bluesky "C:\mydata\bluesky bookstore\";

PROC TEMPLATE;
  list styles /
  stats=all;
RUN;
```

PROC TEMPLATE can also be used to define new style templates. In the next example a new style called *greenYellow* is created setting attributes for the body and title. The style definition is stored in the bluesky library. The new style is applied to a report created in PROC SQL through an ODS statement that precedes the report.

> **Tip:** If you define your style template with selected style elements, all remaining elements are assigned default style attributes. Messages such as those below will appear in your SAS log indicating where default style attributes were used.
>
> ```
> NOTE: Unable to find the "SystemFooter" style element.
>       Default style attributes will be used.
>
> NOTE: Unable to find the "SysTitleAndFooterContainer" style
>       element. Default style attributes will be used.
> ```

```
PROC TEMPLATE;
define style bluesky.greenYellow;

style body /
         font_face=arial
         font_size=8
         background=dark green
         foreground=white;

style SystemTitle /
      font_face=arial
      font_size=10
      foreground=yellow
      font_style=italic;
end;
run;

ODS html style=bluesky.greenYellow;

PROC SQL;
TITLE1    'Current Client List';
SELECT    company 'Client Name' format=$30.,
          cat(cont_fst, cont_lst)'Contact' format=$30.,
          dept 'Department'
FROM      bluesky.client;

ODS html close;
```

Available template styles can also be accessed interactively from within the SAS graphical user interface Results window as shown in the figure below. Both SAS-supplied and user-defined style templates can be listed here. In addition, any of the style templates can be opened and copied, allowing you to create a new style from an existing one very quickly.

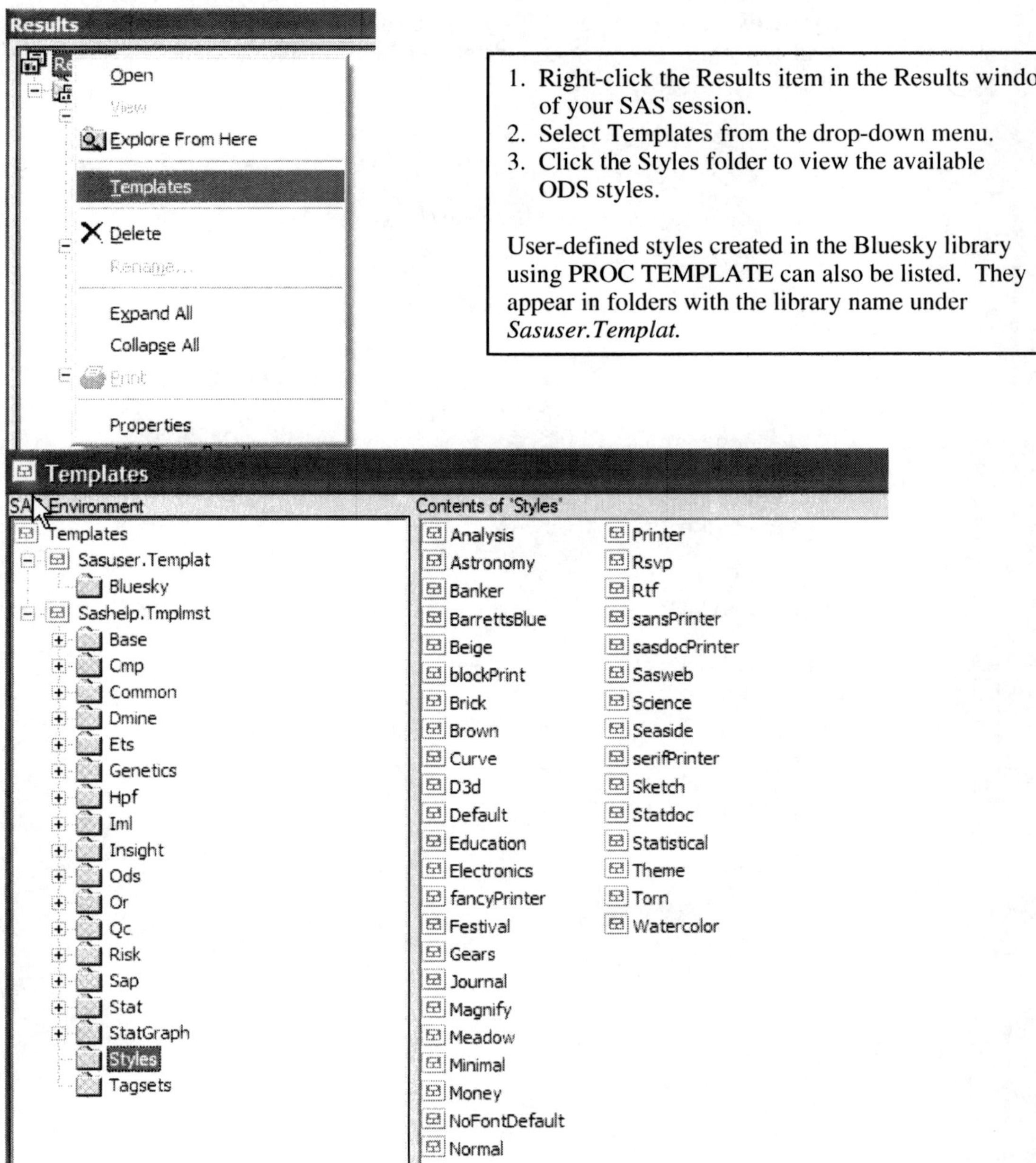

1. Right-click the Results item in the Results window of your SAS session.
2. Select Templates from the drop-down menu.
3. Click the Styles folder to view the available ODS styles.

User-defined styles created in the Bluesky library using PROC TEMPLATE can also be listed. They appear in folders with the library name under *Sasuser.Templat.*

Understanding the SELECT statement

SELECT clause

The translation or remapping of characters required to move data between operating environments that use different encodings is handled by the TRANSCODE option. The TRANSCODE option, with a value of YES or NO, is added as a column modifier in the SELECT clause.

FROM clause

SAS data sets and tables can now be referenced by physical filename rather than the traditional two-level qualifier using a libref and tablename. This flexibility is especially helpful when working with SQL used in interactive applications such as htmSQL. For example, JavaScript can be used to locate a file and return its full physical location and name that can be substituted into an SQL statement in an htmSQL input file.

In the next example the complete directory path and file name are included on the FROM clause in the first SELECT statement. The second SELECT statement draws from the same *orders* table using the traditional two-level qualifier. Both queries are equally correct.

```
SELECT    *
FROM      "C:\mydata\bluesky bookstore\orders.sas7bdat";


LIBNAME bluesky "C:\mydata\bluesky bookstore\";
SELECT    *
FROM      bluesky.orders;
```

Functions

The SUBSTRN function

The SUBSTRN function expands the functionality of the substring function (SUBSTR) and brings it more in line with the ANSI standard. Unlike the SUBSTR function, the new SUBSTRN function allows a result of length zero. The syntax of the two substring functions is the same and the SUBSTR function continues to be available.

Creating and maintaining tables

Formats

The maximum length for format names, both character and numeric, have been increased. The new length for character format names is 31; numeric format names up to a length of 32 are now allowed.

A new informat STIMERw. has been introduced. It is designed to determine the nature of the time value when it is read, distinguishing between hours, minutes, and seconds. It can be used to read the output of the STIMER system option that provides processing time information for PROC SQL and other procedures.

Interactive Applications

Macro variables

Macro variables assigned on an INTO clause can now include a leading zero in their name. The next example includes four macro variable ranges with the first variable in the range assigned a value of 01. As a result, each of the macro variables from 1 to 9 in the series will have a macro variables name with a leading zero. For example, the first two client macro variables will be named client01 and client02.

```
SELECT   clientno, totsale "Total sales" ,
         quantity "Total quantity",
         totsale/quantity "Price per book"
INTO     :client01- :client50, :bksum01 - :bksum50,
         :bkamt01 through :bkamt50, :bkpr01 thru :bkpr50
FROM     bluesky.orders
WHERE    ord_date between '01MAR2004'd and '30MAY2004'd;
```

The scope of a specific macro variable may be checked using one of two new macro functions. The function %SYMLOCAL checks the macro symbol tables to determine if its macro variable argument is local in scope; %SYMGLOBL is used to check for a global macro variable. A third new function %SYMEXIST checks the macro symbol tables to determine if a specific macro variable exists in the tables. These functions are very useful for quickly checking the scope of a single macro variable if your macro results are suspect.

In the example below, the %SYMGLOBL function is included in a %IF-%THEN-%ELSE statement within the macro to check the scope of the macro variable *bksum*. If the macro variable *bksum* is recorded in the global symbol table the function evaluates to 1 or TRUE; otherwise, it evaluates to 0 or FALSE. The outcome of the function determines which message is written to the SAS log, a portion of which is included in the example. A %SYMEXIST function in a %PUT statement is included outside of the macro *orderchk* to check for the existence of the *bksum* variable. Notice that the message written to the SAS log is preceded by a 1, the value returned by the function when it evaluates to TRUE.

```
LIBNAME bluesky "C:\mydata\bluesky bookstore\";
PROC SQL noprint;

SELECT    sum(totsale), sum(quantity) ,
          mean(totsale/quantity)
INTO      :bksum, :bkamt, :bkprice
FROM      bluesky.orders
WHERE     ord_date between '01APR2004'd and '30MAY2004'd;

%macro orderck;
   %if &bkprice > 25.00 %then %do;
        PROC SQL;
        TITLE2   "Average price per book > $25 for the period";
        SELECT ord_date, clientno, prodcode,
               totsale format=comma10.,
               quantity format=comma6.
        FROM   bluesky.orders
        WHERE  ord_date between '01APR2004'd and '30MAY2004'd;
   %end;
```

```
   %if &bksum < 10000 %then %do;
        PROC SQL;
        TITLE2 "Total sales < $10,000 for the period";
        SELECT clientno, prodcode,
               totsale format=comma10.
        FROM    bluesky.orders
        WHERE   ord_date between '01APR2004'd and '30MAY2004'd;
   %end;
   %if &bkamt > 3000 %then %do;
        PROC SQL;
        TITLE2 "Total quantity sold > 3000 for the period";
        SELECT clientno, prodcode,
               quantity format=comma6.
        FROM   bluesky.orders
        WHERE  ord_date between '01APR2004'd and '30MAY2004'd;
   %end;

   %if %SYMGLOBL(bksum)%then %put The macro variable bksum is
       global in scope
   %else %put The macro variable bksum is local in scope;

%mend orderck;
%orderck;
%put %SYMEXIST(bksum) is the value of the function;
```

SAS log:

```
The macro variable bksum is global in scope
1508
1509  %put %SYMEXIST(bksum) is the value of the function;
1 is the value of the function
1510
```

Tip: To return all user-defined global or local macro variables stored in the macro symbol table %PUT _GLOBAL_ and %PUT _LOCAL_ are used. Refer to Chapter 7, "Building Interactive Applications," for more details on %PUT options that are useful when working with macros.

Dictionary tables

Several new dictionary tables and associated SASHELP views have been added. The new dictionary tables together with a brief description are summarized in the following table. In addition, some of the dictionary tables have been expanded to include new columns. A complete description of each dictionary table can be found in Appendix B, "Dictionary Table Descriptions."

Dictionary table name	Description of contents
check_constraints	Information on check constraints
constraint_column_usage	Information on columns associated with integrity constraints
constraint_table_usage	Information on tables associated with integrity constraints
dictionaries	Information on all DICTIONARY tables
engines	Available engines
formats	Formats and informats currently accessible
goptions	Information about currently defined graphics options
libnames	Currently defined SAS data libraries
referential_constraints	Information about referential constraints
styles	Information about known ODS styles
table_constraints	Information about integrity constraints defined in known tables

SAS/ACCESS interface

New options have been added that assist in optimization of SQL queries when one or more of the tables is stored in a database.

MULTI_DATASRC_OPT

The MULTI_DATASRC_OPT LIBNAME option assists in the optimization of joins that cannot be passed to a DBMS for processing, such as those involving tables in different databases. When the option is set to IN_CLAUSE, SAS attempts to generate a set of unique values from one of the tables involved in the join. If both of the tables are stored within an RDBMS, the smaller of the two tables is used to generate the IN clause. If the join is between a database table and a table stored on disk, the table external to the database is used to create the IN clause of unique values.

In the next example the MULTI_DATASRC_OPT is set to IN_CLAUSE in a LIBNAME statement referencing an Oracle database. When the query is processed the smaller of the two tables, *address*, is used to generate an in clause of unique values.

```
PROC SQL;

LIBNAME   orablue ORACLE
          user=scott password=tiger path=master schema=bluesky
          multi_datasrc_opt=in_clause;

LIBNAME   sqlsrvr ODBC
          datasrc='bluesky' user=wayne password=john
          multi_datasrc_opt=in_clause;

SELECT    o.ord_date, o.totsale, o.clientno, a.city
FROM      orablue.orders (sasdatefmt=(ord_date='date9.')) o,
          sqlsrvr.address a
WHERE     o.clientno = a.clientno;
```

Tip: The SAS date format specified in parentheses after the orders table name in the FROM clause of this query is used to control the format of the dates retrieved from the database table. Without this format, the dates are displayed in a date timestamp format. More information on working with dates in database tables is included in Appendix C, "Information for Database Users."

Notice the position of the FROM clause option; it appears after the name of the table it is associated with but before the alias.

DBMASTER

The DBMASTER option is set to the name of the table SAS is to consider the master when an SQL statement includes a join between tables from two different databases. Generally, this is the larger of the two tables.

In the next example the SELECT statement from the previous example has been modified to indicate the larger of the two tables, *orders,* as the master table in the join operation.

```
PROC SQL;

LIBNAME   orablue ORACLE
          user=scott password=tiger path=master schema=bluesky;

LIBNAME   sqlsrvr ODBC
          datasrc='bluesky' user=wayne password=john;

SELECT    o.ord_date, o.totsale, o.clientno, a.city
FROM      orablue.orders (dbmaster=yes
          sasdatefmt=(ord_date='date9.')) o,
          sqlsrvr.address a
WHERE     o.clientno = a.clientno;
```

Tip: When multiple options are set for the same table in a FROM clause, they appear in parentheses separated by a space.

DBSLICE and DBSLICEPARM

The DBSLICE and DBSLICEPARM options are related to threaded reads. A WHERE clause designed by the user to generate suitable query components or partitions for threaded reads is set as the DBSLICE option. The DBSLICEPARM option controls the scope of the threaded reads and the number of threads.

In the next example the DBSLICE option is used to partition the *orders* table in the Oracle database in the order date (ord_date) column. The date format used to specify the DBSLICE criteria is database-specific. For each criterion provided, a new slice of the *orders* table is created and each is handled by a separate thread.

```
LIBNAME     orablue ORACLE
            user=scott password=tiger path=master schema=bluesky;

SELECT      stock.prodcode "Product Code" format=$15.,
            stock.auth_lst "Author" format=$15.,
            avg(orders.quantity) as mnqty
            "Average Quantity" format=comma8.,
            avg(stock.price) as mnprice "Average Price" format=
            comma10.2,
            sum(orders.quantity*stock.price) as smprice
            "Quantity * Price" format= comma10.2

FROM        orablue.orders
            (DBSLICE=("ord_date <'01-JAN-04'" "ord_date >=
             '01-JAN-04'")),
            orablue.stock
WHERE       orders.prodcode = stock.prodcode

GROUP BY stock.prodcode, stock.auth_lst
ORDER BY stock.auth_lst;
```

Tip: These options are available only for DB2 UNIX/PC, ODBC, Oracle, Sybase, and Teradata.

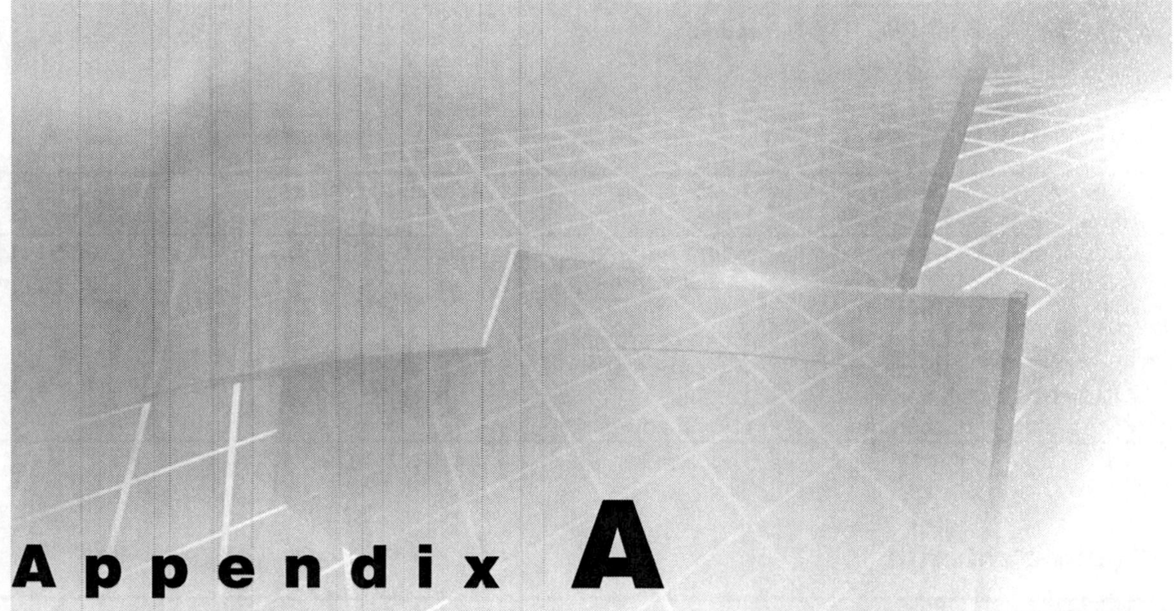

Appendix A

Bluesky Publishing Tables

Address

Description

The *address* table contains a detailed address for each client. Each client is allowed more than one address in the table. As a result, a table row is uniquely identified by a combination of client number (CLIENTNO) and address (ADDRESS).

Columns

Column name	Data type	Description	Associated tables
CLIENTNO	Numeric	Client number	CLIENT, ORDERS, ORDER_2001_2002
ADDRESS	Character	Street address	
CITY	Character	City	
STATE	Character	State or province	
ZIP_POST	Character	Zip or postal code	
COUNTRY	Character	Country	
EMAIL	Character	E-mail address	

Table contents

clientNo	address	city	state	ZIP_post	country	email
1001	6015 Pine Street	Austin	TX	77703-1232	USA	eagleton@usa.com
2010	951 South King Drive	Chicago	IL	60628	USA	Hdavis@cat.org
3007	200 Trinity St.	Cambridge		CB23NG	UK	allace@unimedya.net
4008	6D Lor Ampas	Singapore		328781	Singapore	clements@biz.comp
5005	102S North Terrace	Adelaide		5005	Australia	ebaird@eod.people
6090	Flemmingstr. 270	Berlin		12163	Germany	g_smith@home.com
7008	190 rue de l'Arc de Triomphe	Paris		75017	France	cjennings@medien.print
8003	359 T 41st at Dunbar	Vancouver	BC	V5K2C3	Canada	acaston@usa.com

Client

Description

The *client* table includes contact information for each client. A single client may have more than one contact. As a result, a table row is uniquely identified by a combination of client number (CLIENTNO), last name (LST_NAME), first name (FST_NAME).

Columns

Column name	Data type	Description	Associated tables
CLIENTNO	Numeric	Client number	ADDRESS, ORDERS, ORDER_2001_2002
COMPANY	Character	Client company	
CONT_FST	Character	Contact first name	
CONT_LST	Character	Contact last name	
DEPT	Character	Contact's department	
PHONE	Character	Contact's phone number, including area code	
FAX	Character	Contact's fax number, including area code	

Table contents

clientNo	company	cont_fst	cont_lst	dept	phone	fax
1001	University of Texas	Alice	Eagleton	Administrative	512-495-4370	512-495-4374
2010	Chicago State University	Holee	Davis	Marketing	312-756-7890	
3007	Heffers Booksellers	Marge	Wallace	Sales	01223-568568	01223-354936
4008	National University of Singapore	John	Clements	Administrative	874-2339	
5005	University of Adelaide	Emily	Baird	Information technology	61-8-8303-4402	61-8-8830-4405
6090	Heymann's	Gary	Smith	marketing	49-30-8252573	49-30-8242690
7008	Cosmos 2000	Curtis	Jennings	Information technology	33-14-362-1899	33-14-352-1929
8003	Lawrence Books	Alan	Caston	Information technology	604-261-3612	604-261-3756

Currency

Description

The *currency* table contains historical exchange rates between US dollars and other currencies. For each currency, an average exchange rate for one month is stored. Each row in the table is uniquely identified by the currency (CURRENCY) and the date (CUR_DATE).

Columns

Column name	Data type	Description	Associated tables
CURRENCY	Character (length 3)	Type of currency	ORDERS, ORDER_2001_2002
CUR_DATE	Date	Date of currency exchange rate	
EXCHRATE	Numeric	Currency exchange rate	

Table contents

currency	cur_date	exchRate	currency	cur_date	exchRate	currency	cur_date	exchRate
USD	1-Jan-03	1	USD	1-Aug-03	1	USD	1-Mar-04	1
EUR	1-Jan-03	0.94160	EUR	1-Aug-03	0.89678	EUR	1-Mar-04	0.81540
SGD	1-Jan-03	1.73628	SGD	1-Aug-03	1.75323	SGD	1-Mar-04	1.70165
AUD	1-Jan-03	1.71592	AUD	1-Aug-03	1.53413	AUD	1-Mar-04	1.33446
CAD	1-Jan-03	1.54145	CAD	1-Aug-03	1.39553	CAD	1-Mar-04	1.32894
USD	1-Feb-03	1	USD	1-Sep-03	1	USD	1-Apr-04	1
EUR	1-Feb-03	0.92726	EUR	1-Sep-03	0.88925	EUR	1-Apr-04	0.83267
SGD	1-Feb-03	1.74514	SGD	1-Sep-03	1.74698	SGD	1-Apr-04	1.68325
AUD	1-Feb-03	1.67930	AUD	1-Sep-03	1.51142	AUD	1-Apr-04	1.33851
CAD	1-Feb-03	1.51215	CAD	1-Sep-03	1.36443	CAD	1-Apr-04	1.33898
USD	1-Mar-03	1	USD	1-Oct-03	1	USD	1-May-04	1
GBP	1-Mar-03	0.92637	EUR	1-Oct-03	0.85461	EUR	1-May-04	0.83349
SGD	1-Mar-03	1.75511	SGD	1-Oct-03	1.73361	SGD	1-May-04	1.71124
AUD	1-Mar-03	1.66290	AUD	1-Oct-03	1.44498	AUD	1-May-04	1.41819
CAD	1-Mar-03	1.47608	CAD	1-Oct-03	1.32373	CAD	1-May-04	1.37745
USD	1-Apr-03	1	USD	1-Nov-03	1	USD	1-Jun-04	1
EUR	1-Apr-03	0.92075	EUR	1-Nov-03	0.85405	EUR	1-Jun-04	0.82327
SGD	1-Apr-03	1.77712	SGD	1-Nov-03	1.72961	SGD	1-Jun-04	1.71305
AUD	1-Apr-03	1.63977	AUD	1-Nov-03	1.39728	AUD	1-Jun-04	1.43931
CAD	1-Apr-03	1.45820	CAD	1-Nov-03	1.31250	CAD	1-Jun-04	1.36025
USD	1-May-03	1	USD	1-Dec-03	1	USD	1-Jul-04	1
EUR	1-May-03	0.86563	EUR	1-Dec-03	0.81372	EUR	1-Jul-04	0.81557

Table contents *(continued)*

currency	cur_date	exchRate	currency	cur_date	exchRate	currency	cur_date	exchRate
SGD	1-May-03	1.73571	SGD	1-Dec-03	1.71168	SGD	1-Jul-04	1.71462
AUD	1-May-03	1.54638	AUD	1-Dec-03	1.35421	AUD	1-Jul-04	1.40982
CAD	1-May-03	1.38396	CAD	1-Dec-03	1.31361	CAD	1-Jul-04	1.32778
USD	1-Jun-03	1	USD	1-Jan-04	1			
EUR	1-Jun-03	0.85341	EUR	1-Jan-04	0.79411			
SGD	1-Jun-03	1.73090	SGD	1-Jan-04	1.69837			
AUD	1-Jun-03	1.50509	AUD	1-Jan-04	1.30219			
CAD	1-Jun-03	1.35297	CAD	1-Jan-04	1.29660			
USD	1-Jul-03	1	USD	1-Feb-04	1			
EUR	1-Jul-03	0.87561	EUR	1-Feb-04	0.79293			
SGD	1-Jul-03	1.76712	SGD	1-Feb-04	1.68812			
AUD	1-Jul-03	1.53064	AUD	1-Feb-04	1.28946			
CAD	1-Jul-03	1.38795	CAD	1-Feb-04	1.32906			

Orders

Description

The orders table includes orders placed in the years 2003 and 2004. Each table row is uniquely identified by a combination of client number (CLIENTNO) and invoice number (INVOICE).

Columns

Column name	Data type	Description	Associated tables
PRODCODE	Character	Book product code	STOCK
ORD_DATE	Date	Date order placed	
QUANTITY	Numeric	Number of books order	
TOTSALE	Numeric	Total order price	
CURRENCY	Character	Currency of invoice	CURRENCY
DELCODE	Character	Order delivery method	SHIPPING
CLIENTNO	Numeric	Client number	CLIENT, ADDRESS
INVOICE	Character	Invoice number	

Table contents

prodCode	ord_date	quantity	totsale	currency	delCode	clientNo	invoice
300456	7-Feb-03	300	2850.00	USD	UPS	1001	030207-01
300680	6-May-03	150	2175.00	USD	EXE	1001	030506-01
400178	6-May-03	500	32875.00	USD	UPS	1001	030506-01
500120	6-May-03	600	20700.00	USD	UPS	1001	030506-01
200345	10-Nov-03	1400	76972.00	SGD	EXE	4008	031110-01
300680	20-Oct-03	2900	3390.00	USD	UPS	2010	031020-01
400100	15-Mar-03	125	5468.75	SGD	EXE	4008	030315-01
400128	11-Apr-03	200	6800.00	EUR	UPS	7008	030411-01
400100	11-Apr-03	200	8750.00	AUD	UPS	5005	030411-01
600125	24-Jun-03	350	2432.5	EUR	EXE	3007	030624-01
300456	7-Feb-03	50	475.00	EUR	UPS	3007	030207-02
300678	9-Jan-03	275	4661.25	CAD	GRN	8003	030109-01
100340	9-Jan-03	800	14400.00	CAD	UPS	8003	030109-01
500120	6-Sep-03	1000	34500.00	USD	UPS	1001	030906-01
200345	27-Sep-03	500	27490.00	EUR	EXE	6090	030927-01
600125	1-Feb-04	12	83.40	CAD	GRN	8003	040101-01
600780	1-Feb-04	103	885.80	SGD	EXP	4008	040101-02
100406	7-Mar-04	45	675.00	EUR	EXP	3007	040307-01
100345	10-Mar-04	180	11700.00	EUR	EXP	7008	040310-01
400100	10-Mar-04	350	15312.50	CAD	EXA	8003	040310-02
500500	10-Mar-04	70	1645.00	USD	EXA	8003	040310-02
600125	10-Mar-04	100	1250.00	SGD	EXP	4008	040310-04
200507	8-Apr-04	20	1490.00	SGD	EXP	4008	040408-01
300456	10-Apr-04	55	797.50	EUR	EXP	6090	040410-01
200145	12-Apr-04	700	39375.00	USD	EXE	2010	040412-01
400128	12-Apr-04	1230	41820.00	USD	EXE	2010	040412-01
500238	12-Apr-04	200	4450.00	AUD	EXP	5005	040412-02
600489	12-Apr-04	25	137.50	EUR	EX	7008	040412-03
600125	5-May-04	600	8580.00	USD	EXE	2010	040505-01
500127	7-Jun-04	324	8505.00	USD	EXE	2010	040607-01
500168	20-Jul-04	335	11390.00	AUD	EXP	5005	040720-01
400345	11-May-04	25	2150.00	SGD	EXP	4008	041011-01
100890	12-May-04	260	17940.00	EUR	EXP	3007	041012-01
100340	12-Jun-04	20	360.00	CAD	GRN	8003	041212-01
200678	12-Jun-04	5000	225000.00	EUR	EXP	3007	041212-02
300289	12-Jun-04	30	1080.00	EUR	EXP	6090	041212-03
100601	23-Jul-04	590	15487.50	EUR	EXP	3007	041223-01
400102	23-Jul-04	1500	82500.00	AUD	EXP	5005	041223-02
400178	23-Jul-04	10	657.50	EUR	EXP	6090	041223-03
500116	23-Jul-04	400	13600.00	EUR	EXP	7008	041223-04

Order_2001_2002

Description

The *order_2001_2002* table includes orders placed in the years 2001 and 2002. Each table row is uniquely identified by a combination of client number (CLIENTNO) and invoice number (INVOICE).

Columns

Column name	Data type	Description	Associated tables
PRODCODE	Character	Book product code	STOCK
ORD_DATE	Date	Date order placed	
QUANTITY	Numeric	Number of books order	
TOTSALE	Numeric	Total order price	
CURRENCY	Character	Currency of invoice	CURRENCY
DELCODE	Character	Order delivery method	SHIPPING
CLIENTNO	Numeric	Client number	CLIENT, ADDRESS
INVOICE	Character	Invoice number	

Table contents

prodCode	ord_date	quantity	totsale	currency	delCode	clientNo	invoice
500120	28-Feb-01	120	4140.00	GBP	UPS	3007	010228-01
600451	16-Jan-01	520	6500.00	FRF	EXE	7008	010116-01
400457	5-Jan-01	650	48522.50	USD	UPS	1001	010105-01
400100	5-Jan-01	90	3937.50	USD	UPS	1001	010105-01
100345	9-Mar-01	1250	81250.00	CAD	EXE	8003	010309-01
600780	30-Mar-01	80	688.00	FRF	UPS	7008	010330-01
400100	20-Apr-01	125	5468.75	DEM	EXE	6090	010420-01
400128	20-Apr-01	200	6800.00	GBP	UPS	3007	010420-02
500500	6-Apr-01	200	4700.00	CAD	UPS	8003	010406-01
500500	6-Jun-01	475	11162.5	GBP	EXE	3007	010606-01
200345	26-May-01	500	27490.00	GBP	UPS	3007	010526-01
600780	9-Jun-01	475	4085.00	CAD	GRN	8003	010609-01
100345	21-Aug-01	1500	97500.00	CAD	UPS	8003	010821-01
500120	6-Oct-01	1000	34500.00	USD	UPS	1001	011006-01
200345	5-Dec-01	125	6872.50	DEM	EXE	6090	011205-01
600125	17-Nov-01	300	2085.00	CAD	GRN	8003	011117-01
600780	31-Jan-02	100	860.00	USD	EXP	1001	020131-01
300680	7-Feb-02	125	1812.50	GBP	EXP	3007	020207-01

Table contents *(contineud)*

prodCode	ord_date	quantity	totsale	currency	delCode	clientNo	invoice
300678	27-Feb-02	950	16102.50	FRF	EXP	7008	020227-01
200345	29-Mar-02	300	16494.00	CAD	EXA	8003	020329-01
200678	29-Mar-02	70	3150.00	CAD	EXA	8003	020329-01
600125	29-Mar-02	100	695.00	CAD	EXP	8003	020329-01
400178	9-Apr-02	1000	65750.00	USD	EXP	1001	020409-01
200145	23-Apr-02	25	1406.25	DEM	EXP	6090	020423-01
200145	17-May-02	700	39375.00	CAD	EXE	8003	020517-01
100340	29-Jun-02	1500	27000.00	USD	EXE	1001	020629-01
100601	13-Jul-02	200	5250.00	AUD	EXP	5005	020713-01
600489	31-Aug-02	25	137.50	FRF	EX	7008	020831-01
600125	5-Sep-02	675	4691.25	USD	EXE	1001	020905-01
200345	17-Oct-02	985	54155.30	USD	EXE	1001	021017-01
300680	18-Oct-02	235	3407.50	DEM	EXP	6090	021018-01
100340	5-Nov-02	65	1170.00	AUD	EXP	5005	021105-01
100340	6-Dec-02	890	16020.00	GBP	EXP	3007	021206-01
500500	7-Dec-02	135	3172.50	CAD	GRN	8003	021207-01
200678	28-Dec-02	1200	54000.00	GBP	EXP	3007	021228-01

Reprint

Description

The reprint table contains details on the cutoff levels that trigger when a book is to be reprinted. Each row in the table is unique.

Columns

Column name	Data type	Description	Associated tables
REPRINT	Character	Code corresponding to the cutoff level	STOCK
CUTOFF	Numeric	Inventory level that triggers a print run of a book	

Table contents

reprint	cutOff
A	0
B	10
C	50
D	100
E	500
F	1000

Shipping

Description

The shipping table includes all of the available shipping options and the charge for each. Each row in the table is unique.

Columns

Column name	Data type	Description	Associated tables
DELCODE	Character	delivery code	ORDERS, ORDER_2001_2002
DELTYPE	Character	delivery description	
CHARGE	Numeric	rate charged for delivery	

Table contents

delCode	delType	charge
EXE	2 day Express shipping	15.00
UPS	US postal service	10.00
EXP	express mail	10.00
EXA	express air delivery	15.00
GRN	ground delivery	10.00

Stock

Description

The stock table includes specific information about each of the books published by the Bluesky Publishing Company. Each table row is uniquely identified by either product code (PRODCODE) or ISBN.

Columns

Column name	Data type	Description	Associated tables
ISBN	Character	Library identification number	
TITLE	Character	Book title	
AUTH_FST	Character	Author's first name	
AUTH_LST	Character	Author's last name	
CATEGORY	Character	Book Category	
REPRINT	Character	Reprint code	REPRINT
STOCK	Numeric	Copies of book in stock	
YRPUBL	Numeric	Year book was published	
PRODCODE	Character	Book product code	
PRICE	Numeric	Price per book	

Table contents

ISBN	title	auth_fst	auth_lst	category	reprint	stock	yrPubl	prodCode	price
1-7890-1072-1	Decorative Arts	Greg	Evans	arts	E	1500	1999	300678	16.95
1-7890-2878-7	The Ultimate Philosophy	Cory	Johnson	arts	C	100	1999	300456	9.50
1-7890-1256-2	Democracy in America	Jeff	Thompson	arts	C	55	2003	300289	36.00
1-7890-5477-x	The Underground Economy	Arlene	Tee	arts	E	1000	2000	300680	14.50
1-7890-1209-0	The Art of Computer Programming	Corinna	Keenmon	computer	F	1600	1999	500120	34.50
1-7890-1378-x	New User's Guide to Computers	Jennifer	Mathson	computer	D	350	2003	500127	26.25
1-7890-7648-x	Visual Basic for Beginners	Denise	Kizer	computer	E	600	2003	500168	34.00
1-7890-5634-9	Start a Business Using a Computer	Roy	Wilson	computer	F	1000	2002	500238	22.25
1-7890-3473-6	Introduction to Computer_Science	April	Jensen	computer	D	1000	2002	500890	32.50

(continued)

Table contents *(continued)*

ISBN	title	auth_fst	auth_lst	category	reprint	stock	yrPubl	prodCode	price
1-7890-2829-9	Computer: Beginners Guide	Rosanna	Marossy	computer	D	100	2000	500500	23.50
1-7890-3245-8	Engineering Infrastructure Modeling	Merrill	Frank	engineering	E	2400	1999	200345	54.98
1-7890-1290-2	Space Sciences	Ian	Bishop	engineering	F	1500	2001	200145	56.25
1-7890-5698-5	Managing Water Resources	Brian	Kerwin	engineering	F	6000	2001	200678	45.00
1-7890-1267-8	Materials Science	Andrew	Bole	engineering	C	50	2000	200507	74.50
1-7890-4578-9	Risks in Life - % Gain or Loss?	Paul	Smith	general	F	1000	2000	600123	14.30
1-7890-3468-x	Women Writers	Alex	Paul	general	E	1000	2000	600780	8.60
1-7890-2390-4	Greece and Beyond	Clark	Foutz	general	D	398	2000	600451	12.50
1-7890-3278-4	Mountaineering Skills	Chris	Lillard	general	B	200	2000	600489	5.50
1-7890-3007-2	The Maestro	Alexander	Dixon	general	B	100	2000	600125	6.95
1-7890-4578-9	The 10% Solution	Gabe	Haney	medicine	C	400	1999	400457	74.65
1-7890-5475-3	Tibetan Medicine	Wendy	Perry	medicine	F	2000	2000	400128	34.00
1-7890-3467-1	Medications and Maintenance	David	Barry	medicine	B	30	2000	400345	86.00
1-7890-7893-8	Unconventional treatments	Debbie	Hedge	medicine	C	1000	2003	400102	55.00
1-7890-3479-5	National Library of Medicine	Robert	Saravit	medicine	A	35	2001	400178	65.75
1-7890-3891-x	Medical Education in School	Beth	Miler	medicine	B	300	2000	400100	43.75
1-7890-4567-3	Book of Science and Nature	Allison	Clark	science	F	1000	2003	100890	69.00
1-7890-3478-7	Free Thinking in Mathematics	Ken	McMurry	science	E	900	2001	100601	26.25
1-7890-1280-5	Science and Technology	Kay	Davis	science	D	200	2002	100406	15.00
1-7890-5678-0	Science of Biology	Lisa	Sharr	science	D	500	2000	100345	65.00
1-7890-2876-0	Geology: Volcanos	Jena	Richardson	science	D	400	2001	100340	18.00

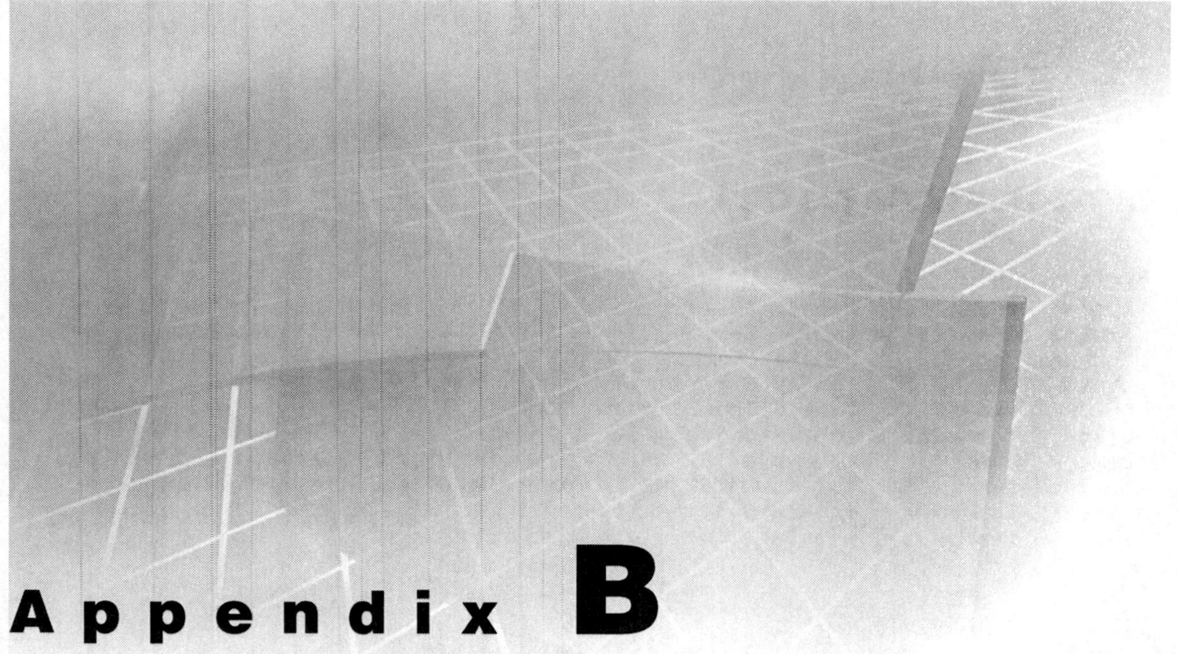

Appendix B

Dictionary Table Descriptions

Each dictionary description was generated using the DESCRIBE statement and edited for readability. All dictionary tables reside in a SAS library called *dictionary*. The example following shows a SELECT statement that is used to retrieve all of the rows from the *styles* dictionary table.

```
PROC SQL;
TITLE " There is no need to include a libref for the dictionary
        library" ;

SELECT  *
FROM    dictionary.styles;
```

The SELECT statements needed to create the associated SAS help views are included for reference.

Note: For dictionary tables available in SAS Version 8, columns and related views new to the table in SAS Version 9 are highlighted. If the entire dictionary table and related views are new to SAS Version 9, a notation to that effect has been added to the table title.

DICTIONARY.CATALOGS

Table description

```
libname  char(8)     label='Library Name'
memname  char(32)    label='Member Name'
memtype  char(8)     label='Member Type'
objname  char(32)    label='Object Name'
objtype  char(8)     label='Object Type'
objdesc  char(256)   label='Object Description'
created  num         format=DATETIME informat=DATETIME label='Date Created'
modified num         format=DATETIME informat=DATETIME label='Date Modified'
alias    char(32)    label='Object Alias'
level    num         label='Library Concatenation Level'
```

SAS Help view:

```
TITLE " SASHELP.VCATALG" ;

CREATE   view sashelp.vcatalg as
SELECT   *
FROM     dictionary.catalogs;
```

CHECK CONSTRAINTS—new to SAS Version 9

Table description

```
constraint_catalog  char(32)  label='Constraint Catalog'
constraint_schema   char(8)   label='Constraint Schema'
constraint_name     char(32)  label='Constraint Name'
check_clause        char(256) label='Check Clause'
```

SAS Help view

```
TITLE " SASHELP.VCHKCON" ;

CREATE   view sashelp.vchkcon as
SELECT   *
FROM     dictionary.check_constraints;
```

COLUMNS

Table description

```
libname        char(8)     label='Library Name'
memname        char(32)    label='Member Name'
memtype        char(8)     label='Member Type'
name           char(32)    label='Column Name'
type           char(4)     label='Column Type'
length         num         label='Column Length'
npos           num         label='Column Position'
varnum         num         label='Column Number in Table'
label          char(256)   label='Column Label'
format         char(49)    label='Column Format'
informat       char(49)    label='Column Informat'
idxusage       char(9)     label='Column Index Type'
sortedby       num         label='Order in Key Sequence'
xtype          char(12)    label='Extended Type'
notnull        char(3)     label='Not NULL?'
precision      num         label='Precision'
scale          num         label='Scale'
transcode      CHAR(3)     LABEL='TRANSCODED?'
```

SAS Help view

```
TITLE " SASHELP.VCOLUMN" ;

CREATE  view sashelp.vcolumn as
SELECT  *
FROM    dictionary.columns;
```

CONSTRAINT COLUMN USAGE—new to SAS Version 9

Table description

```
table_catalog        char(8)   label='Libname'
table_schema         char(8)   label='Table Schema'
table_name           char(32)  label='Table'
column_name          char(32)  label='Column'
constraint_catalog   char(32)  label='Constraint Catalog'
constraint_schema    char(8)   label='Constraint Schema'
constraint_name      char(32)  label='Constraint Name'
```

SAS Help view

```
TITLE " SASHELP.VCNCOLU" ;

CREATE  view sashelp.vcncolu as
SELECT  *
FROM    dictionary.constraints_column_usage;
```

CONSTRAINT TABLE USAGE—new to SAS Version 9

Table description

```
table_catalog       char(8)  label='Libname'
table_schema        char(8)  label='Table Schema'
table_name          char(32) label='Table'
constraint_catalog  char(32) label='Constraint Catalog'
constraint_schema   char(8)  label='Constraint Schema'
constraint_name     char(32) label='Constraint Name'
```

SAS Help view

```
TITLE " SASHELP.VCNTABU" ;

CREATE  view sashelp.vcntabu as
SELECT  *
FROM    dictionary.constraint_table_usage;
```

DICTIONARIES—new to SAS Version 9

Table description

```
memname  char(32)   label='Member Name'
memlabel char(256)  label='Dataset Label'
name     char(32)   label='Column Name'
type     char(4)    label='Column Type'
length   num        label='Column Length'
npos     num        label='Column Position'
varnum   num        label='Column Number in Table'
label    char(256)  label='Column Label'
format   char(49)   label='Column Format'
informat char(49)   label='Column Informat'
```

SAS Help view

```
TITLE " SASHELP.VDCTNRY" ;

CREATE  view sashelp.vdctnry as
SELECT  *
FROM    dictionary.dictionaries;
```

EXTFILES

Table description

```
fileref char(8)    label='Fileref'
xpath   char(1024) label='Path Name'
xengine char(8)    label='Engine Name'
```

SAS Help view

```
TITLE " SASHELP.VEXTFL" ;

CREATE   view sashelp.vextfl as
SELECT   *
FROM     dictionary.extfiles;
```

FORMATS—new to SAS Version 9

Table Description:

```
libname  char(8)     label='Library Name'
memname  char(32)    label='Member Name'
path     char(1024)  label='Path Name'
objname  char(32)    label='Object Name'
fmtname  char(32)    label='Format Name'
fmttype  char(1)     label='Format Type'
source   char(1)     label='Format Source'
minw     Num         label='Minimum Width'
mind     num         label='Minimum Decimal Width'
maxw     num         label='Maximum Width'
maxd     num         label='Maximum Decimal Width'
defw     num         label='Default Width'
defd     num         label='Default Decimal Width'
```

SAS Help view

```
TITLE "SASHELP.VVFORMAT";

CREATE   view sashelp.vformat as
SELECT   *
FROM     dictionary.formats;
```

GOPTIONS—new to SAS Version 9

Table description

```
optname  char(32)    label='Option Name'
opttype  char(8)     label='Option type'
setting  char(1024)  label='Option Setting'
optdesc  char(160)   label='Option Description'
level    char(8)     label='Option Location'
group    char(32)    label='Option Group'
```

SAS Help view

```
TITLE "SASHELP.VGOPT";

CREATE   view sashelp.vgopt as
SELECT   *
FROM     dictionary.goptions;


TITLE " SASHELP.VALLOPT ";

CREATE   view sashelp.vallopt as
         SELECT  *
         FROM    DICTIONARY.OPTIONS
UNION
         SELECT  *
         FROM    DICTIONARY.GOPTIONS;
```

INDEXES

Table description

```
libname  char(8)     label='Library Name'
memname  char(32)    label='Member Name'
memtype  char(8)     label='Member Type'
name     char(32)    label='Column Name'
idxusage char(9)     label='Column Index Type'
indxname char(32)    label='Index Name'
indxpos  num         label='Position of Column in Concatenated Key'
nomiss   char(3)     label='Nomiss Option'
unique   char(3)     label='Unique Option'
```

SAS Help view

```
TITLE   "SASHELP.VINDEX  ";

CREATE   view sashelp.vindex as
SELECT   *
FROM     dictionary.indexes;
```

LIBNAMES—new to SAS Version 9

Table description

```
libname      char(8)    label='Library Name'
engine       char(8)    label='Engine Name'
path         char(1024) label='Path Name'
level        num        label='Library Concatenation Level'
fileformat   char(8)    label='Default File Format'
readonly     char(3)    label='Read-only?'
sequential   char(3)    label='Sequential?'
```

```
sysdesc       char(1024)    label='System Information Description'
sysname       char(1024)    label='System Information Name'
sysvalue      char(1024)    label='System Information Value'
```

SAS Help view

```
TITLE "SASHELP.VLIBNAM  ";

CREATE   view sashelp.vlibnam as
SELECT   *
FROM     dictionary.libnames;
```

MACROS

Table description

```
scope    char(32)     label='Macro Scope'
name     char(32)     label='Macro Variable Name'
offset   num          label='Offset into Macro Variable'
value    char(200)    label='Macro Variable Value'
```

SAS Help view

```
TITLE " SASHELP.VMACRO ";

CREATE   view sashelp.vmacro as
SELECT   *
FROM     dictionary.macros;
```

MEMBERS

Table description

```
libname  char(8)     label='Library Name',
memname  char(32)    label='Member Name',
memtype  char(8)     label='Member Type',
engine   char(8)     label='Engine Name',
index    char(32)    label='Indexes',
path     char(1024) label='Path Name'
```

SAS Help view

```
TITLE " SASHELP.VMEMBER";

CREATE   view sashelp.vmember as
SELECT   *
FROM     dictionary.members;
```

```
TITLE " SASHELP.VSACCES";

CREATE    view sashelp.vsacces as
SELECT    libname, memname
FROM      dictionary.members
WHERE     memtype='ACCESS'
ORDER BY  libname asc, memname asc;


TITLE " SASHELP.VSCATLG " ;

CREATE    view sashelp.vscatalg as
SELECT    libname, memname
FROM      dictionary.members
WHERE     memtype='CATALOG'
ORDER BY  libname asc, memname asc;

TITLE "SASHELP.VSLIB ";

CREATE    view sashelp.vslib as
SELECT    distinct libname, path
FROM      dictionary.members
ORDER BY  libname asc;

TITLE "SASHELP.VSTABLE";

CREATE    view sashelp.vstable as
SELECT    libname, memname
FROM      dictionary.members
WHERE     memtype='DATA'
ORDER by  libname asc, memname asc;

TITLE " SASHELP.VSTABVW ";

CREATE    view sashelp.vstabvw as
SELECT    libname, memname, memtype
FROM      dictionary.members
WHERE     memtype='VIEW' or memtype='DATA'
ORDER BY  libname asc, memname asc;

TITLE " SASHELP.VSVIEW";

CREATE    view sashelp.vsview as
SELECT    libname, memname
FROM      dictionary.members
WHERE     memtype='VIEW'
ORDER BY  libname asc, memname asc;
```

OPTIONS

Table description

```
optname    char(32)      label='Option Name'
opttype    char(8)       label='Option type'
setting    char(1024)    label='Option Setting'
optdesc    char(160)     label='Option Description'
level      char(8)       label='Option Location'
group      char(32)      label='Option Group'
```

SAS Help view

```
TITLE "  SASHELP.VOPTION ";

CREATE   view sashelp.voption as
SELECT   *
FROM     dictionary.options;
```

```
TITLE "  SASHELP.VALLOPT ";

CREATE   view sashelp.vallopt as
         SELECT  *
         FROM    DICTIONARY.OPTIONS
UNION
         SELECT  *
         FROM    DICTIONARY.GOPTIONS;
```

REFERENTAL CONSTRAINTS—new to SAS Version 9

Table description

```
constraint_catalog           char(32) label='Constraint Catalog'
constraint_schema            char(8)  label='Constraint Schema'
constraint_name              char(32) label='Constraint Name'
unique_constraint_catalog    char(32) label='Unique Constraint Catalog'
unique_constraint_schema     char(8)  label='Unique Constraint Schema'
unique_constraint_name       char(32) label='Unique Constraint Name'
match_option                 char(8)  label='Match Option'
update_rule                  char(12) label='Update Rule'
delete_rule                  char(12) label='Delete Rule'
```

SAS Help view

```
title "  SASHELP.VREFCON ";

create   view sashelp.vrefcon as
select   *
from     dictionary.referential_constraints;
```

STYLES

Table description

```
libname  char(8)    label='Library Name'
memname  char(32)   label='Member Name'
style    char(32)   label='Style Name'
crdate   num        format=DATETIME informat=DATETIME label='Date Created'
```

Note: In SAS Version 8, a NOTES column was included in this table. This column was eliminated in SAS Version 9.

SAS Help view

None.

TABLES

Table description

```
libname      char(8)    label='Library Name'
memname      char(32)   label='Member Name'
memtype      char(8)    label='Member Type'
dbms_memtype char(8)    label='dbms member type'
memlabel     char(256)  label='Dataset Label'
typemem      char(8)    label='Dataset Type'
crdate       num        format=DATETIME informat=DATETIME label='Date Created'
modate       num        format=DATETIME informat=DATETIME label='Date Modified'
nobs         num        label='Number of Physical Observations'
obslen       num        label='Observation Length'
nvar         num        label='Number of Variables'
protect      char(3)    label='Type of Password Protection'
compress     char(8)    label='Compression Routine'
encrypt      char(8)    label='Encryption'
npage        num        label='Number of Pages'
filesize     num        label='Size of File'
pcompress    num        label='Percent Compression'
reuse        char(3)    label='Reuse Space'
bufsize      num        label='Bufsize'
delobs       num        label='Number of Deleted Observations'
nlobs        num        label='Number of Logical Observations'
maxvar       num        label='Longest variable name'
maxlabel     num        label='Longest label'
maxgen       num        label='Maximum number of generations'
gen          num        label='Generation number'
attr         char(3)    label='Dataset Attributes'
indxtype     char(9)    label='Type of Indexes'
datarep      char(32)   label='Data Representation'
sortname     char(8)    label='Name of Collating Sequence'
sorttype     char(4)    label='Sorting Type'
sortchar     char(8)    label='Charset Sorted By'
reqvector    char(24)   format=$HEX48 informat=$HEX48 label='Requirements
Vector'
```

```
datarepname  char(170)    label='Data Representation Name'
encoding     char(256)    label='Data Encoding'
audit        char(3)      label='audit trail active'
audit_before char(3)      label='audit before image'
audit_admin  char(3)      label='audit admin image'
audit_error  char(3)      label='audit error image'
audit_data   char(3)      label='audit data image'
```

SAS Help view

```
title "SASHELP.VTABLE";

create   view sashelp.vtable as
select   *
from     dictionary.tables;
```

TABLE CONSTRAINTS—new to SAS Version 9

Table description

```
table_catalog         char(8)   label='Libname'
table_schema          char(8)   label='Table Schema'
table_name            char(32)  label='Table'
constraint_catalog    char(32)  label='Constraint Catalog'
constraint_schema     char(8)   label='Constraint Schema'
constraint_name       char(32)  label='Constraint Name'
constraint_type       char(8)   label='Constraint Type'
is_deferrable         char(1)   label='Is Deferred?'
initially_deferred    char(1)   label='Initially Deferred?'
```

SAS Help view

```
title " SASHELP.VTABCON ";

create   view sashelp.vtabcon as
select   *
from     dictionary.table_constraints;
```

TITLES

Table description

```
type     char(1)      label='Title Location'
number   num          label='Title Number'
text     char(256)    label='Title Text'
```

SAS Help view

```
TITLE " SASHELP.VTITLE ";

CREATE   view sashelp.vtitle as
SELECT   *
FROM     dictionary.titles;
```

VIEWS

Table description

```
libname char(8)      label='Library Name'
memname char(32)     label='Member Name'
memtype char(8)      label='Member Type'
engine  char(8)      label='Engine Name'
```

SAS Help views

```
TITLE " SASHELP.VVIEW  ";

CREATE   view sashelp.vview as
SELECT   *
FROM     dictionary.views;
```

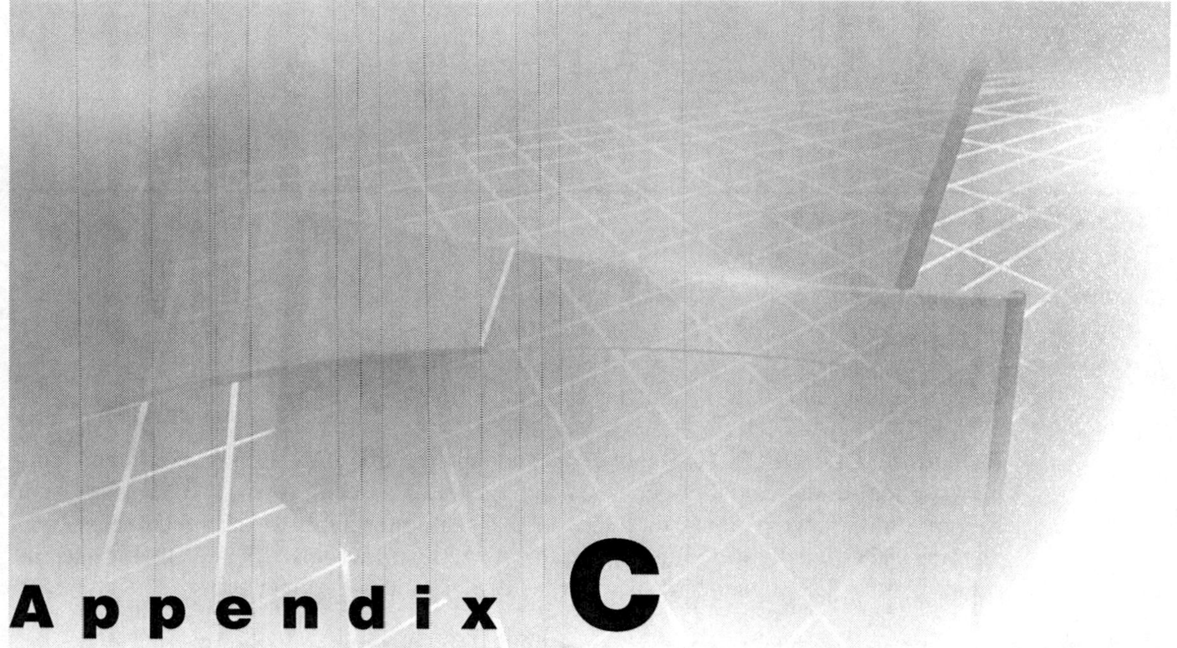

Appendix C

Information for Database Users

SQL Pass-Through Facility

The SQL Pass-Through Facility allows access to the power of a database management system (DBMS) through the familiar SAS interface. PROC SQL statements are submitted to a DBMS, querying tables that reside in the database. In addition to queries, the SQL Pass-Through Facility can be used to create or modify tables and indexes in a database. Database-specific statements can also be issued from PROC SQL.

To use the Pass-Through Facility, you issue a CONNECT statement after the SQL procedure has been invoked with a PROC SQL statement. The CONNECT statement establishes communication with a database, allowing subsequent SQL statements to reference tables and views in that database.

CONNECT statement

General form:

```
CONNECT TO  dbms-name <AS alias>
            <(<connect-statement-arguments>
            <database-connection-arguments>)>;
```

Each time a CONNECT TO statement is encountered in a SAS session, communication between the session and the specified database is established. A single SAS session can support more than one connection to a database or connections to several databases residing either locally or remotely. Each connection is assigned an alias that is used in subsequent SQL statements to specify the desired database connection.

> **Tip:** A default alias corresponding to the DBMS name (for example, ORACLE or SYBASE) is applied if one is not specified. When multiple simultaneous connections are made in a single SAS session, an alias must be specified for each connection. In this situation, the default alias may still be used for one of the multiple connections. However, I recommend specifying an alias for every database connection for clarity, especially when working with multiple connections to the same database.

In the next example, a CONNECT TO statement is used to establish a connection to an ORACLE database. The outer query returns all rows retrieved from the inner SELECT statement, which is executed against the *stock* table in the database. The ORDER BY clause is added to the outer SELECT statement after the closing parentheses of the inner SELECT statement. Additional optional clauses such as WHERE and GROUP BY may also be added to the outer SELECT statement in the same manner.

```
PROC SQL;
CONNECT TO ORACLE as orablue
(user=scott password=tiger path=master);

SELECT   *
FROM     CONNECTION TO orablue
         (SELECT *
         FROM    bluesky.stock
         )
ORDER BY title;

DISCONNECT from orablue;
```

Tip: Optional clauses such as ORDER BY, WHERE and GROUP BY may be added to both the inner and outer SELECT statements.

EXECUTE statement

General form:

EXECUTE (DBMS-specific-SQL-statement) BY dbms-name|alias

Statements other than SELECT are issued directly to a DBMS through an EXECUTE statement. All statements included in an EXECUTE statement are written using database-specific SQL options and syntax. Processing of EXECUTE SQL statements is handled exclusively by the database.

The EXECUTE statement is limited to a single SQL statement such as SELECT, UPDATE, or GRANT. When entering new rows of data into an existing table, a separate EXECUTE statement is required for each INSERT statement.

Tip: The EXECUTE statement provides the ability to submit database-specific SQL statements directly to a database from your SAS session.

DISCONNECT statement

General form:

DISCONNECT FROM <*dbms-name* | *alias*>;

A DISCONNECT statement is issued to sever the connection to a database. If more than one database connection is active, the database alias assigned on the CONNECT statement must be included or all database connections will be terminated.

SAS/ACCESS LIBNAME statement

As of SAS Version 8, the LIBNAME statement can be used to specify a connection to either a DBMS or a traditional SAS library. The parameters necessary to establish a connection with the database are added to the LIBNAME statement or the USING clause.

General form:

```
LIBNAME libref dbms-name
        <(<connect-statement-arguments>
        <database-connection-arguments>)>;
```

A LIBNAME statement associates a libref with a database and allows subsequent SQL statements to operate against that database. The connection parameters needed to establish communication between the SAS session and the specified database can be included in the LIBNAME statement.

A single SAS session can support several LIBNAME statements, each specifying a connection to a database that resides either locally or remotely. Several connections to the same database can be made in a single SAS session as can connections to different databases.

> **Tip:** The LIBNAME statement associates a libref with a database and it remains active for the entire SAS session unless cleared with a LIBNAME libref CLEAR statement. By default, a connection to the DBMS is made when the LIBNAME statement is executed. If the DEFER=YES option is set, a connection to the database occurs when an SQL statement includes the libref a table in the DBMS.
>
> A CONNECT statement establishes a database connection when it is encountered. The connection is automatically closed when another CONNECT statement is encountered or a DISCONNECT statement is issued.

In the next example, a LIBNAME statement is used to establish a connection to an ORACLE database. There is no need for an outer and inner query as shown in the preceding example. Instead, the SELECT statement executes against the *stock* table in the ORACLE database simply by using the libref assigned to the database as part of the two-level name.

```
LIBNAME orablue ORACLE
user = scott password=tiger path=master schema=bluesky;

PROC SQL;
SELECT     *
FROM       orablue.stock;
```

> **Caution:** It may be possible for someone with access to your SAS software programs to connect to your database if the program includes a CONNECT or LIBNAME statement with a user ID and password. There are a few operating systems and/or databases that check the user ID of the

individual submitting the program; however, many do not. Operating system security measures should be employed to ensure that only authorized individuals can access or submit your SAS software programs.

Selected connection options

There are several options available for the CONNECT and LIBNAME statement that can be used to handle the database connection. Most options can be used on either statement; however, some are available only for use with the LIBNAME statement. In addition, not all database connections support or use the same options.

You will find a full discussion on all options available for the LIBNAME and CONNECT statements in the Base SAS documentation. Options of particular importance have been included here for reference.

Important connection options specific to several commonly used database systems are covered in later sections of this appendix. Each of the options discussed below can be added to either the CONNECT or LIBNAME statement. The following table summarizes the availability of each option.

Option	CONNECT statement	LIBNAME statement	Databases not supported
DBPROMPT	√	√	DB2 z/OS, OLE DB
DEFER	√	√	DB2 z/OS, OLE DB
READBUFF	√	√	
DBCOMMIT		√	DB2 z/OS, Teradata, Informix
DB_CREATE_TABLE_OPTS		√	
SCHEMA		√	DB2 OS/390
PRESERVE_COL_NAMES		√	Teradata, Sybase
PRESERVE_TAB_NAMES		√	Teradata, Sybase
PRESERVE_NAMES		√	Teradata, Sybase

A full discussion of all options available for the LIBNAME and CONNECT sstatements is found in the SAS documentation.

Important connection options specific to several commonly used database systems are covered in later sections of this chapter. Each of the options discussed below can be added to either the CONNECT or LIBNAME statement. The following table summarizes the availability of each option.

DBPROMPT and DEFER options

By default, when a LIBNAME or CONNECT statement is initiated, a connection to the DBMS is established. If DEFER=YES is specified on the LIBNAME statement, the database connection is deferred until the libref is encountered in an SQL statement. If it is specified in the CONNECT statement, the database connection is deferred until the first SQL Pass-Through Facility statement is processed.

If DBPROMPT=YES is specified in the LIBNAME or CONNECT statement in lieu of connection parameters, the parameters needed to make a connection to a DBMS are obtained through interactive prompts.

Tip: If you set DBPROMPT=YES, the value of the DEFER option is automatically set to YES, overriding the default. Set DEFER=NO explicitly to make the database connection when the LIBNAME statement is processed; otherwise, prompts will appear each time the libref is encountered.

READBUFF option

The READBUFF option specifies the number of rows of DBMS data to read into the buffer. When this option is set, network traffic may be reduced and performance improved because a number of rows are fetched in a single call to the database and read into the buffer. However, it is important to note that SAS memory usage increases with this option because SAS stores these rows in memory. Moreover, if the tables in the database from which the rows are drawn undergo frequent changes, the data in memory may not represent the most up-to-date data stored in the tables.

DBCOMMIT option

The DBCOMMIT option specifies the number of rows to be processed by an UPDATE, DELETE, or INSERT statement before the changes are committed or made permanent in the database. All changes made prior to a commit can be undone or rolled back. It can be beneficial to set DBCOMMIT to a number that allows you to check your changes before they become permanent.

Tip: If DBCOMMIT is set to zero, a single commit is issued after PROC SQL completes. If a rollback occurs, all changes made with UPDATE, DELETE, or INSERT statements since PROC SQL was invoked are undone.

Caution: If you set another option, AUTOCOMMIT=YES changes made with an UPDATE, DELETE, or INSERT are committed immediately upon execution. In this case a rollback is not possible; changes must be undone manually. I do not recommend this option when global changes to a table are being made.

DBCREATE_TABLE_OPTS option

This option forces PROC SQL to pass all database-specific clauses of a CREATE TABLE statement and the CREATE TABLE statement itself directly to the database. This is useful when creating table columns with data types not available in SAS.

SCHEMA option

By default, the schema accessed through the DBMS connection is that of the user specified in the CONNECT or LIBNAME statement. An alternate schema may be set with the SCHEMA option.

PRESERVE_COL_NAMES, PRESERVE_TAB_NAMES, and PRESERVE_NAMES options

The PRESERVE_COL_NAMES option preserve spaces, special characters, and mixed case in the column names while PRESERVE_TAB_NAMES option does the same for table names. Both options are combined with the PRESERVE_NAMES.

Tip: To use column or table names that are not allowed in SAS, set DQUOTE=ANSI as an option when you invoke PROC SQL.

Oracle interface

Note: SAS Release 6.12 can only connect to Oracle releases 7.3 and 8.0. SAS Release 8 or later is required for connections to Oracle 8*i* and Oracle 9*i*.

The username and password must be enclosed in quotation marks if they contain spaces or nonalphanumeric characters. A default password of NULL is used if the password is omitted.

PRESERVE_COMMENTS option

The PRESERVE_COMMENTS option allows you to pass additional information called hints to the ORACLE query optimizer to direct Oracle to process the query using a specific processing method. The hints are entered as comments enclosed by /* and */ in the SQL query and are passed to Oracle directly.

Tip: The PRESERVE_COMMENTS option must be included in the LIBNAME or CONNECT statement for hints to be passed to Oracle.

The next example illustrates a connection to an ORACLE database assigned the alias orablue. The database path, bluesky is the service name associated with the database in the tnsnames.ora file. A hint INDX is specified after the SELECT keyword to direct Oracle to use the prodcode index when processing the query.

```
PROC SQL;
CONNECT to oracle as orablue
(user=scott password=tiger path=bluesky
 preserve_comments buffsize=500);

SELECT *
FROM connection to orablue

(SELECT /* +indx(prodcode) */
         prodcode, title, stock
FROM     bluesky.stock
WHERE    prodcode = '300456' or prodcode= '300680')
;

DISCONNECT from orablue;
```

Tip: Oracle hints are always preceded by a plus (+) sign.

BUFFSIZE option

The BUFFSIZE option sets the number of rows to be retrieved from a table or view with each fetch. The default value is 250 rows per fetch with up to 32,767 rows per fetch permitted. The upper limit is dependent on the available memory and in most cases the maximum number of rows is not pratical.

Sybase interface

Tip: All connection arguments for Sybase are case-sensitive. Lowercase strings must be enclosed in quotation marks.

The username and password must be enclosed in quotation marks if they contain spaces or nonalphanumeric characters. A default password of NULL is used if the password is omitted.

SYBBUFSZ option

The SYBBUFSZ parameter specifies the number of rows retrieved from a database view or table to be written to the buffer. The buffer size is dynamically set by the SAS/ACCESS interface to accommodate the number of specified rows when data is read from the table or view. The amount of available system memory should be considered in the assignment of this parameter. If this parameter is omitted from the CONNECT statement, retrieved rows are not written to a buffer, which may adversely affect performance.

DB2 interface

Tip: All connection arguments for DB2 are case-sensitive. Lowercase strings must be enclosed in quotation marks.

The username and password must be enclosed in quotation marks if they contain spaces or nonalphanumeric characters. A password must be specified if a username is included, unless the authentication is provided through the operating system.

ODBC, OLE DB, and SQL Server interface

Both relational and nonrelational database management systems may be accessed through Open Database Connectivity (ODBC). A data source is defined for the database in the Windows ODBC manager using an appropriate driver.

QUALIFER option

In addition to the SCHEMA option, a qualifier can be set, allowing a three-part identifier for database objects.

Tip: If you are experiencing difficulties connecting to your database, use the PROMPT option with ODBC. It can be specified in either a CONNECT or LIBNAME statement as shown here:

```
CONNECT to ODBC (prompt);
   LIBNAME bluesky ODBC PROMPT;
```

This option prompts you for your data source, user name, and password using the same windows presented in the ODBC data sources manager.

Data dictionary

Each DBMS has a data dictionary comprising tables and views with information about users and database objects and structures. The data dictionary can only be accessed through SAS/ACCESS and SQL Pass-Through Facility by those with appropriate authorization.

In the next example the Oracle user system queries the data dictionary *dba_users* table to obtain a list of users in the database. The OPTIONS statement limiting the number of user names reported to fifteen is applied after all rows are retrieved from the database table. The WHERE clause added to the inner SELECT statement eliminates system-related user names that contain a dollar sign ($). An ORDER BY clause was added to the outer SELECT statement to generate a sorted list of user names from the rows returned to the SAS session by the inner SELECT statement.

```
PROC SQL;
OPTIONS OBS=15;

CONNECT to oracle as orablue
       (user=system password=manager path=bluesky);

SELECT *
FROM   connection to orablue
       (SELECT  username
       FROM     dba_users
       WHERE    username not like ('%$%')
       )
ORDER BY username;

DISCONNECT from orablue;
```

```
USERNAME
------------------------------
ADAMS
BLAKE
CLARK
CTXSYS
DBSNMP
JONES
KATHY
MDSYS
MTSSYS
ORDPLUGINS
ORDSYS
OUTLN
SCOTT
SYS
SYSTEM
```

Tip: An EXECUTE statement is not required to issue a SELECT statement against a table in a database. Rather, the SELECT… FROM CONNECTION TO database-alias is used to query the data dictionary table. CREATE TABLE AS SELECT … FROM CONNECTION TO database-alias can also be used to capture the information contained in these tables.

Database privileges

User creation and privileges

Users can be created and privileges assigned to them using the SQL Pass-Through Facility EXECUTE statement. All statements issued through an EXECUTE statement are subject to the database security rules.

Tip: The GRANT statement is not supported in PROC SQL. It must be submitted via an EXECUTE statement to the database.

In the next example CREATE and GRANT statements are issued by the *system* user, creating a new user *taylor* with basic connection privileges. A new connection to the database as user *scott* is established and SELECT access to one of Scott's tables granted to the new user. Finally, a connection is made as the new user and a query against the *emp* table is executed.

```
PROC SQL;

CONNECT to oracle as orablue
          (user=system password=manager path=master);
EXECUTE   (create user taylor identified by tim) by orablue;
EXECUTE   (grant connect, resource to taylor) by orablue;


CONNECT to oracle as ora_scott
          (user=scott password=tiger path=master);
EXECUTE   (grant select on emp to taylor) by ora_scott;


CONNECT to oracle as ora_taylor
          (user=taylor password=tim path=bluesky);

SELECT    *
FROM      connection to ora_taylor
          (SELECT   *
          FROM      scott.emp);

DISCONNECT from orablue;
```

Tip: The object schema is specified as a table-qualifer in the FROM clause of the inner SELECT statement when working with the SQL Pass-Through Facility.

When using the SAS/ACCESS LIBNAME statement, you access objects in the default schema for the user unless the SCHEMA option is added to the connection parameters.

Each time a CONNECT statement is encountered, an implied DISCONNECT statement is executed, closing all open connections to the database(s). If you receive an error message similar to the one following, reissue the CONNECT statement.

SAS log:

```
70   PROC SQL;
71   EXECUTE(grant select on scott.emp to taylor) by orablue;
ERROR: The ORABLUE engine cannot be found.
ERROR: A Connection to the orablue DBMS is not currently
       supported, or is not installed at your site.
```

Tip: Add %PUT &SQLXMSG; after your CONNECT statement to view more detailed error messages returned during failed connection attempts when using the SQL Pass-Through Facility.

In the next example a new user is added to a Microsoft SQL Server database called *northwind* and is subsequently granted access to the database. A SELECT statement is then issued against the *sysusers* table to confirm that the new user has been added to the database. Notice that the SQL statements enclosed in parentheses in the EXECUTE statement are quite different from those in the previous example.

```
PROC SQL;

CONNECT to ODBC as sqlsrvr
          (datasrc='bluesky' user=kathy password=kathy);
EXECUTE   (exec sp_addlogin 'wayne', 'john', 'bluesky' ) by sqlsrvr;
EXECUTE   (exec sp_grantdbaccess 'wayne')by sqlsrvr;

SELECT    *
FROM      connection to sqlsrvr
          (SELECT name
          FROM sysusers)
ORDER BY  name;

DISCONNECT from sqlsrvr;
```

Tip: All SQL statements enclosed in parentheses in an EXECUTE statement are database-specific, and the user must have the privileges necessary to execute the statement.

PROC SQL and ANSI SQL 92

ANSI standard naming conventions

The ANSI standard reserves keywords under all circumstances while PROC SQL fully reserves only the CASE keyword. The table below summarizes the keywords reserved under the ANSI standard. None of these keywords can be used as a table or column name when a table is created in a DBMS.

AS	INNER	RIGHT
CASE	INTERSECT	UNION
EXCEPT	JOIN	USER
FROM	LEFT	WHEN
FULL	ON	WHERE
GROUP	ORDER	
HAVING	OUTER	

Tip: The DQUOTE= ANSI option allows for the literal interpretation of non-SAS permissible column and table names existing in a database. All characters are allowed within the double quoted string. Alternatively, the RENAME option can be used to temporarily rename offending columns or tables.

ANSI standard data types

SAS supports all ANSI standard data types listed in the following table.

Bit	Integer	Time
Character	Interval	Varbit
Date	Numeric	Varchar
Decimal	Real	
Double Precision	Smallint	
Float	Timestamp	

SELECT statement

When the SAS/ACCESS LIBNAME statement is used to connect to a database, the PROC SQL SELECT statement is written in the same manner as a SELECT statement issued against tables stored in a native SAS library. With SQL Pass-Through Facility it is important to remember that the inner SELECT statement is passed to the database for processing and must be written in database-specific SQL. The outer SELECT statement is processed by SAS.

Null or missing values

Processing

When null or missing values are present in a column used in a WHERE clause, the results may differ depending on whether SAS or the DBMS processes the clause. ANSI-compatible SQL has three-valued logic, that is, special cases for handling comparisons involving NULL values. Any value compared with a NULL value evaluates to NULL.

PROC SQL follows the SAS System convention for handling missing values: when numeric NULL values are compared to non-NULL numbers, the NULL values are less than or smaller than all of the non-NULL values; when character NULL values are compared to non-NULL characters, the character NULL values are treated as a string of blanks.

The DIRECT_SQL LIBNAME option discussed below can be used to direct processing to your choice of SAS or the DBMS.

> **Tip:** The IS NULL and IS NOT NULL operators must be used in place of IS MISSING and IS NOT MISSING in queries passed to a DBMS.

Sorting

Null or missing values are always included at the beginning of a list sorted in ascending order and at the end of the sorted results in descending order. If the SQL Pass-Through facility is used, the treatment of null or missing values in the sort process varies depending on the DBMS. Null values may be placed at either the beginning or end of the sorted results.

Functions and operators

The SQL procedure allows several SAS functions and operators that are not ANSI standard in WHERE, HAVING, and SELECT clauses. The following list summarizes the differences and restrictions among SAS and ANSI functions and operators:

- The sounds-like (=*), CONTAINS, and the SAS exponentiation (**) operators are not part of the ANSI standard.
- The <> operator rather than NE or != is used to mean NOT EQUAL in the ANSI standard.
- The SQL procedure supports summary functions that are not part of the ANSI standard.
- The automatic remerging of summary functions is not available in the ANSI standard.

> **Tip:** Array functions and the DIF and LAG functions are not supported by PROC SQL. Please refer to Chapter 4, "Functions," for a full discussion of single and summary functions in PROC SQL.

The following tables summarize the functions and operators that are part of the ANSI SQL 92 standard. Each ANSI element listed is supported by Oracle, DB2, SQL Server, and Sybase. Additional or alternate forms of the ANSI element available within PROC SQL are included in each table.

ANSI functions	Available in PROC SQL
AVG	AVG, MEAN
BIT_LENGTH	
CHARACTER_LENGTH	LENGTH
CONVERT	
COUNT	N, COUNT, FREQ
EXTRACT	Similar to SAS Date and time functions
LOWER	√
UPPER	√
MAX	√
MIN	√
OCTET_LENGTH	
POSITION	SCAN
SUBSTRING	SUBSTR, SUBSTRN [1]
SUM	√
TABLE_NAME	
TABLE_SCHEMA	
TRIM	TRIM, LEFT
TRANSLATE	

[1] SAS Version 9.

ANSI operators	Available in PROC SQL
()	√
*, /, +, -, =	√
<, >, <=, >=	√
<>	^=, ¬=, ~=, <>
AND	√
BETWEEN	√
EXISTS	√
IN	√
LIKE	√
NOT	√
NULL	√
OR	√
||	√

In addition to the ANSI standard elements listed above, each database-specific SQL language includes its own unique set of functions and operators. SELECT statements passed to a DBMS for processing may include any functions that are valid in the SQL language of that database.

> **Tip:** All ANSI standard functions may be passed to a DBMS for processing. To use SAS functions that are not supported by a DBMS, use the DIRECT_SQL option discussed in the next section to force SAS to process the functions.

ESCAPE character

Since SAS Version 8.2 an escape character can be specified to allow matching to wildcard characters with the LIKE operator. The escape character forces the interpretation of the next character literally rather than as a wildcard character. A default escape character exists for each relational database system. The LIKE clause escape character may specify either the database default or an alternative escape character for SAS-processed statements. However, for DBMS-specific SQL statements included in an SQL Pass-Through Facility EXECUTE statement, the database default escape character must be used.

ORDER BY clause

By default, an ORDER BY clause sorts each of the listed columns in ascending order. The SORTSEQ option can be used to set an alternate default sorting sequence for PROC SQL. This functionality is not part of the ANSI standard (SQL2).

Working with two or more tables

PROC SQL supports all ANSI Standard (SQL2) subquery, join, and set operators.

PROC SQL also supports an additional OUTER UNION operator. In addition, the SQL procedure allows set operations on tables that do not have the same number of columns with matching data types. This added functionality is made possible through the creation of virtual columns as required to process the operation.

Creating and managing tables and views

When creating tables, the database specific data types must be applied. Default headings and other column modifiers discussed in Chapter 6, "Creating and Managing Tables and Views," cannot be added.

> **Tip:** Neither the COMMIT and ROLLBACK statements are supported by PROC SQL. These statements must be submitted with an EXECUTE statement.

In the figure below a table called *orders* is created in both an Oracle and Microsoft SQL Server database. The connection to the database is made through a LIBNAME statement with connection parameters appropriate to the database. The data types specified in the PROC SQL CREATE statement are translated into database comparable ones. In this example the order date column has been translated to a DATETIME data type appropriate to each database. If you review the description of each of the tables written to the SAS log, you will notice that the ord_date column has been assigned a format of DATETIME20. in the Oracle database and a DATETIME22.3 format in the SQL Server database. You will also note that the format and label specified for the product code table column are ignored in both cases.

Tip: The translation of a SAS date format specified in the PROC SQL CREATE statement into a DATE or DATETIME data type by the DBMS may generate unexpected results. The default DATE or DATETIME data type for the database is used rather than the default SAS DATE format. To force the correct interpretation of the SAS dates, the SASDATEFMT data set option must be used. More information on SASDATEFMT is included later in this section.

```
PROC SQL;
LIBNAME orablue ORACLE user=scott password=tiger path=master
        schema=bluesky;
CREATE table orablue.orders (
         prodCode   char(10) format $6. label="Product",
         ord_date   date,
         quantity   num,
         totsale    num,
         currency   char(3),
         delCode    char(3),
         clientNo   num,
         invoice    char(10));

DESCRIBE table orablue.orders;


LIBNAME sqlsrvr ODBC datasrc='bluesky' user=wayne password=john;
         PROC SQL;
CREATE table sqlsrvr.orders (
         prodCode   char(10) format $6. label="Product",
         ord_date   date,
         quantity   num,
         totsale    num,
         currency   char(3),
         delCode    char(3),
         clientNo   num,
         invoice    char(10));

DESCRIBE table sqlsrvr.orders;
```

SAS log:

```
973  DESCRIBE table orablue.orders;
NOTE: SQL table orablue.orders was created like:

CREATE table orablue.orders  (
     PRODCODE char(10) format=$10. informat=$10. label='PRODCODE',
     ORD_DATE num format=DATETIME20. informat=DATETIME20.
     label='ORD_DATE',
     QUANTITY num label='QUANTITY',
     TOTSALE num label='TOTSALE',
     CURRENCY char(3) format=$3. informat=$3. label='CURRENCY',
     DELCODE char(3) format=$3. informat=$3. label='DELCODE',
     CLIENTNO num label='CLIENTNO',
     INVOICE char(10) format=$10. informat=$10. label='INVOICE'
  );

create table sqlsrvr.orders  (
     prodCode char(10) format=$10. informat=$10. label='prodCode',
     ord_date num format=DATETIME22.3 informat=DATETIME22.3
     label='ord_date',
     quantity num label='quantity',
     totsale num label='totsale',
     currency char(3) format=$3. informat=$3. label='currency',
     delCode char(3) format=$3. informat=$3. label='delCode',
     clientNo num label='clientNo',
     invoice char(10) format=$10. informat=$10. label='invoice'
  );
```

Tip: The following message appears in the SAS log when tables are created in a database:

```
NOTE: SAS variable labels, formats, and lengths are not
written to DBMS tables.
```

If you examine the product code column description in the above example, you will notice that the label and format specified in the CREATE TABLE statement was not applied to the database table.

Working with dates using SAS/ACCESS can be tricky; SAS date values are assumed to be in a format that matches a default DATE or DATETIME data type of the DBMS. In the next example the PROC SQL INSERT statement is used to load several rows of order information into the Microsoft SQL Server table created in the preceding example.

Although these INSERT statements process without error, the dates are set incorrectly as shown in the report generated from the *orders* table.

```
PROC SQL;
LIBNAME sqlsrvr ODBC datasrc='bluesky' user=wayne password=john;

INSERT into sqlsrvr.orders
values('600125','10mar2004'd,100,1250,'SGD','EXP',4008,'040310-
04');

INSERT into sqlsrvr.orders
values('200507','08apr2004'd,20,1490,'SGD','EXP',4008,'040408-
01');

INSERT into sqlsrvr.orders
values('300456','10apr2004'd,55,797.5,'EUR','EXP',6090,'040410-
01');

INSERT into sqlsrvr.orders
values('200145','12apr2004'd,700,39375,'USD','EXE',2010,'040412-
01');

SELECT *
FROM   sqlsrvr.orders;
```

prodCode	ord_date	quantity	totsale	currency	del Code	clientNo	invoice
600125	01JAN1960:04:29:00.000	100	1250	SGD	EXP	4008	040310-04
200507	01JAN1960:04:29:29.000	20	1490	SGD	EXP	4008	040408-01
300456	01JAN1960:04:29:31.000	55	797.5	EUR	EXP	6090	040410-01
200145	01JAN1960:04:29:33.000	700	39375	USD	EXE	2010	040412-01

The SASDATEFMT option can be used to specify the SAS date format when inserting or retrieving rows from a date column in a DBMS table. Compare the query and results in the next example with those of the previous example. The SASDATEFMT option has been added to each INSERT statement, specifying a DATE9. format for the values inserted in the order date (ord_date) column of the *orders* table. The order dates for the newly inserted rows have now been correctly interpreted by the DBMS. The same option has been added to the FROM clause of the SELECT statement to control the display of the dates when the rows are retrieved. Without this option, the dates would be displayed using a DATETIME22.3 SAS format which is a default DATETIME data type in Microsoft SQL Server.

```
PROC SQL;
LIBNAME sqlsrvr ODBC datasrc='bluesky' user=wayne password=john;

INSERT into sqlsrvr.orders (sasdatefmt=(ord_date='date9.'))
values('600125','10mar2004'd,100,1250,'SGD','EXP',4008,'040310-04');

INSERT into sqlsrvr.orders (sasdatefmt=(ord_date='date9.'))
values('200507','08apr2004'd,20,1490,'SGD','EXP',4008,'040408-01');

INSERT into sqlsrvr.orders (sasdatefmt=(ord_date='date9.'))
values('300456','10apr2004'd,55,797.5,'EUR','EXP',6090,'040410-01');
INSERT into sqlsrvr.orders (sasdatefmt=(ord_date='date9.'))
values('200145','12apr2004'd,700,39375,'USD','EXE',2010,'040412-01');

SELECT *
FROM   sqlsrvr.orders (sasdatefmt=(ord_date='date9.'));
```

prodCode	ord_date	quantity	totsale	currency	del Code	clientNo	invoice
600125	01JAN1960	100	1250	SGD	EXP	4008	040310-04
200507	01JAN1960	20	1490	SGD	EXP	4008	040408-01
300456	01JAN1960	55	797.5	EUR	EXP	6090	040410-01
200145	01JAN1960	700	39375	USD	EXE	2010	040412-01
600125	10MAR2004	100	1250	SGD	EXP	4008	040310-04
200507	08APR2004	20	1490	SGD	EXP	4008	040408-01
300456	10APR2004	55	797.5	EUR	EXP	6090	040410-01
200145	12APR2004	700	39375	USD	EXE	2010	040412-01

Tip: Assigning a SAS date format using SASDATEFMT ensures that dates are handled properly by the database When working with date values, test your INSERT statements to ensure accurate results. Consider setting DBCOMMIT to a value that prevents the changes from being made permanent until after you have reviewed the new rows. A SELECT statement may be issued after the INSERT statement to view the newly inserted rows even though they are not yet committed. In the above example, the changes are not committed to the database until the QUIT statement is executed.

ROLLBACK and COMMIT

The ROLLBACK and COMMIT statements are not supported by PROC SQL. In order to use these statements, you must submit them to a DBMS via a SQL Pass-Through Facility EXECUTE statement.

The next example shows some of the differences between SAS/ACCESS and SQL Pass-Through Facility. In this example a connection is made to an Oracle database as the user *scott* to create a new *orders* table in his schema and add rows to that table. Notice that the CREATE TABLE statement includes data types such as VARCHAR2 and NUMERIC that are specific to Oracle. In addition the INSERT statement includes the order date in a format understood by Oracle; there is no need to add a SASDATEFMT option. The first row is inserted and a COMMIT is executed; a second row is then inserted followed by a ROLLBACK.

```
PROC SQL;
CONNECT to oracle as orablue(user=scott password=tiger
        path=master);

EXECUTE( CREATE table neworder (
         prodCode    varchar2(10) ,
         ord_date    date,
         quantity    numeric,
         totsale     numeric,
         currency    varchar2(3),
         delCode     varchar2(3),
         clientNo    numeric,
         invoice     varchar2(10))
         ) by orablue;
```

```
EXECUTE( INSERT into neworder
         values('200145','12apr2004',700,39375,'USD','EXE',2010,'0404
               12-01')
          ) by orablue;
EXECUTE(  COMMIT) by orablue;

EXECUTE(  INSERT into neworder
         values('200507','08apr2004',20,1490,'SGD','EXP',4008,'040408
              -01')
          ) by orablue;

EXECUTE(  ROLLBACK) by orablue;

SELECT    *
FROM CONNECTION TO orablue
          (SELECT *
          FROM neworder);

DISCONNECT from orablue;
```

The output of the SELECT statement is shown following. Only the first row is in the table because the second INSERT statement was rolled back. The rollback affected only the second INSERT statement because a rollback undoes only the statements issued since the last COMMIT statement.

PRODCODE	ORD_DATE	QUANTITY	TOTSALE	CURRENCY	DELCODE	CLIENTNO	INVOICE
200145	12APR2004:00:00:00	700	39375	USD	EXE	2010	040412-01

Tip: The UNDO_POLICY option provides some of the functionality of the ROLLBACK statement when errors occur during table updates. Refer to Chapter 2, "Working with PROC SQL," for more information on PROC SQL options.

VALIDVARNAME option

In previous versions, database column names greater than 8 characters in length were automatically truncated. However, since SAS Version 8 variable names of up to 32 characters have been allowed. If you are using PROC SQL statements written for SAS Version 6 or 7, referencing variable names of more than 8 characters stored with the view are not interpreted correctly in SAS Version 9.

The VALIDVARNAME option is used to control the SAS version variable naming rules that are to be applied to SQL statements used in SQL Pass-Through Facility during the session.

General form:

```
options VALIDVARNAME= V7 | V6 | UPCASE | ANY
```

The V7 setting is the default for all versions of SAS since SAS Version 7. This setting maps column names in database tables accessed through the SQL Pass-Through Facility to a valid SAS Version 7 name. The rules applying to names in SAS Version 7 are described as follows:

- Up to 32 alphanumeric characters and the underscore (_) are allowed in names.
- Mixed case is allowed.
- Names must begin with either a character or an underscore.
- Any non-SAS characters are mapped to underscores (_).
- If truncation results in two or more identical column names, each of the duplicated names is appended with a counter (0,1,2,...) to create a unique name.

VALIDVARNAME=UPCASE

This setting causes all column names referenced in SQL statements to be converted to uppercase when passed to the database.

VALIDVARNAME=ANY

The ANY setting allows the SQL Pass-Through Facility statements to reference column names that do not conform to the SAS naming conventions. DBMS column names incorporating symbols other than the underscore are interpreted by SAS as valid names when this setting is applied.

Tip: If you encounter problems processing a view created in a previous version, use a DESCRIBE VIEW statement. The PROC SQL statements originally used to create the view will be displayed, allowing you to easily recreate the view.

Optimizing PROC SQL performance

Certain operations are passed directly to a DBMS for processing in order to optimize performance of the SQL procedure. When the DBMS processes the SQL statement, only the resulting rows, rather than the entire table, are passed to the SAS session.

Tip: Use the SASTRACE= ',,,D' system option to obtain information on whether all or part of an SQL statement was processed by SAS or passed to the DBMS for processing. The trace information can be directed to a file with the SASTRACELOC=*filename* option:

```
OPTIONS sastrace=',,,D' sastraceloc=dblog
```

If a libref referencing a DBMS is established on a LIBNAME statement or a USING clause is included in an SQL statement, processing may pass to the DBMS. The conditions under which either the DBMS or SAS takes control of processing are summarized as follows:

- All DBMS-specific statements submitted through the SQL Pass-Through facility are processed by the DBMS and not by SAS.
- If SAS/ACCESS can translate a SAS statement into DBMS-specific SQL, the statement is processed by the DBMS.
- A SELECT statement containing an INTO clause is processed by SAS.
- If the DISTINCT operator is specified in a SELECT clause, it is processed by the DBMS. The unique rows are returned to SAS for further processing.
- WHERE clause processing is done by SAS whenever possible.
- If a PROC SQL statement includes data set options, SAS processes the statement.
- If a SELECT statement is written such that it requires remerging of summary statistics, SAS will process the statement.
- UNION joins are processed by SAS.
- Truncated comparisons are processed by SAS.
- If some but not all functions included in a SELECT statement with a USING clause can be passed to a DBMS for processing, the remaining functions may be translated into DBMS-specific functions in order to allow all functions to be passed to the DBMS.

Tip: Review your results carefully if one or more of the columns in your DBMS tables contain NULL values. A DBMS may ignore NULL values when a WHERE clause is processed whereas SAS does not. Refer to the section above on NULL values for more information.

Passing functions to a DBMS

All ANSI-standard functions, such as MAX, COUNT, and MEAN can be passed to a DBMS directly by SAS. In some cases, SAS can translate a SAS-only function into an equivalent function known to the DBMS. For example, a SAS UPCASE function is translated into an UCASE function in DB2 and an UPPER function in Oracle.

Tip: A summary of the ANSI-standard functions versus SAS functions is included earlier in this appendix. For details on functions that can be translated into DBMS-specify functions, refer to the Base SAS documentation for your database.

Passing joins to a DBMS

Performance can be improved when two or more table joins are processed by a DBMS and only the results are passed to the SAS session. Only those rows in the joined tables that meet the join criteria are returned to the session rather than all rows in each of the tables.

Inner joins between two or more tables residing in a DBMS can be processed by the DBMS. Outer joins, on the other hand, must either support ANSI outer join syntax or meet the conditions described in the table below.

DBMS	**Conditions for outer join**
Informix	Outer joins between only two tables
SQL Server and ODBC	Query containing outer joins between two or more tables does not also include inner joins
Sybase	Query containing outer joins between two or more tables does not also include a WHERE clause

Oracle, which does not support ANSI-standard outer join syntax, is an exception; outer joins between two or more tables can be passed to an Oracle database for processing. The Oracle-specific syntax for the outer join is generated from the PROC SQL query when it is passed to the database.

Even if your join meets the guidelines, it may not be processed by the DBMS. A DBMS may reject the SQL syntax generated for one or more reasons, not all of which are obvious. The LIBNAME statement prevents successful processing transfers to a DBMS for reasons such as the following:

- A join between tables stored in different databases cannot be passed to the database for processing. If your query includes librefs from more than one LIBNAME statement referencing a DBMS, the connection parameters such as server and user ID must be the same.
- LIBNAME statements that include options that affect controls such as locking also prevent the query from passing to the DBMS. Give careful consideration to the performance impact before specifying controls.
- Joins will also not pass to a DBMS for processing if data set options are specified in your query, because such options are foreign to a database.

Joins will also not pass to a DBMS for processing if data set options are specified in your query, because such options are foreign to a database.

> **Tip:** If your query is not passed to the DBMS for processing despite meeting all of the conditions, add %PUT %SYSDBRC and %PUT %SUPERQ(SYSDBMSG) into your program to obtain the DBMS error return code and its meaning. Although %PUT &SYSDBMSG can also be used, %SUPERQ masks any special characters that might be returned from the DBMS. More information on macro variables is included in Chapter 7, "Building Interactive Applications."

DIRECT_SQL option

The LIBNAME option DIRECT_SQL can be set to prevent all or parts of SQL statement processing from passing to a DBMS. By default, DIRECT_SQL=YES results in PROC SQL attempting to pass SQL statements to the database for processing. Settings available for this option are summarized in the following table.

DIRECT_SQL setting	Effect
NO	SQL joins are not passed to the DBMS; however, other SQL statements can be passed to the DBMS.
NONE	All SQL is processed by SAS.
NOFUNCTIONS	SAS handles all functions; other operations or clauses in the SQL statement may be passed to the DBMS for processing.
NOMULTOUTJOINS	SAS handles outer joins involving more than 2 tables; outer joins with two tables are passed to the DBMS for processing.
NOGENSQL	SAS handles the entire SQL statement.
NOWHERE	SAS handles the WHERE clause of the SQL statement; other clauses may be passed to the DBMS for processing.
YES	DEFAULT; joins that meet the conditions discussed above are submitted to the DBMS for processing.

In many cases the DIRECT_SQL setting is used to prevent PROC SQL from attempting to pass queries to a DBMS that cannot be processed by that DBMS. For example, DIRECT_SQL=NOMULTOUTJOINS might be used to allow outer joins between two tables to be passed to Informix but not outer joins between more than two tables. If you recall from the table preceding the one above, Informix will reject outer joins involving more than two tables.

The DIRECT_SQL option might also be set to NOWHERE if indexes that would improve the performance of a WHERE clause are available locally but not in the database.

DBINDEX, DBKEY and MULTI_DATASRC_OPT options

If a join cannot be passed to a DBMS for processing, individual queries for each of the tables involved in the join are run by SAS when it processes the join. By default, SAS reads an entire DBMS table before it processes a join between a DBMS table and a SAS data set. For large DBMS tables, the DBKEY, DBINDEX and MULTI_DATASRC_OPT options cause a subset of the DBMS data to be retrieved for the join. As a result, they may improve performance for joins between large DBMS tables and smaller SAS tables.

Tip: The default value for DBINDEX is database specific. DBINDEX is not available for DB2 OS/390.

If DBINDEX=YES is specified as a LIBNAME, data set, or PROC SQL option, a search is made for all indexes in the tables joined in the query. SAS evaluates each index to determine if it is suitable. If an index with the same attributes as the join column(s) exists, it is used by PROC SQL.

Tip: If an appropriate index is known to exist, it can be specified directly with DBINDEX='index-name'.

The DBKEY data set option specifies a key column in a join table in the FROM clause. SAS checks the DBMS table for values matching the key column and only those rows are returned to SAS for processing. The DBKEY data set option is best applied to a small table with an index associated with the key column.

Caution: DBINDEX and DBKEY can degrade performance. Both should be used only when indexes are available. DBKEY is preferred over DBINDEX because DBINDEX must access the system tables to locate all available indexes. Consider using MULTI_DATASRC_OPT rather than DBKEY as it may provide better performance.

The MULTI_DATASRC_OPT = IN_CLAUSE option creates an IN clause from the unique values in the smaller table. The values in the IN clause are then used to restrict the rows retrieved from the DBMS.

The DBINDEX and DBKEY options are mutually exclusive; DBKEY takes precedence over DBINDEX. If MULTI_DATASRC_OPT and DBKEY are both specified, MULTI_DATASRC_OPT overrides DBKEY. The DBCONDITION option overrides all of these options.

DBCONDITION option

This option causes selection criteria in a CREATE VIEW statement to be passed to the DBMS for processing. The WHERE clause of the SELECT statement associated with the view is specified as the value of DBCONDITION.

In the example following a view is created from the *orders* table created in the SQL Server database Bluesky in an earlier example. The WHERE clause specified on the DBCONDITION option is passed directly to the database for processing. The database is also directed to translate the order date (ord_date) into a SAS date format.

```
PROC SQL;
```

```
CREATE VIEW recent_orders as
        SELECT  prodcode "Product Code" , ord_date "Order Date" ,
        quantity "Quantity", totsale "Total Sale", currency
        "Currency",
        delcode "Delivery Code" ,clientno "Client Number"
FROM    sqlsrvr.orders
        (DBCONDITION= "WHERE ord_date > '01JAN2004'"
        sasdatefmt=(ord_date='date9.'))
USING LIBNAME sqlsrvr ODBC datasrc='bluesky' user=wayne
             password=john;

SELECT *
FROM   recent_orders;
```

Product Code	Order Date	Quantity	Total Sale	Currency	Delivery Code	Client Number
600125	10MAR2004	100	1250	SGD	EXP	4008
200507	08APR2004	20	1490	SGD	EXP	4008
300456	10APR2004	55	797.5	EUR	EXP	6090
200145	12APR2004	700	39375	USD	EXE	2010

Tip: If DBCONDITION is specified, both DBINDEX and DBKEY are ignored.

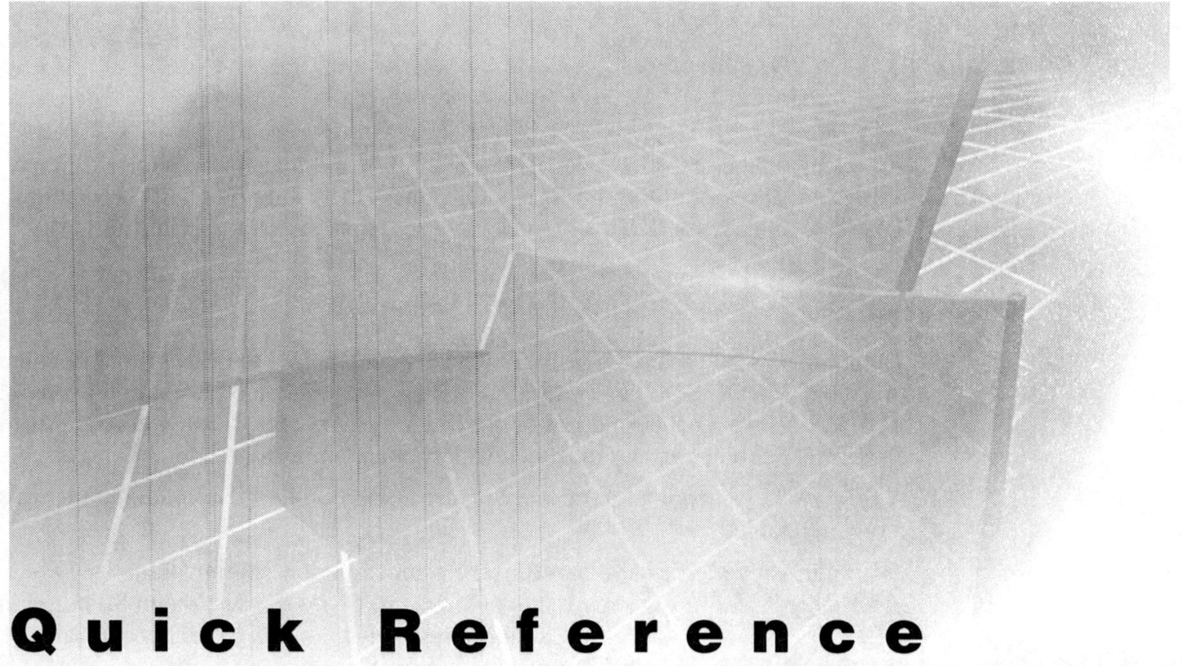

Quick Reference

Chapter 2: Working with PROC SQL

PROC SQL concepts

- PROC SQL can be used to create, maintain, and report from tables and other objects such as views stored in either SAS permanent or work libraries or within a relational database.
- When working within a database, users require appropriate database privileges.

Table structure

- Tables are defined with one or more columns and hold rows of data. They are synonymous with SAS data sets.
- Indexes and constraints can be applied to one or more columns in a table.
- Tables may be created in an RDBMS or in a SAS permanent or WORK library. Tables are accessed through PROC SQL, Base SAS, and other SAS procedures. To create and access RDBMS tables, the user must have appropriate authority.

- Tables may be created in an RDBMS or in a SAS permanent or WORK library. Tables are accessed through PROC SQL, Base SAS, and other SAS procedures. To create and access RDBMS tables, the user must have appropriate authority.

Constraints

- There are several types of constraints that can be applied to one or more columns in a table. PROC SQL can be used to build constraints on tables stored in an RDBMS or in a SAS permanent or work library. In order to apply constraints to an RDBMS table, the user must have appropriate authority.
- A primary key is composed of one or more column values that uniquely identify a row in a table.
- A foreign key enforces a relationship between common column values in two or more tables. If a foreign key relationship is built between two columns stored in different tables, then only values that occur in that column in each of the tables are allowed.
- A UNIQUE constraint can be added to a column in a table to prevent the occurrence of duplicate values in that column.
- A CHECK constraint is used to check incoming column values against a criterion.
- A NOT NULL constraint prevents null or missing values from being input into a column.

PROC SQL versus SAS DATA step

- PROC SQL accomplishes many of the same tasks of traditional SAS DATA steps and procedures. However, the number of statements and procedure calls may be significantly reduced.

PROC SQL naming convention

- The SAS naming convention applies to PROC SQL; however, thought must be given to the ANSI standard reserved words.
- Table names, column names, and aliases can be assigned names of up to 32 characters including alphanumeric characters and the underscore.
- Allowed names for tables, columns, and aliases within a database are impacted by the reserved word list of an RDBMS. The reserved word list depends on how closely the database system adheres to the ANSI standard.

PROC SQL comments

- Comments may be added to PROC SQL statements in the same fashion as comments added to Base SAS statements and SAS procedures.

LIBNAME statement

- A LIBNAME statement assigns a libref or name to a storage location.
- Subsequent SQL statements include two-level names to access tables stored within a particular library.

DESCRIBE statement

- A DESCRIBE statement displays information about the columns, data types, and indexes associated with a table or view.

Working with databases

- PROC SQL statements may be issued against tables and other objects such as views stored in a relational database system using either a SAS/ACCESS LIBNAME statement or the SQL Pass-Through Facility.

SAS/ACCESS LIBNAME statement

- A LIBNAME statement includes a connect string when used to reference a database. One or more LIBNAME statements referencing either database locations or disk locations may be included in your session.
- PROC SQL statements are issued against the database tables by those users with appropriate database privileges.
- Details on the connect strings for selected RDBMS are included in Appendix C, "Information for Database Users."

SQL Pass-Through Facility

- A CONNECT statement containing appropriate connection parameters can also be used to connect to a database. A DISCONNECT statement terminates the connection to the database.
- Database-specific SQL statements can be passed to a database; such statements are referred to as INNER statements. Users must have appropriate authority to work within a database.
- The result set from the database is passed back to the SAS session. Additional SQL statements referred to as OUTER statements are applied to this result set.

- Details on connection parameters for selected RDBMS are included in Appendix C, "Information for Database Users."

PROC SQL options

- Many SAS data set and system options can be applied in PROC SQL.
- In addition to standard output, Output Delivery System (ODS) options are available for reports generated through PROC SQL. Output from PROC SQL can also be used as input to other SAS procedures and DATA steps.

Chapter 3: Understanding the SELECT Table

SELECT statement

- A SELECT statement or query is composed of two or more clauses that control the columns and rows that are reported from a table. A SELECT statement requires a SELECT and FROM clause. All other clauses are optional.
- There is a fixed order in which clauses can be added to a SELECT statement. The order is as follows: SELECT, INTO, FROM, ON, WHERE, GROUP BY, HAVING, ORDER BY, USING.

SELECT clause

- The SELECT clause (mandatory) of a SELECT statement contains a list of the columns and expressions whose contents are to be written from one or more tables.
- Expressions on a SELECT clause may include columns, functions, mathematical expressions, or subqueries.
- Standard SAS label and formatting options may be applied to any column or expression.
- An alias or new variable name may be applied to a column or expression on a SELECT clause.

FROM clause

- A FROM clause (mandatory) contains the names of the tables in which the columns specified in the SELECT clause are located.
- Two-level table names indicating a permanent table stored either on disk or in an RDBMS can be referenced in a FROM clause.

WHERE clause

- A WHERE clause (optional) condition or set of conditions determine which rows of a table are retrieved by a SELECT statement.
- A WHERE clause may reference columns that are not part of a SELECT clause.
- Expressions and functions created in a SELECT clause can be part of a WHERE clause condition if a CALCULATED keyword is included.
- Single functions are allowed in a WHERE clause. Summary functions are not allowed in a WHERE clause.
- A WHERE clause can be used to specify the criteria for joining two or more tables. Table joins are discussed in Chapter 5, "Working with Two or More Tables."

ORDER BY clause

- An ORDER BY clause (optional) sorts the retrieved table rows.
- The SORTSEQ option can be used to modify the default ascending sort order used in the processing of an ORDER BY clause.

GROUP BY clause

- A GROUP BY clause (optional) divides the selected rows by one or more categories and calculates summary function results for each category.
- All columns or expressions on a SELECT clause that are not part of a summary function are commonly included in a GROUP BY clause, although it is not strictly necessary.
- A GROUP BY clause may not necessarily generate a sorted list of results; an ORDER BY clause should be included if sorting is required.

HAVING clause

- A HAVING clause (optional) applies filter criteria to groups or categories of data generated through a GROUP BY clause of a SELECT statement.
- A WHERE clause can be used in conjunction with a HAVING clause; it serves to limit the rows that are passed to the GROUP BY clause for processing.
- Summary functions are allowed in a HAVING clause.

ON clause

- The ON clause (optional) is always included when a FROM clause contains a JOIN keyword. It specifies the criteria for joining two or more tables. Table joins are discussed in Chapter 5, "Working with Two or More Tables."

USING clause

- The USING clause (optional) embeds a LIBNAME statement into a SELECT statement that is part of a CREATE VIEW statement. Detailed information on views and the USING clause are included in Chapter 6, "Creating and Managing Tables and Views."

INTO clause

- Macro variables can be assigned values retrieved by a SELECT statement through the use of an INTO clause (optional). Detailed information on macros is included in Chapter 7, "Building Interactive Applications."

SAS/ACCESS and SQL Pass-Through Facility users

- A table stored in an RDBMS can be accessed directly through PROC SQL if the SAS/ACCESS form of the LIBNAME statement is used. If the LIBNAME statement is incorporated into a CREATE VIEW statement through a USING clause, a connection to the database is made each time the view is accessed. The connection is automatically terminated after the statement referencing the view concludes.
- The SELECT statement information contained in Chapter 3, "Understanding the SELECT Table," applies to statements issued against a RDBMS through SAS/ACCESS. For the SQL Pass-Through Facility it is important to note the following:
  - The SELECT statement clauses and options may be included as part of an outer SELECT statement.

- SAS formatting options can be applied only to columns listed in the SELECT clause of the outer SELECT statement.
- The inner SELECT statement may only include those clauses and options that can be resolved by the RDBMS.

- Appendix C, "Information for Database Users," contains RDBMS specific information for both SAS/ACCESS and SQL Pass-Through Facility users.

Chapter 4: Functions

SAS functions and PROC SQL

- PROC SQL supports most of the SAS DATA step functions and includes an additional function, COALESCE.

Single functions

- Single functions are applied to the value in the specified column in each record of the table. The COALESCE function is a special function available only in PROC SQL.

Summary functions

- Summary functions return a single value for each group of data specified. If a group is not specified, the function returns one value for all records read from the table. Summary functions are commonly used with GROUP BY clauses.

Remerging summary function results

- SAS will automatically calculate a summary function for a group and merge that single value with each record in a table.

SAS/ACCESS and SQL Pass-Through Facility users

- Not all SAS supported functions are available in inner SQL statements submitted against a database when using the SQL Pass-Through Facility. However, they can be added to the outer SELECT query that acts on the results returned by the RDBMS.

- All SAS-supported functions are available when using tables in a database accessed through the SAS/ACCESS LIBNAME statement.
- Some information for database users is included with specific functions in this chapter; refer to Appendix C, "Information for Database Users," for a complete discussion of PROC SQL function use with databases. Refer to Chapter 2, "Working with PROC SQL," and Appendix C, "Information for Database Users," for more information on the inner and outer SELECT queries of the SQL Pass-Through Facility.

Chapter 5: Working with Two or More Tables

Join operations

- Data may be drawn from more than one table by listing all of the source tables in the FROM clause or a combination of FROM-ON clauses. Joins of up to 32 tables are supported.
- An ON or WHERE clause sets out the criteria used to construct the join. A join is categorized as either an inner join or an outer join.

Inner joins

- An inner join matches rows from one table against rows in another table. There are four types of inner joins: cross joins, equijoins, non-equijoins and self joins.

Cross join (Cartesian product)

- A cross join generates a result set that includes all possible combinations of rows from two or more tables listed in a FROM clause. This form of join does not require columns of common values in each of the tables.

Equijoin (simple)

- The equijoin generates a result set that includes only rows from two or more tables that contain matching values in one or more columns. The matching criteria are set out in the WHERE clause. Alternatively, an ON clause can be used to establish the joining column or columns.

Non-equijoin

- The non-equijoin generates a result set that includes rows in one table that meet a criterion established by a second table. The criterion is written with a comparison operator. Rows from the second table are not included in the result set.

Self join

- A table can be joined to itself using a self join or reflexive join. These joins are useful when it is necessary to make a pass through the table to obtain a value or values that become part of the criteria used to select rows in the table. They are similar to subqueries.

Outer joins

- Outer joins match the rows of one table against the rows of another table in the same manner as an inner join. However, outer joins also include unmatched rows from either one or both tables. There are three types of outer joins: left, right, and full.

Left and right outer joins

- Left and right outer joins generate a result set that includes all rows from one table that match rows in another table as well as unmatched rows from the table on the left or right of the operator in the join expression.

Full outer join

- A full outer join generates a result set that includes all rows from one table that match rows in another table as well as unmatched rows from both of the tables.

Set operations

- Set operations are similar to join operations or SAS DATA step merge operations in that they merge rows retrieved from one table with those of another into a single data source. The nature of the merge is determined by the set operator used.
- One or more set operations may occur in a PROC SQL statement with the result or rowset of the first set operation passed to the next set operation.
- An optional CORRESPONDING (CORR) keyword allows SAS to match the columns in each of the tables by name rather than by position.

- By default, all duplicate rows are eliminated; an optional ALL keyword can be used with most set operators to modify the handling of duplicate rows.

Union

- A UNION operation concatenates the rows or rowset retrieved from one table with those of another, reporting the unique rows from each. The common column values contributed from each table are reported in the same column.
- Unless the CORRESPONDING (CORR) keyword is included, the data types of the specified columns must have compatible data types.
- An OUTER UNION operation concatenates the rows or rowset retrieved from one table with those of another, reporting the selected columns for each table separately unless the CORRESPONDING (CORR) keyword is added.
- The CORRESPONDING (CORR) keyword merges corresponding column values of selected columns of one table with those of another table.

Except

- An EXCEPT operation result set includes the rows in one table that do not have matching values for the selected columns in another table.

Intersect

- An INTERSECT operation result set includes the rows in one table that have matching values for the selected columns in a second table.

Subqueries

- A query may include a comparison to one or more values returned from another table using a subquery in the WHERE or HAVING clauses. Comparisons may be written with mathematical operators or the IN operator. There are several special operators available for use with subqueries. A subquery may reference only a single column in its SELECT statement unless an existence test is applied.

Subqueries returning single values

- A single value generated through a subquery may be compared to a value in another table using a mathematical operator such as =, >, or <.

Subqueries returning multiple values

- Several values selected from a single column by a subquery may be compared to a value in another table using the IN operator.

Correlated subqueries

- A value generated in a subquery may be compared to a value in another table on a row-by-row basis for a matching column value. A join between a table in the inner and the outer query is constructed using a WHERE or ON clause in the inner query.

Nested subqueries

- Subqueries may reference other subqueries. All forms of subqueries are available for nesting.

Existence test

- The EXISTS operator tests for the existence of a result from a subquery. If one or more values are returned by the subquery, the existence test evaluates to TRUE and the outer query is executed.
- The NOT EXISTS operator evaluates to TRUE if data is not returned by the subquery.

Quantified tests

- The ALL operator can be used in conjunction with a mathematical operator to test a value against multiple values returned by a subquery. This operator may be used with NOT for the reverse condition.
- The ANY operator used in conjunction with a mathematical operator evaluates to TRUE if the value from the outer table meets the condition for at least one of the values returned by the subquery. This operator may be used with NOT for the reverse condition.

SAS/ACCESS and SQL Pass-Through Facility users

- A table stored in a RDBMS can be joined to a table stored in another RDBMS or to a table created within a SAS session. Options such as DBMASTER or ROLE, new to SAS Version 9 can be set to improve performance. These options are covered in Chapter 8, "PROC SQL Enhancements in Version 9," with additional information for database users provided in Appendix C, "Information for Database Users."

- In systems that don't support the ON clause, inner and outer join criteria are specified in a WHERE clause.
- Join processing may be passed to the DBMS if the SQL optimizer determines that performance would be improved. Information on the SQL optimizer is included in Chapter 6, "Creating and Managing Tables and Views."
- The OUTER UNION set operator is not an ANSI SQL-92 standard. Refer to Appendix C, "Information or Database Users," for more information.

Chapter 6: Creating and Managing Tables and Views

CREATE statement

- A CREATE statement is used to generate tables, views, and indexes.
- Several forms of the CREATE statement are available for tables. An empty table may be created through the definition of a structure, or an existing table may be used as a template. However, often a table is created from selected columns in one or more existing tables and populated with data from those tables.
- The CREATE statement for views may include the USING clause, embedding a LIBNAME statement into the view. Each time the view is accessed, the libref is assigned automatically.
- Constraints such as primary and foreign keys may be defined for a table using in-line or out-of-line syntax. Names can be associated with a constraint only when using the out-of-line syntactical form.
- Labels and formats for each column in a table may be assigned at the time the table is created.

Indexes

- Indexing one or more columns in a table may significantly improve query performance. However, indexes are updated automatically each time existing values in the column upon which the index is built is modified or new values are added.
- Indexes are automatically created for primary key, foreign key, and unique constraints.

- A simple index is built on a single column in a table and must be named consistently with the column.
- A composite index is built on several columns in a table and can carry any SAS allowed name.

SQL optimizer

- The SQL optimizer will automatically evaluate the most cost-effective method of processing an SQL query.
- The SQL optimizer's execution plan is written to the SAS log when _METHOD is added to the PROC SQL invocation statement.
- The index selected by the SQL optimizer is written to the SAS log when MSGLEVEL=I is added to the PROC SQL invocation statement.
- The SQL optimizer can be directed to use indexes with the IDXWHERE option. The IDXNAME option directs the SQL optimizer to use a specific index. These options cannot be used to override the rules concerning index usage.
- Several join methods are evaluated including hash, merge, and index joins. Index joins are considered only when an index exists for one or both of the join columns. Hash joins require that at least one of the tables is small enough to load completely into memory. The join method is indicated in the execution plan.
- The order of the columns is important in a composite index because it can only be selected by the SQL optimizer if the first column in such an index is included in the WHERE or HAVING clause.

ALTER statement

- Additional columns or column modifiers may be added to a table after it is created using the ALTER statement. Columns in the table may also be dropped.

INSERT statement

- The INSERT statement is used to add one or more new rows of data to an existing table. The data may be selected from an existing table or added directly.

UPDATE statement

- An UPDATE statement is used to modify an existing value in a column of a table. The entire column may be updated using the same value or expression. Alternatively, the update action may be completed only for selected rows.

DELETE statement

- A DELETE statement is used to eliminate one or more rows in a table.

DROP statement

- A DROP statement is used to delete a table, index, or view. It eliminates all references to the object within the SAS System.

SAS/ACCESS and SQL Pass-Through Facility users

- The statements presented here can be applied to tables and views stored within a relational database system. However, not all SQL products support the syntax shown nor do they allow the same options. Selected details relating to the usage of these statements in an RDBMS are included in this chapter. Appendix C, "Information for Database Users," includes additional information.
- The USING clause of a CREATE view statement may reference a database location. A connection to the database is made each time the view is accessed.
- Appropriate database authority is required to execute table maintenance statements.

Chapter 7: Building Interactive Applications

Validating SQL statements

- The VALIDATE statement can be used to check syntax of a PROC SQL SELECT statement without running the statement.

Use of macro variables

- One or more macro variables listed in an INTO clause can be assigned variables retrieved from a SELECT statement. These macro variables can then be used as input parameters for macro programs.

Automatic macro variables

- PROC SQL populates several automatic macro variables that can be used to generate meaningful error messages or as input parameters controlling loops.

Screen Control Language (SCL)

- Parameters may be passed to either a macro program or a PROC SQL statement from an SQL-generated interactive window.
- FRAME components such as SCL lists may draw their values from PROC SQL statements or the data dictionary tables.

htmSQL

- PROC SQL statements can be incorporated into HTML web pages using htmSQL.
- Each htmSQL input file includes one or more sections with SQL statements contained within query and update sections. A SAS/SHARE server processes all SQL statements contained in the htmSQL input files

Dictionary tables

- A set of dynamic views containing information about all tables, views, and data sets available during a SAS session are maintained by SAS as a data dictionary.
- Dictionary tables may be queried to obtain table or column names and attributes for programs based on parameters input by a user.

SAS/ACCESS and SQL Pass-through Facility users

- Additional automatic macro variables are assigned values when working with SAS/ACCESS and SQL Pass-Through Facility. They are discussed in Appendix C, "Information for Database Users."
- The dictionary tables also provide information for tables and views stored in a database available during a SAS session.

Chapter 8: PROC SQL Enhancements in Version 9

PROC SQL options

- The THREADS option has been introduced to include parallel processing for sort operations within PROC SQL.

- The number of buffers available for processing a SAS data set or table can be set with the BUFNO option. A permanent buffer page size can be set with the BUFSIZE option.

Output Delivery System (ODS)

- The ODS has been enhanced, providing more custom report formatting for PROC SQL and other SAS procedures.
- The DOCUMENT destination statement provides the ability to selectively control which results are output and the nature of the output format without re-running SAS procedures.
- The TEMPLATE procedure can be used to create style templates that are applied to reports generated by the SQL procedure or other SAS procedures.

SELECT clause

- The TRANSCODE option can be added as a column modifier to translate or remap characters.

FROM clause

- The FROM clause can now include the physical filename rather than the traditional two-level qualifier using a libref and tablename.

Functions

- A new substring function called SUBSTRN is available that allows a result of length zero. The SUBSTR function continues to be available.

Creating and managing tables and views

- Format names have been increased to a length of 32 characters and 31 characters for character and numeric formats, respectively.

Macro variables

- Macro variable names may now include a leading zero.

Dictionary tables

- Several new dictionary tables have been introduced, many of which include information on constraints.

SAS/ACCESS interface

- Two new options have been introduced that assist in the optimization of joins. Both the MULTI_DATASRC_OPT and DBMASTER options are designed to optimize joins that cannot be passed to a database for processing. In each case, the user is able to provide information to the SQL optimizer which helps determine the most cost-efficient processing method.
- The DBSLICE and DBSLICEPARM options provide threaded read functionality.

References

American National Standards Institute. Geneva Switzerland. www.ansi.org.

ANSI INCITS 135-1992 (R1998) *Information Systems - Database Language - SQL* (includes ANSI X3.168-1989) (formerly ANSI X3.135-1992 (R1998).

Codd, E. F. 1970. "A Relational Model of Data for Large Shared Data Banks." *Communications of the ACM* 13(6): 377-387.

INCITS/ISO/IEC 9075-2-2003 *Information technology - Database languages - SQL - Part 2: Foundation (SQL/Foundation).*

INCITS/ISO/IEC 9075-2-1999-*Technical Corrigendum 1 Information Technology - Database languages - SQL - Part 2: Foundation (SQL/Foundation) - Technical Corrigendum* 1:2000 (formerly ANSI/ISO/IEC 9075-2-1999: *Technical Corrigendum* 1:2000).

INCITS/ISO/IEC 9075-2-1999/Amd1-2001 *Information technology - Database languages - SQL - Part 2: Foundation (SQL/Foundation)* - AMENDMENT 1: On-Line Analytical Processing (SQL/OLAP) (supplement to ANSI/ISO/IEC 9075-2-1999) (formerly ANSI/ISO/IEC 9075-2:1999/Amd1:2001).

SAS Institute Inc. 1989. *SAS Guide to the SQL Procedure: Usage and Reference, Version 6.* Cary, NC: SAS Institute Inc.

SAS Institute Inc. 1990. *SAS Language Reference: Concepts, Version 8.* Cary, NC: SAS Institute Inc.

SAS Institute Inc. 1990. *SAS Procedures Guide, Version 8*, 3rd ed. Cary, NC: SAS Institute Inc.

SAS Institute Inc. 2000. SAS Technical Support Document TS-320: *Inside PROC SQL's Query Optimizer*. Cary, NC: SAS Institute Inc.

SAS Institute Inc. 2000. SAS Technical Support Document TS-554: *SQL Joins — The Long and the Short of It*. Cary, NC: SAS Institute Inc.

SAS Institute Inc. 2000. *SAS SQL Procedure User's Guide, Version 8*. Cary, NC: SAS Institute Inc.

SAS Institute Inc. 1999. *SAS/STAT User's Guide, Version 8*. Cary, NC: SAS Institute Inc.

SAS Institute Inc. 2000. *SAS SQL Query Window User's Guide, Version 8*. Cary, NC: SAS Institute Inc.

Index

A

E

G

H

J

U

V

X

Z

Symbols

Books Available from SAS Press

Advanced Log-Linear Models Using SAS®
by **Daniel Zelterman**

Analysis of Clinical Trials Using SAS®: A Practical Guide
by **Alex Dmitrienko, Geert Molenberghs, Walter Offen,** *and* **Christy Chuang-Stein,**

Annotate: Simply the Basics
by **Art Carpenter**

Applied Multivariate Statistics with SAS® Software, Second Edition
by **Ravindra Khattree**
and **Dayanand N. Naik**

Applied Statistics and the SAS® Programming Language, Fourth Edition
by **Ronald P. Cody**
and **Jeffrey K. Smith**

An Array of Challenges — Test Your SAS® Skills
by **Robert Virgile**

Carpenter's Complete Guide to the SAS® Macro Language, Second Edition
by **Art Carpenter**

The Cartoon Guide to Statistics
by **Larry Gonick**
and **Woollcott Smith**

Categorical Data Analysis Using the SAS® System, Second Edition
by **Maura E. Stokes, Charles S. Davis,**
and **Gary G. Koch**

Cody's Data Cleaning Techniques Using SAS® Software
by **Ron Cody**

Common Statistical Methods for Clinical Research with SAS® Examples, Second Edition
by **Glenn A. Walker**

Debugging SAS® Programs: A Handbook of Tools and Techniques
by **Michele M. Burlew**

Efficiency: Improving the Performance of Your SAS® Applications
by **Robert Virgile**

The Essential PROC SQL Handbook for SAS® Users
by **Katherine Prairie**

Genetic Analysis of Complex Traits Using SAS®
by **Arnold M. Saxton**

A Handbook of Statistical Analyses Using SAS®, Second Edition
by **B.S. Everitt**
and **G. Der**

Health Care Data and SAS®
by **Marge Scerbo, Craig Dickstein,**
and **Alan Wilson**

The How-To Book for SAS/GRAPH® Software
by **Thomas Miron**

Instant ODS: Style Templates for the Output Delivery System
by **Bernadette Johnson**

In the Know... SAS® Tips and Techniques From Around the Globe
by **Phil Mason**

Integrating Results through Meta-Analytic Review Using SAS® Software
by **Morgan C. Wang**
and **Brad J. Bushman**

Learning SAS® in the Computer Lab, Second Edition
by **Rebecca J. Elliott**

The Little SAS® Book: A Primer
by **Lora D. Delwiche**
and **Susan J. Slaughter**

The Little SAS® Book: A Primer, Second Edition
by **Lora D. Delwiche**
and **Susan J. Slaughter**
(updated to include Version 7 features)

The Little SAS® Book: A Primer, Third Edition
by **Lora D. Delwiche**
and **Susan J. Slaughter**
(updated to include SAS 9.1 features)

Logistic Regression Using the SAS® System: Theory and Application
by **Paul D. Allison**

Longitudinal Data and SAS®: A Programmer's Guide
by **Ron Cody**

Maps Made Easy Using SAS®
by **Mike Zdeb**

Models for Discrete Date
by **Daniel Zelterman**

Multiple Comparisons and Multiple Tests Using SAS® Text and Workbook Set
(books in this set also sold separately)
by **Peter H. Westfall, Randall D. Tobias, Dror Rom, Russell D. Wolfinger,**
and **Yosef Hochberg**

Multiple-Plot Displays: Simplified with Macros
by **Perry Watts**

Multivariate Data Reduction and Discrimination with SAS® Software
by **Ravindra Khattree**
and **Dayanand N. Naik**

Output Delivery System: The Basics
by **Lauren E. Haworth**

Painless Windows: A Handbook for SAS® Users, Third Edition
by **Jodie Gilmore**
(updated to include Version 8 and SAS 9.1 features)

The Power of PROC FORMAT
by **Jonas V. Bilenas**

PROC TABULATE by Example
by **Lauren E. Haworth**

Professional SAS® Programming Shortcuts
by **Rick Aster**

Quick Results with SAS/GRAPH® Software
by **Arthur L. Carpenter**
and **Charles E. Shipp**

Quick Results with the Output Delivery System
by **Sunil Gupta**

Quick Start to Data Analysis with SAS®
by **Frank C. Dilorio**
and **Kenneth A. Hardy**

Reading External Data Files Using SAS®: Examples Handbook
by **Michele M. Burlew**

Regression and ANOVA: An Integrated Approach Using SAS® Software
by **Keith E. Muller**
and **Bethel A. Fetterman**

SAS® Applications Programming: A Gentle Introduction
by **Frank C. Dilorio**

support.sas.com/pubs

SAS® for Forecasting Time Series, Second Edition
by **John C. Brocklebank**
and **David A. Dickey**

SAS® for Linear Models, Fourth Edition
by **Ramon C. Littell, Walter W. Stroup,**
and **Rudolf Freund**

SAS® for Monte Carlo Studies: A Guide for Quantitative Researchers
by **Xitao Fan, Ákos Felsoválуі, Stephen A. Sivo,**
and **Sean C. Keenan**

SAS® Functions by Example
by **Ron Cody**

SAS® Guide to Report Writing, Second Edition
by **Michele M. Burlew**

SAS® Macro Programming Made Easy
by **Michele M. Burlew**

SAS® Programming by Example
by **Ron Cody**
and **Ray Pass**

SAS® Programming for Researchers and Social Scientists, Second Edition
by **Paul E. Spector**

SAS® Survival Analysis Techniques for Medical Research, Second Edition
by **Alan B. Cantor**

SAS® System for Elementary Statistical Analysis, Second Edition
by **Sandra D. Schlotzhauer**
and **Ramon C. Littell**

SAS® System for Mixed Models
by **Ramon C. Littell, George A. Milliken, Walter W. Stroup,** *and* **Russell D. Wolfinger**

SAS® System for Regression, Second Edition
by **Rudolf J. Freund**
and **Ramon C. Littell**

SAS® System for Statistical Graphics, First Edition
by **Michael Friendly**

The SAS® Workbook and *Solutions* Set
(books in this set also sold separately)
by **Ron Cody**

Selecting Statistical Techniques for Social Science Data: A Guide for SAS® Users
by **Frank M. Andrews, Laura Klem, Patrick M. O'Malley, Willard L. Rodgers, Kathleen B. Welch,**
and **Terrence N. Davidson**

Statistical Quality Control Using the SAS® System
by **Dennis W. King**

A Step-by-Step Approach to Using the SAS® System for Factor Analysis and Structural Equation Modeling
by **Larry Hatcher**

A Step-by-Step Approach to Using the SAS® System for Univariate and Multivariate Statistics, Second Edition
by **Norm O'Rourke, Larry Hatcher,**
and **Edward J. Stepanski**

Step-by-Step Basic Statistics Using SAS®: Student Guide and *Exercises*
(books in this set also sold separately)
by **Larry Hatcher**

Survival Analysis Using the SAS® System: A Practical Guide
by **Paul D. Allison**

Tuning SAS® Applications in the OS/390 and z/OS Environments, Second Edition
by **Michael A. Raithel**

Univariate and Multivariate General Linear Models: Theory and Applications Using SAS® Software
by **Neil H. Timm**
and **Tammy A. Mieczkowski**

Using SAS® in Financial Research
by **Ekkehart Boehmer, John Paul Broussard,**
and **Juha-Pekka Kallunki**

Using the SAS® Windowing Environment: A Quick Tutorial
by **Larry Hatcher**

Visualizing Categorical Data
by **Michael Friendly**

Web Development with SAS® by Example
by **Frederick Pratter**

Your Guide to Survey Research Using the SAS® System
by **Archer Gravely**

JMP® Books

JMP® for Basic Univariate and Multivariate Statistics: A Step-by-Step Guide
by **Ann Lehman, Norm O'Rourke, Larry Hatcher,**
and **Edward J. Stepanski**

JMP® Start Statistics, Third Edition
by **John Sall, Ann Lehman,**
and **Lee Creighton**

Regression Using JMP®
by **Rudolf J. Freund, Ramon C. Littell,**
and **Lee Creighton**

CPSIA information can be obtained at www.ICGtesting.com
Printed in the USA
LVOW11s2055160514

386148LV00007B/41/P